Clinical Psychology as Science & Profession

Clinical Psychology as Science & Profession

Davide Shakow

ALDINETRANSACTION
A Division of Transaction Publishers
New Brunswick (U.S.A.) and London (U.K.)

Second paperback printing 2009

This book is printed on acid-free paper that meets the American National Standard for Permanence of Paper for Printed Library Materials.

Library of Congress Catalog Number: 2006045687
ISBN: 978-0-202-30890-6
Printed in the United States of America

Library of Congress Cataloging-in-Publication Data

Shakow, David, 1901-
Clinical psychology as science and profession / David Shakow.
p. cm.
Originally published: Chicago : Aldine Pub. Co., c!969.
Includes bibliographical references and index.
ISBN 0-202-30890-1 (pbk. : alk. paper)
1. Clinical psychology. 2. Clinical psychology—Study and teaching. I. Title.

RC467.S48 2006
616.89—dc22 2006045687

To the memories of Frederick Lyman Wells,
William McDougall, and Edwin Garrigues Boring,
and to Grace Helen Kent, teachers of both psychology
and psychology called clinical

Preface

For more than four-and-a-half decades (from early in my college days) I have lived on the exhilarating but "perilous" professional borders surrounding clinical psychology. At different periods in this career I have inevitably become involved in teaching, field training, research, and administration related not only to clinical psychology, but also to other "helping" professions such as psychiatry, social work, nursing, and medicine. These endeavors were associated either directly with the institutions in which I was employed, or indirectly as a member of committees or as a participant in conferences devoted to one or another of these topics.

So much preoccupation with this area naturally afforded many opportunities for formulating principles of conduct, testing out techniques, and expressing opinions on the issues involved. The essays which resulted have been published in a wide range of journals and books. Considering the marked growth of clinical psychology during this period and the continuing demand for many of these articles, there appears to be some justification for making them more accessible.

The articles were, of course, written for different occasions over the course of many years. They cannot therefore have the systematic organization or felicitous flow of a volume that is more respectful of the unities. I apologize for the more than occasional overlappings and the actual repetitions—in many instances I have had to crib from myself. (In some instances where the overlapping was too gross I have abridged a few of the papers.) Perhaps in the process of overlooking these, the reader may even be gracious enough to interpret them as merely the reasonable efforts of an author to emphasize important points.

I hope that the consistency of much of the philosophy (bias! for some) which resides in these articles will be manifest. This philosophy derives fundamentally from William James and to some extent from Sigmund Freud, but more directly from a number of my teachers—particularly Fred Wells, William McDougall, Grace Kent, and Edwin Boring.

The papers in this volume are organized into five categories. The introductory series provides both historical background about clinical psychology and discussion of the roles and functions of the clinical psychologist. This is followed by the most extensive section, that dealing with the training of clinical psychologists. The third group is concerned with psychology's professional relations with psychiatry, with psychotherapy as a speciality, and with medicine. The fourth section deals with various aspects of psychology's relationships with psychoanalysis. The volume concludes with the treatment of a broader and more general issue, that of public service.

I am grateful both to the students and colleagues who have taught me so much in the daily round of direct activities, and to the colleagues I have been associated with in committees and in conferences from whom I have learned equally if somewhat differently. To Ruth Ann Van Dyke I am indebted for so efficiently handling the multitudinous problems connected with assembling a volume of this kind.

Contents

Clinical Psychology as Science and Profession

PART I

History and Functions

The first three papers in Part I tend to emphasize in different ways the historical aspects of clinical psychology. No attempt has been made to be exhaustive. Rather, the effort has been to point up areas relevant to the context for which the article was prepared. The next group of papers in this section emphasizes particularly the roles and functions of the clinical psychologist, especially as reflected in his work in the hospital and the clinic.

1. Clinical Psychology: An Evaluation

For its twenty-fifth anniversary, the American Orthopsychiatric Association decided to put out a volume *Orthopsychiatry 1923–1948: Retrospect and Prospect*, of which Lawson G. Lowrey was editor. I was asked to write the following article on clinical psychology, in which I tried to meet the spirit of the volume.

Clinical psychology, having celebrated its fiftieth birthday (Brotemarkle, 1947), is now entering adolescence. Puberty seems to have arrived with a vigor and animation, not untouched with brashness, in marked contrast to the extended, rather asthenic, childhood. Its zeal is in fact creating problems for its parent and more remotely related disciplines. These fields themselves are in a state of postwar reorganization and find it necessary to reorient to this additional pressure. I shall attempt in this essay to follow through the high points of the child's development, evaluate the features of his adolescence, and consider the promise of his maturity.

Reprinted with permission from L. G. Lowrey and V. Sloane (Eds.), *Orthopsychiatry, 1923–1948: Retrospect and Prospect*, 1948 (American Orthopsychiatric Association) Copyright, the American Orthopsychiatric Association, Inc.

Origins

We can agree with Louttit (1939, p. 362) that clinical psychology in any organized fashion dates from the time that Lightner Witmer in 1896 (Fernberger, 1931, p. 11) first established the psychological clinic at the University of Pennsylvania. Despite the tendency for historians (Stevenson & Smith, 1934; Witmer, 1940) of the movement to minimize or neglect almost entirely the role Witmer played, child guidance in this country may with good justification be said to have started with his establishment of the Clinic. It was Witmer, too, who coined the terms "clinical psychology," "psychological clinic," and "orthogenics," terms which have become part of the language. From the beginning he called for the qualitative study of the *individual* patient, not only for diagnostic purposes, but especially for therapeutic ones. The need for detailed consideration of a case was recognized even to the extent of establishing a hospital school (Fernberger, 1931, p. 14) in order to be able to observe children over an extended time. Although in its early period the Clinic's emphasis was almost entirely on the retarded child, in later years its major preoccupations were with the problems of the superior child and with vocational guidance and speech disability. What has since become known as the "team" approach was in some fashion early adopted by the Psychological Clinic at the University of Pennsylvania. Physicians, especially neurologists, collaborated in the study of cases and there was an early and continuing use of social workers.

With respect to training, there was consistent recognition of the importance of providing systematic education in applied psychology and supplying facilities to psychologists, educators, and other students for study in the practical setting. Courses, demonstrations, and practicum facilities in the clinical field for the study of exceptional children were a regular part of the program.

While the Clinic was developing, other influences were at work which were to play roles in the development of clinical psychology. Cattell's (1937) effort at establishing a psychological service at Columbia in the middle '90's had not been successful. At Pennsylvania, where he had founded the Psychological Laboratory and had been Witmer's teacher, he had undoubtedly left some of the psychological atmosphere and influence which grew out of his interest in the study of individual differences.

Although rumblings of the Binet development had started earlier (Seashore, 1942, p. 160) it was not until 1905, with the publication of the first form of the Binet-Simon test, that the influence of this instrument became marked. Among the first to adapt the Binet-Simon Test to American conditions was the Vineland Training School. There, in 1906, Goddard (1943) had started the first laboratory in an institution for the study of the feebleminded.

About 1910, the second psychological clinic in a university setting, modeled on the one at the University of Pennsylvania, was organized by Seashore (1942, p. 124) at the University of Iowa.

At about the same time, Wallin was becoming active in the application of psychological techniques to school children. After some other related activities, he started a psycho-educational clinic at the University of Pittsburgh in 1912 (Wallin, 1914,

p. 32). Wallin (1914, p. 59) emphasized the educational, as opposed to the psychopathological, significance of clinics and recommended that they might best be established in association with departments of education.

Beginning with the latter part of the nineteenth century and through the early part of the twentieth (in the latter period paralleling the tremendous growth of mental testing) a most important development was taking place in the field of psychiatry which had a considerable influence on the course of clinical psychology. The functional point of view was becoming more and more prominent through the activities of such men as Charcot and Janet, but most particularly Freud abroad, and Meyer in this country. This trend led to the development of another type of clinic in this country.

In 1909, William Healy started a Behavior Clinic, in association with the Cook County Juvenile Court of Chicago, for the study of delinquency. It is from this development that the child guidance movement ordinarily dates its origin (Stevenson & Smith, 1934; Witmer, 1940). Healy (1934, p. 2) had been impressed by Witmer's clinic but as is seen by an examination of his trailblazing work (Healy, 1915), his general approach was in many ways different from that of Witmer. As Stevenson and Smith (1934) point out, Healy's emphasis was not precisely that of the present child guidance clinic, but it comes quite close in spirit. Of interest in this connection is the fact that whereas Healy recognized the importance of social workers, he did not have a full-time worker on his staff (Stevenson & Smith, 1934, p. 17). Witmer's clinic, on the other hand, apparently had one from the very beginning (Fernberger, 1931, p. 15). In neither case was psychiatric social work involved, for this field had not as yet appeared as a specialty. The subsequent development of child guidance clinics and the place of psychology in their functioning are described by both Helen Witmer (1940) and Stevenson and Smith (1934).

Despite Lightner Witmer's pioneer status in the field, his early emphasis on training, and the pattern of attack he developed which contained most of the elements of present-day clinics, it is only fair to say that his contribution has had surprisingly little effect on the development of the mental hygiene field, or even on that of clinical psychology. On the other hand, Healy's clinic activity, which came ten years later, has had a marked effect on both fields, particularly the former. Why this difference? It is of interest for us to examine possible bases because they are important for the understanding of the development of clinical psychology.

If the content of the programs of the two clinics is studied, one is struck by Witmer's consistent concern with educational problems, primarily those of the mentally defective. This emphasis on the intellectual-cognitive aspects of personality naturally lead mainly to contact with the educator in the setting of the school or the institution for the feebleminded. Healy, on the other hand, was mainly concerned with social pathology. His primary emphasis was on the affective aspects of personality, which involved contact with a variety of social agencies and institutions. Healy, it turns out, was wiser in his choice, for throughout the history of psychiatry, down to the very present, this study of the feebleminded has been a relatively narrow and distinctly less rewarding field in practically all ways than the study of the personality difficulties associated with psychopathy, neurosis, and psychosis.

Too, when Witmer became interested in the medical aspects of a problem it seemed to be mainly with the physical or neurological, whereas Healy's was primarily with the psychiatric. Retardation and physical defects interfering with school progress, and the physical environment in which school work is done, are recurring themes in issue after issue of Witmer's *Psychological Clinic, A Journal of Orthogenics.*

More important, perhaps, than the nature of the material (or perhaps inextricably woven into the material) is the point of view represented by each. Witmer's approach was essentially segmental and static, one which is relatively uninspiring and plodding compared with the total, seminal, stimulating approach of Healy. Whereas Healy was markedly influenced by the functional psychology of James and the dynamic views of Freud and Meyer, Witmer identified himself rather with the decidedly non-imaginative Wundtian-Kraepelinian approach. A systematic skimming of the full run of the *Psychological Clinic* leaves one with the feeling that Witmer was burdened by a conservatism which temperamentally set him into opposition to what he considered the "unscientific" nature of the newer, dynamic, radical psychology. This is somewhat paradoxical in a person who was himself something of a pioneer. But a consideration of his activity leads to the conclusion that his pioneering was not really in new thinking but rather in new material to which old thinking was applied. Witmer, we must conclude, undoubtedly missed out in his estimate of the future. This is further reflected in the violent attacks which he made on James as a psychologist and as a scientist. Interestingly enough, he is probably correct in many individual aspects of his criticism, but there is no grasp of the spirit and total significance of James in the social scene. One would guess that Witmer had "certain blindnesses" which acted to prevent his choosing the more promising and meaningful leads. He thus failed to make the contributions which he was in the earliest position to produce.

The circumscribed presentation of the material coming from the Pennsylvania Clinic also probably played a role in the limited response to the Witmer approach. He published no systematic book in the clinical field, his major contributions being in the form of papers in his own journal. Holmes' book (1912) describing the clinic's procedure is quite anemic and unimaginative. Healy's *Individual Delinquent* (1915), published only a few years after Holmes' volume, is on the contrary a full-bodied and challenging book.

Three other possible factors in this difference in influence must be considered. The Pennsylvania Clinic may have been considerably handicapped in attaining the social importance which it might have had because it was established in a University setting and was directed by one who was not himself a physician. The association with student training and education may during those early days have prevented its broader use, whereas if it had been established in a medical school, which already was recognized as a therapeutic center, or in the marketplace, like Healy's, having close contact with existing social agencies and meeting their problems, it might have had more general influence. The natural conservatism of people coupled with the newness of the field would seem to be more difficult to overcome in the setting in which it was placed. Despite Fernberger's (1931, p. 10) suggestion that if it had not been Witmer someone else would have started a clinic, perhaps

Pennsylvania got started too early. Too often has it been the fate of early pioneers to miss reaping the benefit of their efforts. All in all, the neglect of Witmer by non-psychological historians seems to a considerable extent justified, even though this neglect may be based on the wrong reasons.

There is one aspect of Witmer's influence which is more directly related to clinical psychology; viz., the effect of his activity on the establishment of university clinics and courses in clinical psychology in the universities. Wallin in 1914 describes the results of a survey he made some years earlier of psychological clinics and courses offered in the clinical field. He found at that time 26 clinics in institutions of learning and many more courses offered in this general field (Wallin, 1914, pp. 22–119).

A parallel development to these clinics which is of some importance in the history of clinical psychology was the establishment of psychological laboratories in hospitals for the mentally disordered. The McLean Hospital, St. Elizabeth's Hospital, the Boston Psychopathic Hospital, and others are among the outstanding. Associated with these institutions are such names as Franz, Yerkes, and Wells (Shakow, 1945a). In some respects the work in these institutions followed along more conservative academic experimental lines. Other aspects of their activities helped to broaden considerably the range of application of test devices. In these centers, too, there was an early association of psychologists with psychiatrists both more extensive and intensive than that found in the Witmer type of clinic.

The American Psychological Association has at various times in its history made attempts to deal with problems related to clinical psychology (Fernberger, 1932, pp. 42–53). In 1895 and the years following there was some interest in the standardization of mental tests. In 1915 a study of the qualifications of mental examiners was initiated. In 1918 a committee appointed to study this problem further, reported favorably on certification of examiners by the Association. A Certifying Committee was appointed in 1920, but by 1923 only 25 members had applied for certification. In 1927 certification was discontinued, apparently because there was not enough interest in the Association to maintain it. This grew out of the fact that it did not contribute enough to those who qualified under the high standards which were established.

In 1931 a more systematic and organized attack on clinical psychological problems began. In that year the Clinical Section of the American Psychological Association appointed a special Committee on Standards of Training for Clinical Psychologists. This Committee circulated a questionnaire among about a thousand psychologists and in 1935 published a report which contained a set of recommendations for training (APA, CTCP, 1935). In 1936 the Psychology Department of Columbia University formulated a tentative curriculum for clinical psychologists which involved two years of graduate work and one year of internship (Poffenberger, 1938). In 1937 the Boston Society of Clinical Psychologists also developed a three-year training program of the same general kind (1937). After 1937, with the formation of the American Association for Applied Psychology, activities of this kind became more numerous, culminating in the Subcommittee report to be discussed later (APA, AAAP, 1945). Important interim considerations of the problem are to be found in the reports of a special Subcommittee of the New York City Committee on Mental Hygiene (1935), of the Special Committee on School Psychologists of the New York State Association of Applied Psychology (1943), and of the Committee on Professional Training in Applied Psychology of the American Association for Applied Psychology (1943). A detailed consideration of these developments will be found in Morrow (1946). Some aspects of the contribution of journals to the clinical psychological field are covered by Symonds (1946).

If we were to characterize the situation at the beginning of this decade, we might say that although a considerable amount of clinical work was being done by psychologists in community clinics and hospitals as well as in university clinics (which had, however, taken a decidedly secondary role), their training for this work was, with few exceptions, unsystematically acquired. Though there was wide concern with problems of training, little that was systematic had been achieved. Whatever background the clinical psychologist had was largely self-organized. It was surprisingly little determined by programs emanating from universities or any other official psychological institution.

The Present Situation

The last several years have seen much preoccupation with the problems of clinical psychology and much thought has been given to its nature and its scope. A great variety of influences from both within and without psychology have resulted in clinical psychology developing into a field which calls upon its practitioners for competence in three major functions: *diagnosis*, the use of procedures directed at acquiring knowledge about the origin and nature of the psychological conditions under investigation; *research*, the systematic experimental or clinical attack on specific problems for the advancement of knowledge; and *therapy*, the use of techniques for improving the condition of the persons who come for help. It is towards these goals that training in psychology is more and more systematically being directed at the present time.

The general pattern of the program of training of the clinical psychologist which is quite generally accepted is that proposed in a report by a subcommittee of the Committee on Graduate and Professional Training of the American Psychological Association and the American Association for Applied Psychology (1945). This program was the natural outgrowth of a long series of efforts, arising mainly in the field centers (Morrow, 1946), to systematize the training which had been unorganized for a long time. The extensive and more intelligent use of psychology during the Second World War and the development of the Veterans Administration (Miller, 1946) and United States Public Health Service programs gave the already going efforts a great impetus and resulted in the adoption almost overnight of this general program. The pattern followed has been the development of existing university departments as central clinical training units and the integration of field training centers into their program. Although several suggestions for the establishment of special professional schools in clinical psychology have been made, present opinion seems to favor working within the framework of existing university departments of psychology expanded to meet the special needs of clinical psychology.

The program proposed by the committee is a four-year Ph.D. graduate training period, one year of which, preferably the third, consists of an internship. On the foundation of basic systematic courses in psychology, courses in clinical and dynamic psychology, practicums, clerkships, and the internship are organized. The emphasis is on training in diagnosis, research, and therapy under close individual supervision.

One of the problems of the past now receiving careful consideration is the recruiting and selection of potentially able clinical psychologists. During the period when universities were not vitally concerned with the problem, there was a tendency on the part of some professors to direct their weaker students, those who did not quite fit and those who would not make "scientists," into clinical courses with the hope that those students would find jobs somewhere. A number of inadequately trained people, generally called "psychometricians," who presumably were nothing more than psychological technicians, thus entered the field. With the growing professional consciousness of psychologists, a distinct change is taking place in the university attitude as well as among those working in the field. The importance of good personality as well as high intellectual qualities for clinical work is receiving recognition. This trend is being aided in two ways. One is through the increasing selection of clinical psychology by high-grade students. In fact, more and more reports are being received from different centers that clinical students stand among the highest level of graduate students in psychology. The other is through intensive programs of investigation of selection techniques. The most prominent and ambitious of these is the study being carried out at the University of Michigan for the Veterans Administration.

In recent years the American Psychological Association has become increasingly aware of the need to set up standards both for training and practice in clinical psychology. As has already been described, some early attempts were made in this direction but nothing definite resulted. The formation of the American Association for Applied Psychology in 1937 (amalgamated with the American Psychological Association in 1944) helped considerably in establishing professional psychology and securing for it proper recognition in the total psychological scene.

The American Psychological Association's Committee on Graduate and Professional Training has in the last several years set up standards for evaluating the training given by universities in clinical psychology. In fact, this Committee has provided the criteria for the selection of universities participating in the Veterans Administration and the Public Health Service programs.

In May, 1947, recognizing that adequate evaluation cannot be carried out on the basis of paper credentials but must rather be based on actual visitation of institutions, the American Psychological Association appointed a new Committee on Training in Clinical Psychology. This Committee is charged with the formulation of an "ideal" training program, and with setting up criteria for the evaluation of institutions before actually undertaking the evaluation. The United States Public Health Service has provided a grant (to be supplemented by the American Psychological Association, if necessary) for implementing this task. It is expected that this

Committee will provide the data which will make possible official accrediting of both academic and field institutions [as it did].

The Board of Directors of the American Psychological Association, its Policy and Planning Board (APA, PPB, 1947), its Committee of Graduate Department Chairmen, and its Committee on Clinical Psychology (a joint committee with the American Psychiatric Association) (APA, CCP, 1946), are all interested in developing adequate clinical psychological training and standards, and from time to time make recommendations to the Association along these lines.

A most important development in psychology is the organization of the American Board of Examiners in Professional Psychology, a board modeled on the specialty boards in medicine and having in general the same standards. In September, 1946, the Association accepted the report of the Committee on the organization of a Board of Examiners (APA, CABEPP, 1946) and in April, 1947, the Board (consisting of nine members) was incorporated. The general plan of the Board is to require five years of acceptable experience in addition to the doctoral degree as a requirement for admission to examination for its diploma.

At one time or another associated groups have been concerned with standards for clinical psychologists. Thus, the American Orthopsychiatric Association, vitally interested as it has been in the problems of standards in the orthopsychiatric field, has been interested in standards for psychologists as one aspect of the problem for the clinic team. The closely affiliated American Association of Psychiatric Clinics for Children is also deeply concerned with these problems, and at the February, 1947, meeting of the Association considered a Committee report on standards which, allowing for the special needs of child guidance clinics, are in many respects similar to those proposed by the Subcommittee.

The combined Committee on Clinical Psychology of the American Psychological Association and the American Psychiatric Association has discussed the problem, and the Group for the Advancement of Psychiatry has established a Committee on Clinical Psychology to study the relationships between psychiatry and clinical psychology. Recently the Macy Foundation held a conference on clinical psychology to explore the basic needs and contributions of the field, with especial respect to therapy. All these efforts have important implications, direct and indirect, for the establishment of standards, accreditation, and certification.

Another aspect of the problem of certification involves governmental bodies. In order to protect the public by setting standards, several attempts have been made to promote legislation for the certification of psychologists by state agencies (Symposium, 1941). In general, psychologists have taken the attitude that such legal certification should be approached slowly and carefully and await the development of standards within the field. Two different types of certification have been under consideration, exemplified by the Connecticut (Heiser, 1945) and Virginia (Finger, 1946) laws. The former calls for the general certification of psychologists with a Ph.D. degree plus one year of experience; the latter provides for the certification of specified kinds of psychologists, in this case, clinical psychologists, with a Ph.D. plus five years of experience. It is believed in the psychological group, as reflected in the recommendation of the Policy and Planning Board (APA, PPB, 1947), that state certification should preferably be on the pattern of the Connecticut plan and that "expert" certification should be left to a professional agency, the Board of Examiners. It is likely that this suggestion will be generally adopted [as it was].

These very active developments in the clinical psychological field did not, of course, occur in isolation. Some of the influences have already been mentioned: those which were a natural result of broad social developments and those which came from within the psychological field proper. Another considerable influence has been the concurrent development in the associated fields of psychiatry and psychiatric social work. Both of these disciplines have been concerned with training and standards for many years. Social work has perhaps dealt with these problems most consistently and adequately, as seen in the establishment of a list of approved schools and the activities of the American Association of Psychiatric Social Workers through its various committees and publications. The psychiatric group, through its conferences on psychiatric education, and the organization of the American Board of Psychiatry and Neurology have gone far toward establishing standards. Activities of both groups have placed a certain pressure on psychology to do likewise—a pressure which has been very healthy.

The Future of Clinical Psychology

Of the three professions mainly concerned with the problems of psychopathology, clinical psychology is the last to establish itself. Psychiatric social work, as has been pointed out, has taken its task most seriously and made the most definite efforts to determine its functions and to train for these in an organized fashion. Psychiatry has in recent years done considerable thinking about the problem and has in a somewhat less organized way also attempted to establish standards of training.

Psychology, in its clinical contacts, has been handicapped by its academic tradition. This background had first to be lived down. After an effective period of revolt, second thought has indicated that it contains important values which could be adapted to the new setting. The revolt was necessary in order to establish the importance of human problems as a field for study. But once this essential principle was accepted, the contribution of academic psychology with its insistence on careful investigation, control, and concern with fundamentals could be recognized for the role it should play in a well-rounded clinical psychology. Clinical psychology has gone through the stage of breaking away entirely from academic psychology in order to establish its field of work on an adequate practical basis, and a trend is now seen toward reamalgamation with its parent body. The other two disciplines did not in this respect have so sharp a contrast with their origins and were therefore able to deal with their problems earlier.

There is a good deal of ferment in the field. In part this is a reflection of the existing social concern with psychopathology generally. But there is a special part which involves the field of clinical psychology. Not only are psychologists themselves interested, but other groups are concerned about its development. The many factors which have played a role in this attitude have already been discussed. The question which now arises is whether this great flood of activity will be productive and lead to a well-formulated program and a distinctive place for the clinical psychologist.

There seems to be good reason for believing that these efforts will bear fruit. The combination of great social need, effectiveness of contribution, and organized and widespread concern about responsibility and standards would appear to make the future position of the clinical psychologist secure. The optimum achievement of this promise, however, will depend on what psychology does about providing training, and how effectively it works out its relationships with associated disciplines in the various settings in which these are involved.

We can perhaps best envisage coming developments if we see them as represented in the clinical psychologist of the not too remote future.

Until psychology becomes fairly well known as a field of vocational choice, it is unlikely that undergraduate prerequisites for clinical psychological training will be made as definite as those now current in medicine. Even then, it is questionable whether rigid prerequisites will be established. In some medical circles questions are being raised about this aspect of medicine's present program. The desirability of a broad scientific and humanistic background would be emphasized. This should include an acquaintance with the principles of science, physical, natural, and social; the principles of logic; an acquaintance with world literature, particularly in the field of biography and character description; and an acquaintance with broad cultural and humanistic fields. Experience with varied human settings such as comes from contacts in factory or camp would be considered an asset. Only elementary aspects of psychology would be included in the undergraduate program, enough to give the student a real "feel" of the content of psychology.

The actual program of training would start with a graduate-level four-year course, one year of which would be spent in an internship, leading to a doctoral degree. The first year would be spent mainly in basic courses common to training in all psychological fields. It would, however, provide opportunities for orienting the student toward life situations. This would be accomplished not through training in special technical skills, such as testing, but rather through situations affording opportunities for the detailed natural observation of a variety of persons, normal and abnormal, in a wide range of situations. The major aim of this aspect of the program would be, besides providing for the student contact with human material, to train him in the accurate description of complex human behavior and situations. To develop such skills, devices such as movies and recording instruments would be used. Instruction in the background of test devices, their theory and history, and practice in the use of simple techniques, would also be part of the program for this year. Some time would be devoted to a course in the experimental approach to problems of personality.

The second year would be spent in the acquisition of background knowledge about and initial training in the administration of the more difficult diagnostic devices. This would be accomplished in clerkship and practicum settings. A first acquaintance with the principles of therapy and more advanced work in some of the phases of the study begun in the first year would constitute the balance of the year's activity.

The third year would be spent in an internship center which offers a rich variety of material and full representation of the various disciplines which play important roles in psychopathology. The major function of the internship would be to provide practical experience of gradually increasing complexity under close and competent supervision. The program would provide a broad base for later specialization by placing the student in full-time diagnostic, therapeutic, and research contact with human clinical material, contact of a much more intensive kind than that provided by the clinical clerkships of the second year. Of great importance is the fact that this study would be carried out in close association with members of other disciplines, from which experience the student would learn the values and techniques of the team approach to the problems of personality. The internship year would also provide an opportunity to do the necessary research for the dissertation.

The fourth year would be devoted to seminars on professional problems, the completion of the work on the dissertation, any additional courses needed by the student to round out his training, and to cross-discipline seminars. In fact, relationships with other disciplines, particularly psychiatry, would be emphasized throughout the four years. The use of representatives of these disciplines in the teaching would help to implement such a program.

Before embarking on this program, the candidate would have to go through a careful selection process by devices which accumulating experience have indicated to be effective. Besides obvious intellectual qualifications, the candidate would need to have certain personality qualifications which had been generally agreed upon as important for clinical work.

The universities and the field training centers would have undergone the same critical evaluation as the student himself and the latter would have available to him data which told him whether the institutions he was considering met the standards of the American Psychological Association.

Having obtained his Ph.D., the student would presumably be in a position to undertake clinical work in an institution where further supervision in advanced or specialized aspects of the clinical field would be available. This would be in the nature of a residency. After a year of such experience, the candidate would be eligible for certification by the state of which he is a resident, certification which carried with it reciprocal privileges in other states. After an additional four years of experience, at least half of which was spent in a recognized center, the candidate would be eligible for the examination of the American Board of Examiners in Professional Psychology, which would, on his meeting the requirements, issue to him a diploma as a specialist in clinical psychology. Sometime during this period he will have gone through some form of intensive self-examination under competent guidance, preferably a psychoanalysis (Shakow, 1945b).

All through his training period, the psychologist would have emphasized the importance of a research attitude, the great need for research in the field, and his special preparation for it. As a result of such an emphasis, it is to be hoped that this function would be considered by the psychologist as a major one.

During the immediate post-doctoral period and beyond, post-graduate courses, ordinarily organized under state or national psychological association auspices, would be available to him to keep him informed of developments in the field.

By means of a program of this kind, there is some assurance to individuals, to society generally, and to related disciplines, that persons who go through this course will be competent to practice. Three types of control would act to assure this: the personal inner control which is a natural result of proper initial selection, ethical training and identification with a respected and competent group; the professional controls which come from membership in the American Psychological Association and from certification by the Board of Examiners; and the legal controls which come from state certification.

The development of clinical psychologists of this type should go far to establish sound relationships with related disciplines and within the field of psychology itself. Within psychology there should result greater integration and cross-fertilization, the expected effect of constant contact between academy and field. The clinical group will be kept in touch with fundamental theory and methodology and the academic group will be kept aware of the nature and complexity of human problems and processes.

With psychiatry and psychiatric social work, its two major teammates, the relations should become more clearly defined. The concurrent efforts of the three professions toward adequate preparation of its members can result in nothing but benefit to their interrelationships. This generally happens when competent persons work together. Most of the disagreements which have in some places existed have arisen from the inadequacies of poor personality or poor professional preparation of one, another, or all the members of the team. In those settings where the teammates have been mature and competent, the problems, personal and professional, have been at a minimum.

As has been observed, the nature of the team approach has changed over the years. With the growth of clinics there has been a tendency for the functions of the three disciplines to overlap considerably, sometimes to make them almost indistinguishable. But it is desirable, and likely, that despite common emphasis on therapeutic activity, there will continue to be specialization in those aspects which the training in the particular discipline emphasizes: by the psychiatrist in handling psychosomatic problems, by the social worker with the social and environmental aspects of problems, and by the psychologist with diagnostic and research aspects. The great value of the team approach lies not in the fact that every patient has to be studied by practitioners of three disciplines, but that all disciplines are available for study in those cases where they are needed, and that the coordinated thinking of the disciplines, each from its own point of view, is available in every case. The problems of disturbed human personality are so complex that single-discipline handling of problems runs the danger of being quite incomplete and inadequate.

With the field of medicine, aside from psychiatry and neurology, clinical psychology should develop more and more extensive contacts, especially in research. Besides association on problems through the psychiatrist, the field of somatopsychics, in which the psychological aspects of physical disease are studied, will become increasingly important as a field of associated endeavor. Industry and education will also provide opportunities for the well-trained clinical psychologist, even to a greater extent than at present.

Settings for Future Work

In the main, the clinical psychologist of the future will work in institutions, hospitals, university and other clinics, public and private, and in other places where he will be associated with members of other disciplines and where material for research is readily available.

In line with what is happening in psychiatry, and partly as a result of this development, there will probably be an increasing amount of practice in private settings. It is to be hoped, however, in view of the considerations already mentioned, that this will not become a dominant trend and that most work will be in the form of group practice; that is, in association with members of other disciplines, particularly psychiatry.

Undoubtedly a certain number of psychologists will be interested in individual practice. Under these circumstances it should be largely on a referral and consultation basis, work with cases sent by psychiatrists and other physicians. Only a limited amount of direct individual practice is possible. The questions raised by the latter stem from the lack of sufficient social control of the situation. At present there is little likelihood that psychologists will be licensed in the sense that physicians are licensed. Until this takes place, and at least for the present, such a step seems undesirable. The social controls, legal and professional, which are available are not sufficiently developed to make direct individual practice by psychologists generally desirable. At least as important as those mentioned here, are the considerations mentioned earlier with respect to the importance of group evaluation in providing the patient with the best treatment. In these respects, the restriction on individual practice holds as well for psychiatric practice.

Clinical psychology, after a long period spent as part of an academic discipline, is in the early stages of becoming a profession. It is going through the natural disturbances and difficulties which attend a growth process of this kind. However, if it selects its students carefully, for personality as well as intellect; if it trains thoroughly, in spirit as well as letter; if it trains broadly, recognizing that "Otis specialists" or even "Rorschach specialists" are not clinical psychologists; if it remains flexible about its training and encourages experimentation; if it does not become overwhelmed by immediate needs at the cost of important remoter goals; if it maintains its contact with its scientific background, remaining aware of the importance of theory as well as practice; if it remains modest in the face of the complexity of its problems, rather than becoming pretentious—in other words, if it finds good people and gives them good training—these disturbances and difficulties need not be of serious concern. Its future, both for itself as a profession and for society in the contribution it can make, is then assured. Fortunately, there are many reasons for believing that these are the prevailing aspirations in clinical psychology.

2. Clinical Psychology

In the early fifties, the Institute of Psychoanalysis in Chicago planned a volume on *Dynamic Psychiatry*, the contributors to be persons who were or who had been associated with it as faculty members, as students, or otherwise. The project was under the guidance of Franz Alexander and Helen Ross. I was asked to contribute the chapter on "Clinical Psychology." Its purpose was to tell something about the nature of clinical psychology and to describe its functioning in a psychiatric setting.

Clinical psychology cannot be defined in a simple clear-cut way. If defined too broadly, its scope overlaps considerably with related fields, such as psychiatry; if defined narrowly, it does not cover areas which are at present definitely within the range of activity of clinical psychologists. In a period of remarkable public interest in the general area of mental health, a restricted and rigid definition might also tend to hinder natural growth.

It can, however, be said that clinical psychology is concerned with the psychological adjustment problems of the individual—more specifically, with the determination and evaluation of capacities and characteristics relating to adjustment and the study and application of psychological techniques for improving adjustment. Clinical psychology approaches these problems from the point of view and with the skills of its particular training, just as adjustment problems are approached by other interested disciplines according to their own background and training.

Clinical psychology as a field in its own right had its beginnings in 1896, when Lightner Witmer set up a Psychological Clinic at the University of Pennsylvania (Brotemarkle, 1947). This step was taken in the setting of a general psychology which has a "long past" dating from the very beginnings of philosophy, but only a "short history," starting about the third quarter of the nineteenth century, as a field for scientific study. Against a background of academic psychology—a psychology that was almost entirely concerned with *general* laws, particularly those relating to sensation and perception—Witmer applied some of the methods of the laboratory to the problems of the *individual* case. An approximation of what has since become known as the "team" approach in the psychiatric area was early adopted by the Psychological Clinic at the University of Pennsylvania. Physicians, especially neurologists, collaborated with the psychologists at the clinic in the study of cases, and there was an early and continuing use of social workers.

During the period in which the University of Pennsylvania Psychological Clinic was developing, other factors were at work which played roles of varying importance in the growth of clinical psychology. Prodromal signs of the Binet development had appeared earlier, but it was not until 1905, with the publication of the first form of the Binet-Simon test, that the influence of this instrument became marked.

Reprinted with permission from F. Alexander and H. Ross (Eds.), *Dynamic Psychiatry*, 1952 (University of Chicago Press).

Beginning with the latter part of the nineteenth century and through the early part of the twentieth, a most important development was taking place in the field of psychiatry which had a considerable influence upon the course of clinical psychology. The functional point of view was becoming more and more prominent through the activities of such men as Charcot and Janet, but most particularly of Freud, abroad, and Meyer in this country.

This trend toward a functional point of view led to the development of another type of clinic in the United States. In 1909, William Healy, in association with the Cook County Juvenile Court of Chicago, started a Behavior Clinic for the study of delinquents (Healy, 1915). It is from this development that the child-guidance movement ordinarily dates its origin. Healy had been impressed by Witmer's clinic, but his general approach was in many ways quite different. The approach to the problem that Witmer developed has had an important but limited effect on the development of clinical psychology, determining its pattern only in the early days. On the other hand, Healy's approach has had a more pervasive effect on clinical psychology, especially in its latter phases. Witmer's consistent concern was with educational problems, primarily those of the mentally defective. This emphasis on the intellectual-cognitive aspects of personality naturally led mainly to contact with the educator in the setting of the school or institution for the feebleminded. Healy's primary emphasis on the affective aspects of personality involved a broader study of the individual and contact with a much greater variety of social agencies and institutions and called for a more profound, dynamic psychology.

A development paralleling the development of these clinics, and one that is of some importance in the history of clinical psychology, was the establishment of psychological laboratories in hospitals for the mentally disordered, beginning as early as 1894 in this country (Shakow, 1945a). The McLean Hospital, St. Elizabeth's Hospital, the Boston Psychopathic Hospital, and the Worcester State Hospital are among the outstanding early examples. In some respects the work in these institutions followed along more conservative academic, experimental lines. Other aspects of their activities helped to broaden considerably the range of application of test devices. In these centers, too, there was an early association of psychologists with psychiatrists, both more extensive and intensive than that found in the Witmer type of clinic.

From these beginnings the scope of activity of clinical psychologists during the last fifty years has been quite broad. This range includes, besides work in child-guidance agencies, work in psychiatric hospitals, mental hygiene clinics, vocational guidance centers, school systems, student personnel services, prisons, schools for the delinquent, general hospitals, neurological hospitals, hospitals for the tubercular, nursery schools, case-work agencies, schools for the handicapped, and agencies working with the alcoholic and with the aged.

Since, as has already been pointed out, some of the areas covered by psychology are overlapping, whereas some are distinctive, it should be instructive to consider the relations of the psychologist to the other members of the staff in the psychiatric setting.

When the team approach was first put into practice, what happened typically was what generally happens in new developments where the participants are relatively untrained. Simplicity, naïveté, and specialization of the highest degree characterized the organization. The psychiatrist as physician made a physical study of the patient; the social worker went out into the community and conducted a social investigation which resulted in a social history; the psychologist gave the mental tests. When the physical, social, and mental-test studies were completed, an evaluation conference, attended by all three, was held, and on the basis of the pooled findings the psychiatrist carried out the indicated therapy with the patient. The patient was usually a child, since it was almost exclusively in child-guidance clinics that the team approach was the standard practice. If, in addition to personal therapy, environmental modifications were indicated, the social worker was called upon for this additional activity.

It soon became obvious that others besides the patient proper—usually the mother—also needed therapy. This task naturally fell to the social worker, since she had already established contact with the outside community. The limited scope of the psychologist's activity was broadened somewhat when it was recognized that certain problems, such as those of speech or reading difficulty, were fundamentally reeducational problems. These were turned over to him as the person best versed in educational procedure. It developed, however, that speech and reading problems were not mere matters of tutoring or habit training but were integrally associated with personality difficulties. Since these problems were already in the psychologist's hands, it was natural for him to continue with them at this broader level, and so the way was opened for the psychologist to work with related problems of general personality therapy. With the gradual broadening of the field of the other members of the team, the psychiatrist extended his own field to include occasional work with the adults in the child patient's environment. Under these circumstances, it was natural for the social worker to feel that age was not a reasonable basis for distinction in her own treatment work, so she began working with children. And the psychologist, on the same general grounds, began to work therapeutically with parents.

Thus what started off as a group whose members each had a very specialized and compartmentalized function became in practice a group of persons having overlapping and sometimes quite similar functions. This overlapping also resulted in the fact that frequently all three members no longer worked on the same case together. Sometimes only one, more frequently two, and, relatively less frequently, all three disciplines were involved in dealing with the same case.

Under these circumstances, what is the division of responsibility which the team situation now calls for? In answering this question, we must recognize that two important factors are involved. The first is the obvious one of the nature of the training provided by each of the disciplines. The second is a factor which is sometimes neglected in formal discussions of the problem but which is of paramount importance in the practical setting. I refer to the personality, interests, and special abilities of the individual staff member. In a field where personality factors play such an important role and where variations in the special background, interests, and abilities of workers are so great, the needs of the patient demand that both these factors be given due consideration.

We can best indicate the division of responsibility and activity among the members of a clinic whose workers are equally well trained in their particular specialities by the consideration of each of the six major functions of a clinic's activity: diagnosis, research, teaching, consultation, community relations, and therapy.

In relation to diagnostic work, each member of the team naturally makes the important diagnostic contributions which arise from the traditional approach of the discipline he represents: the psychiatrist, the medical-psychiatric; the social worker, the social and developmental data, which come from the family background history; the clinical psychologist, the psychological data, which come from psychological tests and situational studies.

In the research sphere, each profession will have problems which fall within its own field and will wish to work with these relatively independently. Problems requiring coordinated attack are taken care of by representatives of the disciplines involved.

With respect to teaching, each profession under ordinary circumstances takes care of its own group of students and also carries the responsibility for that program of training in its own field which is laid out for the students and staff workers in other fields.

In the sphere of consultation (with representatives of other agencies, professional persons, and parents), each profession naturally takes care of the problems which are most relevant to its major competence. Problems of intellectual status, developmental stages, special abilities, and defects are usually the task of the psychologist; problems of a social and socioeconomic type, the task of the social worker; and problems of psychiatric and psychosomatic character, the task of the psychiatrist.

Community relations, which involve contact with other social agencies, with professional persons—such as ministers, physicians, and teachers—and with the lay public, are best established by each profession in its own field insofar as lectures and other group contacts are concerned. Presumably, any of the members of the staff would be prepared to give talks on the general problems of mental hygiene.

In relation to therapy, all three types of workers concern themselves with one or another of the various forms of psychotherapy, with an understandable concentration of effort by the social workers on cases where the problems are mainly social, by the psychologist where they are mainly educational, and by the psychiatrist where they are primarily psychosomatic.

Although in the six major clinic functions there is participation by all the disciplines, in three of these functions—namely, therapy, research, and community relations—one or another particular discipline is more prepared by training and predominant interest to take the major role.

The leadership in therapy rests in the hands of the psychiatrist because of his medical background, with its social and legally recognized responsibilities for treatment, and because of his great concern with this problem. The leading role in research would generally fall most naturally to the psychologist because of his special preoccupation with this aspect and because of his training, which places emphasis on investigative approaches. Predominant concern with community relations is the obvious responsibility of the social worker because of her extensive community contacts, her wide acquaintance with social organization, and her concern with the social forces in the community.

A clinic organized to take advantage of the different specialized backgrounds of the disciplines involved, as well as of their common skills, and, in addition, to take advantage of the special background and competence of its individual staff members can be said to meet the true meaning of the "team" approach. Such an approach involves a coordinated attack based on coordinated thinking about the mental hygiene problems of the individual and the community.

I have mentioned the range of activities that the psychologist is involved in as a result of his special training. It would be profitable to examine this training briefly. The last several years have seen much preoccupation with the problem of training in clinical psychology. A great variety of influences both from within and from without the field have caused clinical psychology to call upon its practitioners for competence in three major functions: *diagnosis*, the use of procedures directed to acquiring knowledge about the nature and origin of the psychological conditions under investigation; *research*, the systematic experimental or clinical attack upon specific problems for the advancement of knowledge; and *guidance and therapy*, the study and use of techniques for improving the condition of the person who comes for help. It is toward competence in these three functions that training in psychology is being more and more systematically directed at the present time.

The generally accepted pattern of training of the clinical psychologist is that proposed in the report of the Committee on Training in Clinical Psychology of the American Psychological Association (1947). This program is the natural outgrowth of a long series of efforts, arising mainly in field centers (Morrow, 1946), to systematize the training which had remained in an unorganized state for a long time. The extensive and more intelligent use of psychology during the second World War and the development of the Veterans Administration (Miller, 1946) and the United States Public Health Service (Felix, 1948) programs gave already going efforts a great impetus and resulted in the adoption of a general program. The pattern followed has been somewhat different from that of psychiatry, in that it has emphasized more the development of existing university departments as central clinical training centers and has encouraged the integration of field training centers into the university programs (Harrower, 1947). Although several suggestions for the establishment of special professional schools in clinical psychology have been made, present opinion seems to favor working within the framework of existing university departments of psychology expanded to meet the special needs of clinical psychology.

One of the problems of the past which is being given careful consideration at present involves the recruitment and selection of potentially able clinical psychologists. The importance for clinical work of good personality characteristics as well as high intellectual qualities is receiving recognition (Kelly, 1947).

Until psychology becomes fairly well known as a field of vocational choice, it is unlikely that undergraduate prerequisites for clinical psychological training will be made as definite as those now current in medicine. Even then, it is questionable whether rigid prerequisites will ever be established. The desirability of a broad scientific and humanistic background is recognized. This is expected to include an acquaintance with the principles of science, physical, natural and social, and with the principles of logic; an acquaintance with world literature, particularly in the field of biography and character description; and an acquaintance with broad cultural and humanistic fields. Experience with varied human settings such as comes from contacts in factory or field is considered an asset. Only enough of the elementary aspects of psychology are included in the undergraduate program to give the student a real "feel" for the content of psychology.

The actual program of training consists of a graduate-level four-year course which leads to a doctoral degree (APA, CTCP, 1947). This is ordinarily followed by five years of experience, at least half of which is spent in a recognized training center. Such a program makes the candidate eligible for the examinations of the American Board of Examiners in Professional Psychology, which issues diplomas of specialization in clinical psychology.

The contributions of the psychologist in the psychiatric setting will be discussed in relation to the three major areas already considered in the description of team activities and training, but mainly in relation to two of them, diagnosis and research.

It is probably fair to say that there is, on the one hand, a tendency on the part of the psychiatrist to pay too much attention to diagnostic contributions from the psychologist and, on the other, not to take these contributions seriously enough. In the field of psychiatry, where diagnosis and judgment depend so much on qualitative bases, it is natural to place rather exaggerated importance on quantitative scores of some aspect or other of the personality when these are made available. On the other hand, owing to the fact that the qualitative observations of the psychologist frequently fall into the same general categories as those of the psychiatrist, there may be a tendency to pay less attention to this aspect of his contribution.

In the diagnostic[1] realm, what questions should be put to the psychologist to which he may legitimately be expected to have a reply? Before answering this query, it should be understood that the answers which the psychologist gives should ordinarily be considered to be of suggestive, complementary, or corroborative significance in the context of findings provided by a number of disciplines. Only occasionally can they be considered definitive. Frequently, the covert psychological examination provides data on characteristics and traits which are not elicited by the ordinary overt psychiatric examination.

The psychologist, on the basis of the diagnostic devices which he uses, can with varying degrees of completeness and assurance, depending on the problem and the conditions of the examination, provide answers to questions which fall into four major areas: intellectual aspects of the personality, affective-conative aspects of personality, certain aspects of diagnosis, and certain aspects of disposition.

In the intellectual sphere some of the questions may be: At which level of intellectual activity is the patient functioning? What relationship does this level

[1] By "diagnostic," the author means, of course, a good deal more than mere "pigeon-holing." Diagnosis is here concerned with the origin, nature, and especially the dynamics of the conditions under study and with suggesting hypotheses as to outcome under varying forms of disposition.

have to his optimal level? What specific intellectual abilities and disabilities does he have?

With respect to the emotional-activity aspects of personality, the questions may be: What are the patient's fundamental traits and characteristics? What are his dominant preoccupations? What are his latent trends? How much do these characteristics aid or hinder the achievement of his intellectual or other capacities?

With respect to diagnosis, such questions may include: What kind and what degree of disturbance does he manifest in intellectual functions generally and in specific functions, such as memory, reasoning, or association? What kind of syndrome do the psychological tests show? What evidences of change in function does he manifest now (e.g., following a course of therapy or a long illness) as compared with his functioning at an earlier period?

With respect to disposition, the questions may be: What educational recommendations can be made? What vocational recommendations are indicated? What are the prognostic possibilities of the use of his capacities in a vocation or in education or in life generally, with or without therapy?

The above are broad questions, the answers to which depend on the use of a variety of psychological procedures. Some of these procedures or devices attempt to obtain information primarily on intellectual functioning, some on emotional functioning.

The essential scientific methods available to both psychiatry and clinical psychology are, of course, naturalistic observation and experiment.[2] The former is the naturalist's standard approach, in which conditions are accepted as given and generalizations are made from selected observations. The latter, on the other hand, attempts to set up the conditions to be observed, trying insofar as possible to control all variables but one, and then to make generalizations.

In the field of psychology a widely used method has developed which falls somewhere between these two. I have reference to the use of tests. This method resembles the experiment, in that the conditions are set up by the experimenter but the control of the variables is only moderately achieved. Various forms of statistical control have, therefore, to be introduced as substitutes for the experimental controls.

If we compare the methods used by psychiatry and those used by clinical psychology in the diagnostic realm, it appears that the predominant method used in psychiatry is that of naturalistic observation, whereas that of clinical psychology is testing. In the case of psychiatry, one deals mainly with the case history, which consists essentially of observational data obtained vicariously through relatives and acquaintances or from self-observation by the patient. These data are recorded either by the psychiatrist himself or by a social worker. In addition, the psychiatrist makes use of clinical observation, that is, contemporary observations made either by himself or by his surrogates, such as nurses.

The psychologist, although he depends on clinical observation to some extent—

[2] A more detailed discussion of the investigative methods of the psychologist will be presented later in the context of a consideration of research.

I refer to the observation of behavior during the course of the examination—places major dependence on testing procedures. In order to make the tests informative and dependable, three types of controls are set up: pre-examination controls, examination controls, and post-examination controls. These controls are set up in order to reduce the amount of dependence placed on the observer. Not having these controls, psychiatry puts a tremendous burden on the observer as the recording and evaluating instrument. Although the burden on the psychologist still remains great, these control devices help to reduce the amount of this dependence.

Let us examine the various types of control in order. The pre-examination controls involve the standardization of tests, in relation to both material and methods, until satisfactory criteria of adequacy have been met. With few exceptions, acceptable test devices go through a long period of preliminary study and trial before they are finally ready for use. A large body of tentative material is worked through, and final selection of content is made on the basis of the discriminative quality of the items to evaluate the function tested. In addition, considerable experimentation goes on with respect to the manner of presentation of the material, resulting in a standardized set of instructions. By these methods there is achieved at least some reduction in the variables which might be introduced by the observer or examiner into the situation.

The second of these types of control—those established during the examination proper—relates to the problems of "representativeness" and "optimity" of results. It is concerned with the determination of where the patient's present performance places him in relation to his potential present performance and to his fundamental capacity. An attempt is made here to determine how good a sample of the patient's optimum ability, insofar as tests are able to get at these capacity-capability levels, has been obtained during the present examination.

Psychometric determinations, even more than physiological determinations such as oxygen-consumption rate and blood pressure, are affected by the condition of the subject during examination. It is therefore essential to evaluate the adequacy of the examination results. If these are reasonably close to the *optimum* performance of which the subject was capable at *any* time, they may be considered both optimal and representative. If the results obtained are the best which the patient can obtain during the more or less immediate period of the examination (and if, at the same time, they are lower than those he could obtain at the time of his best performance), the results may be considered representative but not optimal. A consideration of the many factors which must be taken into account in arriving at this important judgment will make the distinction between the two clearer.

The factors disturbing representativeness are generally of a temporary nature. Some are under the partial control of the subject: effort, interest, self-confidence. Others are almost entirely outside the subject's control: a psychotic episode (temporary manic, excited, or hallucinatory conditions), an emotional upset, marked anxiety, physical handicap (loss of sensory aids, such as glasses, etc.), passing physical illness (headache, etc.), fatigue, poor test conditions.

The actual quantitative changes produced by these temporary factors, that is, the unrepresentativeness, is to be seen in their effect on mental age in various groups. In a study (Roe & Shakow, 1942) carried out on a variety of mental disorders, the average additional decrease in mental age level, over and above the effect of the disorder, was found to be about 13 per cent. The decrease varies considerably, however, with the type of mental disorder. Thus in a feebleminded group having an associated psychosis, the difference was negligible, whereas in chronic alcoholism with psychosis it was about 20 per cent, and in dementia praecox, simple group, about 30 per cent. The importance of taking into account the factor of representativeness is thus clearly indicated.

The optimity of the examination is affected not only by all the factors of a temporary kind mentioned in the discussion of representativeness but also by a group of factors of a relatively permanent nature, such as physical disability (uncorrected deafness, paralysis, etc.), psychotic state of a prolonged type, chronological age beyond approximately forty, and language disability.

A judgment of "unrepresentative" or of "not optimal" is not, of course, automatically made when some or even all of these factors are present. Rather, the examiner should consider the presence of such factors as cues for further investigation. He must then examine them carefully in relation to test performance and evaluate the role which each may have played in affecting the results. It is conceivable, though not actually likely, that many of these interfering factors may be operating and the examination results may be evaluated as optimal.

For purposes of illustration, let us take one of the factors—chronological age. Numerous studies (Miles, 1933, 1939) have indicated that certain psychological functions begin to show a decline at approximately the age of forty. The curve of function is, of course, based on an *average* tendency in the general population. In some persons the decline comes earlier, in some later. It is important for the examiner to be aware of this contingency in order to evaluate the performance of the particular subject with respect to the possible effect of age on performance. If the evidence, such as a considerably lower proportionate score on immediate memory items as compared with the score on reasoning items and vocabulary, is in the direction of decline, then a lack of optimity is indicated.

In relation to this problem, the most difficult factor to evaluate is the effect of mental disorder. As stated earlier, when the patient is in a psychotic or other disturbed episode, the representativeness should be questioned, but when the disordered state is more permanent, the optimity is also questioned. It is obviously difficult to distinguish between, or to set arbitrary limits for, episodes and more permanent states. The examiner must keep in mind the primary purpose of making these judgments, namely, to evaluate fairly the person's psychological *capacity*. At the same time, it is necessary to determine his *functioning* ability, that is, what he has to work with at the present time. If, from all the evidence available with regard to his psychotic condition, the person's performance today is the best he would be likely to achieve during the approximate period of the next several weeks or more, then the examination is considered representative. A statement to this effect means that, in the opinion of the examiner, the patient is functioning at a level of performance as high as he is likely to attain if examined during the reasonably near future. When the examiner, however, has some basis for believing that the patient could achieve a higher level of performance within such a period of time, he must consider the examination unrepresentative.

The judgment of optimity in relationship to mental disorder is particularly difficult and requires a kind of clinical judgment which only extended clinical experience can provide. The question placed before the examiner here is really: What more or less permanent effects has the disorder had on the psychological functions which prevent the present measure from being as high as the highest which the person would have obtained at some earlier time, that is, at a period of optimum performance? If there is any evidence in the history or psychiatric record or internal evidence in the test itself that the best performance has not been obtained, the examination is not considered optimal. It must again be stressed here that the presence of mental disorder does not *ipso facto* result in the judgment of "unrepresentative" or "nonoptimal." Occasionally there are cases of even long-standing psychoses in which some of the functions measured by tests appear to be little or not at all affected.

Representativeness is, of the two, the more easily determined. Optimity can to some extent be gauged from internal evidence provided by the tests, but to a greater degree it is determined from the factors mentioned above, together with an evaluation of the educational and vocational achievement and, when available, previous psychometric results.

The third type of control is the post-examination control. This has to do with the problem of norms, relating the performance of the patient to that of other persons in a particular group. With few exceptions, tests are not considered adequate until explicit norms of this kind have been established on certain samples of the population.

There is need for care in sampling the group in order to avoid bias. If we wish to be able to say that X is better or worse than the average, and perhaps even say *how* much better or worse, then we must be sure that our average is a real average and not due to age, sex, race, personality, or occupational or other forms of selection. Complicated statistical methods for selecting adequate standardization groups, which we need not go into here, have been developed. Any group may be used for standardization purposes if it is clearly defined and carefully selected. Usually the norms are based on a variety of samples. To give a few examples, they may be age norms established on persons of different ages or autogenous norms based on racial, handicapped, or diagnostic groups.

Scores obtained by subjects may be expressed in norms in a variety of ways. Norms may be given in terms of age. In this case a statement is made about the score being the equivalent of such and such a chronological age or mental age level (or a derivative of this in terms of I.Q. level). In other cases the norms may be given in terms of centile standing or in quintiles, quartiles, or deciles. We may say, for instance, that a person's score falls into the lowest quartile of those for his age group. In still other cases the norms may be given in terms of standard deviational units, a statistic which is particularly adaptable to the kinds of distributions of functions which are obtained in psychological studies. An individual score could be described as falling one standard deviation above the average score of the group, which would mean that it falls at about the upper 15 per cent mark.

The important point for our purpose, whichever norms are used, is that dependence is not placed on the individual examiner's privately established norms (in other words, his "judgment"), but rather upon objectively obtained criterion data. Any adequate estimate of a subject's psychological capacity must therefore be based on an evaluation in terms of two standards: Where does the person stand in relation to the *group?* Where does he stand in relation to his optimum *self?*

The difference in the predominant emphases of approach of psychiatry and psychology to the problems of the study of the person makes a combined attack by the two disciplines desirable. Although there is indeed some overlapping in the methods used and in the area covered, the major differences lead to obtaining both complementary and supplementary data with checks and counterchecks. In an area where the difficulty of obtaining dependable data is relatively great and the phenomena dealt with complex and difficult, the need for such control is obvious.

In emphasizing the "objective" character of tests, it is not my intention to minimize the importance of the "subjective" controls. These controls are essential if the greatest advantage is to be gotten from the objective characteristics. Psychological examining is not a matter of machine-tending; it is a complex human relationship calling for all the skills and sensitivities demanded by any situation requiring the establishment and maintenance of rapport. The examiner must recognize when tests are called for and when they should not be used. He needs to know what tests and combinations of tests are required in specific problems, and what their limitations are, as well as their strengths. Besides having an insightful knowledge of the diagnostic and prognostic aspects of his test findings, the examiner must be sensitive to their therapeutic implications. In fact, it is necessary that he have a "therapeutic attitude" in his testing, that is, one which avoids probing and the carrying-out of misplaced therapy. In keeping with good testing procedure and without violating the controls, he must leave the patient better rather than worse for the test experience. The examiner must have a sense of balance between the extremes of rigorous, pedantic exactness and slovenly "guessing." He must recognize that different problems lend themselves to differing degrees of control and that there are times (in certain stages of development of a problem) when a rough negative correlation appears to obtain between psychological significance and degree of control. While always working for reasonably greater control, he must be honest both in designating the degree obtained at the particular time and in admitting ignorance and tentativeness when such are the case. The psychologist must have enough security, on the one hand, not to escape into exactness about the insignificant and, on the other, not to escape into meaningless profundities because he is overcome by the complexity and difficulty of the significant. He must have a sense of responsibility about his test findings—an appreciation of the fact that they make a real difference to a particular individual and to those involved with him. The psychologist must recognize that he carries this responsibility as well as the broader social-scientific one of awareness of the research implications of his findings for advance in a field which needs much further work.

Having considered the general principles of testing, we may now discuss some of the available tests. The degree to which psychological testing has permeated our culture in the last twenty years is striking. There are in existence at least five thousand different tests of a psychological nature. An estimate made recently indicates that in 1944 some sixty million psychological tests were given to twenty million persons. For our purposes it is sufficient to become acquainted with the general categories of tests and to understand something about the most prominent tests used in the psychiatric clinical setting. I shall therefore consider first the problem of the classification of tests.

Tests are designed not only to study different functions, an aspect which we shall take up shortly, but also to study various groups of persons. These may include persons in different age ranges; groups of persons with different kinds of handicaps, such as deafness, blindness, psychosis, and neurosis; groups having special vocational characteristics. Some tests are intended for persons at a high level of functioning, some for persons at a low level; some tests use language as a means of communication, others deliberately avoid the use of language, employing instead other types of symbols or performance. Some tests emphasize underlying capacity, whereas others deliberately attempt to study the achievement or acquired knowledge of the person. Again, some tests emphasize intellectual characteristics, whereas others are primarily devoted to a study of nonintellectual or affective aspects. Some are intended for individual administration, whereas others are intended for groups.

We are here concerned primarily with those tests that attempt to measure characteristics that appear mainly to derive from underlying capacity and from the natural maturation of the organism, rather than with tests that are directed at determining the level of achievement derived from specific training. In the latter category fall those tests which attempt to measure educational achievement, skills in school subjects and vocational fields.

The capacity tests may be divided into four major groups: psychomotor, intelligence, nonintellectual aspects of personality, and special aptitudes.

Psychomotor tests generally deal with simple functions, such as steadiness, speed of tapping, and reaction time. Ordinarily, tests of this kind are little used in the clinical psychiatric setting except when organic functions appear to be affected.

The next major category, tests of intelligence, is one of the most important. This area is, in fact, the most highly developed area of the testing field. Intelligence tests fall into two major types: those dealing with composite aspects of intelligence and those dealing primarily with single aspects of intelligence. Among the former are such tests as the Stanford-Binet (Terman, 1916) and the Terman-Merrill (Terman & Merrill, 1937)—respectively the 1916 and 1937 revisions of the Binet—and the Wechsler-Bellevue (Wechsler, 1944). Here also are included group tests of intelligence, such as the Otis Self-administering Test of Mental Ability and the Miller Mental Abilities Test. Among the individual tests falling into the second type of this major category are special tests of such single functions as thinking and memory. Commonly used tests of this kind are the Vigotsky Test (Hanfmann & Kasanin, 1942), a test of conceptual thinking, and the Wells Memory Test (Shakow, Dolkart, & Goldman, 1941).

A third category involves those tests dealing with nonintellectual aspects which have loosely been called "personality" tests. These are mainly of two types: questionnaire and projective. The questionnaire type, of which the Thurstone Personality Schedule and the Bernreuter Personality Inventory are good examples, provides descriptive statements with regard to personality and asks the person to identify himself with either the presence or the absence of the attitude or behavior described. The responses are scored according to available norms. In general, tests of this kind have many defects—primarily in that they tend to elicit unconscious halo effects—and have therefore only limited usefulness. The projective tests of personality are among the most important devices available. In recent years they have taken a very prominent place in the batteries of tests used in the clinical setting. The major instruments in this area are the Rorschach Test (Klopfer & Kelley, 1942), which emphasizes the formal characteristics of personality, and the Thematic Apperception Test (Murray, 1943), which emphasizes the content aspects. The well-known Word Association Test is one of the earliest forms of projective test.

The last category under this major grouping of capacity tests is the one concerned with tests of special aptitudes. These tests aim to get at underlying aptitudes for special fields, such as art, music, mechanics, medicine, and aviation. The test items are based on an analysis of the major functions necessary for the achievement of particular vocational and avocational goals. The attempt is made to determine potential skill in these fields before the person has had any actual training in them. In the clinical setting, these tests are relatively unimportant. Further, the tests themselves have reached only a limited stage of development.[3]

We are now ready to consider some outstanding examples of tests in the intelligence and personality areas.

We may take two examples of the individual intelligence test—the Revised Stanford-Binet Intelligence Scale and the Wechsler-Bellevue Intelligence Scale. In 1916 Terman published the first Stanford Revision of the Binet Test, and in 1937 the further revision here referred to. The test is designed to determine the general level of mental ability of the person tested. It consists of a large number of items arranged from the two-year to the superior adult level. In the case of the younger children, such tasks as building block towers, naming objects, etc., are used; at the higher levels, items involving functions such as reasoning, both verbal and numerical, are employed. Tests of memory are included throughout the scale. The test results are reported in terms of mental age and I.Q. In general, the Stanford-Binet Intelligence Scale is the most valuable for use with children, for whom it was mainly designed.

The Wechsler-Bellevue Intelligence Scale was organized to measure intelligence in adults and adolescents and is given orally to individual subjects. It consists of ten subtests, five of which are primarily verbal and five primarily performance. The verbal tests depend on language both for giving directions and for the responses of the subject. In the performance tests, only the oral directions given by the examiner depend upon language. The five verbal tests cover information, comprehension,

[3] A detailed discussion on the use of tests in diagnosis is to be found in Rosenzweig (1949).

arithmetical reasoning, memory span for digits, and recognition of similarities. The five performance tests involve arranging pictures in a proper sequence, completing incomplete pictures, imitating a design with blocks, assembling a disassembled object, and learning pairs of associated symbols and digits. An alternate verbal test—vocabulary—aims at obtaining a measure of the person's past learning ability. The Wechsler-Bellevue Scale has been standardized on a large number of children and adults, ranging in age from ten to sixty. The results are given in terms of verbal and performance I.Q.'s and a combined I.Q.

The projective tests of personality, in contrast to those we have just discussed, do not require "correct" responses and allow for freedom and spontaneity in answer to the specific stimuli. Since the answers may be considerably elaborated and freedom for the expression of unusual trends is permitted, they are of particular value in the psychiatric setting.

We may now consider two of these tests—the Rorschach Test and the Thematic Apperception Test. The Rorschach Test consists of a set of ink-blots to which the subject is requested to give associations. The scoring of these responses is carried out on the basis of four types of analysis: (*a*) number of responses; (*b*) location of responses: whether a given response is to the whole blot or to only part of it; (*c*) determinants of response: whether form, movement, or color or a combination of these is perceived; (*d*) content of the interpretations: whether human, animal, landscape, etc., was seen. A psychogram is made from these scores which takes the interrelationship of these various kinds of response into account, that is, the individual record is considered as a whole, not as a set of isolated scores. On the basis of this psychogram, considerable information about fundamental personality characteristics is made available. Intellectual creativity, autism, richness or poverty of associations, capacity for outwardly directed affectivity, egocentricity, capacity for social rapport, degree of control over intellectual processes, adaptability, introversiveness and withdrawal, self-appraisal, stereotypy, aggressiveness, orderliness, conformity—these are some of the characteristics on which the Rorschach may throw light. In addition, the test may be of aid in diagnostic classification, since certain combinations of response types are found empirically in particular personality and diagnostic groups.

The Thematic Apperception Test consists of a series of pictures arranged in separate groups for male and female subjects and for adults and children. The subject is instructed to regard each picture as an illustration and is then requested to tell a story to go with it, identifying the characters, explaining their relationship to one another, and giving the background for the situation and its outcome. The material is recorded verbatim and is then analyzed according to the major themas which are revealed. As far as the subject knows, this is a test of creative imagination. He ordinarily believes that he is discussing entirely impersonal material; actually, he provides the examiner with considerable information about his own background, preoccupations, and latent trends, including his attitudes, ideals, and needs and his relationships to important persons in his environment. One obtains from the analysis of these data an understanding of the content of the person's thinking, that is, with *what* he is concerned. The Rorschach, on the other hand, primarily provides a statement about the formal characteristics of the personality, that is, *how* the person reacts and expresses his concern. These tests are thus complementary, and therefore the use of both together is a particularly desirable clinical practice.

The attempt to understand the dynamics of the individual maladjusted personality brings into focus the need for relating his problems both to his resources and to his methods of dealing with such problems. What contribution can the psychological examination make to this task?

In the task presented by the integration of data from the various disciplines frequently concerned with the study of a patient—particularly in bridging the gap between extremes provided by psychiatric and physiological-biochemical data—the psychological material is in a favorable position. Its position is strategic because, on the one hand, its more controlled and objective nature makes it adaptable for correlation with physiological and biochemical material and, on the other, its behavioral and higher-level functional nature makes it directly comparable with the psychiatric and social data.

In addition to the final goal of integrating the psychological findings with those of the other disciplines, the psychological program has another aim, that of establishing a unified psychological portrait of the individual patient. This picture is derived from a battery of tests. Certain general principles of the sampling of psychological functions lie behind the selection and administration of a test battery. These principles involve sampling (1) in different areas (2) for content as well as for formal aspects (3) by overlapping devices and, where possible (4) under conditions of stress as well as under ordinary examination conditions.

In the present consideration of sampling, it is unnecessary to go beyond the simple but useful tripartite classification of cognitive, affective, and conative, using these terms in their conventional meanings. Although any device employed inevitably taps all three areas to some degree, certain devices are especially useful for investigating functions predominantly in one or another of these areas.

The same generalization holds for the structural-contentual dichotomy. Some devices are more adequate for investigating the formal or structural aspects of personality, that is, the *how;* others for exploring the contentual aspects, that is, the *what.* A general weakness in many investigations of personality, especially in those of a psychometric nature, has been the emphasis on the formal aspects of the personality at the expense of content. Although this one-sided emphasis is understandable and in some respects justifiable, the result of it has been to disregard a most important source of information about personality. Although the realm which one necessarily enters when one becomes involved with content is less objective and quantifiable, the broader understanding of the particular personality which study of this aspect affords is impressive.

The third principle of sampling—the inclusion of overlapping devices—is essential in any attempt to sketch a broad psychological portrait on the basis of necessarily limited sampling. It is a most useful way of increasing the reliability of the personality evaluation. The proper evaluation of personality cannot be achieved through the employment of any single device, and in this connection the importance of a battery of tests cannot be overemphasized. Frequently one device, for example, the Rorschach, provides the most revealing data for one patient, whereas, for another, one of the other devices, for example, the Thematic Apperception Test, provides the most dependable and productive material, while the Rorschach results are relatively barren. Whether this is due to differences in the relative sensitivity of persons at various personality levels or to some other cause, the fact remains that no one device is always productive, and even at best no one device is sufficiently broad and dependable to give reasonably complete and reliable data. Only by means of a battery of tests can one approximate a relatively extensive, integrated, and dependable personality analysis.

The fourth principle—testing under stress conditions—is found to be of value in adding significant detail to the picture of the patient. Although it is true that almost any testing situation involves stress to some extent, the concern here is with situations which attempt to place unusual pressure on the subject. Stress—whether in the sense of distraction, failure, or frustration, whether it be hypothetical or real, personal or impersonal, peripheral or central, or physiological or psychological—is bound to reveal additional characteristics of the person under study. Stress also serves to bring out differences between persons which examination under ordinary conditions would not reveal. The data derived from testing under stress conditions gain from the integration of the separate findings. This is accomplished by disregarding the boundaries of individual tests, by comparing one with another, and by cross-checking for congruences and differences. The aim is to obtain as complete a psychological analysis of the patient as possible—an analysis which covers attitude and intellectual and affective-conative aspects of personality structure and content.

The attitude of the patient is revealed in his involvement with the tasks put before him. His effort, attention, and expenditure of energy, his mood, general cooperativeness, and responsiveness, play roles here. The representativeness and optimity of the results obtained and the handicaps from which the patient suffers that may have affected the test results are also important.

Personality structure is considered from two points of view: intellectual and nonintellectual. In the former, the quantitative results, such as M.A., I.Q., and percentile rank, are discussed. The qualitative findings are analyzed with respect to the light they throw on comprehension, judgment, thinking and reasoning, learning, memory, imagery, etc. In the latter, consideration is given to such items as affective responsiveness, anxiety, security, maturity, and goal behavior (ventureseomeness as opposed to cautiousness, realism as opposed to unrealism of approach, plasticity as opposed to rigidity, consistency as opposed to variability). An evaluation is made of the subject's reactions to stress situations as they affect these characteristics.

Content is analyzed through a consideration of the major sentiments and complexes revealed by the subject. Particular attention is paid to those which relate to (*a*) family—paternal, maternal, filial, fraternal, and conjugal relationships; (*b*) sex—prenubile and nubile heterosexual attitudes, homosexual and other aberrant attitudes; (*c*) aggression—manner of expression of aggression, whether direct or indirect, externally or internally oriented, punished or unpunished (need for guilt and expiation), and reciprocated or initiated; (*d*) ideals—social and vocational;

(*e*) any other sentiments and complexes which appear to be of special importance to the subject.

Following the analysis, a summarizing evaluation may be made, giving a tentative dynamic and structural synthesis derived from the mass of psychological data. This evaluation is available for comparison with the evaluations made by the representatives of the other disciplines.

A condensed case study, that of patient W., has been selected to illustrate the use of a test battery in some of its aspects.[4]

During the examination W. cooperated well, manifesting some degree of interest in each of the variety of tests, but his responses were given in a slow and hesitating manner. Numerous signs of "tension," such as humming, drumming on the chair arm, and occasional laughing, were present.

The patient attained a "superior" intellectual rating. Vocabulary achievement was at the top decile level for adults. The poorest performance was on items involving rote memory and conceptual thinking. In the latter, although he did not actually give evidence of the concrete thinking often associated with schizophrenia, he substituted vague generalizations for true concepts. The results were considered representative of the general state of the patient at the time of the examination, but there was some question as to whether they could be characterized as optimal.

In other formal aspects of personality, there was evidence of marked constriction, as shown by data from the Rorschach Test. Many fissures in the constrictive wall indicated that this manner of defense was not entirely effective. These manifested themselves in various forms of "looseness," e.g., bizarre responses and variation in the quality of responses (initial poor responses which, on second thought, he would replace with good responses). There were, however, several Rorschach Test signs which called for favorable interpretation. Conventionality of response, interpreted as evidence of contact with the environment, was seen in a high number of popular responses. The improvement in the quality of responses on second thought (already mentioned) and some degree of "warmth" as indicated by his color responses were also in his favor. An attempt to attain a higher level of mental activity than he was capable of was manifested both in the Rorschach Test and in a certain pretentiousness which appeared in the Stanford-Binet vocabulary responses.[5] This was also shown in his general manner of expressing himself on the Thematic Apperception Test. His exceptional interest in small details and in human and animal parts shown on the Rorschach Test was also manifested on the Thematic Apperception Test.

In "goal behavior," W.'s outstanding characteristic was one of cautiousness associated with some rigidity. In a motor task, the successive aspirations he set for achievement also indicated a cautious approach associated with rigidity.

The effect of placing the patient in stress situations was to create a considerable disturbance of expression in the formal aspects of his personality. In tasks involving goal behavior, after repeated failure he still rigidly maintained the aspiration level adopted during success. With further prolongation of failure, however, the rigidity broke down, and W.'s behavior fluctuated between undue cautiousness and an

[4] A more detailed discussion of this case as well as the principles of study here presented will be found elsewhere (Shakow, Rodnick, & Lebeaux, 1945).

[5] E.g., "hysterics" is defined by him as: "state of nervous exhaustion associated with persons suffering a mental breakdown due to external harassment."

unrealistic return to the highest aspiration level set during success. This fluctuation may best be interpreted, perhaps, as due to a conflict between an unrealistic reluctance to accept a lowered aspiration level and a realistic need to be cautious in a situation of repeated failure. In a learning situation under stress he showed considerable disturbance; there was a cessation of further learning, even in trials not involving stress.

An analysis of the content in the test material, based mainly on the Thematic Apperception Test, indicated that his major problems revolved around the areas of family, sex, and aggression, all of which appeared to be closely interlinked. The stories revealed considerable conflict with respect to filial relationship. Although benevolent familial attitudes are described in several instances, there seemed to be an inability on the part of a child character ever to accept both parents at one time, or to accept an originally described familial setting as satisfactory. There was a distinct trend for existing family constellations to disintegrate. This occurred in one of three ways: (1) One of the parents (usually the mother) was blamed, and the child accepted living with the other, with whom he went away to another setting. (2) Both parents were eliminated either by death or by being characterized as inadequate in their method of bringing up children. This was followed by the youngster's being adopted, or at least brought up, by somebody else. The surrogate parent was sometimes male and sometimes female. (3) The central character escaped entirely from the family environment to new people and surroundings.

Stories involving the relationship between the sexes were apparently embarrassing to the patient and usually given with some hesitation. In general, they emphasized the distinction which he consistently drew between passion ("carnal" relations) and love. He showed little concern for more permanent love relationships, while temporary love and "carnal" relationships seemed to occur only in connection with primitive or foreign persons.

The aggression expressed in the stories was weak and usually associated with "badness" and ignorance; it appeared only as an attribute of inferior persons. In the main, the central character was the object of assault or the object of unfair treatment. He tended to be passive, suppliant, or bewildered, and when aggression was evidenced it would quickly become attenuated or generalized, e.g., a specific physical attack on the central character was changed into a battle between the power of intelligence and ignorance. The reaction to such aggression was generally one of seeking support and guidance from others to attain strength. Frequently, however, the central character would leave the field entirely as a solution to the problem.

In relation to goals the central characters very consistently showed marked dependence, frequently turning to protective figures to help them out of difficulties. The need for "affiliation" and "succorance" seemed great. The goals were weak, uncertain, conventionalized, and not clearly defined. Only one goal, namely, marrying a "nice girl," was mentioned more than once, but even then quite tentatively and with little force.

Several other trends which seemed to be of importance should be mentioned. There was much preoccupation with details of physiognomy and bodily characteristics. The reference to physical characteristics as indicators of moral and psychological characteristics, usually of a negative type, was frequent. Although this trend was more marked for male figures, it was found also with respect to female figures. In a superior manner, W. described characters as of "low" nature, although they appeared quite clearly to be projections of himself. There was, too, an interest in the general details of the background, some emphasis on the unreality of the pictures, and a sensitivity to the part which the photographer played in their making. Some of the elaborative details of the themas given by W. revealed an underlying suspiciousness.

In summarizing and evaluating the psychological findings, the following points stood out. W. appeared to be a person of superior intelligence who had not quite settled down to a definite way of handling his problems. Three trends were discernible: (1) a realistic, at least superficially socialized, trend which gave evidence of a continuing contact with the environment; (2) a constrictive trend which served to shut out the environment and to permit him to build himself up to a superior status; (3) a loose, unorganized trend, manifesting loss of control. The first trend seemed fairly weak, and the major battle appeared to be between the latter two. The central problems revolved about the relationship between aggression and the familial triangle situation. There was some ground for tentatively suggesting the following hypothesis: Basic to his then existing condition was a marked confusion and bewilderment concerning his relationship with his mother as a source of satisfaction for his unconscious needs, with a resultant turning to the father figure for the satisfaction of these needs. A similar pattern was present in the closely related aggressive trends. Tentative attempts at aggressive expression which had met with rebuff apparently led to bewilderment and to a search for support in some kind of positive action. The various types of solution, however, were not clearly differentiated and seemed to be milling around in a confused mass, none of them having sufficient underlying force to go anywhere in particular. The similarity of this pattern to the earlier description of the formal aspects of W.'s personality is striking.

At the time when the above psychological report, based entirely on independently derived test data, was made, the following material was reported by staff members representing other disciplines.

According to the physicians' statement, W. had been committed to a state hospital in 1941, because of "depressed appearance, extreme apathy and untidiness, a belief that his mind is being read, great thinking difficulty."

The history obtained by the social worker, before the commitment was, in brief, as follows: W., 33 years old, was born in a small town, the youngest of nine siblings, three brothers and five sisters, who appear to be in good physical and mental health. As a small child he was considered unusually cross and shy but was much superior intellectually to the rest of the family. He achieved excellent marks in school and was given piano lessons beginning at the age of 10. His father was a heavy drinker and a domineering person, toward whom W. apparently developed considerable antagonism which he generally covered up. The father died of arteriosclerosis and angina pectoris at the age of 68 when the patient was about 17. The mother, aged 73 at the time of the history, was in good health. W. graduated from an outstanding secondary school with honors and entered a well-known college. The whole family helped him financially with his schooling. This was supplemented by money borrowed from the college and by what he earned through working in one of the dining-rooms and at the post office during the school year and vacations. It is reported that he studied very hard throughout this whole period and that he had very little outside recreation. He is said to have had a marked feeling of responsibility and to have been sensitive to the pressure exerted by the family. He had feelings of inadequacy and considered himself unable to measure up either to their expectations or to the standards of his college. At various times he stated that the work was very difficult for him and that he never felt that he had an adequate grasp of the situation.

Always considered a quiet, seclusive, introspective type of person, he had but one close friend at college, from whom he drifted when the latter married. He was interested in the piano, which he played fairly well, but he avoided playing for others. One of the informants described him as an "idealist, very hard to talk to" and as having difficulty in expressing his ideas. After graduation, he continued to work in a post office for a short time and then held successive positions in brokerage offices, at a department store, and finally at one of the railroads. He was employed by the department store for three years and did quite well in the cashier's office. He became discontented in the latter department, however, and insisted on being transferred to the merchandising department against the advice of his superiors and colleagues. As was expected, he did not get along well there. He finally left the department store and was given a job as a baggage master of a small railroad station near his home town on the strength of his father's previous good work record for the railroad. It was while he was on this job that he was drafted into the army. The record at the railroad indicated that his adjustment had not been of high quality.

W. had not been considered to be an altogether healthy person. He was slightly deaf; and there was some possibility that he had suffered from convulsions as a baby. At the age of 25 he was involved in a serious automobile accident but suffered no obviously severe injuries.

There is a report that during the 26–27 year age period a "change" occurred in the patient's personality. He became indifferent to the Episcopal church to which he belonged and had formerly attended regularly. W. no longer cared to play the organ as he used to do, and he began worrying about world conditions and became "pessimistic." He grew careless of his personal appearance, was moody, indifferent, and preoccupied, and readily gave up his jobs. He began to "run wild" and became involved in financial difficulties through gambling, especially on horse races. His stated purpose at the time was to try to make money rapidly in order to pay back his school debts. Although abstinent with respect to alcohol before graduation from college, he now became a social drinker, but never to the point of intoxication. At this period, and for the first time in his life, he began to associate with girls. He contracted gonorrhea, for which he was treated but toward which he reacted violently with anxiety and guilt feelings. At about the same time he was going out regularly with a girl whom his family had selected for him and whom they were very desirous that he marry. After three years of association, however, this relationship faded out; the family never knew quite why.

The patient was drafted in one of the first registration groups. After he registered, the family noticed that he was very depressed and unhappy about it and apparently dreaded going into the army. When he was notified to report for the draft he suddenly disappeared without a word to anyone and was not heard from for several weeks. At this time his home town police were notified that W. had been picked up in Florida, in a confused and dazed condition. He was brought back and taken almost immediately into the army, where he was unable to adjust himself to camp routine, repeatedly returning home AWOL. Within a month, more positive symptoms developed, and he was sent to the army station hospital. There he stated that for years he had had peculiar experiences and that people had been reading his mind. He remained at the camp hospital for about four months, when he was transferred to a state hospital.

During this hospital period he was described as preoccupied, emotionally unresponsive, slow, vague, and indefinite in his thinking, and possibly hallucinated. He was tried at various occupations but showed no particular interest in his work and often sat reading a paper rather than working. After 27 months spent at this hospital with relatively little change in condition, he was transferred to another hospital at which he was given the intensive study here described.

The relevant physical and physiological findings reported at this time were a suggestion of hypometabolism, low blood-vitamin level, and a slight degree of "tension" in each of three oral glucose tolerance tests: a control, under stress in a pursuitmeter situation, and under stress in an interview situation.

The outstanding psychiatric data reported were a stiff and rather manneristic attitude, some disturbance in associations, and strange ideas about circumcision and about being used as a test case in a murder trial. He showed some unresponsiveness, fear, irritability, and inappropriate affect. There was reason to believe that he experienced auditory hallucinations. His delusional formations dealt with persecutions, thought influence, and thought transference. He indicated that his heterosexual adjustment was not adequate; that he had attempted intercourse only with prostitutes and that this had not been satisfactory. He reported being strongly attracted to a girl whom he had met while working as baggage master. Actually he had established no contact with her, although she was the subject of many of his fantasies.

One important group of preoccupations centered around telepathy and ideas of influence and reference. He felt that he could project his thoughts into people and that he was used as a transmitting agent. Reports made over the radio, he felt, sometimes referred to him. Thus in a recent broadcast he had heard Lowell Thomas describe a submarine rising to the attack, as a "long, low, flat, extended shape." W. felt that "low," "flat," and "shape" referred to him: "low" because people think he is low morally; "flat" because the people supporting him are flat-broke; and "shape" because he is interested in the shapes of women and not so much in the sentimental side of love.

On the basis of the assembled data, the staff made a diagnosis of "Schizophrenia, Other Types." Some staff members, however, emphasized the predominant paranoid content. The prognosis was characterized as "guarded." It was considered poor for "social recovery," but it was believed that after a time he would be able to make a limited adjustment in the community. The staff recommendation was that he remain in the hospital for treatment, which was to consist of psychotherapeutic interviews combined with occupational and vitamin therapy. Further physiological studies were to be carried out, and, if these indicated its desirability, thyroid therapy was to be added.

The major purpose of giving the case report here is the exposition of psychological procedures. It is, therefore, not possible to consider in any detail the integration of psychological findings with those derived from other sources. The report has been concerned primarily with integrating the material obtained from the variety of psychological devices used. The numerous correspondences between the independently obtained psychological data and those obtained through social service investigation and psychiatric study will no doubt have been noted. Even though the latter are necessarily presented in mere outline, the attempt has been made to provide sufficient material to permit appreciation of the manner in which the psychological data corroborate and complement the other data—the combination of which results in a fuller and more sharply focused portrait of a living patient.

So many questions relating to reliability and validity, so many problems relating to manner of presentation and communication, arise in the process of attempting to compress an extensive body of psychological data—data concerned so largely with both present cryptic activity and with inferences respecting past activity—that a report such as the present one must necessarily be made with some hesitation and reservation.

In material of this nature, the reliability and validity of any one generalization depends on a synthesis of amassed cues, major and minor, direct and inferential, presentative and symbolic, provided by many disciplines. Generalizations are composed from these varied reflections of the same facet of the personality by the different techniques which attempt to describe it. In the study of W., certain generalizations seemed to have adequate foundations. Unfortunately, even the addition of material which was available but not discussed in this report, material from psychiatric, physiological, social work, and psychological sources, did not permit the further generalizations which the delineation of W.'s portrait required.

Studies of this kind make available to the student of personality a body of data which even the most complete verbal report of psychosomatic events cannot convey. A report such as this one, despite its attempts to supply a systematic framework, is, even so, able only to provide relatively isolated, and at most partially corroborated, samples of behavior. These samples of quantifiable and unquantifiable behavior, taken from different areas, frequently lose their significance because viewed out of context, and they inevitably make such a report inadequate in many respects. The difficulty is enhanced by the many obstacles to facile communication in the sphere of personality. Such problems as are raised by theoretical biases—the attenuation of scientific concepts by common-sense language, the lack of rigorous use of terms, both within psychology and among related disciplines, as well as many other handicaps—are generally acknowledged.

I recognize the existence of the difficulties which undoubtedly give rise to errors or ambiguities in generalization. Despite these handicaps, a field so complex as personality study demands perseverance in the attempt to integrate the independent data obtained from different disciplines. Continued study and research are also needed both in the development of an adequate language and in the fundamental problems of personality uncovered by individual studies. Fairly extensive experience with the types of procedures described here results in the conviction that they contribute considerably to the understanding of the individual personality by laying bare both superficial and more deep-lying personality characteristics and content. Furthermore, they accomplish this task frequently in relatively less time than is required by other methods, and they offer pertinent cues for further investigation of the particular personality both to the psychiatrist and to the psychologist.

I have tended to emphasize diagnostic aspects. More and more, however, the clinical psychologist is becoming concerned with the pressing and limitless range of research needs in the field of personality. Although the research interest of psychology has always been great, growing out of its background as an academic discipline, the focus of its concern has not been in the area of motivation until recently. However, a marked shift of interest in this direction has taken place in the last several decades. This must largely be ascribed to the remarkably pervasive influence of Freud and his concepts on psychology not only in the area of abnormal behavior but also in the wider areas of personality, learning, and social relations. With the gradual growth of facilities for adequate training in psychology, increasing numbers of persons are entering the field who, in addition to a background in fundamental research, have also the essential attitudes and points of view that derive from clinical experience in diagnosis and therapy and from exposure to the complexities of human motivation that such experience gives. Such a background will, on the one hand, give some assurance of preoccupation with significant problems and, on the other, sufficient concern with rigor in investigation as to lead to studies fitting more obviously into the body of current biological research, broadly conceived.

The methods of investigation used by the psychologist are in essence not different from those generally used in biology. The differences which do exist lie in the problems created by, and the advantages accruing from, work with subjects of greater complexity and having well-developed symbolic functions. We may roughly classify the methods into four groups, even though in actuality they shade off one into the other and are, therefore, not always clearly distinguishable. These are: (1) naturalistic observation, (2) seminaturalistic observation, (3) free laboratory, (4) controlled laboratory.

The first method provides for the study of the organism in a relatively free, natural habitat in which the widest range of stimuli and responses growing out of the particular setting are observed. These observations are made as completely and as accurately as possible, usually by an outside observer. Thus in a hospital setting it may be desirable to study group behavior as it naturally structures itself on the ward or to study the complex therapeutic situation with the free give-and-take of the patient-therapist dyad through the use of devices such as sound movies.

The second method, the seminaturalistic, may be provided for either by a "natural habitat" or by a laboratory situation. In the former, the degree of freedom is somewhat limited as compared with the first group; in the latter, the degree of freedom as compared with the two following groups of laboratory approaches is greater. In either case the stimuli are varied, and the degrees of freedom of response permitted are considerable. Some controls and limitations on the situation are, however, set up in order to direct behavior along certain lines. In the field of test procedures, the analogous device is the projective technique. In the experimental area an investigation directed at studying the susceptibility of schizophrenic subjects to environmental stimulation (Rickers-Ovsiankina, 1937) might be cited in exemplification. In this situation various objects having different degrees of interest-demand character are left around a room into which the patient is introduced. He is told that the examiner will return shortly after he has completed another piece of work. The patient is observed in this relatively "free" situation for a stated period of time, and a detailed record is made of the range and intensity of his preoccupation with the objects and with himself.

In the third type of approach, the free laboratory, although some degree of variation in the stimuli and degree of freedom of response is still maintained, they are considerably reduced as compared with the former two methods. Here specific instructions are given the subject to respond in certain definite ways to stimuli, and recordings may be made of various physiological functions accompanying psychological response. An example of this kind of situation is a variation of the Luria experiment (Huston, Shakow & Erickson, 1934), in which the subject is required to respond orally to the stimulus words of a free association test. At the same time he is required to press on a tambour with one hand, and a recording is also made of finger tremor from the other hand and of respiration and galvanic skin response.

The fourth type, the controlled laboratory approach, carries the degree of control still further. Here both the stimulus and the response are quite fixed and limited. Studies of the latent time of the patellar tendon reflex (Huston, 1935) at the lowest psychological level or of reaction time (Huston, Shakow & Riggs, 1937) or simple psychomotor learning (Huston & Shakow, 1949), at a higher level, fall into this category.

It is obvious that the methods of investigation described lend themselves to the accumulation of relevant data for methodological and descriptive purposes as well as for theoretical ones. It is likely that for some time in the future considerable effort will have to be expended by the psychologist in sharpening old tools and devising new ones. The problems in the field are so complex that considerable ingenuity will have to be devoted to this task. The psychologist need not, of course, limit himself to the study of the disordered person. Depending upon the nature and needs of the problem, he may use normal or even animal subjects, setting up, for greater control, situations which nature provides reluctantly or in too complex a setting.

Besides the accurate descriptions of behavior that are, of course, the essential basis for any theoretical development, there are some special problems of description to which the psychologist can make a special contribution. I refer here to objective studies in the evaluation of the effects of therapies or other modifications of behavior. The activity of the psychologist should, however, be mainly directed to the exploration of the fundamental aspects of personality with a view toward developing comprehensive theories of personality. Hypotheses along these lines may be derived directly from experiment or from clinical experience and study, preferably from thoughtful integration of both. The great growth of Freudian hypothesis and theory, based upon years of broad clinical experience and insight, now calls for a period of systematic experimental study in order to consolidate it into the body of psychological knowledge.

The important problems calling for study in the area centering around psychopathology and personality are numerous. They involve both factors of a structural kind and those of a functional nature. Because of the manifold effects of disturbances in the needs upon the ego structure, reflections of these disturbances are found in almost all aspects of the psyche. For this reason, besides the immediate problems of motivation, the areas of receptive and perceptive processes, the mechanisms of response, learning and memory, thinking and imagination, intelligence and social and group behavior call urgently for study, in both their cross-sectional and their longitudinal aspects.

In some of these areas experimental work may be carried out independently by the psychologist. But in most areas collaborative work with psychiatrists, neurologists, physiologists, internists, and other specialists is a necessity in order to obtain the most productive use of the material and to make the most meaningful advances (Shakow, 1949c).

This chapter can close on no more appropriate note than the above. An acquaintance with the relative states of development of the social sciences when compared with the physical, or even biological, sciences and close knowledge of the development of the sciences concerned with interpersonal relations must force the student to conclude that one of society's greatest present needs is research in this area. In this research, each of the disciplines closely or even remotely related to these problems must make its individual, but particularly its joint, contribution to the understanding of the fundamental processes. The increasing cooperation in the day-by-day diagnostic and therapeutic activities should serve the additional function of providing background and experience for some of these joint research efforts.[6]

[6] The volume edited by Watson (1949) contains a catholic presentation of articles dealing with several of the topics touched upon in the present contribution.

3. Clinical Psychology

This chapter is part of an article written at the request of the editor of the *International Encyclopedia of the Social Sciences* for the new, 17-volume encyclopedia which appeared in 1968.

For our present purposes, since the essential history before what is called "Recent developments" in this chapter has already been dealt with in the preceding two papers (No. 1 and No. 2) the overlapping material has been omitted.

Clinical psychology, a branch of psychology, is that body of knowledge and skills which can be used to help persons with behavior disabilities or mental disorders to achieve better adjustment and self-expression. It encompasses the applied areas of diagnosis, treatment and prevention, and the basic area of research. (In British countries, the term "clinical psychology" is more or less interchangeable with "medical psychology.")

In function, clinical psychology overlaps such fields as psychiatry, a medical specialty, and social work, a more specifically treatment-oriented calling; it borders on those of sociology, particularly in its social-psychological aspects, and the ministry, when it assumes the "helping" role. Clinical psychology's relation to anthropology is remote, except for the analogies which can be drawn between patterns of collective behavior and forms of individual pathology.

The content of clinical psychology includes large portions of psychopathology, abnormal psychology, and similar areas. It is particularly dependent upon personality theory and psychoanalysis for its theoretical underpinnings.

Recent Developments

Since the 1940's there has been much preoccupation with the problems of clinical psychology. The play of a great variety of forces, both within and without psychology, has made clinical psychology into a field which calls upon its practitioners for competence in three major tasks: *diagnosis*, acquiring knowledge about the origin and nature of given psychological conditions through the use of tests, measurements, standard interviews and like procedures; *research*, the advancement of knowledge by a systematic attack—be it in the laboratory or in the field setting—on specific problems capable of controlled, experimental resolution; and *therapy*, the intricate art and science of improving the condition of clients. Beyond these tasks lies always—implicitly at least, but increasingly at an explicit level—the important problem of prevention.

Present doctoral training for these tasks calls for a minimum program of four years, one year of which (preferably the third) consists of an internship. On a foundation of basic courses in theoretical, clinical and dynamic psychology, practicums, clerkships and internships are organized. The type of training program now generally accepted was initially proposed by the Committee on Training in Clinical Psychology of the American Psychological Association in its 1947 Report (APA, CTCP, 1947), and, in its major outlines, further supported in conferences at Boulder (Raimy, 1950), Stanford (Strother, 1956) and Miami (Roe, 1959). (A fourth conference was held in the spring of 1965.) The 1947 Report called for centering clinical training in existing university departments, and the integration of field training units and university programs. Although proposals to establish special professional schools in clinical psychology have been made, the solution still generally favored is to expand existing university psychology departments to meet the needs of clinical psychology. Such a plan underscores the model of the clinical psychologist as a scientist-professional and supports the motto that a clinical psychologist is a psychologist first and a clinician second.

As the professional consciousness of psychologists has developed, however, universities and field centers have come to recognize the importance of appropriate personality qualities and high intellectual abilities in clinical work. In the past, some professors had a tendency to direct their weaker students—those who did not have the makings of "scientists"—into clinical courses with the hope that they would then be able to find jobs in clinical settings. A number of poorly trained people, generally called "psychometricians," who presumably were nothing more than psychological technicians, thus entered the field. The present attention to selection and recruitment problems, however, has led to an increase in competently trained researchers and practitioners. Most have come from institutions where standards have been maintained and where a reasonably comfortable relationship exists between academic and clinical psychology. Some have also come from centers where the standards have not been of the highest level, but where exceptionally good people have managed, in one way or another, to educate themselves.

The American Psychological Association has, in recent years, taken an increasingly greater role in setting up standards for evaluating both training and practice in clinical psychology. The Committee on Graduate and Professional Training, (APA & AAAP, 1945) was followed by the Committees on Training in Clinical Psychology (APA, CTCP, 1947, 1948, 1949) and more recently by the Education and Training Board (Roe, 1959). These Committees have provided the criteria for approving universities, and for recommending their participation in the Veterans Administration and the Public Health Service programs.

To consolidate and advance standards, the American Board of Examiners in Professional Psychology was organized and, in April, 1947, incorporated. It was modeled on the specialty boards in medicine and had similar standards. The Board generally requires five years of acceptable experience in addition to the doctoral degree for admission to examination for its diploma. A "grandfather" clause, which expired December 31, 1949, allowed for certification of qualified persons on the basis of experience rather than actual examination.

With protection of the public in mind, governmental bodies have made several attempts to set the standards for certification of psychologists. The two types of legislation that have been under consideration by state agencies are exemplified, in essentials, by the early laws of Connecticut and Virginia. The former provides for the general certification of psychologists with a Ph.D. degree plus one year of experience; the latter entails the certification of specified kinds of psychologists with a Ph.D. plus five years of experience. The consensus among psychologists is that state certification should follow the Connecticut pattern and that "expert" certification should be left to a professional agency, for example, the American Board of Examiners in Professional Psychology.

Present Picture

Since 1947, the growth of clinical psychology in the United States has been phenomenal. This is reflected, to a small degree, in the following statistics: (1) membership in the Division of Clinical Psychology of the American Psychological Association has risen from 787 in 1948 to 2,883 in 1964; (2) the number of schools fully approved by the Committee on Training in Clinical Psychology of the American Psychological Association has increased from 20 in 1948 to 55 in 1963; (3) there were an estimated 742 graduate students enrolled in doctoral training in programs in clinical psychology in the academic year 1947–48 compared to 3,340 in 1962–63; (4) the number of clinical psychologists certified by the American Board of Examiners in Professional Psychology has increased from 234 in 1948 to 1,793 in 1963 (of the total, 1,116 are "grandfathers"); (5) 28 states, and four provinces in Canada, have established some form of statutory control; 18 states have set up non-statutory control.

But this unusual growth has not come about without much travail. An increasing number of questions have arisen, questions which psychology and clinical psychology will have to answer forthrightly (Shakow, 1965) in the coming years.

1. Can psychology train persons with both professional and scientific goals in mind?

2. How much application can there be in a field where basic knowledge is still so meager?

3. Should not clinical psychologists be devoting more time to research?

4. How can socially unprofitable trends toward private practice be curbed?

5. Should training for research and teaching be separated from training for the applications of psychology?

Outside the United States (David, 1958), there are signs of increasing interest in clinical psychology. However, growth rates for the countries differ, and the pace is decidedly less rapid than that of the United States.

In Canada training has consisted of a combination of American and English patterns. In Britain, the pattern has, in general, been less structured than in the United States. Formal programs, where they do exist, have been modeled on the Maudsley (University of London) pattern, which consists of one year's internship and a doctoral dissertation. The 1948 National Health Service development led to an increase of clinical psychologists (Summerfield, 1958, pp. 171–76). Whereas at the end of 1945 there were 77 professional psychologists in the British Psychological Society working in mental health, by 1958 the number had increased to some 400. University training facilities have been extended and the taking of higher degrees has been encouraged.

The situation in the Western continental countries is not as encouraging. A strong medical tradition still holds sway, limiting a good deal of the practice of clinical psychology (and particularly of psychotherapy) to physicians. In the last few years, however, these countries have made increasing inquiries about American training programs, and one can expect some growth of clinical training along American lines.

In Eastern continental Europe, medical influence is even more pervasive. Particular emphasis is placed upon physiological functioning with a corresponding denigration of the place of psychological testing, objective or subjective, and of the study of individual differences generally. Rapid growth of clinical psychology appears far from likely.

In Japan, noteworthy among Eastern countries (McGinnies, 1960, pp. 556–62), psychology is in an active ferment. Despite a number of handicaps, as for instance, the rigidity of the university system and the over-representation of physicians in clinical psychology, the field is developing rapidly. Thus at the 1958 meeting of the Japanese Psychological Association, of the 619 papers in 11 areas presented, clinical psychology ranked fourth in number, being preceded only by perception, education, and learning.

On the whole, there has been a tremendous growth of clinical psychology in the United States and a moderate growth, along similar lines, in other countries. The hope is that countries will work out patterns suited to their own needs and not be guided too much by the patterns established in the United States—patterns that have brought with them problems of their own.

Prospects

What about the future of clinical psychology? A large number of major problems have to be solved by both psychology and clinical psychology if clinical psychology is to make its proper contribution to the needs of society and to develop its potential as a profession. These include training both for old and new areas of endeavor, evaluation of both training institutions and individuals, and improvement of existing programs. Specifically, the issues that have to be faced are:

1. *Training for Research.* The role of the university, the role of the field center, and the relationship between the two types of institutions need elaboration. Concomitantly, the content of research needs redefinition so it will encompass the most rigorous laboratory research, systematic naturalistic observation, and a serious attitude of inquiry leading to deliberate efforts to obtain answers to questions which arise during clinical operations.

2. *Application of clinical psychology to institutional and community settings.* The function of each of the training agencies and the way to integrate their work need careful spelling out.

3. *Delineation of important areas for clinical research and practice.* This calls for much imaginative thinking. New methods of therapy, new methods of diagnosis, and—particularly—preventive methods of education are becoming increasingly important. Clinical psychology must do everything it can to cultivate persons with the resourcefulness to meet problems in this unconventional area. It is clear that the personnel shortages in the area of mental health will be enormous and far from filled by present-day mental health professionals. Much thought and experimentation must go into making use of a much larger pool of persons, for example, younger persons with the ideals and resourcefulness represented in Peace Corps volunteers, older persons such as mothers whose children do not now need their attention (see the experiment by Margaret Rioch [Rioch, Elkes, Flint, Usdansky, Newman & Silber, 1963]), and teachers, whose effective use is crucial in the mental health area. In addition, new methods of therapy and prevention must be constantly invented for and tested on groups—especially the underprivileged—which have heretofore received little consideration in mental health projects.

4. *University training programs.* The proper university settings for training in clinical psychology should be described and the importance of programs coming from unified departments considered. The nature of the doctoral degree granted to clinical psychologists—whether strictly professional (say a Ps.D.) or a combined research degree (the Ph.D.)—calls for special discussion. The place and nature of post-doctoral programs, especially such programs for psychotherapy training, should be given equal thought.

5. *Evaluation and regulation.* The composition, responsibilities, and standards of committees that evaluate the performance of institutions, both universities and

field centers, and those that regulate the activities of individuals, such as the American Board of Examiners in Professional Psychology and state licensing and certification boards, should be reexamined.

6. *Upgrading research and practice.* The holding of periodic regional conferences to consider the details of existing and potential training programs would be an effort in this direction. The kind of professional eclecticism proposed by Kubie (1954), or the intensive, integrated approach discussed in detail at the Gould House "Conference on an Ideal Program of Training for Psychotherapists" (1963) may be possibilities. In addition, methods for making the private practice of psychology more effective and socially useful should be reviewed.

The major problems of clinical psychology continue to lie within the parent field, psychology. Clinical psychology, after a long period spent as part of an academic discipline, has been through the early stages of becoming a profession as well. It is going through the natural disturbances and difficulties which attend a growth process of this kind. However, if it selects its students carefully, for personality as well as intellect; if it trains thoroughly, in spirit as well as letter; if it trains broadly, recognizing that narrowly educated specialists are not true clinical psychologists; if it remains flexible about its training and encourages experimentation; if it does not sacrifice remoter goals to the fulfillment of immediate needs; if it maintains its contact with its scientific background, remaining alert to the importance of theory as well as practice; if it keeps modest in the face of the complexity of its problems, rather than becoming pretentious—in short, if it finds good people and gives them good training—these disturbances and difficulties need not be of serious concern. Its future in society and as a profession is then assured.

4. The Functions of the Psychologist in the State Hospital

Because of an apparent growing interest by psychologists in the field of mental disorder, it seemed appropriate for a person who had had some experience in this area to consider briefly some of the possible functions of a psychologist in a mental institution. The paper was presented at the September, 1938, meeting of the American Association of Applied Psychology.

From numerous directions there is evident a growing interest in the field of mental disease. Associated with this is a recognition of the need for a concerted attack on its problems by various disciplines. Psychology is showing a legitimate interest in this endeavor, as witnessed by its increasing concern with the clinical field.

More than nominal acceptance of the psychologist into the team of workers in

Reprinted with permission from the *Journal of Consulting Psychology*, vol. 3, 1939.

psychopathology will depend on what contributions he can make. Thus far, with some exceptions, contributions to this field by persons who have been called "psychologists" have been predominantly at a level which cannot be considered higher than that of the technician. This has in some respects contributed less to the future advancement of psychology in its relations with psychiatry than would have no psychology at all.

It is the purpose of the present paper to discuss in broad outline the possible—and necessary—contributions of the psychologist to the study of mental disorders, particularly in relation to state hospitals, and to consider, in passing, some requisites of the psychologist for this work.

The contributions of the psychologist will be discussed with respect to three major types of activity: *diagnosis*, *teaching* and *research*.

The first of the functions of the psychologist to be considered is *diagnosis*. By this is meant not simple classification but the descriptive and interpretive data which the psychologist can supply, largely on the basis of objective devices, that may help in understanding the patient and his disturbance. On examination, this diagnostic contribution is found to be of three kinds: (1) The description of what the patient in his various conditions is like in certain relevant psychological functions, that is, *what he is*. (2) The implications which the psychological studies have for therapeutic (educational, vocational, personality, etc.) policy, that is, *what to do*. (3) The determination of the effects of whatever therapy may have been used on psychological functions, that is, the evaluation of *what has been done*.

The psychologist, although concerned with these three types of problems, uses essentially the same devices for obtaining the answers to all of these questions.

Because of the great variety of subjects, situations and conditions which he is called upon to meet, it is important that he be prepared to employ a great many procedures. Before applying these, however, it is most important that he establish in himself an attitude with respect to them quite different in many ways from that which he is customarily trained to have in dealing with normal subjects.

He must be prepared to make frequent modifications in his devices, since in general they have been standardized on children or other inappropriate groups. He must be prepared to exercise ingenuity in dealing with "uncooperativeness" and to recognize the part which emotional factors may be playing in determining the results. Because important findings frequently do not come out in quantitative scores, he must be especially sensitive to the varieties and nuances of qualitative response, for it is often in these that major cues appear.

With an attitude some of the components of which were just mentioned, he is ready to face the actual problems which he is frequently called upon to meet. Some of these are: (1) determination of levels and patterns of intellectual functioning, (2) determination of the existence and nature of special defects such as amnesia, aphasia, agnosia, etc., (3) diagnosis of feeblemindedness or various types of psychoses, (4) determination of the presence and extent of deterioration, (5) diagnosis and classification of personality characteristics, (6) determination of the effects of therapy or of medication, (7) recommendation of vocational, educational or therapeutic programs.

But it is not only with adult patients that the psychologist in the psychiatric hospital has to deal. Frequently children are admitted to the hospital or to its out-patient department. Here the problems may be even more concerned with therapeutic recommendations. Not infrequently, too, the psychologist is called upon to study the employees of the hospital, particularly the attendant group, with the purpose of more careful selection, promotion, etc.

It will be gathered from what has been said that it is essential for the psychologist to do the kind of diagnostic work which will impress upon the psychiatric staff the necessity of consulting the psychological department in a way different from that to which they are accustomed in the case of the conventional chemical laboratory. The latter is used, in most hospitals, as a purely technical service to which specimens are sent for routine tests on which figures are reported back. The use of a psychology laboratory in a similar way, namely, as a purely technical service for "doing I.Q. tests," should be discouraged and actively fought.

The acceptance of these diagnostic responsibilities will do much toward achieving for the psychologist a proper status in the hospital setting. To take care of these responsibilities adequately, however, considerable training is necessary. This training, although it may be obtained in part elsewhere, cannot be truly satisfactory without a relatively lengthy period of concentrated study in a psychiatric hospital.

Besides training members of his own profession the state hospital psychologist must take part in the training of other groups concerned with psychopathology. These two kinds of student groups require separate consideration.

The first stages of the training of a *psychologist* for the psychiatric field, insofar as the state hospital psychologist is involved, have already been presented in some detail elsewhere (Shakow, 1938). An internship year at a state hospital was recommended. The thesis advanced was that an internship year has four major purposes: (a) to give the student facility in the use of already acquired techniques, (b) to saturate the student with experience in the practical aspects of psychopathology, (c) to intensify the psychologist's customary experimental-objective attitude, in the clinical setting, (d) to make the student acquainted with the types of thinking and attitudes of colleagues in other disciplines, such as psychiatry and social work.

To achieve these purposes, a setting is required in which the student can be given considerable opportunity not only for psychometric contact with patients and training in a wide assortment of techniques, but an opportunity for listening to and partaking in discussions of the psychiatric aspects of cases, an opportunity for carrying on research projects, and an opportunity to participate in seminars and courses on the practical and theoretical aspects of psychopathology.

To give a course of training having this general content should be accepted as a responsibility by every *psychologist* now working in a psychiatric institution. This is especially necessary since there is at present a dearth of centers available for such training. In addition, for those who are interested in becoming associated with the psychiatric hospital itself, there should be an advanced year of training within the hospital. For those interested in other branches of psychiatric-psychological work, the additional year should be spent in another appropriate center.

There are *other members of the hospital staff* who should have psychological teaching. The psychologist might very well take advantage of every informal and formal pedagogic opportunity afforded him in connection with these.

To the psychiatric staff he can informally convey psychological points of view and make psychological contributions during the discussion of cases at staff conferences. Formally, the psychiatrists, particularly the psychiatric interns, should be given courses in general psychology, psychometrics, abnormal psychology, and experimental psychopathology, as indicated by the particular circumstances. Wherever the material lends itself, it should be organized around actual cases and the psychiatric implications of psychological studies elaborated.

The other groups with whom the hospital psychologist is most likely to have special pedagogic contact are the social workers and occupational therapists. Whatever courses he gives to these should also be organized about clinical material, insofar as this is possible, and special attention paid to the interests of the particular group. Occasional lectures on important psychological topics and developments, and the presentation of case studies and research projects are other ways in which he can keep his contact with the staff.

Besides the diagnostic and teaching functions of the hospital psychologist, there is a third which is at least of equal importance—in some ways, of greater importance. This is *research.*

The kinds of research which the psychologist can carry on, either by himself or in collaboration with other staff members, are various. Parenthetically, it might be suggested that at least some of the psychologist's research, if possible to arrange, should be carried on in collaboration with psychiatrists or other members of the staff, in order to develop closer relationships among the disciplines concerned. The research activities may be roughly classified into four types: (1) diagnostic, (2) psychotherapeutic, (3) theoretical, (4) administrative.

The practically unlimited opportunities for the psychologist in all of these fields need be no more than mentioned.

With respect to *diagnosis*, the necessity for new discriminative procedures and for the further appreciation of already existing analytic psychological procedures in relation to all the problems mentioned under the discussion of diagnosis is great.

In the *therapeutic* field there are also possibilities for the adequately prepared psychologist. There are many problems of therapy which for solution require an experimental-clinical approach, problems whose answers can be obtained more readily in such a way than by means of the more time-consuming, conventional clinical one. The psychologist is in a peculiar position to carry on such studies. Whether by selection, by training or by both he is frequently more fitted than the medically trained person for *psychotherapeutic* work. Such aptitude, when present, together with his experimental attitude places him in a peculiarly strong position for doing fundamental research in therapy.

In the way of *theoretical* research—research on the basic problems of psychopathology—psychologists can make a considerable contribution. As opposed to the study of the particular symptoms of a particular patient, a field more legitimately that of the clinician, they have a more fundamental interest than other groups in general principles.

In both the therapeutic and theoretical fields there is an important section which has thus far barely been touched—a section which offers opportunities to both the social psychologist and the sociologist. Reference is to the need of studying the state hospital as an institution to whose employees, patients, and procedures the patient has to make adjustments.

It is in this region that there is considerable overlapping with the field of research termed *administrative*. The hospital, especially the psychiatric hospital, has been entirely neglected by industrial psychologists. Personnel is by far the most important factor in the treatment of mental disease and if psychiatric hospitals are to make the advances they should, more attention will have to be given to the problems of personnel and personnel relations. The state hospital is not only a fertile field for all kinds of administrative research, but it offers sufficiently different problems from industry so that it ought to have a special attraction for those interested in this aspect of applied psychology.

This short survey of the functions of a state hospital psychologist has touched upon the three major fields in which he must work, namely, diagnosis, teaching, and research. The program laid out may seem quite formidable for institutions with limited personnel and facilities. In practice, however, it is possible for each adequately prepared state hospital psychologist to make some contribution to most of these fields. It would appear that such a contribution is essential if psychology is to establish its place in the study of mental disorders.

5. Administration of Psychological Services in Institutions for the Mentally Disordered and Mentally Retarded

In 1948 or thereabouts, D. H. Fryer and E. R. Henry organized a two-volume *Handbook of Applied Psychology* (published in 1950) for which they invited the present article.

The agencies concerned with the psychological study of mentally disordered and mentally retarded patients in institutions are varied in nature, but the administrative problems are essentially the same. This is true whether the institution is a psychopathic hospital which takes patients only for short-time observation, a hospital for psychotics which takes patients for longer periods, a school for the feebleminded, or a psychiatric out-patient department in a psychiatric or general hospital. The administrative differences are mainly in the emphasis which is placed on one or another of the functions.

The successful administration of a psychological department in any of these institutions is dependent upon two fundamentals: the recognition of well-defined objectives and the establishment of an efficient organization to carry out these objectives. The importance of the former is overlooked so often, with objectives therefore left unformulated, that a considerable part of the discussion which follows will be concerned with it.

Psychological Functions

The institutions for the mentally disordered and retarded are usually made up of most or all of the following professional departments: psychiatric and medical, nursing, social service, occupational therapy, pedagogical, and psychological. The functions of the psychological services fall mainly into three major categories: examination, education, and research. A fourth, therapy, falls somewhat outside the usual requirements and will be given consideration separately.

Psychological Examination

The psychological examination comprises not merely classification but the descriptions and interpretations which the psychologist can provide, based largely on findings from objective devices, to help in the understanding of the patient and his disturbance. The examination contributes essentially (1) a description of what the patient is like in his various states with respect to certain relevant psychological functions, that is, what he is; (2) implications which these psychological studies have for a therapeutic (educational, vocational, personality) program, that is, what to do; and (3) the determination of the effects of whatever therapy may have already been used on psychological functions, that is, the evaluation of what has been done. The psychologist uses the same devices for obtaining the answers to these questions as are used in all clinical psychological practice.

It is important that the psychologist be prepared to employ many different procedures because of the diversity of subjects, situations, and conditions which he is called upon to meet. Before applying these, however, it is essential that he develop an adaptive attitude with respect to their use, an attitude in many ways quite different from the more rigid one which he is customarily trained to have in dealing with normal subjects, an attitude which recognizes that procedure must be appropriate to the situation without sacrificing objectivity.

The actual tasks of the hospital psychologist include: (1) determination of levels and patterns of intellectual functioning; (2) determination of the existence and nature of special defects, such as amnesia, aphasia, and agnosia; (3) classification of feeblemindedness or various types of psychopathic conditions; (4) determination of the presence and extent of deterioration; (5) description of personality characteristics; (6) determination of the effectiveness of therapy or of medication; and (7) recommendations for vocational, educational, or therapeutic programs.

Where adults are the dominant concern, the classificatory and descriptive functions may be emphasized; where children are in the majority, the problems may revolve more about therapeutic considerations. Not infrequently, too, the psychologist is called upon to study the institution's employees, particularly the attendant groups, for the purpose of aiding in selection or promotion. No matter what the setting, however, it is essential for the psychologist to make a contribution which will lead to the use of the psychological department in a consultative capacity. The psychologist is not a technician merely turning out I.Q.'s or test scores.

Educational Function

The psychologist contributes to the education of other groups working in psychopathology. He can best convey psychological points of view and findings to psychiatrists informally during discussion of cases at staff conferences. He gives courses to psychiatric residents and psychological interns in general psychology, psychometrics, abnormal psychology, and experimental psychopathology. Other student groups with whom the hospital psychologist is most likely to have special educational contact are social workers, nurses, and occupational therapists. All courses are best organized about clinical material in which the interests of the particular group are exemplified. Occasional lectures on important psychological developments, cases of psychological interest, and research projects inform the hospital professional staff of functions served by the psychological department.

Research

The research carried on by the psychologist alone or in collaboration with other staff members is likely to be varied and can be roughly classified into four types: (1) diagnostic, (2) therapeutic, (3) theoretical, and (4) administrative.

Diagnostic.

There is always a need for new discriminative procedures and for the evaluation of already existing procedures in relation to the specific hospital problems.

Therapeutic.

There are many problems of therapy which require for solution an experimental clinical approach, problems whose answers can be obtained more readily by psychological experiment than by the more time-consuming, conventional clinical method.

Theoretical.

Psychologists can make a substantial contribution through research on the basic problems of psychopathology as opposed merely to the study of the symptoms of particular patients.

Administrative.

The hospital may be studied as an organization to whose employees, patients, and procedures the individual patient has to make adjustments. Thus considered, the psychiatric hospital has been seriously neglected by those specializing in industrial psychology. Proper personnel is by far the most important factor in the treatment of mental abnormality, and more attention needs to be given to personnel relations in hospitals. Administrative research in hospitals offers sufficiently different problems from industry to be especially attractive to industrial psychologists. Another aspect of this field are the problems connected with the occupational placement of patients. Psychologists in schools for the feebleminded have already done a good deal toward determining the relationships between mental level and occupation.

Therapeutic Function

Actual therapy and rehabilitation (including personal, educational, and vocational therapy) are functions of the psychologist which are not clearly defined in hospitals. The therapeutic functions of the psychologist depend upon the particular institution and the particular psychologist. In institutions for the feebleminded, psychologists have as one of their functions not only organization of programs of therapy but actual execution of such programs. The practice of assigning such programs to the psychologist in psychiatric hospitals has in the past not been widespread. It was generally true in these hospitals that therapy, when done by psychologists, was primarily for research purposes. Increasingly, however, psychologists in such hospitals are playing a role in both the individual and group therapeutic programs.

Personnel

A department of psychology organized to accomplish the aims outlined above requires the following personnel: a chief psychologist, research psychologist, one or more psychologists, and psychological interns. The expansion or diminution of this group will be determined by the needs and available resources.

Standards

Standards for personnel and occupational designations vary from place to place but the general requirements for psychological personnel in psychiatric hospitals and institutions for the feebleminded are about as follows: The chief psychologist has a doctor's degree in psychology and some three to five years of experience in the field of psychopathology. The research psychologist has the doctor's degree and in addition has two to three years of research experience in general experimental psychology and in psychopathology. The clinical psychologist has at least a master's degree in psychology, with a few years of experience in psychometric work. However, the time is fast passing when clinical psychologists without the doctor's degree will be generally acceptable. Psychological interns are with few exceptions at the graduate student level in universities, preferably in the third year of a four-year program.

Appointments

Appointments to positions in psychology are generally made by the head of the hospital or institution on the advice of the head of the psychology department. This may be either from a civil service list or from applications received directly. Selection is based on education, on experience, and occasionally on an examination. The usual tenure regulations apply if the position is on civil service. Ordinarily this involves a period of probationary appointment of six months or more during which time the incumbent may be dismissed for reason of inefficiency or questionable moral character. Upon the achievement of full civil service status, the incumbent may be dismissed for these reasons only after a hearing if requested, or because of the abolition of the position. If the position is not on civil service, tenure is dependent upon the personnel policies of the particular administration, which vary considerably.

Responsibilities

The chief psychologist's responsibilities consist of (1) administration of the department, (2) maintenance of professional and teaching relationships within the staff and throughout the institution, (3) supervision of routine psychological work, and (4) direction of research. He must delegate some of these functions at least in part to his assistants. The research psychologist is concerned primarily with research upon problems of psychopathology determined as essential to the institution. The senior clinical psychologist is responsible for (1) the training of the interns in diagnostic testing, (2) the supervision of contacts with the psychiatrists on specific cases as part of his supervision of the psychometric work, and (3) the interpretation of findings to the hospital staff. The clinical psychologists, under supervision of the senior clinical psychologist, work with the more difficult diagnostic problems, those not assigned to interns, and aids in the supervision of the latter. The interns, who are at the institutionsprimarily for training, carry a certain amount of the diagnostic work in order to obtain necessary experience, attend courses, staff meetings, and seminars, and take part in research projects.

Administration

The process of administration of a psychological department is made easier by the preparation and use within the department of a manual of standard practice. Such a compendium of the accumulated experiences of the group adds immeasurably to efficiency through the orientation of interns and new members and saves much time on the part of members of the department in verifying exact procedure. It includes the standard practices for the major problems which arise in the administration of a psychological department, viz., regulations and experience in general practice, in special examination of patients, and in research. A presentation in outline of the contents of such a manual as prepared at the Worcester (Mass.) State Hospital, and as used there and at the Illinois Neuropsychiatric Institute, will illustrate the various aspects of administration.

General Practice

In connection with the regulations and experience in general practice the following may be emphasized:

1. *Administrative organization and regulations:* Included here are organization items and regulations covering the physical and personnel set-up of the whole institution, such as the procedures in handling of patients, the use of case records, keys, and staff maintenance. The trivial but necessary first things with which one has to become acquainted in order to become a smoothly functioning member of an institutional community are mentioned. Similarly, general departmental regulations are included with respect to hours of duty, absence from duty, routine duties in the maintenance of the department, and manner of use of departmental property.

2. *Examination of patients:* Descriptions of the kinds of patients who are generally referred for psychological examination, both intramural and extramural, are included, and procedures for obtaining patients and managing them while in the laboratory.

3. *Routine of psychological examinations:* A general discussion of the routine of examination includes the psychological problems involved in the determination of handicaps, the observational techniques to be followed, organization of test batteries, order of tests in battery, use of "shock-absorber" tests, changes in standardized techniques of tests, scoring procedures and organization of batteries for multiple sessions; use of hospital and department case records in relation to the psychological examination; procedures in reporting the results of examinations, such as form, steps in supervision and approval, reports of unsuccessful examinations; and procedures in the examination of employees and other normal subjects.

4. *Reading and study:* Under this heading are descriptions of facilities of the institution and of the training program for interns with its intradepartment aspects of psychometrics, research, courses, and seminars and with its extradepartmental aspects of general orientation, acquaintance with special institution procedures, courses, staff meetings, case conferences, and special lectures.

Special Practice

The descriptions of the steps to be followed in examinations are considered as follows: (1) *Schedules of tests:* Suggested basic schedules are included for different types of patients and situations, such as the illiterate, the specially handicapped, the various diagnostic medical types, and the various psychological problems. (2) *Psychological record:* Descriptions of the content of the psychological report are provided which include identifying data, handicaps, attitudes, special findings, examiner's remarks and impressions, interpretations, recommendations, comparisons with previous examinations and summarizing statements. (3) *Record-keeping and filing practice:* Detailed presentation of procedure in record-keeping and filing is given.

Instruction

A test instruction manual supplies the description, instructions, scoring keys, and norms for the variety of tests used in psychological examination in the institution. It contains the standard test procedures and any modifications of these procedures in the way of presenting instructions, scoring, and use of norms. It is especially valuable for the assembly of the data on performance tests ordinarily not found in any collected form.

Research

A general discussion of research principles and the special problems which arise in carrying on research in the institution is included in the manual of standard practice. The various steps in research are considered in detail, among which are discussed the organization of the project and use of a project outline, giving the object, justification, method of investigation, required records and reports, required personnel, duration, and cost. Further considerations include suggestions for the collection and analysis of data, for reporting, and for the selection and maintenance of apparatus.

EQUIPMENT

The physical requirements of a psychology department depend, of course, on the number of its personnel and the scope and nature of its program. An average set-up provides a suite of well-lighted and relatively sound-proofed rooms in a central location so that patients can be brought to it most conveniently from all parts of the institution, and adequate professional equipment.

Space

The rooms are of different sizes to serve the following purposes:

Examination. Plain undecorated rooms containing only the furniture needed for examination purposes.

Experimentation. Rooms required for research are those usually found in psychological laboratories.

Observation. At least one room is required with a one-way screen or mirror and an intercommunication system for the observation of patients and for the instruction of interns and students.

Offices. The department offices include small private rooms for staff members and a large central office, if separate rooms are not available, for the interns and students. A separate room is required for the clerical force, for storing test materials and for filing the psychological records of institutional patients. Only originals of reports are sent to the institutional offices. It is desirable that all original records of examinations be kept permanently in the department files, together with carbons of the reports. This is necessary for research and reference purposes.

Professional Equipment

The following professional equipment is necessary:

1. A well-stocked and varied supply of paper and performance test materials of all kinds. A clinical psychologist in an institutional setting is called upon to work with such a great variety of subjects and problems—all ages, all stages of literacy, all states of physical health and all stages of mental disorder—that extensive test materials are essential. A sample file of the testing materials available on the market is a further aid in selecting examination devices suitable to meet these demands.

2. The experimental equipment needed will depend on the nature of the psychological problems of the institution, and usually apparatus will have to be specially constructed for experimentation. A small shop in connection with the laboratory adds considerably to the efficiency of the experimental set-up.

3. A well-stocked library in the laboratory is necessary. It should contain dictionaries and handbooks on testing, experimental psychology, psychiatry, statistics, physiology and medicine for reference use by department staffs, interns, and students.

4. A set of record blanks specially devised to meet the needs of the institution is needed for use in the recording and reporting of test results.

Coordination

A psychological department which has the facilities discussed above is in a position to perform numerous services and make numerous contacts with the rest of the institution. The psychological department is directly responsible to the superintendent of the institution in administrative matters, to its clinical director in professional matters and teaching, to its director of out-patient departments for extramural work, and to its research director for research work. Thus, the psychology department has many lines of coordination with the various divisions of the institution. Through these numerous contacts the psychologist is afforded an incomparable opportunity to develop attitudes conducive to professional psychological service in psychiatric hospitals and institutions for the feebleminded.

6. The Psychologist in the Clinic Setting

During the 1947 meetings of the American Orthopsychiatric Association, a symposium on "The Psychologist in the Clinic Setting" was held under the chairmanship of S. J. Beck. Among others, David Rapaport and Saul Rosenzweig participated. I was asked to discuss the evolution of the "team" approach to clinic problems.

CHAIRMAN: There is a great diversity of clinic settings. Constantly, however, something is happening which some of us may be overlooking because we are part of the events. I refer to the evolution which has been taking place in the clinic set-up. From earlier ideas as to the roles of the professional personnel, there have been important shifts in thinking. The shifts have been both to the left and to the right; they have drawn clearer lines about our early, vague formulations and have also opened up some new vistas as to the potential of each discipline in the unit as a whole. On our panel is one member who has been in a strategic position to observe this evolution. In fact, he has himself been responsible for some of the events. This is the next speaker, Dr. David Shakow.

DAVID SHAKOW, PH.D.: When the team approach was first put into practice, what happened was what generally happens in new developments where the participants are relatively untrained. Simplicity, naïveté and specialization of the highest degree characterized the practice. The psychiatrist as physician made a physical study of the patient; the social worker went out into the community and conducted a social investigation resulting in a social history; the psychologist did the mental tests. When the physical, social, and mental test studies were completed, an evaluation conference, attended by all three, was held. On the basis of the pooled findings, the psychiatrist carried out the indicated therapy with the patient. Usually the patient was a child, since it was almost exclusively in child guidance clinics that the team approach was the standard practice. If, in addition to personal therapy, environmental manipulation was called for, the social worker manipulated.

It soon became obvious that others, usually the mother, also needed therapy. This task naturally fell to the social worker since she already had the contact. Such additional responsibility increased the worker's satisfaction in her job and was warmly welcomed by her. The quite limited scope of the psychologist's activity was broadened somewhat when it was recognized that certain problems, such as those of speech or reading difficulty, were fundamentally reeducational problems. These were turned over to him as the person best versed in educational procedure. It developed, however, that speech and reading problems were not mere matters of tutoring or habit training, but were integrally associated with personality

Reprinted with permission from the *American Journal of Orthopsychiatry*, vol. 18, 1948.

difficulties. Since the problem was already in the psychologist's hands, it was natural for him to continue with it at this broader level. So the way was opened up for the psychologist to work with problems of general personality. With the gradual broadening of the field of the other members of the team, the psychiatrist became somewhat restive and extended his own field to include occasional work with adults. Under these circumstances, it was natural for the social worker to feel that age was not a reasonable basis for distinction in her own therapeutic and case work, and she began working with children. The psychologist, feeling the same way, began therapeutic work with parents.

What started off as a group whose members each had a very specialized compartmentalized function, became in practice a group of persons having overlapping and quite similar functions. This overlapping also resulted in the fact that frequently all three disciplines no longer worked on the same case together. Sometimes only one, more frequently two, and relatively less frequently all three were involved in handling the same case.

On the basis of what is actually happening in practice, it is obvious that our conception of what we mean by the "team" approach must be reformulated. How shall this be done? What is the division of responsibility which a revaluation of the situation calls for?

Two factors play a role. The obvious one is the nature of the training provided by each of the disciplines. The second factor is often neglected in formal discussions of the problem, but in the practical setting is of paramount importance. I refer to the personality, interests, and special abilities of the individual staff member regardless of the group of which he is a member. Certainly in a field where personality factors play such a great role and where variations in the special background, interests, and abilities of workers are great, the interests of the patient demand that these factors be utilized to the fullest. Although the discussion which follows will naturally emphasize the former, in the particular situation it is natural and desirable that the latter be given its due value.

We can best determine the division of responsibility and activity among the members of a clinic, whose workers are equally well trained, by the consideration of each of the six major functions of a clinic: therapy, diagnosis, research, teaching, consultation, and community relations.

Therapy. All three types of workers may concern themselves with one or another of the various forms of psychotherapy in general personality problems; with an understandable concentration of effort by the social workers on cases where the problems are mainly social; by the psychologist where they are mainly educational; and by the psychiatrist where they are psychosomatic. So far as clientele is concerned, there seems to be no reason for making distinctions on an age basis.

Diagnostic. Each group will naturally continue to make the important diagnostic contributions which arise from its traditional approach: the medical-psychiatric, the social and developmental data which come from the family history, the psychological data which come from psychological tests and experimental situations.

Research. Each group will have problems which fall within its own field and will wish to work with these relatively independently. Problems requiring coordinated attack could best be taken care of by a committee representing the disciplines involved.

Teaching. Each group will under ordinary circumstances take care of its own group of students as well as carry the responsibility for the program of training in its own field which students and staff workers from other fields should have. Clinics would do well to increase the amount of "other-discipline" teaching they do. In general, each of the disciplines has been weak in acquainting their colleagues from the other two professions with its philosophy and techniques. Although a certain degree of such acquaintance results from joint staff meetings, it is surprising how much ignorance of each other's basic philosophy and methods exists among the three groups working so closely together. With this in mind, there should be short-term clerkships in the others' departments for the staff members as well as for the students of a particular discipline. In addition, there are, of course, general topics of interest to the whole staff for which plans should be arranged by a coordinating committee.

Consultation. This should be with representatives of other agencies, professional persons, and parents. Each profession would naturally take care of the problems which are most relevant to its major competence. Thus problems of intellectual status, developmental stages, special abilities and defects, might very well go to the psychologist; problems of a social and socioeconomic type to the social worker, and problems of a psychiatric and psychosomatic kind to the psychiatrist.

Community relations. This involves contact with other social agencies, professional persons such as ministers, physicians, and teachers, and the lay public, and could best be established by each group in its own field insofar as lectures and other group contacts are concerned. Presumably, any of the members of the staff would be prepared to talk on general problems of mental hygiene.

Although in all six fields there is participation on the part of all disciplines, the three fields in which one or the other of the disciplines is prepared by training and major interest to take a role of leadership are therapy, research, and community relations.

The leadership in therapy naturally rests in the hands of the psychiatrist because of his medical background, with its social and legally recognized responsibilities for treatment, and his major concern with this problem. Leadership in research would seem most naturally to fall to the psychologist because of his special preoccupation with this aspect, and his training which places so much emphasis on investigative approaches. In community relations, leadership is an obvious responsibility of the social worker because of her extensive community contacts, her wide acquaintance with social organization, and her concern with the social forces in the community.

A clinic organized with these overlapping functions, taking advantage of the specialized backgrounds of the disciplines involved, as well as of their common skills, and of the special background and competence of its individual staff members can be said to meet the true meaning of the "team" approach. It involves a coordinated attack through coordinated thinking on the mental hygiene problems of the individual and his community. One then has a clinic where competence is permitted to express itself for the benefit of the patient, where the checks and balances provided by differing approaches, *the* great value of the team approach, work most freely; in other words, a clinic which instead of being staff-centered has truly come of age because it is patient-centered.

7. The Role of the Psychologist

In February 1963 the Mount Sinai Hospital, New York, honored the opening of its Institute of Psychiatry by holding a two-day Dedication Conference on the "Current and Future Role of the Psychiatric Unit in a General Hospital." The paper below was one of a panel of presentations on this occasion. It was published as part of the volume of the proceedings edited by M. Ralph Kaufman. This volume contains further discussion of the topic of this paper, as well as many others, of course.

The principles which will guide my discussion will necessarily involve consideration of the standards that psychiatry should set, those that psychology should meet, and the several needs, present and future, that the institution has to meet.

Although our chairman, in his invitation to participate, called for a "blueprint," I am sure that he did not intend us to be as rigid as this word would ordinarily imply. He undoubtedly merely wanted us to provide a general architectural drawing of the possibilities in the field, a drawing of sufficient detail to serve as a useful guide to immediate practice but sufficiently flexible to allow for the changes which are likely to occur in the course of social developments over the years. Above all, in trying to meet this request, I know that I am not making suggestions for the establishment of a psychiatric unit in an *ordinary* general hospital. The primary personnel for such an institution are psychiatrists, psychiatric nurses, and perhaps social workers. Other groups of professionals are more or less useful, but not essential. However, in the kind of hospital represented by Mount Sinai, other disciplines and services *do* become essential. I am cognizant of Mount Sinai's high standards; consequently, in making suggestions for psychology, I am thinking of Mount Sinai's achieving a position in relation to psychology of the kind achieved by the Menninger Clinic among private hospitals and Worcester among state hospitals. Essentially, I am guided by thinking of the place of psychology in an ideal institution (to borrow part of the title of a well-known report).

Reprinted with permission from M. R. Kaufman (Ed.), *The Psychiatric Unit in a General Hospital,* 1965. (International Universities Press).

General Considerations About the Psychiatric Unit

The basic structures and functions that relate to a general hospital psychiatric unit are fairly clear. There are the in-patient and out-patient psychiatric units for adults and children. Primary concern is with acute patients who remain in the hospital for a relatively short period; service to these is a major goal, with consultation, however, being almost equally important. Teaching and research are inevitable parts of such an advanced institution.

Since there is still so much that the psychologist has to do in order to define his position with regard to the existing situation, I shall limit myself for the most part to a consideration of the hospital as it is. Over the next decade there will probably be very little change in the general pattern of care except that which comes through the improvement of psychodiagnostic and therapeutic methods. It is possible that with the increase in the amount of preventive work, and the greater use of home and local community facilities for the care of mentally disordered patients, there may be some decrease in their number in general hospitals. My own guess is, however, that this latter trend will have its major effect on the special hospitals, such as state and private hospitals for the mentally disordered, and that the problem of taking care of acute cases will remain for the general hospitals. In fact, the proportionate burden for such hospitals may even increase.

Before going on to the psychologist himself, it is necessary first to consider the general attitudinal background of the psychiatric unit. It is the psychiatrist who sets the essential tone. Certain cardinal characteristics describe the modern psychiatrist. Foremost among these is the recognition of the importance of *attitudes* in interpersonal relationships. Without the central acceptance of the all-importance of the patient and *his* attitudes, integral to which is the possession by the psychiatrist himself of a warm but objective approach toward patients, it is difficult to see how a psychiatrist can function optimally.

In addition to this pervasive quality, the psychiatrist should have fully integrated into his approach to professional problems a working acceptance of a combination of the following five principles underlying the understanding of personality: (1) the *genetic* principle, which acknowledges the importance of antecedents in the genetic series to account for present manifestations of personality; (2) the recognition of the *cryptic*, of unconscious and preconscious factors as crucial determiners of behavior, the recognition that behavior has underlying motivations which are rarely perceptible to the actor, and frequently not even to the trained observer except with the use of special techniques; (3) the *dynamic* notion that behavior is drive-determined, that underneath behavior ultimately lie certain innate or early developed drives; (4) the general *psychobiological* assumption that the personality is integral and indivisible, that there is a pervasive interrelationship between psyche and soma; this involves the acceptance of an organismic principle of total rather than segmental personality; (5) the *psychosocial* principle, which recognizes the integration of the individual and his environment as a unit, which recognizes that drives and their derivatives are expressed in individual response in a social context and that the social is of equal importance with the individual in the determination of behavior.

The Psychologist

The psychologist should be a *clinical* psychologist, with the general orientation just described. Before going on to consider his specific roles and commitments, we must be clear about the clinical psychologist. In recent years his image has become confused, with the clinical psychologist himself contributing to this confusion. There has been much talk recently about behavioral and social sciences in the field of mental maladjustment. Out of this has developed a tendency in some circles to stereotype the clinical psychologist as a kind of paperback psychiatrist. The psychiatrist, overimpressed with the therapeutic demands of the psychologist, has a tendency to view him merely as a less well-trained edition of himself. The social scientist, on the other hand, generally called upon to do a research job and being a relative newcomer in the field, without historical knowledge of clinical psychology's varied role over the years, has tended to view the clinical psychologist, with the psychiatrist and social worker, as grubbers in the soil of service.

The psychologist has himself added to these misconceptions largely because many who have gone through clinical psychological training have not been made fully aware of the goals originally laid out for clinical psychology programs by the Committees and Conferences on Clinical Training (APA, CTCP, 1947; Raimy, 1950; Roe, 1959). These goals called for a background of general psychology combined with intensive training in service (diagnosis and therapy) to serve as a basis for a career of continued concern with the clinical and investigative problems, as well as the service opportunities, which the field offers. It was further agreed that this training approach was most effective when carried out in an environment, such as a hospital, where persons came for help and were thus motivated to bring real phenomena for study. The plan was that after a period of deep and serious immersion in the study of individuals by this clinical method the psychologist interested in generic problems would be in a much better position to undertake research studies of significance. The image projected by this plan was the clinical psychologist as primarily a psychologist who chose to approach the problems of psychology through the very rich data provided by the clinical individual approach in preference to segmental laboratory study dealing with generalized man. There was a recognition that psychology could advance most rapidly by way of both paths simultaneously, the clinical psychologist from the study of the individual and the laboratory psychologist from an emphasis on problem areas. It had, of course, been assumed from the beginning that after such combined general and clinical training, a certain number of persons would devote themselves entirely to service, others entirely to investigation, but it had been hoped that the majority would combine both functions. Although to train persons in both a science and profession is a difficult task, the idea remains a realistic one, and I trust it will be basic in the setting up of a psychology group at Mount Sinai.

I have emphasized that the psychologist should be a *clinical* psychologist. In the present context, all that is meant by this is that his background should include substantial experience with clinical material so as to insure that he is *patient*-oriented. He must recognize that in the service-oriented setting, his primary responsibility lies in his technical contributions to the understanding of the individual case so that optimal service for the patient is insured. Having accepted this fundamental obligation and met it optimally, he can then take care of his other major functions: to see the implications of his findings in individual cases for theory and to contribute to research and teaching.

Areas of Function

Thus cognizant of his primary responsibilities, the psychologist in a setting of this kind functions in four major areas: service in psychodiagnosis, service in psychotherapy, teaching, and research. His service functions are clear. In the teaching area, he makes his contribution to the education of staff, residents, interns, medical students, as well as persons from his own discipline. His research activities may be directed at administrative, at applied, and at basic research, the last dealing with both clinical and nonclinical material.

Psychodiagnostic Function

Let us first consider the *psychodiagnostic* function. I might begin by making the trite but frequently neglected point that personality is an important variable not only in relation to psychiatric problems but also in the more strictly medical illnesses. Only in the case of extreme medical emergencies do both psychology and psychiatry become irrelevant. There is, therefore, a place for the psychologist not only in relation to the psychiatric service but also in the context of the more strictly medical facilities: general medicine, neurology, pediatrics, and various areas of surgery. It is to be expected that recognition of the more strictly psychological factors will continue to grow as it has in the psychiatric consultations at Mount Sinai over the years.

Psychiatric patients who come to the general hospital setting are acute and, with rare exceptions, short-term cases. In long-term cases, perhaps those undergoing psychoanalysis or extended psychotherapy, much data relating to personality structure and function are uncovered during the long process of therapy. Since this is not true for the acute case, psychodiagnostic techniques are particularly valuable here. For prognostic and selection purposes, such methods, of course, remain of value with all cases.

With what kinds of problems can the psychologist in his psychodiagnostic role be of aid? One area concerns some aspect of *capacity level.* It includes such problems as that of intellectual level, latent resources or ego strength, underlying schizophrenic or other psychotic process, capacity for change, and the detection of disturbed capacity not uncovered in the ordinary psychiatric examination. Another is the area of *capacity use*, which deals with such questions as how concrete or atomistic is the patient's thinking, how effective are the defenses which hamper his ego function, and how fixated are these defenses. Further areas relate to problems of affective evaluation, the determination of whether one is dealing with an organic or neurotic problem, the establishing of areas of greatest present conflict. Still another major area involves the evaluation of the course of treatment, the changes taking place in the patient as a result of therapy, whether psychotherapy or pharmacotherapy. It may, indeed, involve the primary question as to the desirable intensiveness of psychotherapy or whether drugs should or should not be given. In relation to the more strictly medical illnesses, it is often important to ascertain, for example, psychogenic factors involved in contemplated plastic surgery, whether psychotherapy should be associated with medical treatment, whether a patient should be hospitalized or treated as an out-patient.

Evaluation of Tests

In the environment we are considering, where the primary emphasis is on the individual patient rather than the problem or the technique, certain general standards related to psychodiagnostics should prevail. The psychologist, being skilled in the administration and understanding of a wide variety of tests, will be able to keep in mind their limitations as well as their strengths. He will be able to appreciate when tests are called for and when not, what tests and combinations of tests are required in specific problems. While having a sensitivity to the diagnostic and prognostic aspects of his test findings, he should also be sensitive to their therapeutic implications. In fact, it is necessary that a "therapeutic attitude" underlie his testing, that he avoid probing and misplaced therapy, as well as violation of the situational controls. In keeping with the spirit of good testing procedure, he will leave the patient the better, rather than the worse, for the experience.

In assessing the results of tests, the psychologist should have some sense of balance between the extremes of rigorous pedantic exactness and slovenly guessing, recognizing that different problems lend themselves to differing degrees of control, and even acknowledging that there are times and stages in the development of a procedure when a rough negative correlation appears to obtain between psychological meaningfulness and degree of control. Although he should be continually working for reasonably greater control, the psychologist should also be appreciative of the great importance of honesty about the degree of control obtained at a particular time, admitting ignorance and hypothesizing when such is the case. It is expected that he will have enough security neither to escape into exactness about the insignificant nor to resort to meaningless profundities when confronted by the complexity and difficulties of the significant.

There are so many questions relating to the reliability and validity of data concerned with present cryptic activity and inferences for past activity, so many problems relating to manner of presentation and communication in attempting to compress an extensive body of psychological data into an abbreviated account, that it would be rather presumptuous to report any findings without some hesitation and reservation. Any examiner who has had experience with psychodiagnostic material recognizes that the reliability and validity of any of his conclusions depend on a synthesis of amassed cues—major and minor, direct and inferential, presentative and symbolic—coming from various sources which represent reflections of the same facet of the personality. It is further true that even the most complete verbal report of events cannot adequately convey the whole body of data available to the examiner. Despite attempts to supply a systematic framework, the generalizations which compose a report are still able to provide only relatively isolated, partially corroborated samples of quantifiable and unquantifiable behavior that could easily lose their significance when viewed out of context. This difficulty is enhanced by the many obstacles to facile communication which exist in the sphere of personality. Such handicaps include the attenuation of concepts by common speech, the lack of rigorous use of terms within the discipline, and the specialized use of terms based on theoretical bias.

Consultation with Referring Physician

The acuteness and the relatively short-term stay of the cases create a special need in general hospitals for speed in carrying out consultations. It is therefore desirable that the psychological examiner arrange for early personal conference with the referring physician and make the results of the examination available as quickly as possible thereafter in written form.

Another problem which must be dealt with is the amount of information with which the examiner should be provided. In some institutions the practice is to have psychologists examine all patients practically "blind." In others the opposite policy is followed: the examiner has available to him the social history as well as a group of problems that are posed for him by the referent. My own preference is not to have any fixed arrangements but, rather, to let the needs of the particular case determine the conditions for examination. There may be occasional instances in which "blind" conditions seem desirable. Then there may be others in which all available information should be in the hands of the psychologist. The psychological examination is not a game to see who can find out most about the patient. Neither is it a situation in which the psychologist is under the strain of having to do without the minimal amount of descriptive and clinical knowledge which would help him make his contribution. What is needed is decision about the particular requirements in an individual case, with provisions being made for the psychologist to obtain the least amount of information which can enable him to make the greatest contribution with a minimum of wasted effort.

Psychotherapeutic Function

In addition to psychodiagnosis, the other service area for the psychologist is psychotherapy. The great social need for psychotherapists has already been detailed in the report of the Joint Commission (1961), so I need not develop that theme further.

My fundamental position, in line with the report of the Joint Commission, is that the practice of psychotherapy should not be determined by a person's particular discipline. Many years of observation in this area have led me to believe that so far as psychotherapy is concerned, the order of importance of the three factors integrally involved is first, the personal qualities of the therapist; second, the nature of the patient and his problem; and, third, the nature and adequacy of the therapist's training, especially in areas related to human psychology and motivation. Particular professional identification is not necessarily involved in these three.

In fact, in relation to medicine as professional background for psychotherapeutic training, I have often wondered whether conventional medical training does not sometimes serve as a hindrance rather than as an aid to optimal preparation for psychotherapy. While experience in dealing with patients certainly has its helpful aspects, there is some danger that acting as a healer of physical ailments may serve to desensitize the student to the subtleties of psychological and social factors. (It is to be hoped, however, that the increasing emphasis on psychosocial factors in medical training will eventually reduce this liability.) While the long experience that medicine has had in inculcating ethical principles affords a considerable advantage over other, younger fields, nevertheless it is important to recognize that ethics is not a medical monopoly and that its major mainstay lies in the personal character of the practitioner. Actually, I wonder whether social work, through its selection program and the nature of its training, has not done the best job in this respect. Given the proper selection principles, both self-selection and external selection, and proper safeguards in the form of internal and external superego controls (the details of which I have described elsewhere [Shakow, 1949c]), this problem is reasonably well taken care of.

One of the tests with regard to professional selection is, I suppose, for one to examine one's own criteria. In the actual situation of having to recommend a psychotherapist for a person for whom I have personal regard, I have found myself making recommendations largely on the basis of the personal qualities of the therapist and the general competence of his training. I have paid little attention to whether he was a psychiatrist, a psychologist, or a social worker. I wonder whether the experience of many of you is not too dissimilar. (I might add that in the case of psychiatrists, I have often been struck by the incongruity between their individual behavior and the positions they take in group assembled.)

When I speak of personal qualities, I include particularly those attributes of personality which we designate as honesty, integrity, and fundamental human sympathy. I cannot think of any field of work in which these qualities are more important than in psychotherapy. It is important, however, not to minimize the value of training background. I cannot say that I am entirely satisfied with the training given either to psychologists or to physicians, or, for that matter, even to social workers. I would feel most comfortable if we had persons, properly selected, of course, who had gone through a training program of the general nature recommended by Kubie (1954), which combines the advantages of the various kinds of training. Whether society can ever overcome its rigidities and consider such a plan seriously, I do not know. In any event, given present training methods, it would seem to be advantageous for the advancement of the field of psychotherapy to have persons come to its practice from a variety of backgrounds.

Thus disembarrassed of its political aspects, psychotherapy practice would be determined strictly by the broader social criteria of competence of the practitioner. Here I can merely point to the great opportunities afforded an organized hospital such as Mount Sinai to provide the proper social controls, for in such a setting the proper level of supervision can be provided, whether it be direct detailed supervision, occasional supervision, or merely general supervision and consultation. In the context of always available consultation, the dangers which exist in private practice for *all* practitioners, whether medical or nonmedical, are minimized. The kind of group practice provided by a well-organized hospital has the advantage of encouraging the maintenance of both ethical and technical standards and fosters awareness of the dangers that lie in individual practice. We must recognize that everyone's superego needs repeated bolstering and nourishment, especially in a field where knowledge is meager compared with ignorance. In such a setting, group practice provides additional support to inner control to a degree not provided by legal licensing or malpractice strictures.

Teaching Function

A third major area of activity for the psychologist lies in the teaching sphere. In a setting such as is provided by Mount Sinai, this would include teaching residents in psychiatry, residents and interns in other medical specialties, general practitioners who come for special training in psychiatry, medical students (when Mount Sinai has its own medical school), and students in psychology.

The most effective training is probably conducted in a center which, in addition to staff from a variety of professions, has a comparable range of students. In such settings there is considerable stimulation toward development of insight and skill as a result of the working relationships established on the same case material, the differential demands made for common understanding of case material, and discussions between and among the students of the various disciplines. This type of training program is also conducive to the development not only of identification with one's own group but also of additional identification with a common enterprise, with the team of workers, the group that transcends the individual discipline. It is important to recognize the fundamental contributions in this direction which come from well-qualified cross-discipline teaching.

Teaching the Psychiatric Resident

Of the groups involved, let us first consider the psychiatric resident. Although psychiatric residents vary considerably in their backgrounds, it is clear that the resident does not come to the hospital with a *tabula rasa* concerning psychology. Increasingly, he comes with some background in the behavioral and social sciences, and those who teach psychology should be aware of this.

The training of the resident in psychodiagnosis should be directed at the integration of material provided by other fields and disciplines with his own data. The training he receives in diagnostic activities should therefore be based not only upon his own observations and data but also on data provided by others. Learning to understand the contributions from others presumably calls upon the resident to go through two quite different processes. The first requires his actually having the experience of obtaining the data as the person representing the other discipline obtains it; the second involves acquiring experience in integrating the material provided by others with his own. The discussion which follows will deal with possible contributions from psychology toward accomplishing these purposes.

It is especially important that the experience in psychology be oriented realistically, if not entirely ideally, to both content and method. The program should be organized to fit in with the present, generally accepted, primary goal of residency training in psychiatry: the development of competent clinical psychiatrists who have certain attitudes and a knowledge of descriptive and dynamic psychiatry basic to diagnosis and treatment. Since this goal is most effectively achieved in a program that is centered predominantly on concrete case material rather than on the didactic and abstract, psychological teaching is most effective when it employs a similar approach.

A substantial part of the plan should consist of supervision of the residents in systematic observation and description of personality. Some acquaintance with resident training leaves me with the conviction that before actually beginning serious diagnostic work the resident should have a preliminary period devoted to naturalistic observation and description, the procedures on which sound diagnosis is necessarily based. Because so much of psychiatry depends upon the description of the complexities of behavior, it is reasonable that a definite portion of the resident's time be set aside for training in careful observation and report. For this purpose, one-way screens, paired observers, and recording devices of both sound and visual types should be used in settings in which individuals and groups are under observation in both free and controlled situations. Repeated checking of observers' reports against each other, against supervisors' observations, and against mechanical devices might be considered standard practice. Since high standards of succinctness and accuracy of terminology are essential to an adequate report, this period of practice in observation should be both preceded and accompanied by a systematic study of personality description schemes in which the meanings of the terms used are carefully considered. What is emphasized here is that the resident develop a healthy respect for careful observation and report, for he is going to work in a field where, with rare exceptions, the major, and not infrequently the only, instrument is the observer himself.

The psychological group should also provide systematic training in the evaluation of personality by psychodiagnostic testing. The purpose of this course should certainly not be to make expert examiners out of the residents; instead, it should be intended to give them sufficient insight into the meaning and mechanics of psychodiagnostic testing to develop an appreciation of the contributions that tests make but, at the same time, to make them cautious and soundly critical of their uses. While such a program should include a certain amount of theoretical material about the nature of tests and measurements in psychology, it should have a predominantly practical orientation, main emphasis being given to the demonstration of tests and batteries of tests actually being used with patients. These could range from simple lecture demonstrations to the actual administration of a test battery to a group of residents or to one of a resident's own patients viewed through a one-way window. In the instance in which a resident's own patient is involved, the resident should afterwards follow through the process of scoring and the analysis of the material with the psychologist. Insofar as possible, test data should be considered in relation to actual patients on whom other clinical material is available.

"Laboratory" work, consisting of the resident himself being given a battery of tests and the opportunity to practice on other students, might also be included. At more advanced stages the resident might be given some consistent training which would enable him to examine a limited number of patients. The resident should also be made acquainted with simple devices, such as the Kent EGY, which he might learn to use regularly as part of his own "mental status" examinations.

At the residency level, the major goals of training in research should probably be the development of skill in the critical evaluation of reports in the literature, a beginning skill in the organization of new studies, and the development of alertness to research problems. The contributions from psychology here may be along several lines.

A seminar in methodology, including primary statistics and experimental design, might be conducted around the critical evaluation of published studies. Better yet would be its organization around an ongoing research project in the hospital. During the process of evaluating such studies by the seminar method, alternative and possibly improved experimental designs might be considered. Statistical methodology and design introduced in this fashion has many advantages over a didactic course, one of them being that few residents manifest a sufficiently strong need or enduring interest in formal material in this area to make a didactic course productive.

It is important to avoid, insofar as possible, the assignment of a project to a student. It is much preferable to encourage him to be sensitive to problems which arise during his own clinical work and to assist him in formulating testable hypotheses from this material. If the student can be helped through the whole process of investigation: being faced with a problem, formulating it, setting up the design for at least a limited study of the question, carrying out the actual experimental or clinical investigation, and then making the final analysis and writing up the results, then the utmost in research initiation will have been accomplished.

Teaching Other Medical Groups

Concerning teaching opportunities with other medical groups, the same philosophy of case orientation and learning by doing that I have expressed in relation to psychiatric residents should prevail in the teaching of residents and interns from other medical specialties and of general practitioners who come for special training in psychiatry. There may be occasions when didactic lecturing with these groups is appropriate. However, decisions to use this kind of instruction should be given careful thought before they are adopted. Ordinarily, courses should as much as possible be of a seminar type, case-oriented, and be accompanied by demonstrations.

The teaching of medical students presents a quite different and broader problem, for it involves the participation of the psychologist in the four years of medical training. I can do no more here than emphasize that the psychologist has a contribution to make in each of the medical school years. The participation of the psychology staff is profitable in basic courses on personality development and dynamic psychology through courses of a "laboratory" type, whether these be in experimental approaches to psychodynamics or in psychodiagnostics. The program might be under the aegis either of a behavioral sciences department or a division in the department of psychiatry. My own preference at the present developmental stage of psychology would be for the latter. I believe that psychology's eventual contribution will be greater if it continues to combine clinical and generic interests in an integral fashion, rather than prematurely attempting to establish itself as a basic medical science department.

The training of clinical psychologists is, of course, a very special problem, and it strikes me as a major responsibility of an institution like Mount Sinai. I have already on several previous occasions (APA & AAAP, 1945; Shakow, 1946, 1957) considered in detail some general aspects of this problem which are relevant for the Mount Sinai situation. It is sufficient here to emphasize that although there are many other types of organizations carrying on such activities, there are relatively few general hospitals with the proper facilities for training psychologists. Because of continually increasing needs for clinicians, the provision of clinical training at the third-year internship and graduate levels in an active general hospital such as Mount Sinai would be extremely beneficial.

Research Function

We have considered three major areas of function: service in psychodiagnostics, in psychotherapy, and teaching. The fourth and perhaps most important function of the psychologist is research. As well as having a sense of personal responsibility about his findings, an appreciation of the fact that his findings make a real difference to a particular individual and his immediate family, the psychologist should recognize that he also carries a broader social and scientific responsibility. He must be aware of the inadequacy of the methods, the data, and the theory in the field. He should, therefore, be constantly sensitive to the research implications of his findings and his techniques, and be on the lookout for significant problems and investigative methods, attacking these problems in order to be able to integrate his data with the fundamental body of psychological knowledge. My own view is that if psychologists were forced to limit their contributions to one area, I would like to see it be research. The need for knowledge in the field of personality and mental health is so great that it seems almost unnecessary to stress the reasons for this emphasis. The kind of training I have described for the psychologist, combining as it does both practical and research experience, should enable him to make a valuable contribution to the advancement of knowledge in this field.

Of the three major research areas, two are applied and one is basic. The problems in the two applied areas are those connected with the individual devices used in the examination and treatment of patients, and those centered on the processes which may roughly be called administrative. The basic area is concerned with the general theoretical understanding of the personality factors related to health and disease. I shall mention only a few examples in each of these fields of investigation.

In the *patient-oriented applied* area, there is much to be done with psychodiagnostic procedures. We have a large armamentarium of devices which can be used for examining any one of the multiple facets of personality, in fact, a plethora of such devices. But our knowledge of these instruments, which are so vital to clinical psychology, is far from dependable. While both the objective and projective devices we use appear to have logical rationales—sampling of behavior under controlled and standardized conditions based on norms, on the one hand, and the projective hypothesis added to these, on the other—we are far from having established their dependability. One must, however, avoid the danger of falling prey to the simplistic solutions of easy statistics to solve these problems. Before we attempt this stage of analysis, we must carry out searching clinical studies, using the knowledge which can come only from detailed analysis of individual cases.

Aside from general problems of reliability and validity, the greatest amount of research is now needed in the systematic follow-up of cases which have not borne out test predictions, in order to trace factors that might have played a role in the aberrant results. At present, there seems to be little regard for the constant checking of negative cases. Consequently, a great deal of psychodiagnostic work is carried out and then forgotten.

Therapeutic devices are even more problematical, perhaps because research in therapy is so much more difficult to carry out. The questions that arise are endless. There are problems of the different varieties of therapy and their appropriate use, problems of assessment of change, of controls, of defining the significant variables, of analyzing the therapeutic relationship, problems of methods of expression and communication, and the problem of the learning processes involved in the therapy situation. These are only some of the areas which call for investigation, whether it be investigation directed at the study of psychotherapy or at other forms of therapy.

Of the many areas of applied *administrative* research, there are some in which the social scientist is expert. The psychologist, however, is especially equipped to deal with problems relating to personnel selection and to certain aspects of residency training.

The first of these is clear, although the problem itself is complicated and must be approached with more sophistication than it has been previously. The second, that related to residency training, is not so obvious. Largely because of the tremendous time investment that goes into the training of the resident, it is important to evaluate the conditions conducive to most effective learning at this level. This involves an examination of the program content, the nature of the teachers, and the teaching methods. Psychologists can be of considerable aid in this area by providing careful observations on present situations and by making suggestions for modifications which may lead to more efficient learning. It is important to approach the problem experimentally, to attempt to separate the largely personal factors which affect teaching and learning from those which are of general applicability. Recent work in the field of group dynamics, with which both psychologists and sociologists are acquainted, may have some contributions to make to the general improvement of teaching. This knowledge is most particularly applicable, however, to the productivity of staff meetings and conferences, activities constituting so large a part of training programs.

The nature of the supervisory process, of special importance at the residency level, also deserves systematic study. Social workers have already made a substantial empirical contribution to this area, and their experience should be called upon. It is possible, however, that more systematic study by psychologists interested in social and communication problems would be profitable.

The realm of *basic* psychological research in personality in its broadest sense is so immense that it can be no more than mentioned here. Developmental process, motivation and ego function, perception, psychomotor functions, cognition, learning, and conditioning are a few outstanding examples of basic research areas. Studies in these should be carried out under ordinary conditions, under stress conditions, and in relation to their physiological and constitutional concomitants. The wards of the general hospital provide an unusual opportunity for study of a great variety of "nature's experiments" in highly selective disturbances, and the psychiatric facilities provide many such "experiments" in general psychological disturbance. It is, however, most important that the study of hospital cases be balanced by the study of normal persons as controls, an area too much neglected in psychiatric work. This optimal use of the potential of the general hospital setting would then afford an unusual facility for making contributions to the understanding of the factors which play a role in both abnormal and normal personality.

Summary

In the preceding remarks I have outlined a fairly substantial program for the psychologist. Against a background of certain general attitudes, he is expected to contribute in four major areas: psychodiagnostics, psychotherapy, teaching, and research. While it is obvious that no one person can carry out such a program, a training program which has these goals in mind can develop persons who, given an opportunity to express their dominant interests, can as a group represent all of these important functions. Such a *department* of psychology can then, in the context of the contribution from other professions and disciplines, make its own legitimate contribution to achieving the goals of the "ideal" general hospital, present or future.

PART II

Training Objectives and Programs

This group of nine papers is devoted to the great variety of problems that arise in the development and execution of training programs.

8. An Internship Year for Psychologists

I wrote this paper after approximately ten years of experience in directing internship programs at the Worcester State Hospital. This followed on my personal experiences as intern under Grace Kent at Worcester in 1924–25 and under Fred Wells at the Boston Psychopathic Hospital in 1925–26.

There is a growing recognition of the need for an internship in the training of clinical psychologists.[1] The value of full-time experience with clinical problems has been demonstrated in medical and, to some extent, in social work training, and the possible value of similar experience with psychological material has been realized by workers in clinical psychology.

The major purpose of this paper is to discuss the content of an internship year. However, before proceeding to this, a brief consideration of the course of which the internship would be a part seems desirable.

Clinical Training Course

The first question which arises is: At which point in the course should the internship come? Two other disciplines, medicine and social service, have each apparently found a different stage of the training program most desirable for the internship.

Reprinted from the *Journal of Consulting Psychology*, vol. 2, 1938, with permission of the American Psychological Association.

[1] The question might indeed be raised as to whether an internship is not desirable for all psychologists and necessary for those who teach abnormal psychology.

In medicine, the student is given fundamental science training which is followed by clinical courses. It is only after this formal training is completed that he has his internship period. Thus, concentrated work with case material, usually of a particular kind, comes at the *end* of the regular course. In psychiatric social service, at least as represented by an outstanding school, the student has her internship (or externship, as the case may be) relatively early, interspersed with periods of didactic training. At this school, Smith College, a summer's formal school work is followed by nine months of concentrated field work (the internship) and completed (for those with previous social work experience) by an additional summer of academic work. A third plan, used by some social service schools, attempts to supply a substitute for the internship by part-time academic work and part-time field work carried on simultaneously. Since this program would not meet adequately the requirements of an internship, there will be no further discussion of it.

A consideration of both plans leaves one much more impressed with the possibilities of the medical system for the psychologist, although one recognizes that the Smith system has its advantages. The nature of the internship training in psychology would probably have to be somewhat different depending on which of the two plans was adopted, but the difference should not be great. Even if not adopted, the Smith plan offers a suggestion to psychology which should be given serious consideration. It indicates the possibility of taking advantage of summers for study. This may perhaps be the solution to the problem of combining work for a doctor's degree with clinical training which, according to one suggestion (Poffenberger, 1938), would lead only to a certificate. Thus work for a degree might involve three winters and four summers for those wishing to compress the course, or four winters and one summer for those interested in using only the usual school year. The certificate course would presumably be shorter by a full year.

Assuming that the internship comes at the end of the course of training, the question arises as to what preparation in psychology the student should have for it. Briefly, besides a background in general and experimental psychology, which may be assumed, a student should have *as a very minimum*—in order to take advantage of the various possibilities of the internship training—courses in abnormal psychology, clinical psychology, statistics and psychometrics, and field courses in clinical psychometrics and remedial work.

We may now go on to the discussion of the internship period, assumed for the present as being optimally a year in length.[2]

The Content of the Internship Year

The suggestions to be made refer especially to psychiatric hospitals and are to a considerable extent based on the practices followed at the Worcester State Hospital. With regard to the limitations introduced by the type of the institution, obvious substitutes could be made for other types of institutions; with regard to the

[2] It is very probable that a year's internship will soon be found inadequate for the training deemed necessary. However, for the present, discussion may be limited to a program involving a year's training.

limitations imposed by the special institution, enough is perhaps gained from the experience on which it is based to compensate for any bias which inevitably enters.

From the institution's standpoint, the purpose of an internship is presumably not to teach new techniques (although a certain amount of such teaching is unavoidable no matter how well prepared the student comes to the internship), but rather to give the student facility *in the use of already acquired techniques*. There are, however, at least three other equally important purposes. One of these is to *saturate the student with experience* in the practical aspects of psychopathology. Throughout this emphasis on the clinical side, however, considerable effort should be expended to retain and develop further that characteristic in which the psychologist by his training is different from the psychiatrist and social worker, namely, in the more *experimental-objective attitude* which he takes. The fourth purpose is to get the student *acquainted with the types of thinking and the attitudes of his colleagues in other disciplines* with whom he works most closely, that is, the psychiatrists and social workers. The program of training may now be discussed in relation to these four desiderata.

For facilitation in the use of techniques, even at the risk of repeating material already gained in field and other courses, the student should, after a period of orientation to the institution and the department, be placed at the double task of brushing up on already acquired psychometric techniques and on the study of the various modifications in procedure followed at the institution. During this period, too, the student should learn any of the standard techniques with which he is not already familiar.

After undergoing an examination on the techniques, the student should be ready for a course of practice testing. When the supervisor believes the student to be ready, the latter is permitted to take part in the psychometric work of the department, being assigned to the easiest cases at first, and being permitted, with accumulating experience, to go on to the more difficult cases. Throughout the internship period, the psychometric work should be done under supervision, both in laying out the program of examination and in reviewing its results and implications.

Psychometric practice should be rounded off by a seminar on clinical psychometrics in which the application of tests to clinical problems is studied by the case method.

The second purpose of the internship, *saturation of the student with clinical contacts*, could be achieved in various ways. The student would be required to attend all staff meetings where he would have an opportunity to hear discussed from different points of view a great variety of cases. He could also attend the courses in psychiatry and related subjects which active institutions always have for various student groups such as nurses, occupational therapists, etc. In these, a further opportunity is given him to become acquainted with the variety of psychiatric problems but in a more systematic fashion than in the staff meetings. In addition, it would be desirable to have each student follow, as a kind of psychiatric aide, at least one patient therapeutically under the guidance of a psychiatrist. In a state hospital, where so few patients get the necessary intensive therapy because of dearth of personnel, such an arrangement should not be difficult to make. In a child guidance clinic, remedial work might be substituted.

The third function of the internship, *the intensification of the experimental-objective attitude* of the psychologist, might be advanced by having the student carry through a research problem of an experimental nature, quantitative or objectively qualitative. Participation in a seminar on experimental psychopathology or on the psychologist's approach to psychopathology, in which the emphasis is placed on the objectification and experimentalization of clinical material, should be the counterpart of the research activity.

The fourth function of the internship year, *the development of insight and understanding into the attitudes of the psychologist's clinical colleagues*, could be accomplished in various ways. The staff meetings already mentioned in another connection are fundamental for bringing out the differences and similarities of the various approaches. In addition, it would be wise for the intern to become acquainted with the ways in which the psychiatrist as medical clinician works. Medicine has developed certain procedures for dealing with clinical problems which are ordinarily foreign to the psychologist and which could be quite suggestive to him. With this in mind, the student should be given the opportunity to attend a certain number of medical case discussions, clinical-pathological conferences, general physical examinations, neurological examinations, etc., not with the purpose of acquainting him with the language of medicine, but rather to give him insight into the thinking processes and methods of the clinician. (He might very well sit through a meeting without understanding the technical language but still get considerable understanding of the methods by which the problems are attacked.) Acquaintance with psychiatric techniques and procedures would come largely from the staff meetings mentioned and conferences on individual cases.

The other group of workers with whom the psychologist is most closely associated are the social workers. Besides becoming acquainted with social service procedures during staff meetings, special conferences on cases of common interest should be arranged with this group. The possibility of having an intern accompany a social service worker during a few of her investigations and family interviews should also be considered.

Although the latter three purposes of the internship do not lend themselves to as detailed discussion as does the first, they should not for this reason be considered the less important.

Besides its value to the individual psychologist, the internship year offers certain advantages to the profession of psychology itself, advantages difficult to obtain otherwise. The conditions of an internship are quite stringent in the demands for adjustment which it places on one. Not only is there the problem of adapting oneself to a variety of abnormal people, but there is also the necessity for adjusting oneself to one's associates in a much greater degree than is necessary in almost any other position in which the person may be placed, in some instances not even excepting his own family. Having to eat, live, and work with the same people for a period of about a year puts sufficient strain on a person to make it possible to tell from the way in which he meets this experience whether he is or is not fitted for clinical work. The gain for psychology in weeding out candidates temperamentally unfitted for clinical work should significantly advance the professional standing of psychology.

It is believed that any internship which adequately carries out the four purposes mentioned will complement the formal training in such a way as to place in the clinical field psychologists who are prepared to take on responsibilities in clinical psychology analogous to those which medical interns are ready to assume at the same stage of training.

9. The Training of the Clinical Psychologist

I prepared this paper for a meeting of the Clinical Section of the American Association for Applied Psychology in September, 1942, which was unfortunately not held because of war travel restrictions. The article was widely circulated and then, because of the amount of interest expressed, was published.

Introduction

The problem of the professional training of the psychologist (Shakow, 1938) has recently come to the surface with a rush of volcanic proportions after an extended period of underground rumbling.[1] One of the earlier signs of expressed interest was the organization of the American Association for Applied Psychology. More recent indications are to be found in the pronouncements of various leaders in psychology: English (1941) in his Presidential Address to the American Association for Applied Psychology in September, 1940, Hunter (1941) in his Presidential Address to the Eastern Psychological Association in April, 1941, and Yerkes (1941) in his address to the American Philosophical Society in April, 1941. Additional evidence is provided by the announcements which come from all directions of the establishment of internship training programs.

Although psychology has been quite slow in *accepting* itself as a profession, it does not follow that the same degree of retardation should characterize the process of *establishing* itself professionally. A psychology with a receptive attitude is in the

Reprinted with permission from the *Journal of Consulting Psychology*, vol. 6, 1942.

[1] Because of the number of persons to whom the writer is indebted for criticism of the program described in the present paper, individual acknowledgments are dispensed with. Special mention must be made, however, of the Conference on the Training of Clinical Psychologists which met on two occasions in 1941. It was the meetings of this group which encouraged the writer to organize notions long dormant and it was the criticisms by members of this group, as well as by others, which have resulted in much improvement over the first formulation of the scheme.

fortunate position of not having to pass through too wide a range of experimentation to determine the proper program of training necessary for the attainment of professional status. Without servilely following all their procedures, psychology can glean many serviceable suggestions from the experience of those fields of endeavor which have undergone a similar process of professional self-establishment during recent years, namely, medicine and social work (Commission on Graduate, 1940; Commission on Medical, 1932; French, 1940).

The science of psychology has responsibilities in the matter which cannot be evaded. The need for applied psychological work is great and unless psychology can provide adequately trained personnel, other disciplines, which recognize both the need and the responsibilities, will take over the functions which are more properly the province of the psychologist. The scope of activity expected from the clinical psychologist has generally been quite limited. The suggestion has frequently been advanced that this limitation was primarily due to the poor training of its practitioners and the low standards in the field generally. Whether this is so or not, certainly any real broadening of the scope can come only from the institution of truly professional training and standards.

From one standpoint it might be argued that clinical psychology is the groundwork for *all* professional psychology, whether educational, industrial or consulting. (It might even be held with considerable cogency that a training in clinical psychology is a not unessential part of the training of all except a few academic psychologists.) For the present purposes, however, we shall limit ourselves to the training of the clinical psychologist, per se.[2] The attempt will be made to present comprehensively, if somewhat sketchily, what are considered the important principles of training, from the undergraduate through the postgraduate period. The problems connected with the inauguration and maintenance of standards at the various stages will be discussed and a plan for action suggested.

Goal of Training

Before any specific recommendations for a program of training are proposed, it is essential to formulate the goal toward which this training is to be directed. The most obvious decision to be made is with respect to the level of contribution to be expected from the clinical psychologist. By this term we must mean a person of professional level capable of acting in a consulting rather than in a technical capacity. Although a demand for technicians exists, psychology cannot afford to concern itself with this peripheral problem at a time when the importance of establishing itself professionally is central. Granted this, the question becomes one of determining the kind of trained person who, at the present stage of development of the profession and

[2] In presenting this program for the training of the clinical psychologist, it is recognized that the training is weighted in the direction of psychopathology, especially as it is represented in the psychiatric hospital. This is in part deliberate and in part due to the background and experience of the writer. With relatively few changes, however, the general scheme is adaptable to other clinical fields and even to the educational and industrial fields.

with the present needs of the field, would most adequately represent and advance clinical psychology. Such a person would seem to be one who, besides meeting certain basic personality requirements and having a breadth of educational background, is competent to carry a triad of responsibilities: diagnosis, research, and therapy. It is important to recognize that for most clinical psychologists entering the field the stage of specialization in any one of these has not as yet been reached.

The Educational Program—General Principles

With respect to the educational program for the training of the clinical psychologist, there are certain general principles which it seems reasonable to stress:

1. The program should be organized and planned in such a manner that there is direction towards a fairly specific goal from the beginning of graduate work and to some extent even from undergraduate days on. Although clinical psychology is not so well-known and defined a field as medicine, and therefore cannot expect prospective students to be aware of their interest in it early in the undergraduate period, there is good reason for setting up some ideals of training for this period as a rough guide. This would help to lay the ground for greater control, in the future, of preparation for the field.

2. The program should be organized around an integrated combination of academic and field work.

3. The program should not, for the present at least, be too rigidly organized, since considerable experimentation with respect to persons, background, and content is essential for the development of the most adequate program. Much can be learned about the progress which stems from such an elastic attitude by an examination of the approaches of the medical and social work professions to a similar problem.

4. A process of careful discrimination in the choice of content is essential if the program is not to become impossibly broad and dilute. It may be anticipated that considerable pressure will be brought to bear on organizers of training programs to include a great variety of subjects and content; almost everything remotely related to the field will undoubtedly be thought of as important. Even though everything *is* of some value, the obvious fact must constantly be kept in mind that some work is more essential for the particular goals to be attained than other.

5. Except at the level of elementary courses and such fixed courses as physics and chemistry, the philosophy and manner of teaching, as well as the content, are important. Little of significance, obviously, can be surmised from the mere title of a course. Until there is some supervision and evaluation of instructors and instruction, as well as of course titles, considerable liberality will have to be shown in this respect. (The writer will be forgiven for stressing an educational truism so frequently found untrue in practice.)

6. The program of training should be at least as rigorous and extensive as that for the Ph.D. It should include the equivalent of the requirements for the Ph.D. plus an additional year of internship.

Educational Program—Pre-psychological (Undergraduate)

The pre-psychological program is the stage of preparation about which the least specificity is possible. However, there are certain general suggestions as to the content of the program which may be advanced:

1. A major in the biological (and physical) sciences. (The pre-medical course is on the whole along the right line, but distinctly greater emphasis should be placed on the biological rather than on the physical sciences.)
2. A minor in the social sciences (sociology, history, anthropology, economics, etc.).
3. Some work in mathematics, philosophy, and comparative literature.
4. Four or five introductory courses in psychology, for example, elementary general, elementary experimental, elementary dynamic. (Professional and advanced courses in the field should in general not be open to undergraduates. The student must, however, be permitted to take a sufficient number of psychology courses to enable him to acquire a fair acquaintance with the content of the field of psychology.)
5. Languages. (French and German preferably. Some consideration should, however, be given to languages which may play a greater role in the future, e.g., Spanish and Russian.)
6. Statistics. (To include the statistics of small samples.)

It will be gathered from the above that the training is thought of as *pre-professional* in character and includes as little as possible of work which is to be done later at a professional level. The aim of undergraduate training is to lay the general scientific background for the student's work in psychology proper.

The undergraduate program cannot be appraised according to credit hours or in relation to specific courses. Each candidate's record has to be examined on its own merits to see how far it meets the spirit of the background requirements of broad training, preferably concentration in the biological sciences, and at least introductory acquaintance with the social sciences. The more detailed study of the latter field might well be left for the graduate period, at which time the student is more mature and better able to grapple with its greater uncertainties.

Educational Program—Professional (Graduate Level)

For the professional training, greater specification of content is possible. Although the requirements for entrance into the training course should be left fairly flexible, and inadequacies corrected by conditioning the student, the professional training course should be organized so as to give a thorough fundamental training in psychology and its applications to the clinical field. It is here, especially, that all suggested courses (many more than can possibly be included) should be scrutinized carefully and rated according to their potential contribution to the training of a soundly prepared clinical psychologist. It is very simple to smother the student in a multiplicity of courses and even leave him, in the end, a badly trained technician. Rather, the stress should be on fewer, well-integrated courses which subtly but inevitably leave the student with a sound philosophy—a foundation on which special techniques can easily be built.

The professional program is viewed as one extending over four years (one year of which is to consist of an internship) and leading to a doctorate. It is expected that the program will be as exacting as that ordinarily required at present for the Ph.D. Although to some extent modeled on the medical school program, it is intended that the training will at the same time meet the standards of the highest quality of graduate study, viz., study which encourages initiative and individualization with the aim of developing more self-reliance than ordinarily results from the narrowly prescribed medical course.

First year.—The primary purpose of the first year of graduate work is to lay the systematic foundation of knowledge of psychology and to achieve the degree of acquaintance with the medical sciences needed for clinical work. To reach this goal, the following program is suggested:[3]

Courses	*Semester Hours*
1. Systematic General Psychology—lectures (fundamental theory, sensation, perception, learning, etc.)	6
2. Systematic Dynamic Psychology—lectures (personality, motivation, abnormal, psychoanalysis)	6
3. Developmental Psychology—lectures (genetic and comparative; child, adolescent, late maturity, individual differences)	6
4. Medical Sciences—lectures and laboratory (special aspects of anatomy, physiology; especially neuroanatomy, autonomic nervous system, endocrinology, etc.)	12

Second year.—The program of the second year of graduate work is mainly directed at providing the student with the necessary background in the experimental, psychometric, and therapeutic approaches to the problems of clinical psychology. Although a certain amount of teaching is still in the form of lectures, the major emphasis is on direct contact with patients or other subjects, either in the psychometric or in the experimental setting. Clerkships in different settings are essential elements of this year's training program. From the point of view of pedagogic technique, the participative, rather than the didactic method, should be employed as much as possible. The actual courses suggested are as follows:

Courses	*Semester Hours*
1. Experimental Dynamic Psychology—laboratory (experimental attack on dynamic problems—perhaps four minor projects during the year)	6
2. Theory and Practice of Intelligence Tests—lectures and clinical practice (training with a variety of problems: feebleminded, child guidance, special abilities and disabilities, psychotic and neurotic, etc. Short training periods —clerkships—should be provided at various centers).	6

[3] The semester hours are not intended to be taken too rigidly. They are given merely as suggestions to indicate relative weightings.

3. Theory and Practice of Projective Devices—lectures and clinical practice (training in a variety of settings—see above) 6
4. Therapeutic Theory and Methods—lectures and discussions (introductory course in therapy) 3
5. Educational Theory and Practice—lectures (fundamentals of educational philosophy) 3
6. Introduction to Clinical Medicine—lectures (introductory course in clinical medicine similar to that given medical social workers) 3

In addition, the advisability of a "didactic" analysis, which should be made optional, might seriously be considered as part of the work for this year.[4]

Two changes in the above outlined program for the first two years, involving no change in the number of hours but merely in the arrangement of courses, are worthy of serious consideration. The first is that of splitting the medical science course and carrying it over the two years; the second is that of carrying the systematic dynamic and the experimental dynamic psychology courses over the two years, running them concurrently. The advantage of the first is that it reduces the heavy weighting on medical topics in the first year; the advantage of the second is that it permits a greater integration of the systematic and experimental approaches and also starts the student off in the first year of graduate work with an experimental attitude, which is highly desirable.

Third year.—The third year of training should be devoted to the internship—a full year of work (usually with maintenance provided) to be spent away from the university at some institution.[5] The internship is placed at this period in the program because of the belief that most students are then at the optimum stage for profitable use of such opportunity.[6] The student has had a taste of clinical work and is anxious really to sink his teeth into it. He is also ready to consider a research topic for his dissertation and can take advantage of the material which is available at the institution. The internship (Shakow, 1938) has been made an integral and required part of the training rather than a voluntary one because it is felt that no preparation for clinical psychology, just as no training in medicine, is complete without intern experience. The major aim of this part of the program would be to give the student a broad base for later specialization by throwing him into full-time contact with human clinical material, contact of a much more intense kind than he can

[4] If psychoanalysis is accepted as part of the program, special care will have to be taken to select analysts who are relatively free from doctrinairism and who have an interest in psychological theory as well as in therapy.

[5] For the present, it is probably wise for psychology not to concern itself with providing both internships (training for general application) and residencies (training for specialities). The internship here considered is a combination of both of these as the terms are used in medical circles. Concern with the problem of specialization within clinical psychology may come later—only after a fundamental training program of a broader kind has been well established.

[6] The third year has been chosen for the internship after considerable weighing of its relative advantages when compared with a fourth-year internship, i.e., after the graduate work and the dissertation have been completed. The preference was determined by the several arguments which will be found under the discussion of the third- and fourth-year training programs.

possibly have during the clinical clerkships of the second year. This aspect of the training should be organized around the *case material* to be found in the institution, that is, the patient rather than the pathological condition should be made the center of the work which is done.

The activities which comprise the internship fall into four categories: clinical psychometrics, research, courses and conferences, and therapeutics.

1. Clinical psychometrics—practice under supervision, in the administration, interpretation, and reporting of psychometric and other psychological studies.[7]

2. Research—experimental attack on a problem in clinical psychology or psychopathology, the data to be used for a doctorate dissertation which is jointly supervised by the university and the training center.

3. Courses and conferences—(*a*) clinical psychiatry, neurology, and psychosomatics—lectures and demonstrations; (*b*) approaches of various disciplines to clinical psychology and psychopathology—case discussions mainly (approaches of the social worker, adult and child psychiatrist, internist, pastoral worker, etc., to the problems of the field); (*c*) seminar in clinical psychology—case method (psychopathologic and psychotherapeutic problems exemplified in cases); (*d*) psychiatric staff conferences—adult and child; (*e*) journal club—consideration of current literature on clinical psychology and related fields; (*f*) special conferences—clinicopathological, neurological, autopsy, etc.

4. Therapy—therapeutic work with a few cases, carried out under adequate psychiatric and psychological supervision.

From the pedagogic standpoint, the problem arises as to whether this program is better carried out by a concurrent or block system of occupation by the student with these four major activities. Long experience with systems emphasizing one or the other (neither one of these can practically be carried through in pure form) results in the impression of the much greater effectiveness of the distributive, concurrent method. Despite the possible advantage of protection from encroachment by other activities which the block plan may offer, the loss of contact and variety occasioned by its adoption is in the final analysis not compensated for. However, the practice of devoting certain definite hours during the day for special purposes should be encouraged.

Although in some ways the psychological intern may congratulate himself on the fact that he does not have many of the odd and routine responsibilities which fall to the medical intern in the clinical setting, it must be recognized that the medical intern grows considerably in resourcefulness and self-reliance from such demands made upon him. Some thought will have to be given to securing for the psychological intern opportunities for the exercise of similar responsibilities. However, constant vigilance must be exercised to keep service responsibilities secondary to educational opportunities, a danger particularly apt to occur in institutions not

[7] The importance of competent supervision, especially in the early stages, cannot be exaggerated. This holds for all the aspects of training but particularly for the practicums of the second and third years. Lack of supervision in the early stages has too frequently been the basis for the establishment of the strangest practices in psychometrics, as any person who has had contact with "trained" psychometrists can testify.

thoroughly organized on an educational basis. With respect to the problem of responsibilities, the student should be given as much opportunity as possible to participate in the teaching programs of the department for such groups as nurses and occupational therapists and to take over part of the responsibility for training less advanced psychological students.

The importance of an internship year along the lines here described cannot be emphasized sufficiently. Although the urgency of twenty-four hour presence on the job is not as great for the clinical psychologist as for the medical man, since the latter's work is frequently of an emergency nature requiring twenty-four hours' coverage, still the values which come with full-time domicile in an institution are many.[8] Some of the advantages of internship are as follows:

1. It offers the student an opportunity to get away from the academic atmosphere for an extended period, usually a very healthful and much appreciated opportunity after some eighteen successive years of academic work.

2. It affords training in carrying a full-time position.

3. It is an unsurpassable trying-ground for intellectual and personality fitness for clinical work. (The special strains which institutional work and living place on a person offer the supervisor and the trainee an unusual opportunity for the evaluation of interest and fitness for this work.)

4. It offers an opportunity for consistent and full-time occupation with the clinical field. There is not, in contrast with part-time externships, the confusion and strain which come with shifting back and forth from the clinical to the academic settings. The gain in wholeheartedness of occupation more than balances whatever gain may be had from the continued contact with the university.

5. It offers an opportunity for *real* acquaintance with the aims, principles, and technics of clinical psychology, an opportunity to get not only the "feel" and the "know" of psychology, but the "feel" of other fields, as well, through both professional and personal contacts. This is of inestimable value in preparation for later work in the clinical field.

6. It permits (as against short-term internships or externships) the more detailed study of the unfolding and development of a case—the kind of opportunity which psychologists generally do not have.

7. It permits twenty-four hour residence in an atmosphere permeated with a psychology of a living kind and appears to have more potentiality for the maturation of the personality than almost any other experience ordinarily available to the psychologist.

8. The choice of institution is not limited by accessibility, as it is in a part-time program. This permits the use of desirable institutions at some distance from the universities.

Where full-time internships are not available, the next best arrangement would probably be that of full-time externships. These do not have the disadvantages, mentioned earlier, of part-time internships.

[8] It is understood, of course, that mere domicile—the provision of maintenance in return for a certain minimum of service, frequently nonpsychological in character—is not under consideration here.

When, at a later date, the time arrives for the consideration of more extended internships, the advisability of setting up the rotating types of internships might be considered. Except for those institutions with limited facilities and types of problems, a well-organized psychiatric teaching hospital (Shakow, 1939) has more than enough to keep an intern profitably occupied for a year without rotation.[9] There is danger of a considerable loss of time and unprofitable occupation with the warming-up and tapering-off stages in a program of rotation. This is especially true in psychology, since rotation here would really be "revolution." The situation is likely to be quite different from that of medicine, in which rotation is, with few exceptions, from service to service within the same institution; in psychology, rotation would mean "revolving" from institution to institution, with all the complications which arise from constant reorientation. Even under the relatively satisfactory medical situation, the limitations of rotation have been found to be many (Commission on Graduate, 1940, pp. 40–42).

Fourth year.—The fourth and final year should be spent at the university. The advantages of this proposal are manifold:

1. It enables the student to complete the analytic and final work on his dissertation.

2. It permits the final integration of the experiences acquired during the internship with the theoretical principles emphasized by the university.

3. Such return of graduate students should act as a force integrating the university and the field training center. (It might serve the further purpose of acting as an educational influence upon the non-clinical university group!)

4. It places the student geographically handy to the agency which is already established for placement, namely, the university placement bureau. This is of considerable importance, since institutions such as field training centers are ordinarily not in a position to be of much help to their trainees in job placement.

The program of the fourth year would include the following:

1. Final work on dissertation.

2. Cross-discipline seminars (psychology, anthropology, sociology, psychiatry, and so forth) which devote themselves to the place of psychology among the sciences concerned with the adjustment problems of the individual and the group. The purpose of these seminars should be to integrate the major principles of the previous years' study and point out the broader implications of the course of training for the personal and social scenes.

3. Seminar on professional problems—standards, ethics, etc.

4. For those who have had a "didactic" analysis during the second year, a

[9] Numerous objections to institutions as training centers have been raised. Some of the points made are that the prevalence of cases with poor prognosis is discouraging to the student, that the types of patients are limited, that the institution is frequently isolated, that the student cannot see a patient through from the beginning to the end of the contact, that there are certain limitations on the contacts which they can establish with other specialists such as teachers, probation workers, etc. These weaknesses, although frequently present, are not inherent in all institutional situations and when present can frequently be eliminated. They must, however, be kept in mind when institutions for training are being selected.

"control" analysis might be arranged for during this period; for those who have not, a "didactic" analysis might be made optional at this point.

Certain auxiliary devices for integrating the whole program deserve consideration but will here only be mentioned: (*a*) the appointment by the university of a field supervisor whose responsibility would be to hold scheduled conferences with the interns in order to maintain the contact with the university and perhaps help to supervise the dissertations;[10] (*b*) annual or semiannual conferences of students from various centers who are undergoing internship training, for the purpose of considering common problems and for reporting research or case studies.

Students should be encouraged to use their summer holidays for special work, for undertaking optional parts of the program, or for any employment which brings them into close contact with the average run of human beings, whether it be in the factory, the field, or the laboratory.

Postgraduate Training

It seems desirable also to suggest some plans for postgraduate training. Because of the constant advances being made in the field, provision should be made for postgraduate opportunities to keep abreast of these developments. It would appear to be the function of the university to provide the necessary courses during summers and at other times convenient to persons engaged in the full-time practice of professional duties.

Evidences of achievement.—At the various levels, some distinct signs of achievement seem necessary. The following are suggested as steps:

1. Bachelor's degree following pre-professional training.

2. Doctor's degree following the four-year course of professional training. Although there are some professional groups, notably the legal, which practice on the basis of bachelor's degrees, there are certain considerations which make it doubtful if anything less than a doctor's degree would be satisfactory for the practice of clinical psychology. The kind of doctor's degree to be awarded is difficult to decide. Although there are some reasons for adhering to the Ph.D. degree, the argument for a truly professional degree, for example, a Ps.D., are many and should be given careful consideration.

3. A third stage of the process of recognition should be that of membership in the professional association of the group—the American Association for Applied Psychology. Two grades of membership should be available: the first, associateship, open immediately upon the attainment of the professional degree; the second, fellowship, obtainable after a definite number of years of experience and the submission of evidence of contribution to the field in the form of publications, etc.

4. A fourth stage in the process, closely linked with postgraduate work in many ways, would be the establishment of a board modeled in general on the specialty boards of the medical field. Such a board, an "American Board of Clinical

[10] Compare with Smith School of Social Work practice.

Psychology," appointed from among the leaders in the field by the professional associations, would have as its function the certification of candidates who have had a definite number of years of actual experience and who have passed examinations ih stated aspects of the field of clinical psychology. Diplomas or certificates of the Board would be evidence of competence in the actual practice of clinical psychology.

Such steps in voluntary certification and approval would seem to precede logically any attempts at governmental certification. The latter, however, should be kept in mind as a necessary step in the future.

Evaluation and Selection

If clinical psychology is to establish itself as a recognized profession, then, throughout the process leading up to the degree and even beyond, during professional practice, the psychologist should be under scrutiny as to fitness. To accomplish this end, a rigorous process of selection of candidates for the course of training and some system of later supervision is necessary. In these respects the practices of the medical group offer numerous suggestions.

The process of evaluation and selection should be concerned not only with the candidates but also with the universities and field training centers. The selection of the first should perhaps be in the hands of both the universities and the training centers, and the approval of the latter two in the hands of a committee of the American Association for Applied Psychology.

The inadequacy, or rather the entire absence, of selective standards at the present time has led to confusion in the field and to an insufficiently high esteem for psychology's contribution on the part of associated disciplines.

Candidates.—The first evaluation of the candidate should come at the point of application for professional training, namely, entrance to the graduate school, and should be repeated at the end of each year's work. This evaluation should be made by the university with the assistance of the field training supervisor at the end of the second and third years.

What requirements should be set up for candidates? The following, aside from the educational requirements already discussed, are important:

1. Breadth of cultural background.
2. Scholastic achievement in the upper quarter of the class in college and graduate school.
3. Deep interest in psychology, with special interest in clinical psychology.
4. Genuine aptitude for clinical psychology; promise of making worthwhile contributions to its advance.
5. Superior intellectual ability.
6. Demonstrated industry and originality.
7. Integrity, tact, self-control, and discriminating sense of ethical values.
8. Readiness to make personal sacrifices to acquire well-rounded training.
9. Demonstrated interest in persons as individuals and not merely as material for manipulation.

Schools.—The schools should be judged on their ability to meet requirements set forth earlier in the discussion of training. Not only the formal meeting of standards with respect to courses given, but also the quality of the courses, as it relates both to content and instruction, should be carefully scrutinized. Perhaps this could be done most effectively through a committee of the American Association for Applied Psychology, as already suggested. This national approving body should rate students and grade schools on the basis of how closely they meet the standards. The committee could very well model itself on the American Medical Association committee which serves this purpose for the medical field.

Field training centers.—The centers for internships should be given the same careful scrutiny as the schools.[11] The standards as to content, quality and quantity of supervision, facilities (personnel, clinical, library, teaching), living arrangements, and so forth, should all be carefully set up. It is necessary to consider also the problem of integration with the university work. It would be good policy to discourage the concentration of students from one school at certain internship centers. A distribution in point of origin of students in an internship training center appears to increase the profit to be obtained by individual interns from their period of study.

Postgraduate training.—This aspect of training needs considerable thought and should be placed under the supervision of a special committee of the American Association for Applied Psychology for the purpose of working with the universities and training centers in an advisory capacity on desirable courses and standards.

Suggested Immediate Program

The program laid out above may seem formidable, but it is difficult to see how clinical psychology can expect to attain recognition as a profession unless it traverses the difficult country indicated.

It must be admitted, however, that in some respects the program which has been suggested represents a long-time ideal. The question arises then: What are the immediate steps to be taken? It would appear reasonable that the first step would be appointment by the American Association for Applied Psychology of a committee on "Professional Training for Clinical Psychology" to consider some such plan as here proposed.[12] Such a committee, together with representatives of the American Psychological Association, should, after an investigation of the available schools which have recognized their responsibilities for training in professional, as well as academic, psychology, designate these schools for training. The field training centers, after similar investigations, may be designated somewhat later. At first the program should be limited to an experimental group of students. A relatively small number of trainees, carefully selected from a list of candidates, should be put through the whole

[11] The same committee, or a subcommittee, might well undertake this function.

[12] At the September, 1941, meetings of the A.A.A.P., a Committee on Training in Applied Psychology with three sections—clinical, educational, and industrial—was set up.

training program under the supervision of the committee.[13] The selectees should be considered as members of a trial group and be carefully scrutinized throughout the training program for their qualities as potential representatives of a real clinical psychology, representatives able to meet in unquestioned fashion the triad of requirements set up earlier: diagnostic, therapeutic and research ability. If possible, the plan should be financed through a foundation or through the use of fellowships extending over the four-year period, so that financial considerations would not limit the range of candidates.

Beyond this, the committee's responsibility would be primarily educational. Its function would be to educate universities to the need for professional training and advise with them on the necessary steps in the process of preparation for clinical psychology. The committee would also encourage responsiveness to the changing need of psychology by holding conferences of the various workers in the field, both from the university and from the field training centers, at which such problems as standards, curriculum and technics would be considered.

The very pertinent question arises as to how rapidly persons with this improved training will be absorbed into the clinical field. Although the opportunities at present are probably not numerous, there is some reason for believing that with improvement in the quality of the candidates will come an increase in the quality of the positions available to them. It has not been the function of this paper to consider the problem of employment opportunities in the clinical field but rather to suggest some plan of adequate training if psychologists are to enter the field at all.

[13] Some suggestions might be obtained from an examination of the Junior Fellow Plan at Harvard.

10. The Worcester Internship Program

This paper was written about the time I left the Worcester State Hospital after eighteen years there as Chief Psychologist and Director of Psychological Research. During this period, some one hundred psychological interns received their training.

The present Worcester internship program is a gradual outgrowth of a program initiated by the writer in 1928 when he came to the Worcester State Hospital as Chief Psychologist. It was based on two similar programs of which he had been a part: one at the same hospital under Dr. Grace H. Kent, and the other at the Boston Psychopathic Hospital under Dr. Frederick L. Wells. To both of these pioneers in clinical psychology a good deal of what may be of value in the present program may be traced. During these eighteen years over one hundred students have gone through the internship training. The course of specialized education which they received

Reprinted with permission from the *Journal of Consulting Psychology*, vol. 10, 1946.

has varied in many respects over the years, but throughout this period there was one underlying premise: namely, that no psychologist, especially no clinical psychologist, was adequately trained, who had merely acquired knowledge *about* people; direct personal contact with human material in an intensive way was essential. This the internship attempted to provide.

Although most of the present goals were implicit in the original plan, the years have emphasized the need for making some explicit and prominent. Others needed modification, while still others proved inadequate.

To describe with exactness the goals of the program is difficult, for they tend to be part of a total philosophy of approach. Outstanding principles may, however, be distinguished. There is considerable emphasis on the molar aspects of behavior, with a persistent attempt at their objectification. This trend has become more prominent with the years and has gradually replaced the more molecular approach which characterized the program in the early days. At the same time there has been a shift from a relatively large degree of laissez-faire freedom to a more directed freedom. This grew out of the demands of the students themselves. The earlier philosophy had been that the institution was teeming with possibilities for study, both of a human and technical nature; it was expected that the intern would spontaneously exploit these. However, whether because of the relative immaturity of the student, or for other reasons, such a development did not generally take place. Time after time, students would ask for more controlled direction because they found themselves floundering. After considerable pressure of this kind, the principle of more direction was adopted.

Another principle emphasized from the beginning was the social responsibility which contact with patients involves. The fact that the intern's findings might actually play a significant role in the disposition of a case required not only an appreciation and respect for the subject as a person, but also an understanding of the social implications of his examination. With the years, too, increasing emphasis has been placed on the need for cooperative working with specialists representing other disciplines—the "team" approach.

Close individual supervision has from the beginning been a cardinal principle of the program. We believed that only through close contact between the supervisor and the student could relatively high standards be maintained. This task, even under the best of circumstances, has its unpleasant and difficult aspects and is for such reasons avoided. It was our firm conviction, however, that the maintenance of reasonable standards in a field where the opportunity for slipshodness is so great was impossible without such supervision.

Although in the earlier years there was considerable liberality about accepting students for short-term—for example, summer, or part-time internships—accumulating experience indicated that the results were not generally satisfactory. In later years, interns were, therefore, not accepted unless they came for a full year. Exceptions were occasionally made for fully qualified persons who were interested in broadening their experience either clinically or experimentally with the kind of material available at the institution, and who could work independently without supervision.

Whether because of the successful achievement of these goals or because a year's residence in a state hospital is a profound educational experience, it almost universally turned out that the year's internship resulted in considerable growth on the part of the intern. This growth he recognized to some extent during and at the end of the internship. Its full force usually did not strike him until he had been away from the institution for a while. In some instances this secondary gain was by far the most valuable contribution which the institution made.

The program, of course, had many obstacles to overcome. In evaluating the relative prominence of those arising from the hospital administration, those arising from the psychological staff, and those arising from the intern group itself, it is surprising that the degree of difficulty was inverse to the order here given.

Considering the relative novelty of the idea, the ordinary rigidity of state systems, etc., the administration of the hospital was unusually receptive to the notion of the training of psychologists and did a good deal which was untraditional in aiding the program. There were certain obstacles with respect to maintenance which occasioned temporary, and even permanent, difficulties, but with respect to professional activities, it was sometimes necessary to restrain the administration from pushing some aspects of the program too fast!

The difficulties stemming from the psychological staff were occasioned mainly by the difficulty in obtaining competent supervisory personnel. The relative unavailability of personnel of the caliber required, the low salary scale, and the unwillingness to come on a maintenance arrangement all played a role in this situation. However, despite these hindrances, it was possible to attract a number of very competent persons to come for short periods—a year or two. Such an arrangement is, of course, far from satisfactory where close supervision and a special philosophy are such important aspects of the program. We were fortunate in finding as frequently as we did supervisors who so quickly adopted and helped to carry out the spirit, as well as the formal aspects of the program.

Our greatest problems were created by the student personnel who took part in the program. Although we frequently had about ten times as many applications for internships as there were available openings, we still ran into difficulties in the quality of the applicants. The variation in this respect was considerable. In part, the greater than expected proportion of poor material was occasioned by the notion held by some academic psychologists that clinical work was a field for those students who couldn't make the grade in academic psychology, in part by poor judgment on the part of references with regard to the persons they recommended, and in part by the intrinsically poorer quality of too large a proportion of those interested in clinical work.

One aspect of this variation in quality was the very marked variation in preparation and background. Until fairly recent years the situation was such that we did not accept any preparation in psychometrics with which the student came at face value, but insisted rather on training him ourselves in the techniques with which he was presumably acquainted.

Fairly frequently we had difficulty, too, with the lack of balance between the theoretical and applied manifested by the students when they came. Sometimes the student would come to us indoctrinated either with a particular theoretical viewpoint, or with the single importance of theory, accompanied by very little tolerance and understanding of clinical problems. Others would come to us in a thorough state of revolt against academic notions and interested in nothing but the "practical." In both types the additional task was thrown on us of establishing some sort of balance between theory and practice, teaching the student the values and the differences in the goals of each, and the enriching effects of one on the other.

A problem which created considerable difficulty in isolated instances—but still too frequently to be pleasant—was the need for dealing with relatively severe personality problems. Apparently the notion seemed reasonable to some university teachers that institutions such as ours were the most appropriate places in which to deal with maladjusted personalities among their psychology students, and so would recommend them for internships. We were placed in the position of having to struggle with a serious dilemma: on the one hand, if we were not ready to deal with personality problems among psychologists or would-be psychologists, who would be? On the other hand, we owed a responsibility to the patients in the hospital. Our ability to deal with them was strengthened by the normality of the environment in which we worked and lived. This strength was dissipated if we had to use some of our therapeutic reserve on colleagues. After attempting therapeutic work with several of these interns, sometimes enlisting the help of the other members of the department, we came to the definite conclusion that it was unwise to accept intern candidates who suffered from more than very minor personality deviations, because of the cost to the rest of the group. We scrutinized credentials carefully from this point of view. When, for one reason or another, they got through the screening, we felt it wise to sever the relationship at an early date. As much persuasion as possible was used to get the person to seek therapy outside the institution before attempting to return to psychology.

Another aspect of the personality problem has to do with characteristics which fall within the normal range, but which affect work habits. This manifested itself particularly in the contrast between the discursive and obsessive personalities—those so overwhelmed by the wealth of opportunity presented by the institution that they flitted from one activity to another with little accomplishment along any line, and those who despite the opportunities offered were so tied down to one line of work that they could not budge from it. Through constant supervision and encouragement, it was frequently possible to achieve greater stability on the part of one and greater fluidity on the part of the other.

However, considering the situation as a whole, I think it is fair to say that we came out in the end with a surprisingly high average. With the recent developments in psychology and the great impetus given to the program of training in clinical psychology, the difficulties with personnel here mentioned are very likely to have less prominence. The attention of internship training centers can then more singleheartedly be given to the problems of training which are more peculiarly their special task and competence.

Present Program

The above remarks may serve as the necessary background for the appreciation of the existing program. The latter will be considered with respect to the content of the orientation period and the internship proper in its various aspects: clinical psychometrics, special study, research, therapy, administration, teaching, and the integration of psychology with other fields. A final section will discuss the program as viewed particularly from the administrator's standpoint.

An important aspect of the speedy adjustment of the intern to the whole program is dependent upon the activities of the *orientation period.* At Worcester the first two or three weeks are considered to be a period which the student requires in order to orient himself to the new environment—physical, employee, and patient—and to the general aspects of his peculiar approach as a psychologist to the problems presented by the institution.

After the student is physically settled in his quarters on the first day, he comes for a conference with the department head, during which his background and previous experience, academic and clinical, are discussed and his interests gone into. The general nature of the program for the year is outlined and there is an opportunity to consider any questions about the internship which he may have. He is then taken on a tour of the hospital, during which he obtains his keys and visits the various divisions—wards, industrial shops, therapy suites, etc. The tour is organized around the patient—the way in which he comes into contact with the various departments during his hospital stay.

In the course of the first few days the intern commences his regular attendance at the variety of hospital staff conferences, some held to discuss individual patients, others to consider research studies. During this week, too, the student begins his acquaintance with the department proper by studying the standard practice of the department, the physical layout, the nature of the research projects which are in progress, and, if time permits, he begins the study and reading connected with psychometric procedure. During the second and third weeks the intern has direct and intensive contact with patients through spending half his time on one of the wards as a recreational attendant. This activity not only familiarizes him with hospital organization, but, more important, serves to bring him into close contact with patients, who in anticipation are usually quite threatening objects. We have found that this experience does a great deal toward bringing interns around to a natural adjusted approach to patients, a goal which is reached much more slowly through the contacts which the intern may have during the course of his ordinary professional activities. During ward work, the student is required to write objective behavior sketches of the activities of about six patients, relying entirely upon observation of overt behavior and casual conversations with them.

The other half of his time during these two weeks, aside from conferences which he may attend, is spent in observing (through one-way vision mirrors) the examination of patients by established members of the department. He writes brief behavioral reports on these patients and discusses these with a department member.

The two types of reports serve to emphasize the necessity for accurate and acute observation of behavior, both with respect to gross and to minimal cues. He continues during this period, too, the early orientation with regard to psychometric techniques.

Sometime during the third week the training program proper, in its various aspects, may be said to begin. With respect to clinical psychometrics, the intern becomes deeply involved in training in the use of psychological test devices and procedures. The order of the steps in the process for each procedure, following upon those which he has already taken in part, that is, reading and observing, are: practice of the procedure on the other interns, independent practice on sample patients, and examination of a "practice" patient while under observation by a staff member. During this stage the intern also takes a written examination on the test device.

Essentially the same general program is followed with the major procedures which the intern is expected to learn during the course of the year. The sequence of study, aside from changes made in exceptional cases, is roughly as follows: (*a*) individual intelligence scales; (*b*) techniques for assessing deterioration; (*c*) devices for the determination of malfunctioning on an organic basis; (*d*) performance scales; (*e*) tests of special functions; (*f*) personality tests. Work with the Rorschach and TAT procedures is introduced by a course of didactic instruction, followed by individual supervision; the others are taken care of mainly in the latter manner. Also, the intern is expected to obtain a passing acquaintance with a large variety of other tests on which he is not required to pass any formal examination.

When a reasonable degree of skill is acquired in the administration of the simpler elements of a battery of tests, the intern takes his place in the rotating schedule of case assignment, examining only those patients on whom examinations requiring test procedures which he is competent to administer are requested. As his skill widens, he gradually takes his due portion of the examination requests, consideration being given to an equitable distribution among the interns of variety, number, and intensiveness of the battery required. The emphasis is, in general, on the intensive study of relatively few cases, rather than on the superficial study of many. Even if very few test procedures are used with a patient, the intern is encouraged to make a thorough analysis based on his findings. In the standard practice manual, in the supervisory interviews which follow his scoring of the test results in early cases, or in the interview which follows his writing of a report in his later cases, the emphasis is on sensitizing him to as many of the facets of the psychological test situation as possible so that he may get the maximum in meaning from the examination which he has carried through—the maximum in objective analysis and interpretation with respect to capacity and personality characteristics as they relate to diagnosis, prognosis, and disposition.

After the first few examinations, the intern is encouraged to write his report before seeing the supervisor. It has been our experience that strictness and insistence on high standards for report-writing has been one of the most valuable contributions made by the internship. It has also been one of the sources of greatest difficulty in handling interns. With very few exceptions, however, interns have in the end been grateful for having had to submit to this discipline, and have felt that they have gained considerably in the ability to analyze and synthesize case material.

The supervisor's responsibility in this respect is of prime importance. It is not his task to check for simple errors in technique or arithmetical errors. These, with few exceptions, will have been taken care of by the automatic checking system which has been a part of our program from the beginning. (After the examiner has scored his test results, he turns them over to another person in the department—interns usually to other interns—for checking of scoring and arithmetical computations.) Rather, it is the supervisor's task to criticize the evaluations made by the intern, to consider points which have been missed, wrong interpretations, etc., and to indicate ways in which the exposition of the findings is inadequate. After mutual consideration of these points, the intern rewrites his report and returns it for further criticism. The supervisor may insist on as many rewritings as he deems necessary. It is also his task to keep the interns to a fairly rigid time schedule of handing in written reports. The natural tendency to procrastinate in writing reports must be dealt with from the very beginning. It has been our practice to make the intern responsible also for seeing to it that the written report reaches the record office for typing and that one copy gets into the case record and another comes back to the laboratory for filing in the department file within a reasonable time.

In addition to writing his report, the intern is encouraged to discuss personally with the referring psychiatrist (usually the resident) the findings and their implications. We have found this to be one of the best points of contact between the students in the two disciplines and an enriching experience for both.

In the early stage of the internship, the student depends upon some senior member of the staff to report his examination results at staff conferences. As he attends more and more conferences and becomes increasingly proficient in his testing, he is gradually led into reporting at conferences, starting with the simpler diagnostic conferences, and toward the end of his internship period, reporting at major teaching conferences. In this way he is given increasing administrative responsibility and is actually learning to carry a staff member's functions.

Although the rate of progress in the outlined program is necessarily determined by the background and ability of the intern, it is ordinarily expected that he will at least be able to take part in the administration of intelligence scales to regular caseload patients by the end of the second month. He should be able to take part in the administration of the major projective tests by the end of the sixth month. The assumption of responsibility for staff conference reports ordinarily does not come until about the eighth month.

From the description of the clinical psychometric program here given, it will be seen that considerable dependence for its successful outcome is placed on the quality and amount of supervision provided. Although during the process of training a considerable amount of necessary service work gets done, and it is important that it should be so, the goal of training cannot be forgotten. From the institution's standpoint, the investment is worthwhile, for in the latter half of his internship the student is sufficiently well prepared so that he can make a definite contribution to the institution's needs.

Another important part of the student's training is the general teaching to which he is exposed and the opportunities for *study* which are afforded him. Some aspects of this program, having to do with training in clinical psychometrics, have already been considered. These, however, are related to or grow out of the individually supervised program. Here I wish to consider the more formal, less individualized teaching which goes on both in the department and in other parts of the hospital.

Within the department it has been the practice to have anywhere from one to three seminars, running concurrently through the academic year. These have varied considerably in content, sometimes theoretical, sometimes experimental, and sometimes practical considerations have been emphasized. During the last year, as an example, one seminar considered the systematic findings of an experimental psychological and psychometric attack on schizophrenia, another discussed in considerable detail the technical and theoretical aspects of a series of therapy cases carried by interns and staff members, and still another considered Rorschach and TAT data in specific cases as they relate to psychodynamic problems. The interns are encouraged to take an active part in the seminar discussions and whenever possible to make presentations of material.

In order to avoid a lapse in study habits, the students are encouraged to use both the departmental and the hospital library freely, especially in following up questions of a psychiatric, psychological, or physiological nature which arise during their daily activities. Various bibliographies on test devices, experimental procedures, etc., are provided as guides to systematic reading. During some periods, weekly journal clubs have been held at which interns have reported in rotation. For complex test procedures, such as Rorschach and TAT, and for newly developed test procedures, special didactic courses are held.

On occasion, too, the interns have seen fit to run staff meetings of their own at which all of the available data on the case would be presented very much as it would be at the hospital staff conference. The students were encouraged to do this on their own because it afforded them an excellent opportunity to express freely notions which they would hesitate to express in the presence of persons with more advanced standing, to say nothing of the opportunity it gave them to get out their aggressions, dissatisfactions, and disagreements with the staff. However, if they so desired, they had the privilege of inviting a senior staff member to attend.

In other departments of the hospital, numerous opportunities are available to the student in the form of staff conferences, lectures, lecture courses, and demonstrations. During the last year, for instance, the following conferences and seminars were available:

1. A semi-weekly psychiatric teaching staff conference.
2. Four weekly new staff conferences.
3. Four weekly diagnostic case conferences.
4. Weekly research case conferences.
5. Weekly seminars in psychiatry.
6. An eight-week course in neurophysiology.

7. A bi-weekly research seminar at which talks were given by prominent specialists in fields related to psychopathology.

It has also been the practice for staff members from other departments, social service, occupational therapy, biochemistry, pathology, and psychiatry, to demonstrate procedures and explain techniques used in their special fields, such as shock therapy, drug therapy, electroencephalography, hypnosis, and autopsies. Child guidance clinic conferences are also open to the student.

The interns are encouraged to take advantage of any opportunities outside the hospital of a psychological or psychiatric nature, such as society meetings, or seminars at nearby universities.

Each student is expected to carry a *research* project, the subject of which is determined during a conference with the head of the department held after the intern has been at the hospital for about three months, when he has established himself well in the routine. An attempt is made to have the student suggest a topic which in a general way fits into the research in progress, with which by this time he is acquainted. If he has no definite suggestions, he is offered the choice of one of several projects of interest to the department. These are limited in character so that they can be completed within the internship year. However, even if not completed, the student is required to write up his findings and submit a report on the study at the end of his internship. On occasion, such researches have been employed for doctor's or master's dissertations.

After the topic is decided upon, the student draws up a detailed project outline, according to a standard form, in which he is required to give the rationale, procedure and material requirements for the research. This is discussed with the head of the department and plans are laid for prosecuting the study. During the weekly conferences which are held, the supervisor keeps in touch with developments and provides the necessary guidance. When the project is sufficiently advanced, the results are usually presented to the department at a seminar.

With increasing experience, it has been found advisable to insist on projects being written up, whether completed or not, before the intern leaves. Experiments in permitting students to take data with them for completion have, with few exceptions, turned out unsuccessfully.

Of all the elements of the program, *therapy* has offered the greatest difficulties. At least it is the aspect in which we feel we have made the least satisfactory progress. With few exceptions, students who come to the internship show more discrepancy between aspiration and preparation levels in this respect than in any other. For a long time the desirability of therapeutic experience as part of the training of the intern has been accepted in principle, but until very recently no practical way of achieving this goal was worked out. Among the many factors accounting for this situation, the chief ones were the inadequate theoretical, as well as practical, preparation for therapy with which the student arrived, and the fullness of the existing program in its other aspects. In the last few years, however, with the greater recognition of the important part which therapeutic activity can play in helping to develop theoretical formulations and the growing wish the psychologist has to make himself useful in a field where the needs are so much greater than the facilities to take care of them, a beginning has been made in providing therapeutic opportunities for interns.

Therapy is concentrated during the second six months of the internship, after the student has become well acquainted with the handling of psychiatric patients and has been exposed to conferences, discussions, and seminars on this topic. By an arrangement with the clinical service, a suitable case is jointly selected by the clinical director and the chief psychologist. A program of therapy is worked out with the supervisor, an experienced therapist, and conferences are held on the progress of the case. These come at least weekly, the frequency depending on the developments. The student is required to keep detailed records of the work for report to his supervisor, as well as for report to the therapy seminar when his turn for report comes. In some instances a report is also presented to a general staff conference.

From the beginning, an integral part of the program has been training in *administration.* Aside from responsibilities which are placed on the student for necessary routine department activities, such as the maintenance of record files, care of test materials and office supplies, and care of the department library, more professional responsibilities are placed upon him as his ability to handle them grows. We have already discussed the increasing burden in relation to representing the department at staff meetings for which he is made responsible, and his responsibility in checking the reports of other interns. After the intern has reached some degree of competence in psychometrics, the supervision program is somewhat modified to include an additional step, namely, supervision by a student on a weekly rotation basis. It is the task of the student whose weekly turn it is to read all the interns' reports for the week to make criticisms which are discussed with the writer of the report. These then go to the staff supervisor, who discusses the criticisms with both the student supervisor and the examiner. We have found such a procedure valuable not only in developing supervisory attitudes but also in reducing the tensions created by being exclusively on the receiving end of criticism.

Interns, too, are used as much as possible in the supervision of the training of more recent newcomers to the internship or in the training of clinical clerks or other workers who are less experienced. It has also been our practice to put the various administrative problems which naturally arise in the course of running a department before the group as a whole for discussion. With few exceptions, the group decision has been adopted, at least experimentally. We have found this participative approach very effective in smoothing out difficulties, both within the department and in its relationship with other departments.

An important aspect of the administrative problem is the relationship with members of other disciplines, a point which has, to some extent, already been discussed. Our policy has been to encourage as much contact as possible between the interns and the other students and staff members in psychiatry, medicine, chemistry, social service, occupational therapy, etc., regarding such relations as an important part of the educational experience of the intern. An innovation along this line is at present being experimented with. About the end of the second month the intern begins to follow about three patients through from the time of admission (the case being referred to him shortly after the new case arrives) to the time of discharge from the hospital or to the end of his internship term (if the patient is not out by that time). During this period he keeps in close contact with the social worker, psychiatrist, nurse, and occupational therapist responsible for the patient, following at close range, the collection of anamnestic data and the treatment and care of the patient. The intern undertakes the handling of the psychological studies on the patient at each point in the process when a psychological examination appears necessary. He keeps a log of the behavior and progress of the patient, relying on the various sources available with which he has contact, and prepares brief progress reports at weekly intervals. The object of this program is to make him aware of the variety of problems concerning the patient, seen in their proper perspective, and to get him to appreciate how the different departments operate in dealing with the patient as a whole. Arrangements are made for the intern to observe and assist in interviews with the patient and his relatives.

Too, the intern is encouraged to keep a daily log of his activities, particularly about patients whom he has examined, in order to determine for himself in which respect his experience needs supplementation. On occasion interns competent to do so are afforded the opportunity of delivering lectures to nursing or lay groups on topics of psychological or mental hygiene content.

Program For Future

As one looks to the future and sees the program as part of a relatively standard program of training approved by the American Psychological Association and its relevant committees, with the resultant recruiting of more adequately prepared persons, certain changes and additions seem indicated.

The first of these would be a greater proportion of time spent on history and interview procedures, in which respect, up to this point, the program has been weak. Another change would be the provision of additional opportunities for therapeutic work. In the diagnostic field, more emphasis should, in the future, be placed upon blind diagnosis and written predictions, checked at suitable intervals. In the non-professional aspects, some effort should be made to improve maintenance and provide a modest remuneration for interns.

With these changes and with the general improvement of the quality of training which will inevitably come when the national professional group becomes interested in this and similar programs, Worcester should continue to make its contribution to the development of clinical psychology in this country.

Graduate Internship Training in Psychology

This report (by the Subcommittee on Graduate Internship Training to the Committees on Graduate and Professional Training of the American Psychological Association and the American Association for Applied Psychology, published in the *Journal of Consulting Psychology*, 9, 1945, 243–266) was the work of a committee I chaired. The other members of the Committee—Brotemarkle, Doll, Kinder, Moore, and Smith—played a substantial role in its preparation. It was accepted and approved by both Associations and served a significant role in the 1947 report of the Committee on Training in Clinical Psychology (see Chapter 11). Because both its spirit and content are so well represented in the later report, it is omitted here.

11. Recommended Graduate Training Program in Clinical Psychology

The first paragraph of the following report[1] and its subparagraphs give some of its background. Carl Rogers, then president of the American Psychological Association, came to see me at the University of Illinois to ask if I would undertake the responsibility of the chairmanship of the Committee on Training in Clinical Psychology. I accepted and the rest of the Committee was then appointed: Ernest Hilgard, Lowell Kelly, Bertha Luckey, Nevitt Sanford, and Laurance Shaffer. We had only a short time (four months) in which to work on the report, which was only the first of the four responsibilities that the Committee was charged with. All of the members of the Committee were involved heavily in its preparation. It was submitted at the September, 1947, meeting of APA.

At the meeting of the Board of Directors of the American Psychological Association in Ann Arbor, March 28–30, 1947, the President was authorized to appoint a special Committee on Training in Clinical Psychology to perform the following tasks:

a) Formulate a recommended program for training in clinical psychology.

b) Formulate standards for institutions giving training in clinical psychology, including both universities and internship and other practicum facilities.

c) Study and visit institutions giving instruction in clinical psychology, and make a detailed report on each institution.

d) Maintain liaison with other bodies concerned with these problems, including

Reprinted with permission from the *American Psychologist*, vol. 2, 1947.

[1] The Committee wishes to acknowledge with gratitude the aid received from the following persons who read preliminary drafts of the report: Mrs. Ethel L. Ginsburg, Mrs. Elizabeth H. Ross, Drs. Alan Gregg, Robert R. Holt, James G. Miller, and David Rapaport.

the committees of the American Orthopsychiatric Association, the National Committee for Mental Hygiene, and others.

The undersigned persons constitute the Committee as finally appointed. The Committee, because of the relatively short period that it has had to work, has limited itself in this report to presenting a recommended program of training in clinical psychology.

The work of our Committee insofar as it relates to a training program grows naturally out of the activities of several previous committees and groups. The historical aspects of the development of clinical psychological training has been thoroughly covered by Morrow (1946). Of particular relevance are the 1943 "Proposed Program of Professional Training in Clinical Psychology" of the Committee on Training in Clinical (Applied) Psychology (AAAP, 1943) and the 1945 Subcommittee Report on "Graduate Internship Training in Psychology" (APA & AAAP, 1945). A recent issue of the Menninger Bulletin (July, 1947) describing "The Menninger Foundation School of Clinical Psychology" and the July, 1946, "Internship and Externship Programs" issue of the *Journal of Consulting Psychology* are also of considerable importance in this context. The report of the Committee on Graduate and Professional Training (Sears, 1947), although more directly related to future activities of our Committee, in some respects also bears on the present report.

The program here presented is especially timely because of the existing ferment in the field of psychology, particularly in the area of clinical psychology. The Harvard University Commission's report (Gregg, 1947) suggests some of the possibilities which lie ahead of psychology in the near and distant future. With respect to clinical psychology, one sees on the one hand the breathless preoccupation with actual training which has resulted largely from the Veterans Administration and United States Public Health Service programs, and on the other hand the deep concern with the goals and trends of this training both within the Psychological Association and on the part of organizations interested in the field with which clinical psychology is associated. The Josiah Macy Jr. Foundation has held the first of a series of Conferences on Clinical Psychology (Harrower, 1947); the American Psychiatric Association and the Group for the Advancement of Psychiatry have Committees on Clinical Psychology, and the American Orthopsychiatric Association and the National Committee for Mental Hygiene are engaged in activities which in one respect or another involve the evaluation of the functions of clinical psychologists. It is, therefore, especially desirable that the Association set forth its own official policy in this important matter of training and that it play the major role in determining the content and goals of such a program.

We are cognizant of the great difficulties which the shift from an academic to a professional program involves in a university setting. We recognize that this change must take much effort and time and that even were it possible to set up a fairly fixed schedule of training, such a step would at present be both premature and ill-advised because of the great need for experimentation in ways of implementing a sound program. We are therefore emphasizing the goals and principles of what we consider a desirable program rather than attempting to lay out a detailed blueprint. We have decided to limit our present consideration of training to a program at the four-year doctoral level because of our firm conviction that professionally qualified persons cannot be given adequate background training in less time. This is in line with a decision independently arrived at by the Policy and Planning Board (APA, PPB, 1947) that further training of clinical psychologists at the M.A. level be discontinued. It should be emphasized, however, that this decision does not preclude the training of persons to apply psychological principles in specialized areas such as remedial teaching, vocational and educational counseling, educational testing, etc. However, such persons are in our opinion not clinical psychologists and the present report is not concerned with their training. We have further decided not to let our program be determined in any way by present practices in training which arise from special situations such as those created by the financial arrangements of the Veterans Administration. We have, rather, tried to present what we consider ideally desirable in the present state of our knowledge, and we have left to the university the practical working out of the program according to local conditions.

Pre-Professional Requirements

In that wise volume, *Medical Education*, Abraham Flexner says:

> . . . the medical school cannot expect to produce fully trained doctors; it can at most hope to equip students with a limited amount of knowledge, to train them in the method and spirit of scientific medicine and to launch them with a momentum that will make them active learners—observers, readers, thinkers, and experimenters—for years to come. . . . The general arrangement of the curriculum, if sound, can make this task a bit easier, or if unsound, a bit harder; but in general much more—very much more—depends on teacher and student than on curricular mechanics or teaching devices [1925, p. 176].

If we substitute clinical psychology for medicine, this statement expresses the essential point which we wish to make in this report. Our task is to find good teachers to give good students good training that will start them off in the first stages of their careers as clinical psychologists. This report will be concerned in some detail with ways of meeting the problems that arise in attempting to achieve this task.

What specific goals do we have in mind in the preparation of the clinical psychologist? Clinical psychology seeks to acquire systematic knowledge of human personality and to develop principles and methods by which it may use this knowledge to increase the mental well-being of the individual. If we recognize that clinical psychology is both a science and an art calling for scientific rigor tempered by personal and social sensitivity, we can specify these goals fairly clearly. The more carefully the present scene is examined and the more thoughtfully the future is viewed, the more convinced are we of the need for preparing the clinical psychologist with a combination of applied and theoretical knowledge in three major areas: *diagnosis*, *therapy*, and *research*. The purpose is not to develop persons with encylopedic proficiencies nor is it directed at disproving the contention of some that the scientific and therapeutic attitudes mix poorly in the same person (a view which we are unwilling to accept until definite proof is forthcoming). Rather is it our purpose to see that the necessary broad training is provided that will make later specialization on a sound foundation possible. It becomes increasingly clear that persons having a specialized background in only part of one of these fields, for instance, Rorschach testing, or counseling, or electroencephalographic research, cannot function adequately. We go even beyond this and say that broad training, if it is in only one of the three major areas, is quite inadequate for ordinary clinical psychological work, to say nothing of teaching and preventative endeavors, two major fields of activity which require special attention.

The ability to carry out effectively the combination of functions called for depends upon the clinical psychologist's being the right kind of person, a person who has a relevant informal experience background into which has been integrated the proper formal education, both undergraduate and graduate.

What characteristics does the "right kind" of person possess? As yet, we do not know definitely, for research on this important problem has only begun. It is generally agreed, however, that especially important are the personality qualifications represented by a reasonably well-adjusted and attractive personality. Until dependable research data are available, the following list, which includes the kind of specific qualities experienced observers believe clinical work calls for, may be useful:

1. Superior intellectual ability and judgment.
2. Originality, resourcefulness, and versatility.
3. "Fresh and insatiable" curiosity; "self-learner."
4. Interest in persons as individuals rather than as material for manipulation—a regard for the integrity of other persons.
5. Insight into own personality characteristics; sense of humor.
6. Sensitivity to the complexities of motivation.
7. Tolerance; "unarrogance."
8. Ability to adopt a "therapeutic" attitude; ability to establish warm and effective relationships with others.
9. Industry; methodical work habits; ability to tolerate pressure.
10. Acceptance of responsibility.
11. Tact and cooperativeness.
12. Integrity, self-control, and stability.
13. Discriminating sense of ethical values.
14. Breadth of cultural background—"educated man."
15. Deep interest in psychology, especially in its clinical aspects.

The list is formidable but in the present state of our knowledge, represents the kind of selection goals toward which we must work. Characteristics of this type seem a necessary foundation for work in a field which requires so much in the way of maturity, sensitivity, and knowledge.

How are we to obtain such persons for training? Problems of both recruitment and selection are involved. The problems of recruitment are more difficult than they are in such major professional fields as medicine and law, since the latter are well-established and known to youngsters from quite early years. For the present, the major effort in recruiting will have to be made at the college level through teachers of psychology and vocational advisors who are on the lookout for promising candidates. In coming years, growing general acquaintance with the field and the multiplication of earlier courses in psychology at the secondary level are likely to lead the student to think of clinical psychology as a life-work. The first rough selection could then come in the secondary schools.

Beyond the problem of recruiting a sufficiently large number of persons to maintain the necessary supply of clinical psychologists lies the major task of proper selection at the point of entrance into graduate work. Here, besides the ordinary selective devices such as are provided by the credentials of the candidate, the Graduate Record Examination and the devices which are being developed in the "Research Project on the Selection of Clinical Psychologists under contract with the Veterans Administration" under the auspices of the University of Michigan (Kelly, 1947) should be of help in selecting the best candidates. It is not necessary to elaborate on the obvious point that besides rigorous selection at the point of entrance into graduate work a process of selection must go on throughout the program.

Given the proper kind of person, what may we expect of him in the way of informal background experience which may be considered relevant? For the present we shall devote our attention to the non-academic experiential background of the person. Since it seems reasonable to expect the clinical psychologist to be interested in people and have a broad base of human contacts, he should have had experiences, particularly in his college years (summer holidays and other spare time), involving close relations with both ordinary and unusual persons in field, factory, institution, or laboratory. In addition to direct contact with people of various kinds, he should have had the indirect acquaintance with people that comes from immersion in great literature, because of the emphasis which such portrayals place on the molar aspects of behavior and the insights into human nature that they give. Anything that reading may accomplish to broaden his acquaintance with the wide range of psychological expression, whether in relation to individuals or cultures, is so much relevant background for him.

What can we say about the formal educational background which we may expect from the candidate who is entering the graduate program? Two distinct points of view are generally expressed. On the one hand, there is some demand that students come with a common, fairly defined background, especially in psychology, in order to make graduate instruction easier. On the other hand, some hold that for the broad development of the field, to cast all the participants in the same mold would be undesirable. Medicine, the proponents of this view indicate, has experimented with a rather rigid prerequisite program but is raising more and more question about its desirability. The solution probably lies somewhere between the two points of view. It seems to us that certain general requirements for the undergraduate program which the student could ordinarily be expected to meet can be laid down. In exceptional cases, provision to waive these should, of course, be made.

The undergraduate program must be recognized as at most *pre*-professional. The professional and the more advanced courses in psychology should in general not be open to the undergraduate. The undergraduate program should be directed at providing a broad cultural and scientific base for specialized graduate study. The courses should help the student to attain a first insight into the structure and dynamics of human behavior, an understanding of the biological and social development of the individual, and a preliminary acquaintance with the principles and methods of collecting and evaluating data.

More specifically, as an example of what a basic undergraduate program might include, the following is presented:

1. *Psychology*. An approximate optimum of twenty semester hours, to consist essentially of courses for undergraduates. The student must be permitted to take a sufficient number of psychology courses to enable him to acquire a fair acquaintance with the content of the field of psychology, both in its general and in its laboratory aspects, but he should not be permitted to concentrate heavily in it. The main emphasis should be on courses in dynamic psychology[2] which consider crucial human problems at a fairly rigorous scientific level. Mass "titillating" courses directed at the general student body are definitely not what we have in mind here.

2. *Biological and physical sciences*. Approximately twenty semester hours of which the major part should preferably be in biology, including genetics, and the balance in physics and chemistry. Satisfactory secondary school preparation in the latter two would reduce the amount required at the college level.

3. *Mathematics and statistics*. Approximately nine semester hours in mathematics and statistics, with special emphasis on their logical principles.

4. *Education*. Approximately six semester hours in the fundamentals of educational philosophy, and experimental didactics in the form of practice teaching if this can be arranged.

5. *Social sciences*. Approximately twelve semester hours in sociology, anthropology, and economics. (Political science or history might be substituted for the last.)

6. *History of culture*. Approximately nine semester hours in history of civilization, comparative literature, comparative religion, philosophy, etc.

7. *Psychology as revealed in literature*. Approximately six semester hours in "literary psychology" if this can be arranged.

8. *Languages*. Reading knowledge of French and German. (Some consideration should, however, be given to the desirability of substituting other languages, for example, Spanish and Russian.)

We wish to emphasize that the undergraduate program cannot be appraised according to credit hours or in relation to specific courses. Each candidate's record must be examined on its merits to see how far it meets the spirit of the background requirements of breadth, good introductory acquaintance with psychology, and fair

[2] We shall have repeated occasion to refer to "dynamic psychology," a term which has to some extent taken on the "blessedness" of James' old lady's "Mesopotamia." Because of this, the term is not in good repute with some persons. However, we find no term so satisfactory for describing what we have in mind—the "how" and "why" of human behavior as opposed to the static, structural "what." Without getting involved in what would in the present context be merely irrelevant semantics, the definition given in Warren: "A systematic interpretation of mental phenomena, regarded as a succession of causes and effects with emphasis upon internal drives and motives," or the definition provided by one of us: "Fundamental theories of motivation, conflict, and resolution of conflict, applied to an understanding of normal and abnormal behavior" essentially describes what we refer to as "dynamic psychology."

acquaintance with the biological and social sciences. If a choice is to be made between the latter two groups, there seems some reason for postponing further study of the social sciences to the graduate period. The student, being more mature at this time, is better able to grapple with its relatively greater uncertainties.

Graduate Professional Program

General Principles

The general principles which underlie the graduate program appear to us of primary importance—in fact much more important than the details of the program. If clarity in the formulation of goals exists, there should be relatively little difficulty about agreeing on the means for implementing them. As has already been indicated, it is the opinion of the Committee that the setting up of a detailed program is undesirable. Such a step, if accepted generally, would go far in settling clinical psychology at a time when it should have great lability. Considerable experimentation with respect to the personality and background of students as well as the content and methods of courses will for a long time be essential if we are to develop the most adequate program. Our aims are rather to achieve general agreement on the goals of training and encourage experimentation on methods of achieving these goals and to suggest ways of establishing high standards in a setting of flexibility and reasonable freedom. We also hold that the goals should not be determined by special situations and special demands, but should be oriented toward the question of what is the best training for the clinical psychologist.

Against this general background, the principles which we consider important are the following:

1. A clinical psychologist must first and foremost be a *psychologist* (APA, PPB, 1947) in the sense that he can be expected to have a point of view and a core of knowledge and training which is common to all psychologists. This would involve an acquaintance with the primary body of psychological theory, research, and methods on which further training and interdisciplinary relationships can be built.

2. The program of education for the doctorate in clinical psychology should be as rigorous and extensive as that for the traditional doctorate. In general this would represent at least a four-year program which combines academic and clinical training throughout but which includes intensive clinical experience in the form of an internship.

3. Preparation should be broad; it should be directed to research and professional goals, not to technical goals. Participants should receive training in three functions: diagnosis, research, and therapy, with the special contributions of the psychologist as a research worker emphasized throughout. Although many will probably tend to specialize in one or another of these areas after obtaining the degree, the Committee feels strongly that there should be training in each of these areas during the graduate period. We are particularly concerned that training shall be of such a quality as to eliminate the possibility that a technician, whether in the sense of a directive or

nondirective counselor, a Multiphasic specialist, a Binet tester, a Rorschach specialist, or a remedial instructor, will be turned out as a clinical psychologist, and so depended upon for a range of work he will be unable to do.

4. In order to meet the above requirements, the program calls for study in six major areas: (a) general psychology; (b) psychodynamics of behavior; (c) diagnostic methods; (d) research methods; (e) related disciplines; (f) therapy. Such a program should go far toward reducing the dangers inherent in placing powerful instruments in the hands of persons who are essentially technicians, persons who from the standpoint of the academic group have no real foundation in a discipline, and who from the standpoint of the clinical group have no well-rounded appreciation of the setting in which they function.

5. The program should concern itself mainly with basic courses and principles rather than multiply courses in technique. It is simple to organize a program that includes innumerable courses of the latter type and come out in the end with a poorly trained person. The stress should be laid on fewer, well-integrated courses which subtly but inevitably leave the student with a sound background, on which he can build knowledge of techniques as he needs them. The courses should be so arranged that more advanced courses really call for knowledge acquired in preceding courses and are built on these. This has too infrequently been true in psychology graduate programs, with the result that students have not had the clear notion of progress toward a goal that law students and medical students have. The relationship of the course material to personality theory should be constantly emphasized and unless the whole program is oriented in this direction we doubt its final effectiveness for achieving the stated goals.

6. Courses should be scrutinized for their content, rather than judged by their titles. Equally important is the way the content is handled, that is, the quality of the teaching. Other factors to be evaluated are the internal integration of the course and its integration with other courses, both academic and field. Departments of psychology have perhaps been too much concerned with providing their instructors with freedom to organize their courses as they saw fit under an assigned title. This has frequently resulted in considerable duplication in courses and in the omission of important areas. In either case, the student suffered. Without in any way infringing on the instructor's fundamental freedom, it would seem possible, through department and individual conferences, for instructors to lay out courses which are complementary and supplementary to the others given, rather than overlapping because they are ignorant of the general content of colleagues' courses. Courses should as much as possible involve active student participation in preference to merely requiring listening or even watching demonstrations. Individualization of instruction, detailed personal supervision, and the encouragement of initiative and self-reliance must be recognized as important aspects of the teaching. The student should come in contact with a number of instructors representing a variety of points of view and types of experience.

7. The specific program of instruction should be organized around a careful integration of theory and practice, of academic and field work, by persons representing both aspects. Just as there is great danger in the natural revolt against "academic"

dominance, of ending up with a "practical" program, so is there danger in the continued dominance of the academy. It is important to break down the barriers between the two types of approach and through their smooth integration impress the student with the fact that he is taking *one* course of training provided by *one* faculty.

8. Through all four years of graduate work the student should have contact, both direct and indirect, with clinical material. This can be accomplished in the theoretical courses through the constant use of illustrative case material with which the instructor has had personal contact. The student should from the first year be provided with opportunities for actual contact with human material in naturalistic, test, and experimental situations in the setting of practicum, clerkship, and internship. Throughout, the effort should be made to maintain and to build upon that most valuable quality, the naïve enthusiastic interest in human beings with which the student first comes into the training program.

9. We have just made the point that the student should have contact with clinical material throughout the four years of training. Equally important is the need for contact with normal material. Opportunities should be provided to enable the student to become acquainted with the range of normal and borderline persons who never establish clinical contacts. Such training is essential in order to keep the student balanced in his interpretation and understanding of the abnormal.

10. The general atmosphere of the course of training should be such as to encourage the increase of maturity, the continued growth of the desirable personality characteristics earlier considered. The environment should be "exciting" to the degree that the assumed "insatiable" interest in psychological problems is kept alive, the cooperative attitude strengthened, and the passivity usually associated with so much of traditional teaching kept at a minimum. The faculty must recognize its obligation to implant in students the attitude that graduate work is only the beginning of professional education.

11. A distinct weakness in the training of psychologists, when compared with that of physicians and social workers, is the lack of sufficient feeling of responsibility for patients and clients.[3] The program should do everything possible to bring out the responsibilities associated with the activities of the psychologist. There should be persistent effort to have the student appreciate that his findings make a real difference to a particular person and to that person's immediate group.

12. A systematic plan should be laid to use representatives of related disciplines for teaching the trainee in clinical psychology, and opportunities for joint study with

[3] The words "patient" and "client," although not quite satisfactory terms for the person with whom the psychologist establishes "interpersonal relationships," are used throughout this report, either together or singly, but always interchangeably. Because of the variety of situations in which the clinical psychologist is called upon to work—medical and non-medical, normal and abnormal—neither term accurately designates all the persons with whom he deals. The old psychological term "subject" is sufficiently broad, but unsatisfactory because of its implications of exaggerated dominance and direction; the other old term "observer" is even more unsatisfactory because of the implication of emotional distance and marked non-dependence which it carries. For the present, to avoid awkwardness in expression, we must be satisfied with "patient" or "client," with the understanding that either term carries the broader meaning here indicated.

students in these disciplines should be provided. Through these approaches the student learns to work closely and in cooperative fashion with those whose methods may be different but whose goals are quite similar. In these settings he learns to acquire modesty about his own contribution, and to value the "team" approach to the problems of both a service and research nature that he meets, problems which, because of their difficulty and complexity, require a concentrated group attack. In the service aspect he must learn that the team approach calls for the coordinated thinking of various specialists on the problems of a particular patient and that participation in such group activity involves not only immediate, but continuing, responsibility for the client, whether direct or delegated, on the part of all of the members of the team.

13. Throughout the course of training there should be an emphasis on the research implications of the phenomena with which he is faced, so much so that the student is finally left with the set constantly to ask "how" and "why" and "what is the evidence" about the problems with which he is faced. There is probably no more important single task placed on the teaching staff than this direction toward research.

14. In addition to the research implications of the data, he should become sensitive to their social implications; he must acquire the ability to see beyond the responsibilities he owes to the individual patient to those which he owes to society. Medicine has developed a code which is admirable so far as concerns responsibility to the individual patient, but has paid relatively less attention to the other type of responsibility. It is our hope that psychologists will gradually acquire more of the medical attitude toward individual patients but develop a high degree of social responsibility as well.

Program of Graduate Training

As has already been indicated, the program of graduate training falls naturally into six major instructional areas: general psychology, dynamics of human behavior, related disciplines, diagnostic methods, therapy, and research methods. For purposes of exposition of the general plan, it seems best to consider the program according to these categories rather than by school year. Under each heading will be discussed the progressively advancing courses falling roughly into the particular category. The classification is, of course, arbitrary and there is a considerable amount of overlapping in both the theoretical and practical aspects. The description of an experiment in perception, for instance, can be significant not only because it points up fundamental perceptual theory, but it can also do the same for psychodynamic theory, research methodology, and physiological relations and—it is not inconceivable—for therapy.

Although it is not our intention to encourage filling up the student's time with courses to so great an extent as is the present practice, for instance, in the medical program, it is still our belief that graduate students in this program can carry heavier schedules than are ordinarily called for by graduate schools. The students must be given time to read and think but we believe these goals need not be sacrificed—in fact they might even be strengthened—if the program were thought of as requiring more semester hours of teaching contact through the year in order to get in *necessary* course work.

A. *General Psychology*. In view of the fundamental tenet accepted by the Committee, namely, that clinical psychologists are primarily psychologists, it is clear that due attention must be paid to preparation in the general aspects of psychology. It is our hope, however, that in the presentation of the general courses now under consideration instructors will keep in mind the need for including material related to personality theory and that they will consider the implications of the phenomena they are discussing in the context of total behavior. It is our hope, too, that the trend of the past toward emphasizing the segmental aspects exclusively will be considerably reduced. The courses[4] in this category which should generally be included are:

1. General, physiological, and comparative psychology.
2. History of psychology and contemporary schools of thought.
3. Developmental psychology—fundamental theories of genetic development: child, adolescent and adult; individual differences.
4. Social psychology.

B. *Psychodynamics of Behavior*. If we are to develop the kind of clinical psychologist this program aims for, considerably more emphasis than in the past will have to be placed on permeating the program with theory of personality and psychodynamics. There is no other aspect of the program that is more important and that has so many ramifications. If a dynamic orientation is what we are after, then there can be no half-measures. To accomplish such a purpose it is necessary that as many of the instructors as possible be well acquainted with psychodynamic theory and that they present their material in the light of such theory both in the classroom and in the field. The suggested courses in this area are:

1. Dynamic psychology—fundamental theories of personality and motivation of normal and abnormal behavior.
2. Experimental dynamic psychology—conferences and laboratory work. Starting with a selected group of classical experiments in general psychology that bring out fundamental experimental principles, the course might go on to the consideration of the theory and design of clinical research and experiments on personality characteristics and dynamics. It should also involve the critical analysis of published studies and the application of experimental techniques to actual problems in the clinical field. Some university might perhaps be interested in the experiment of conducting this course concurrently with the previous course—conceivably even as a single unit.
3. Psychopathology—the consideration of symptoms and symptom complexes in various mental disorders, with emphasis on nosology to some extent but more

[4] At this point and elsewhere when specific courses are considered we have deliberately refrained from indicating the semester hours to be devoted to them. We conceive of some of these as being three-hour courses and others as much as twelve-hour courses. The decision as to their length had best be left to the individual university.

particularly on the mechanisms and dynamics behind symptoms. The course should be organized largely around actual case presentations.

C. *Diagnostic Methods.* Diagnostic study has taken on an increasingly important role in the functioning of the clinical psychologist. This statement may seem somewhat anomalous considering the fact that for a long time "testing" was widely considered the only function of the clinical psychologist. The difference lies in the fact that whereas the functions of the clinical psychologist have been broadened considerably, there has been an equal broadening of the concept of what testing involves and a great expansion of the variety of procedures available to him. Besides standard tests, there are work samples, psychodrama, real life segments, and situational tests among the methods now at his command. At one time diagnosis implied merely a type of "pigeon-holing." At present this represents only a minor aspect of what is called for. Now diagnosis concerns itself with the origin, nature, and especially the dynamics of the conditions under investigation, and with suggesting hypotheses as to outcome under varying forms of disposition. Its important contribution to personality research, to psychiatric diagnosis, and to therapy are being recognized increasingly. The need for detailed and intensive training in this area is obvious. How shall this training be carried out?

There is a certain logical order in the steps of training which seem to us to be essentially these: principles and theory, demonstrations, preliminary laboratory experience (in the sense of practice by students on each other and on any other available subjects), practicums in the form of clerkships (organized short periods of part-time training at established field centers), and internships (organized, full-time, extended periods of training at established field centers).

The devices with which the student should become acquainted and in which he should attain proficiency are many and of varying degrees of difficulty. Increasing experience with students in this field convinces us, however, that before actually beginning to work on diagnostic devices the student should have a preliminary and fairly extensive period of training devoted to naturalistic observation and description, procedures on which these devices are fundamentally based. Because so much of clinical psychology (and psychiatry) depends on the description of the complexities of behavior, we would recommend that a considerable portion of the time to be set aside for diagnostic devices in the first year be spent rather in training students in careful observation and report. For this purpose, one-way screens, paired observers, and recording devices of both sound and visual types should be used in settings where individuals and groups are under observation in free and controlled situations. Constant checking of observer's reports against each other, against supervisor's observations, and against the mechanical devices should be standard practice. It is important that a healthy respect for careful observation and report be developed in students who are going to work in a field where a good share of the time the major instrument, in both respects, is the observer himself. With regard to reporting, both in this connection and in connection with diagnostic study, strictness and insistence on high standards of succinctness and accurate terminology are essential. A further argument for early training in observation is suggested by a reading of Flexner (1925, p. 253), who, quoting Wenckebach's statement, "Das Wissen verdrängt das

Sehen," points out the dangers which come from the early acquisition of technical terms and how frequently such knowledge serves as a barrier to accurate observation of the conditions with which the student is concerned.

Concurrent with the observational field work of the first year might come a broad survey course in clinical psychology whose purpose it would be to provide the student with a perspective of the whole field of clinical psychology. This would include a consideration of the varieties of duties and responsibilities which may be involved in different settings in relation to clients, other professions, and the public. Such a course might be followed by instruction in the technique of taking histories and interviewing, at least in part given under the guidance of experienced social workers and psychiatrists. The preparation of an autobiography during this period is also to be recommended.

After this preliminary background, which has emphasized molar techniques and has provided acquaintance with some clinical material, there follows naturally a systematic course in the theory and practice of diagnostics. Such a course should begin with a consideration of the theory and philosophy of diagnostics; it should provide an understanding of the place of diagnostic procedures in systematic psychology, its relationship to other forms of directed acquisition of knowledge such as naturalistic observation and experiment, its history in detail, and its strengths and weaknesses as a scientific method and as an applied technique. A presentation of the theory and practice of test construction might follow.

The student should then acquire an extensive, if superficial, acquaintance with the wide variety of test and other diagnostic devices: sensory and motor; intelligence: verbal and performance, individual and group; educational and vocational guidance; personality: objective, projective, and situational; and some general notions about their applicability, roughly in the stated order. He should, of course, have a more intensive acquaintance with the selected devices generally used in clinical settings. Whereas he may acquire knowledge of the former from general test survey courses, his knowledge of the latter should be acquired from specialized courses devoted to these techniques. In this connection, the faculty must resist pressure from the students who will put up considerable clamor to be permitted to do projective testing (just as some press for therapy) before they have the necessary relevant clinical and theoretical background for the proper use of these complex techniques. Knowledge about tests should not be derived from didactic teaching alone nor from occasional practice on fellow-students tacked on to the course. Practicums and clerkships, as has repeatedly been emphasized, must be recognized as essential and integral parts of the university training, and periods of practice with subjects in clinical settings must be provided. The general emphasis during the university period should, however, not be on too intensive practice in any one device nor with any one type of subject; rather, it should be directed toward getting across to the student the "feel" of contact with a variety of types of patients as well as the "feel" of a variety of types of test procedures. With this in mind, the university should have available many neighboring clinical centers for clerkships, such as schools, child guidance units, schools for the feebleminded, psychopathic and other psychiatric hospitals, mental hygiene clinics, general medical and surgical hospitals, educational and sensory-motor disability clinics, prisons, industrial units, and vocational guidance centers. Each student should rotate among at least four of these.

During the internship or externship it is inevitable, and in fact desirable, that a certain amount of the activity of the previous years is duplicated. The student should at the time he commences the internship have, besides a general background in basic general and dynamic psychology, a broad acquaintance with test techniques and an elementary appreciation of their application. He has now come to a setting whose major contribution is to throw him into direct, constant, and intensive contact with human material—a setting in which he can apply both his theoretical knowledge and his beginning skills.

In this environment, where the emphasis is on the individual patient, rather than the problem or the technique, there are certain goals related to test procedures which one expects the student will reach. It is exqected that besides acquiring skill, through repeated practice, in the administration and understanding of a wide variety of tests, he will learn when tests are called for and when they are not, what tests and combinations of tests are required in specific problems, and that he will learn their weaknesses as well as their strengths. Besides acquiring a sensitivity to the diagnostic and prognostic aspects of his test findings, one hopes that he will become sensitive to their therapeutic implications as well. In fact, there should be an effort to develop in him a "therapeutic attitude" toward his diagnostic work; an attitude that involves learning to avoid probing and carrying out misplaced therapy; an attitude that involves leaving the patient the better rather than the worse for the experience—this without violating the controls or the spirit of good diagnostic procedure. It is expected that he will acquire some sense of balance between the extremes of rigorous pedantic exactness and sloppy guessing, that he will recognize that different problems lend themselves to differing degree of control, and that there are times and stages of development when a rough negative correlation appears to obtain between psychological meaningfulness and degree of control. It is to be hoped that he will learn that what is important, while working always for reasonably greater control in the clinical setting, is to be honest about the degree of control obtained at the particular time, to admit that one is ignorant or merely hypothesizing when such is the case. His supervisors should strive to have him attain enough security about presenting tentative conclusions so that he does not escape into meaningless profundities or into exactness about the insignificant when he is overcome by the complexities and the difficulties of the significant.

These courses are suggested for the diagnostic series:

1. Observational techniques and reporting.
2. Survey of clinical psychology.
3. Methods of case study, case analysis and interviewing.
4. Theory and practice of psychological diagnostics:
   a) Theory of testing and test construction,
   b) Verbal "intelligence" tests,
   c) Non-verbal ability tests,
   d) Tests of sensory and perceptual function,
   e) Tests of motor function and motor skill,

f) Educational achievement tests,
g) Vocational tests,
h) Clinical tests of psychological deficit, aphasia, conceptualization, etc.,
i) Projective and other personality procedures,
j) Clinical analysis and integration of diagnostic devices.

D. *Therapy.* It is our thesis that no clinical psychologist can be considered adequately trained unless he has had sound training in psychotherapy.[5] The social need for the increase of available therapists is great. Clinical psychologists are being called upon to help meet this need, as well as the greater research need, and we anticipate that many will devote a part of their time to some form of psychotherapy. Our strong conviction about the need for therapeutic experience grows out of the recognition that therapeutic contact with patients provides an experience which cannot be duplicated by any other type of relationship for the intensity and the detail with which it reveals motivational complexities. A person who is called upon to do diagnostic or general research work in the field of clinical psychology is seriously handicapped without such a background; a person who is called upon to do research in therapy (a field to which psychologists of the future must, for various reasons, devote themselves prominently) cannot work at all without such a background.

Many important problems of an interdisciplinary, social, and legal nature are raised by such a program, questions which are not pertinent to the discussion here. There is no reason, however, why these cannot be taken care of eventually by the various committees and conferences concerned with the problem. We feel that members of other groups, such as psychiatrists, psychoanalysts, and social workers, who have been concerned predominantly with problems of therapy should be called upon, to as great an extent as possible, to take an important role in the teaching of the clinical psychologist. A by-product of this association could not help but be a reduction of some of the difficulties raised by the mentioned problems.

Because of the greater complexity and inexactness of the therapeutic process, it would seem reasonable that study in this area begin not before the second year. The work might be introduced by lecture and discussion courses on theory and methods, followed by practicums on simpler therapeutic techniques and on problems such as those which are involved in remedial work and guidance. Therapeutic activity of a more advanced (though still simple) kind should perhaps be left for the internship and fourth years of the program. During the internship, the student should be in an institution where detailed and close supervision is available. In the fourth year he has gained sufficiently in background, maturity, and appreciation of his responsibilities to the client, and to his own and other professions. Really advanced training in therapy is, with few exceptions, a problem of the post-doctoral period which requires considerable thought devoted to it.

The courses which should be included are:

[5] Psychotherapy is a process involving interpersonal relationships between a therapist and one or more patients or clients by which the former employs psychological methods based on systematic knowledge of the human personality in attempting to improve the mental health of the latter.

1. Therapeutic theory and methods—lectures and discussion: introductory course in therapy and counseling; methods and techniques; evaluation of results. There should be considerable emphasis on different points of view in therapy and on common factors in the various forms of therapy.

2. Remedial aspects of special disabilities—lectures and systematic supervised practice.

3. Techniques of guidance and counseling—lectures and systematic practice under supervision in individual personality guidance and counseling of minor problems.

4. Personality therapy—detailed consideration of case material in seminars; carefully supervised practice.

5. Techniques of group therapy—lectures, systematic participation, and supervised practice.

E. *Research Methods*. Because of the academic background of psychology, a natural development has been that of all the disciplines in the mental hygiene field it is psychology which has been most concerned with research. It is important that this interest in research on the part of psychology continue, for as one surveys the scene the likelihood that the major burden of research will fall on the psychologist becomes clearer. If he permits himself to be drawn off into private therapeutic practice as has the psychiatrist, or into institutional therapeutic work as has the social worker, the outlook for research is dim in a field where the need is enormous. As has already been indicated, if a social need for therapy exists, then the need for research is even greater. The fact that there is not equal pressure for the latter is mainly due to the excusable but still short-sighted outlook of the public. The universities, with their more far-sighted orientation, have a serious responsibility to develop research interests and abilities in the clinical psychologists they train. The interest should be in research on the laws of human behavior primarily and on technical devices and therapy secondarily. Throughout the course of training, research attitudes and problems should permeate all aspects of the program, in the diagnostic courses and in therapy, as well as in the courses in general psychology and psychodynamics. The emphasis on personality theory, already mentioned, is closely related and should serve as further support to this point of view. Only from a concentrated attempt to build up such an attitude can we expect to draw from our training programs a substantial number of psychologists who will be interested in devoting themselves primarily to research, and a further number who will devote at least part of their time to such activity.

The courses in this area should include:

1. Experimental psychology—conference and laboratory course of a basic kind in experimental techniques, devoted mainly to the consideration of the more meaningful problems in general psychology, for example, learning, reaction mechanisms, work activity, etc. Consideration should be given to variability of response—to the significance of the extremes of the distribution as well as to the modal and typical response—and to the clinical implications of these general problems.

2. Advanced statistics and quantitative methods in psychology and psychopathology.

3. Research in dynamic psychology—conference and laboratory course which considers the theory and design of experiments in personality characteristics and dynamics; application of experimental and other research methods to the problems in the clinical field.

4. Dissertation—preliminary work on the dissertation including the setting of the problem, preparatory reading, and the outlining of the project in detail during the second year. Actual experimental work on the dissertation carried out during the third (internship) year under joint supervision of university and field center. Final work on the dissertation during the fourth year.

F. *Related Disciplines.* Because of the problems with which he is constantly faced, there is no psychologist who needs a broader background than the clinical psychologist. He works in a setting with medical specialists of many kinds: psychiatrists, physiologists, neurologists, to mention the most prominent, and with representatives of other disciplines such as social workers and educators, with all of whom he has the closest contacts. On the one hand, his work may have specific physiological implications, on the other, broad educational and social aspects. He cannot be narrow; he must be able to meet his colleagues on common ground and at the same time see what the remoter implications of his findings are. That an adequate training program could be organized which does not include in it some of the background which such an assignment calls for is inconceivable. It has already been suggested that some of this background should have been acquired during the undergraduate period. But the greater part must necessarily come during the graduate period. Here, too, representatives from other disciplines should be used as much as possible in the training; in fact, it cannot be carried out without them.

The program should include:

1. Physiological sciences—lectures and demonstrations: selected aspects of physiology and anatomy; especially neurophysiology, neuroanatomy, autonomic nervous system, endocrinology, etc.

2. Introduction to clinical medicine—lectures: introductory course in clinical medicine to acquaint the psychologist with the major characteristics of the clinical pictures of various diseases and with technical medical procedures which he will hear about in the settings where he works. Special attention should be given to those diseases which today are usually referred to as psychosomatic.

3. Social organization and social pathology—lectures and field visits: a course to acquaint the psychologist with social structure; the pathological aspects of this structure as seen in crime, poverty, etc., and the agencies set up to take care of these. The major part of this course could most effectively be given by psychiatrically oriented social workers rather than sociologists.

4. Influence of culture on personality—lectures on cultural anthropology's contribution to the understanding of personality.

We might summarize what has been presented in the preceding section, which covered the content of the program according to areas, by a brief statement of the content according to year levels.

The primary purpose of the first year of study is to lay the systematic foundation of knowledge of psychology, to achieve some degree of acquaintance with the physiological and other sciences needed for professional clinical work, and to train the student in good observational technique.

The program of the second year of graduate work is directed mainly at providing the student with the necessary background in the experimental, diagnostic, and therapeutic approaches to the problems of clinical psychology. Although a certain amount of teaching may still be carried on in the form of lectures, the major emphasis is on direct contact with patients, clients, or other subjects, either in the diagnostic or in the experimental setting. Practicum courses and clerkships in different clinical settings are essential elements of this year's program.

The third year consists of an internship whose content is discussed in fuller detail in a later section. The Committee believes that the third year spent in an internship and the fourth in a final year at the university is the most desirable arrangement, although other patterns should be experimented with. The advantages of this proposal are many: (1) The student is enabled to complete the analytic and final work on his dissertation at the university. (2) It permits the final integration of the experiences acquired during the internship with the more theoretical principles emphasized by the university, and emphasizes the unity of the course of training. Otherwise the internship may be considered as a mere appendage. (3) The return of graduate students with internship background to the university should have some influence in integrating the kind of training provided by the university and the internship center. It might also serve as a reciprocating educational influence upon the non-clinical university group, both students and instructors. (4) The student is placed geographically close to the agency which already has an established placement service and is therefore in a better position to aid him in the consideration of employment opportunities.

The program of the fourth year should be relatively elastic and could include most of the following:

1. Final work on dissertation.
2. Cross-discipline seminars (attended by representatives of psychology, anthropology, sociology, social work, psychiatry, etc.) that devote themselves to the discussion of psychology's relation to the other sciences concerned with the adjustment problems of the individual and the group. The purpose of these seminars should be to integrate the major principles of previous study and to point out the broader implications of the course of instruction for the personal and social scenes.
3. Seminar on professional problems—standards, ethics, etc.
4. Additional courses in psychology as needed to round out the individual student's program.
5. Additional courses in related fields as needed to round out the individual student's program.
6. Advanced therapeutic work, if indicated.
7. A program of self-evaluation, if indicated. (See later discussion of the problem of personal analysis.)

Special Problems

Since certain aspects of the program raise special questions, they are considered in this section. The first of these is the internship.

Internship. What are the aims of a psychological internship?[6] Underlying all of its aims is the principle now recognized for the whole clinical psychology program, but particularly true for the internship, namely, that the knowledge essential to the practice of clinical psychology cannot be obtained solely from books, lectures, or any other devices which merely provide information about people or about ways of studying them. Rather, extensive and intensive experience *with* people is held to be essential if the student is to acquire a proper perspective and the ability to apply effectively the scientific facts and techniques which he has acquired in the academic setting. It should be pointed out that the internship is not a "repair shop" in which the failures of the academic center are taken care of. The university must adequately carry out its function of providing the necessary training in tool subjects so that the student may take the fullest advantage of what the internship is set up primarily to provide, namely, material on which to use these tools. Before he can become either a competent practitioner or investigator, the student must become sensitive to the many relevant aspects of the real person under actual study and learn to view him as an individual. In this process, he also learns to view himself as an essential instrument in the study of other persons. Because of the recognition of these needs, clinical clerkships and internships, the only devices that can accomplish these goals adequately, have been made integral parts of the program.

The major contribution of the internship is the provision of extended practical experience of gradually increasing complexity under close and competent supervision. The building up of an apperceptive mass of experience which gives concrete meaning to general principles can be attained only by volume and variety of contact with actual clinical problems in association with other disciplines. The program should provide the student with a broad base for later specialization by throwing him into full-time contact with human clinical material, contact of a much more intensive kind than he can possibly achieve during the clinical clerkships of the second year. This aspect of the instruction gains its value from being organized around the case material to be found in the institution, that is, the person rather than the condition is made the center of interest. Not only is the person seen in cross-section but it is possible to follow him longitudinally, either as the psychological processes develop and unfold, or as they may have been previously conditioned.

The content of the internship program comprises two major categories of activity: that involving contact with the patients or clients and that involving the acquisition of experience in the administrative sphere.

Contact with clients is of two types: *direct*—the acquisition of information from

[6] The term internship (residence appointment) is used in this report interchangeably with externship (non-residence appointment).

the patient by the investigator himself; *indirect*—the acquisition of information from and about the patient through other investigators and sources.

In direct contact with clients, the main avenues of approach are those concerned with diagnosis and those concerned with disposition. Each of these requires separate consideration.

A most important aspect of the education of the intern is the further instruction he receives in the use of *diagnostic procedures*, the procedures directed at acquiring knowledge about the origin and nature of the patient's condition. Under this heading are included a great variety of techniques of different levels of objectivity and degrees of complexity among which history-taking, interviewing, clinical psychometrics, and analytic and projective techniques are of particular importance.

An equally important aspect of his direct contact with clients is that involving *disposition*: what is to be done about the presented problem on the basis of the findings obtained through the use of the various diagnostic procedures. The worker himself may be directly concerned with disposition or he may serve in the role of consultant. In the former, the direct execution of the implications of the diagnosis may be at a technical aid level, at a therapeutic aid level, or at a quite advanced professional therapeutic level. In the latter instance, when the intern acts as a consultant, the recommendations which frequently are part of a much broader set of recommendations deriving from studies made by several disciplines, are carried out by another person. In such a case, the intern should have the opportunity to find out how effective are the actions taken with respect to the recommendations he has made, that is, he should at least be able to follow the case through written or oral reports. One of the advantages of the full-time internship is that the student is in a position to follow personally the evaluation and disposition made of the patient whom he has studied. A major disadvantage of part-time appointments is the likelihood of lapses in this follow-up process—the experience in too large a part consists of a succession of unclosed gestalten.

The direct contact with subjects just discussed lends itself to two different types of approach, each with a different end in view. The first is the *service* approach, that is, the study of the patient with the aim of solving his particular problem without regard for the general implications involved. Most of the work which is done by the intern is at this level. The second is the *research* approach, that is, the study of the patient not only for himself but for the general implications which his particular problem presents to psychology and psychopathology. This may be based either on a very thorough study of the client as an individual case or as a unit in a series of cases. Research experience, as has been indicated, is an essential part of the background of the clinical psychologist and a considerable part of the intern's time—perhaps up to one-third—should be devoted to the study of a problem on which he can accumulate a body of data during the course of the year's internship. This material, as suggested earlier, may very well be used for a dissertation. One of the most valuable contributions of the internship is the repeated opportunity which it affords for intensive team work, for intimate association with members of related disciplines on specific cases and problems. Such practical opportunities for co-ordinated activity and thinking are indispensable for proper training.

In addition to these direct contacts with clients, a considerable part of the instruction which the student receives involves only *indirect* contact with them, that is, is about patients with whom he himself has had no direct association. This includes experience of three kinds: (1) individual—about a particular subject; (2) general—about classes of subjects; and (3) technical—about methods used with such subjects.

Indirect contacts with *individual* patients may arise either within the setting of the institution's psychology department or outside the department. In the former are included conferences and department staff meetings which consider the diagnostic or therapeutic aspects of cases carried by other members of the department. In this type of relationship with clients, the extradepartmental contributions are usually the more extensive. A major contribution to the student's education is the knowledge which he acquires from regular attendance at the institution staff meetings which consider patients for initial orientation, for diagnosis, for disposition, or for special pedagogic purposes. At these, the student has the opportunity to become acquainted with the contribution made toward the understanding of a case by other disciplines, such as psychiatry, social work, pediatrics, education, occupational therapy, or nursing, and the manner in which the various contributions integrate with the psychological findings.

Contact of the *general* kind, that is, about general problems and classes of subjects, is obtained by the intern both in and out of the institutional psychology department through lectures, courses, and seminars in one or more fields such as psychiatry, psychosomatics, neurophysiology, experimental psychopathology, and re-education and rehabilitation, and in the approaches to the problems of clinical psychology from the standpoints of particular disciplines, namely, social work, neurology, psychiatry, internal medicine, pediatrics, education, pastoral work. The student thus continues his "academic" education in the setting of concrete material and personal day-by-day meaningful illustration. This education has the further advantage of being carried on without the interruptions which shifts back and forth in geographical setting entail. During the internship year, opportunity is afforded for extensive seminar study of advanced techniques in therapy, and advanced work in diagnosis with such devices as the Rorschach and the Thematic Apperception Test, techniques about which only the first essentials are actually learned in the first courses which are taken at the university.

Another aspect of this indirect contact with patients is the instruction which may be provided in sessions which consider new *technical* procedures. Here, too, the emphasis should be on the exemplification of the techniques by case material from the clinical setting.

An important point which administrators of internship centers must keep in mind is the necessity for constantly providing experience with normal material. The institutional personnel, by serving as subjects in psychological experiments and tests, frequently offer a rich source in this respect.

There is one other type of experience which is of some importance. We refer to the *administrative* aspects of department activity, including the mechanics of relationships with colleagues, superiors, members of other disciplines, and the institutional administration. At the start of the course of internship, the supervision should be close and the supervisor should assure himself of the ability of the student to handle even the simplest problems or procedures. As the student shows increasing competence, the supervision should be proportionately reduced and greater responsibility placed on the students to supervise each other with only a final check by the supervisor. The latter should, however, always be available for consultation. The importance of competent supervision cannot be overemphasized and any institution which accepts the responsibility of providing an internship program must recognize this as one of its important tasks. In the intradepartmental sphere, each intern should carry some of the responsibility for departmental functions. This may be in the nature of assisting in the supervision of other interns (rotated regularly among the group), the teaching of students who are serving clinical clerkships, and the care of departmental records of patients.

A fundamental purpose which must lie behind the process of instruction of the intern is the gradual development in him, through judicious supervision, of a sense of a responsibility and self-reliance in handling clinical problems. The program as a whole should be organized to provide the student with increasing responsibilities commensurate with his growth in the ability to accept these. Such a task requires constant knowledge by the supervisor of the state of the student's progress through active contact; absentee, routinized, or overloaded supervision cannot achieve this goal. The optimum number of students that a supervisor can handle depends on the nature of his other responsibilities; in general, five is about right. As soon as possible, the student should become a productive staff member, one who contributes practically to the service activities of the department. Even if his contribution is limited, as it necessarily is at first, the psychological effect on the student in giving him a sense of responsibility and a feeling of usefulness is great. Such contributions also make the administrators of internship centers more receptive to the establishment and maintenance of internship opportunities.

Another important aspect of the problem of the mechanics of instruction is the way in which the internship is organized. A full consideration of the various types (concurrent as opposed to block or consecutive, straight as opposed to rotating) leaves the Committee with the judgment that the block system, in which a full year is devoted solely to the work at the institution, especially that involving residence there, is to be preferred. As suggested earlier, other forms should, however, be experimented with. For the present, too, it seems preferable to concentrate on the straight internship, if for no other reason than because of the much greater simplicity of its organizational aspects as compared with the rotating type. (In the latter, the problem is complicated because the student has to move at intervals from institution to institution.) In the medical field, rotation has in many instances been found to result in a "smattering of knowledge." This, as well as many other important aspects of the problem, is discussed in some detail in the Subcommittee Report (APA & AAAP, 1945), and should be referred to.

What kind of institution is to be preferred for the internship—child or adult, state or private, mental disease or mental deficiency, out-patient or in-patient? Careful consideration of the problem impresses the Committee that it is not the type of institution which should be the major determining factor but rather the nature of the particular institution. "Good" institutions, that is, those providing opportunities for diagnosis, research, and therapy with a reasonably varied population under adequate supervision, of any type are better than poor institutions of what might be considered a favored type.

These general goals can of course most easily be achieved in large training centers where various disciplines are represented. Too much training in psychology has gone on in starved environments and a change in this respect is long overdue. A major characteristic of the "rich" environment is that concurrent training is provided in a variety of related disciplines such as psychiatry, social work, nursing and occupational therapy, as well as in psychology. For the latter, it is most important that at least the first two be represented. Such a setting provides the possibility for students of several disciplines to work jointly, under supervision, on common cases. Some of the most profitable learning about the case itself, about the relative and complementary contributions of the different disciplines, and about ways of working together effectively for the benefit of the client comes from these contacts. Besides the appreciation of the complexity and many-sidedness of the problem which comes from the different philosophies and points of view which are ordinarily represented, there is considerable learning by example from the other disciplines. Instances of this are the appreciation of rigorous experimentation that is derived from the physiologist and biochemist, the appreciation of the importance of meaningfulness as represented in the systematic viewpoint of the psychoanalyst toward molar data, and the sensitivity to the practical social implications of a problem that comes from the social worker.

Optional Courses. Although the four-year program should have a common core for all those training in clinical psychology, and should in general be similar for all students in the program at a particular university, it is important that a certain degree of option for special courses be permitted. This can ordinarily be worked out most satisfactorily in the fourth year, but should be possible at other points in the program. One may expect that the concept of what constitutes desirable clinical training programs will change with the years and it is best to permit students, through elective courses, to do a certain amount of experimenting with their programs as one aspect of this search for the most satisfactory program.

Dissertation. Because of our interest in developing a research-oriented professional person, it is quite important to retain the feature of the dissertation as part of the requirements for the doctorate. However, universities will have to rethink the whole question of the nature of the dissertation and its proper function, especially as it relates to the present type of program. With respect to its place in the proposed program, advantage should be taken of the opportunity provided by the internship to carry out a research project in the field of major interest to the student, both because of this interest and because it is important for him to obtain research experience in the clinical field. The student can learn as much about the nature and rigors of methodology and make an equally significant contribution to knowledge in working on some problem in personality or in psychopathology as he can in the more conventional fields. Although a dissertation on some aspect of personality which is based on normal subjects in the university laboratory should of course be acceptable, the Committee feels that preference should be given to projects involving clinical material, since the student must receive as much training as possible in research with such material. The present program is so organized that research on clinical material could probably be carried out most economically in time if the internship period were utilized for this purpose. In the ordinary course of events, the student would, during his second year, do whatever preliminary work was necessary on his dissertation: he would select the problem with the aid of the faculty and the supervisor at the prospective internship center, and draw up a project outline. If preliminary experimentation is necessary, it might be possible to carry this out at the university or at one of the clerkship centers. During the internship year, the student would collect the data for the dissertation. Supervision of his project should continue a joint responsibility of the university and the field training center. When the student returns to the university for his fourth year of work, he would be in a position to do the final analytic work and writing.

It is our hope that as a result of the more extensive and careful selective devices which this program is advocating, the dissertation will become much less of a major hurdle than it has heretofore been. As in professional schools, the student should by the end of the second year be so certain of having been carefully screened and of having met the requirements as to capacity and achievement that, given conscientious attention to the balance of his program, there should be little doubt about his completing the course. The development of such an atmosphere would do a great deal to reduce the anxiety with which the latter part of the Ph.D. program is so heavily laden, an anxiety which is largely created by the multiple and generally illogical uncertainties connected with the dissertation. If such an atmosphere can be developed, the productivity of students during this period would certainly become greater.

Integration of Academic and Field Program

After what has already been said in different sections of this report, it is unnecessary to discuss further the importance of integrating the two parts of the program. The techniques of implementation, however, require additional consideration. The problem of integration arises with respect to three aspects: (1) content, (2) supervision, and (3) accrediting and certification.

For the program to be most effective, the content provided by the two teaching centers must be well integrated. In this respect, faculty members have in the past been quite lax. They have left too much to the student the task of correlating and integrating the material in the variety of courses which he has taken at the university. The integration of university and field center activities has been neglected even more. If training is to be optimally effective, strenuous effort will have to be directed at correcting the situation. In order to achieve such integration, the whole group must become essentially *one* faculty. Arrangements for reciprocal visits and conferences between the staffs should be made to discuss such problems as the points of view to be emphasized, the techniques of teaching, and the avoidance of overlap.

It is most important for the instructors at each place to know the general content of the teaching at the other. Such mutual acquaintance would go far toward making easier for the student the transition to the internship center and back to the university.

In the matter of supervision, an integrated program must also be achieved. The supervisor at the internship center must obviously be held responsible for the major part of the student's activity. If the candidate is to use his available research time at the institution for work on his dissertation, a very close relationship between supervisors and agreement as to the division of supervisory responsibilities must be achieved by the two groups. The appointment by the university of several of its instructors, on a rotating basis, to act as field supervisors should be considered. It would be their responsibility to hold scheduled conferences with the interns in order to maintain contact with them and help supervise their dissertations.

All of the aspects requiring integration point to the obvious need for a combined responsibility in setting and maintaining standards. Such unification can only be achieved by accepting the internship center as an institution of comparable status with the university and in some respects an integral part of it. This can be achieved by interchange of personnel, joint conferences, and by interchange of student visits. There is no better way of achieving integration than through an interchange of staffs. The teaching staff of the university should be encouraged to spend summers or other periods at the institution on guest appointments. The staff of the institution should be given temporary full-time or permanent part-time appointments at the university on a regular faculty or lectureship basis. The latter arrangement is generally quite practicable and does not become too involved in the problems of university administration.

Self-evaluation. As psychologists become more involved in the clinical field, they become increasingly impressed with the importance of the observer as instrument. An important aspect of this problem, one which arises particularly in dealing with motivational questions, is the degree to which one's own biases, affects, and problems, frequently only different from the patient's in intensity, color the material provided by the patient. It has become obvious to those working in the clinical field that some kind of control of this source of error is necessary. Psychiatrists and social workers, from their more extended experience with this type of material, have long accepted the principle of the need for intensive self-evaluation as a prerequisite for their work, especially their therapeutic work.

Psychologists, in our opinion, must come around to the acceptance of some kind of intensive self–evaluation as an essential part of the training of the clinical psychologist. We are not prepared to recommend any special form of such procedure, although some of us believe that whenever possible this should take the form of psychoanalysis because of its relative completeness. Others of us believe that shorter methods of self-evaluation, because they may be less time-consuming and less indoctrinating, are preferable. Whatever the form, training should include detailed self-examination under the competent guidance of persons relatively free from dogma who have an interest in psychological theory as well as in therapy.

Psychologists can adopt from social work practice a procedure that has been found effective in achieving at least partial self-knowledge. We refer to their use of detailed case supervision of students. As a result of almost daily contacts with the student on his own cases, a relationship is established between the sensitive supervisor and student which may indirectly have therapeutic benefits. Such a setting makes it possible for the student to examine critically his own behavior and interpretations as they grow out of his handling of case material, and provides an opportunity for considerable personal growth. The profit from these personal contacts is increased when backed up by classroom discussion of cases on a less personal motivational basis.

Administrators of training programs should make an effort to promote such supervisory practices and canvass the possibilities for the more intensive type of self-evaluative experience in their own regions. Students, during the last part of their doctoral training, or immediately after this training, should be encouraged to undertake such a program.

Professional Responsibilities. No group can become a profession overnight, a fact which clinical psychology is in the process of discovering. What really counts in the making of a profession—professional ideals and practices—cannot (un)fortunately be taught in courses. Proper technical training, professional certification, and state certification, of course, play important roles. More important, however, are identification with a group having high ideals, and constant association in the actual work situation with persons having professional goals. It is in the work relationship that the student can learn to think of himself as a professional person. It is here that the student can gain an appreciation of how people meet such problems as maladjustment, illness, and handicaps and in this context gain a feeling of responsibility about his work because he understands that his findings really make a difference in what happens to a particular individual and his family. It is here that he learns to carry, in addition to this responsibility for the individual, the broader social one which transcends the need of the individual patient. It is in this setting, too, that another important aspect of professional training, his relationship with other professions, is constantly brought to his attention. He learns the techniques and importance of the group attack on problems: how best to work with other professional groups for the benefit of the individual client and the frequent necessity for identifying himself with a group even broader than his own professional group, namely, the "team."

If the student, after having achieved strong identification with psychology, learns to divest himself of this identification in order to become part of larger wholes for the benefit of a patient or a group, then he may be said to have achieved true professional growth. It is in this setting that ethical problems constantly arise and that the greatest learning in dealing with them naturally occurs. When this opportunity for "field" learning has been afforded, then "talk" learning becomes profitable. Seminars on professional and ethical professional problems have a contribution to make and should generally be made available during the fourth year. In these courses, the ethical problems that arise from relationships with clients, and those that arise from relationships with other psychologists and with other professions and the public should be considered, especially as they develop from concrete situations.

Student Relationships. We have stressed, in one context or another, the importance of the development of a sense of responsibility. Such a sense comes only in proportion to the opportunities for practice afforded a person. Besides those we have already discussed, another area where students may exercise responsibility is in helping to shape the program in which they are enrolled. Such thinking about professional problems, whether group or individual, should be encouraged, as should the organization of colloquia which the students themselves administer. The opportunity to express themselves freely on policy will insure reduction in the dissatisfactions and irritations which naturally arise in any program.

Another aspect of this problem has to do with the individual problems of the students—whether personal, or connected with the program. Provision should be made for adequate conferences on such problems when they arise. In fact, each student should have an active advisor whose responsibility it would be to keep track of the student's progress and who would be readily available to consider his individual problems.

Evaluation of Accomplishment. A problem which necessarily follows the organization of a program such as the one outlined is that of accrediting and certification, that is, the official recognition of the adequacy of those who take part in it—the student, the university, the field center.

For the student, at the various levels of individual advancement, some appropriate symbols of achievement seem necessary. The following are suggested:

1. Doctoral degree following the four-year course of professional preparation. Although there are some professional groups, notably the legal, which practice on the basis of a bachelor's degree, there are various considerations which make it doubtful if anything less than a doctoral degree would be satisfactory for the practice of clinical psychology.

2. Membership in the special division of the professional association of the group, the American Psychological Association's Division of Clinical and Abnormal Psychology. The first grade of active membership, Associateship, as recommended by the Policy and Planning Board (APA, PPB, 1947), would come for participants in this program, with the attainment of the doctorate; the second, Fellowship, with an additional five years of acceptable experience—essentially at the level of diplomate as discussed later.

3. After a year's post-doctoral experience would come state certification as recommended in the Policy and Planning Board Report (APA, PPB, 1947). Closely linked with the problem of study beyond the doctoral degree is that resulting from the establishment of the American Board of Examiners in Professional Psychology (APA, CABEPP, 1946). This Board has as its function the certification of candidates who after five years of actual experience, three years of which have been spent in recognized training centers, have passed examinations in stated aspects of the field of clinical psychology. (The nature of this advanced residency type of training requires special consideration and is not directly pertinent to the present problem. We hope to consider the matter in a later report.) Diplomas of the Board would serve as evidence of competence in the specialty of clinical psychology. Such a program emphasizes the important point that the attainment of the doctoral degree is only a step in the process of professional education, an education which continues through to specialist rating and beyond; in fact, throughout professional life.

Training universities and field centers as well as students must be evaluated. The universities should be evaluated according to their ability to meet the requirements set forth by this program. (Our Committee has been charged with such an evaluation and hopes to be able to commence this task shortly.) Not only the formal meeting of standards with respect to the courses given but the actual quality of the courses, as it relates both to content and instruction, should be carefully scrutinized.

The field centers should be given the same careful scrutiny as the schools. Standards as to content, quality, and amount of supervision, facilities (personnel, clinical, library, teaching), and living arrangements, should all be carefully set up and used in the evaluation. Since it is likely that the degree of expansion of clinical psychological training will depend to a great extent upon the number of really adequate internship centers which are available, considerable effort should be directed by universities to encouraging their development.

Recommendations

The Committee on Training in Clinical Psychology believes that the program outlined in the present report, if effectively carried out, should provide the basic background for clinical psychologists who will undertake both teaching and practice functions in the diagnostic, therapeutic, and research aspects of the field. This program, it believes, should also prepare persons who can eventually contribute to its preventive aspects, a goal toward which more and more of our future efforts must be directed.

The Committee on Training in Clinical Psychology therefore recommends to the Council of Representatives:

1. That the present report be endorsed.
2. That the program here outlined be presented to the universities offering doctoral training in clinical psychology as a recommended program.
3. That the report be recommended for publication in *The American Psychologist.*

Respectfully submitted,

ERNEST R. HILGARD
E. LOWELL KELLY
BERTHA LUCKEY
R. NEVITT SANFORD
LAURANCE F. SHAFFER
DAVID SHAKOW, *Chairman*

Training for the Clinical Application of Test Techniques

Shortly before the American Psychological Association's Committee on Training in Clinical Psychology was appointed, the Macy Foundation held a conference on training in clinical psychology. It was planned as one of a series; unfortunately the others never materialized. The conference was held on March 27–28, 1947, and was chaired by Dr. L. S. Kubie. It was attended by outstanding psychiatrists, psychologists, psychoanalysts, social workers, and foundation representatives. My paper, *Training for the Clinical Application of Test Techniques*, was included in the publication that resulted: M. R. Harrower (Ed.), Training in Clinical Psychology. New York: Josiah Macy, Jr., Foundation, 1947, pp. 21–27. Since its contents have largely been included in Paper No. 2 (pp. 14–38), it is being omitted here.

12. Problems in the Clinical Training of the Clinical Psychologist

At the 1949 meeting of the American Orthopsychiatric Association, one of the Round Tables was on the "Treatment Problems of the Psychologist." This paper constituted my discussion of George Gardner's paper on "Problems in the Clinical Training of the Clinical Psychologist."

I am generally in hearty agreement with the points made by Dr. Gardner. In fact, he makes *too* many relevant points and so I shall have to limit myself to discussing only a few.

Dr. Gardner discusses the problem of when training in therapy shall begin. He argues for its coming late, rather than early, in the training program. With this I agree, if we add that numerous other contacts with clinical material should have preceded, whether these be in the way of observation, interviewing, testing, or all three, including a variety of indirect contacts with patients. However, in arguing for the fourth year for the internship rather than the third, I think that Dr. Gardner is describing not quite completely many, or even most, of the present programs in clinical psychology. The Committee on Training in Clinical Psychology recommended a third-year internship for a number of reasons, not the least of which was a recognition of the peculiar need in psychology training at this stage to bring back

Reprinted with permission from the *American Journal of Orthopsychiatry*, vol. 20, 1950.

into the university persons who had had considerable clinical contact. This, it was thought, would serve to make the academic group face the real problems presented by the clinic and aid in the development of rounded and integrated programs. It is important to realize that it was never intended that the third-year internship should follow on purely academic work in the first two years. Actually, to some extent in the first year, but particularly in the second year, programs are generally organized to provide several types of clinical clerkship experience to students, to give them what Dr. Gardner calls the "basic diffuse clinical orientation" such as is given to third-year medical students. By the time the student gets into his internship, he will ordinarily have had *at least* half a year of such experience.

Because of my own prejudices, I find myself very sympathetic to Dr. Gardner's insistence on the mental hospital as a place for internship. The point made by Dr. Gardner about psychologists and mental hospitals holds, of course, equally for psychiatrists and social workers. I remember the discussion some years back at one of the Association's meetings when training of psychiatrists for child guidance work was being discussed. Considerable opposition was then expressed toward a requirement of state hospital experience. It seemed to me at the time that the argument was confused because no clear distinction was made between the state hospital as a *desirable* place for training and the *inadequate* hospital experience that was so frequently provided and called training. In the present office-practice oriented psychiatric training, one is impressed with the lack of appreciation of marked pathology and of the understanding of end-processes which can come only from mental hospital experience. Aside from this, the wholehearted occupation with sick persons which comes in such an environment is most important for any professional group.

What I have just said is immediately related to Dr. Gardner's next point. He deplores the acceptance of what he calls "the split internship" year. He here puts his finger on a weakness in psychological training to which we must give serious consideration. Psychologists are just becoming aware of field work as an important part of their training. For that reason they have not as yet begun to appreciate fully its meaning and implications. For too many, it is still quite subordinate to the program that goes on in the university. A true understanding of what that peculiarly concentrated type of field activity—the internship—is, is even less prevalent. There is not enough recognition that there is all the difference in the world between undivided absorption with real people who are suffering and part-time more or less flitting contacts with them. There is, further, insufficient appreciation of the amount of understanding and persistent supervision that a true internship involves. The concern about whether an internship year is an academic year or a full year merely reflects some of the underlying ignorance and lack of appreciation. How anybody who has any extended experience with internships can be satisfied with less than the full year, considering all that has to be crowded into this period, is difficult to understand. I agree with Dr. Gardner that the internship is at best merely the beginning of the student's training. The Committee on Training in Clinical Psychology has emphasized the point that the four-year training program should be considered as only the beginning of training, a period in which a foundation is laid for the continued training which comes in the post-doctoral period, the period when professional competence is really developed.

Theoretically I agree with Dr. Gardner's statement that students should be required to carry at least six cases in treatment. As I have seen it work out in practice, however, if proper standards of training are maintained, such a program will probably be at the cost of work on the dissertation. To get in the necessary work in diagnostics, dissertation research, and therapy seems almost impossible during the course of even a full year. Considering the many important other activities that go on in a live center, activities in which the student should take part, such as staff meetings, conferences, seminars, etc., some choice will have to be made. The choice should be made in conference with the student and the university on the basis of opportunities which can be provided best elsewhere in the program at a later time. A major value of including this amount of therapeutic work with patients during the internship year is secondary, but actually a primary gain. I refer to the gains which come from the self-evaluation which is inevitably involved—the kind of value which social workers have most systematically exploited.

In relation to one point I am somewhat surprised at Dr. Gardner's statements. I refer to his discussion of the desirability of overlapping functions in the clinic. I feel that he does not recognize how far practice is ahead of legislation in this respect, as I have pointed out elsewhere, and as the Committee on Membership Standards has found in its studies. Actually, such overlapping of function as is described by Dr. Gardner has surprisingly wide prevalence so far as staffs of clinics are concerned, and to a lesser extent insofar as students in the three disciplines are concerned.

Dr. Gardner puts his finger on perhaps the greatest problem facing the development of clinical psychology today—the dearth of supervising personnel. I believe that this dearth is generally recognized over the country. But sometimes I wonder whether the *importance* of this dearth is sufficiently recognized. Here, too, the university-oriented tradition probably plays a part. The scarcity exists in all areas of supervising personnel—but particularly in therapy. Dr. Gardner suggests the organization of an A.O.C.S.—an association of competent supervisors. Some obvious problems arise in the formation of such an association! The problem might be handled in other, less dangerous, ways. The Committee on Training in Clinical Psychology is, and has been, very much concerned about the problem, and has had in mind various ways of dealing with it. One of these is along the line of the other suggestion of Dr. Gardner, that is, the development of post-doctoral programs in which one of the major tasks would be the development of clinical supervisors. Some thought and planning are already going into the development of such programs.

I have said enough, but I cannot resist commenting on the point about the relationships between the university and the internship center with regard to the selection of interns. Dr. Gardner rightfully calls attention to the medical practice where the selection of the intern is entirely the prerogative of the internship centers. At most, the university may provide a list from which the interns will be selected. This is an attitude which needs emphasizing in psychology because some universities have not recognized it as a problem. They have assumed that internship centers must take the students that the university sends them. I was rather interested in seeing an outline of University of Chicago policy in this regard recently. There the problem was recognized and the center's responsibility in the selection of interns was accepted. With the establishment of approved lists of centers by the Committee on Training, there should be a greater integration of the two kinds of programs—university and internship—with a greater understanding and appreciation of each other's problems and needs.

13. The Improvement of Practicum Training and Facilities

Some five years or so after the Boulder Conference (Raimy, 1950), the field seemed ready to reconsider the principles laid down at that 1949 meeting in the light of the intervening experience. The rapid growth of the mental health movement during this interval was also having considerable effect on psychology. Clinical psychology, with the support of the National Institute of Mental Health, therefore held the Stanford Conference on "Psychology and Mental Health" in August, 1955. The present paper was one of the seven core papers which served as the basis for extended discussion.

When I was invited to take part in this conference I debated with myself for some time whether to undertake the task. I recognized, first, that I was no longer involved in training. More important, however, I asked myself if I had anything new to say. I finally accepted because of the opportunity the conference afforded to express some reactions I had about how things had gone since the time I originally became associated with training programs. This included both some shifts in my previously held views and some old ideas which would not die, ideas which I still believe sound.

I am not going to stick closely to the topic listed in the program. I think there has been enough talk about the details of courses, methods of training, syllabi, etc. I am going to deal with my topic in a general way and range into other parts of the program, undoubtedly trespassing upon the topics of others as I hope they will upon mine. We are here, I understand, to talk about *programs* and to reexamine our goals and ways of best implementing them, rather than to deal with technical details.

After going into history a little, I want to spend my time discussing the internship, or what we call the internship for want of a better term, and particularly the internship in its place in the total program of training. This calls for a reexamination of relationships between the university and the internship training centers, and it is to this aspect that I shall devote my major time. What little I have to say about

Reprinted with permission from C. L. Strother (Ed.), *Psychology and Mental Health*, 1957 (American Psychological Association).

laboratory and clerkship training—the other parts of practicum training—will come out implicitly in the context.

In October, 1944, a committee met at Vineland to consider the topic of "Graduate Internship Training in Psychology." Bob Brotemarkle, Bruce Moore, and I are the only ones present here from that group. The report of the Committee was published under that title in the *Journal of Consulting Psychology* in 1945 (APA & AAAP, 1945). The Committee made the recommendations to the APA and to the AAAP that they implement a few experimental training programs in clinical psychology which would include an internship as an integral part. These programs were to be supported, if possible, with foundation help, the fellowships to be given to students especially selected for the program. It was our feeling then that although there had previously been some sporadic training in clinical psychology, the time had arrived for experimentation with systematically organized programs. It was our thought that after several such programs had been in effect for some years we could be in a better position to evaluate the direction in which training in clinical psychology should go and then perhaps work towards its expansion.

However, history took the matter out of our hands and, in the process, pushed psychology around quite a bit. The war was followed by a period which brought with it warborn demands from the Veterans Administration and the Public Health Service for psychological services. We then went through what the 1947 report called a time of "breathless preoccupation with actual training." The unusual opportunities offered psychology by both these programs were, of course, beneficial in innumerable ways. But I wonder if in some respect it was not unfortunate that these developments came at that particular time. It prevented us from going through the period of slow and careful experimentation which might have resulted in educating ourselves about what was desirable in training programs. For we were not then ready in the training institutions, whether universities or field centers, to deal with training problems satisfactorily. Our inadequacies and insecurities resulted in compensatory claims under which the more moderate of us were merely ready to take over the earth, and the more ambitious, the cosmos. (We were not alone in this, of course; some of our sister professions showed the same symptoms.) Slower development would also have made easier the task of developing an understanding of clinical psychology by the non-clinical psychological faculties. The overwhelming character of the clinical influx, growing out of its suddenly acquired wealth, could not help but contribute to the development of negative attitudes toward the clinical parvenus, attitudes which continue to plague us considerably even today.

It is in this context that the 1947 report of the Committee on Training in Clinical Psychology (APA, CTCP, 1947) appeared. The Committee presented a program and tried hard to say about it (perhaps not most effectively, but still saying it): "Here is the *kind* of minimum program toward which we should strive. This is the *sort* of thing which training should be like, etc., etc." However, despite these efforts to establish such a common attitude, the report was perceived differently by different universities. Some perceived it as intended. Some became quite negativistic; nobody was going to tell them how to run their universities! And some took it as Sinaitic—a *second* set of commandments handed down from on high. It took much self-control on the part of the Committee not to be seduced into actually accepting this tempting Jehovic role. Perhaps the Committee members don't deserve any personal credit for this restraint; it should go rather to their introjected APA Council/Board of Directors' superego. You know we were already then on our way toward trying to be a "good" profession and our governing bodies had standards.

The report and the visits of the Committee during this early period helped to set a general pattern for training programs. And the pattern set was not *too* bad. After not having read the 1947 report for several years, I reread it recently for the purposes of this meeting. I must say I still like the way some things were said. In fact, so far as the principles delineated are concerned, I don't think much exception can be taken, although there undoubtedly are many ways in which these could have been better implemented.

In 1949 the Boulder Conference (Raimy, 1950) was held. This conference came out with essentially the same recommendations as the report. But it was a most important conference since it put the program on a much broader base and spelled out many of the aspects that had been left implicit in the report. More than anything else it gave the representatives from the universities and the field centers an opportunity to think through their programs. This results in the kind of understanding which no committee recommendations can ever achieve.

Shortly after the Boulder Conference, the Committee on Training was replaced by the Education and Training Board with its various subcommittees. I know little about the detailed activities of this Board. I am sure that it has been able to see training in clinical psychology in a much broader context than had been possible for the earlier committee. I am indicating my lack of acquaintance with the E and T Board activities because I want to make clear the basis on which my subsequent discussion is based. I might add, however, that until approximately a year ago I had close relationships with both a field training center and a university, so that I have some knowledge of at least some programs up to that time.

There is no need to tell *this* group what a difficult job psychology undertook when it set up the type of program it did for training in clinical psychology. The attempt to train persons in *both* a science and a profession at the same time is not an easy one. How well we have carried out our task will, I presume, come out at this conference. What I will have to say is based on the assumption that this double goal *remains* the goal of our training programs, and that we are continuing to search for ways of achieving it as effectively as possible.

Since I consider the internship the single most important part of the training program, I shall spend the rest of my time talking about it in one way or another. At this point I wish merely to make some general comments about the internship and leave my detailed discussion for the context of field center-university relationships.

In order to get on to my major theme, I am tempted to leave this topic with merely the trite admonition that the internship should be "good." Although definitions of such high-quality internships have been provided in many places, I cannot leave the subject without a *few* comments about "goodness."

What about the setting of the internship? It should, of course, be carried out in a place devoted to training. It should have a research atmosphere. It should be a place where the quality of the staff and the clinical work of the staff is high: a place where there is a variety of staff, both in psychology and in other professions and disciplines, and where there is an opportunity for much informal as well as formal contact. In other words, it should be a center with high osmotic qualities in which absorbent students are more or less constantly being bombarded with nutrient elements whether they are immediately aware of this or not. (I know that there are great advantages to throwing a bright young student into an undeveloped place, but let us not over-rationalize this expediency.) Such an atmosphere, built around a core of much direct and intensive work with clients, but preferably *patients* (because medical settings at the present time offer the richest experiences), with whom the student works diagnostically, therapeutically, and in research under competent supervision, provides an opportunity for guided learning, but mainly for *self*-learning, which cannot avoid becoming a main foundation of the student's training. Under such conditions, he has the opportunity to learn to recognize how little *he* knows and how relatively little more is known by others. Such a setting helps both to minimize the psychologist's too-ever-readiness to escape into verbalization or exercise his tendency for compensatory omniscience. And I don't mean that our choice then lies between a Uriah-Heepish humility and an equally defensive nihilism —I mean just good substantial self-criticalness. (I notice that this is the second time I have said something about grandiosity. I have, because unfortunately we have had too much of it in clinical psychology. However, I promise not to mention it again.)

All right, *I* have provided a good internship, and the other speakers will, I am sure, provide a good *university*. Now let's get to the heart of the problem—how do we get a good *program*?

What I am going to be asking repeatedly is: Can we have a really good program—one that comes anywhere near to achieving our two-fold goal—until we have worked out our university-field center relationships in such a way that the most effective use is made of the integrated facilities of the two types of institutions?

I don't see how this can come about, however, until psychology faces squarely the issues raised by the internship itself. And psychology, I believe, has *not* really faced these issues in the past. I know, of course, about all the various committees and reports on the topic. What is called for is the facing of issues, not with lips or even with cortex, but with guts. (I have recently come across a word new to me: *penetralia*. Its meaning is I believe self-evident. Perhaps *that's* with what the issues must be faced, with our penetralia!) In fact, I believe that many of the issues have not even been clearly recognized. And when recognized they have often either been evaded or at most dealt with superficially. This is understandable since the problems are not easy to deal with, let alone to solve, at *any* time. They have been especially difficult to handle in a period requiring sudden growth, growth from practically nothing. What *are* these issues?

They fall into two main groups: those relating to the internship itself, and those involving the relationship between the internship and the university centers.

I do not have any statistics for what I am about to say about the importance of the internship experience. It is based on my own experience long ago as a student and on many years of talking with our interns about their training. With rare exceptions—I can think of none now—students have told me that the internship was for them the most significant part of their training experience. This was told to me both at the end of the internship experience and on subsequent informal follow-ups as much as five to ten or more years later. The consistency of these reports and the relatively spontaneous way in which this communication occurred, leads me to believe in their correctness. I realize, of course, that for the "teacher-knows-best" school of thought, this attitude on the part of the student does not have much validity. However, belonging myself to the "student-*generally*-knows-best-when-given-a-fair-chance" school I have been and am impressed, especially since I see good reasons for the students having felt the way they did. I shall have something more to say about student attitudes in a later context.

Another problem has to do with the appreciation of how expensive good internship training really is. We are far from recognizing this fact—a fact so well known to the medical group. I remember how I used to tear my hair in despair—forgive the alliteration!—when I sat on committees concerned with considering the expenditure of funds for training. I remember how difficult it was to get psychologists having little experience with practicum facilities to recognize the differences in the cost of maintaining university programs and that of maintaining hospital programs. The arithmetic was so obvious to them: divide the total budget or the total grant by the number of students being trained in each kind of place. The answer then was clear—internship training is unreasonably expensive and uneconomical! I say we must be ready to face the fact that internship training is highly individualized training and the price of providing adequate facilities and supervisory personnel comes high.

Then there is the semantic problem. Does "practicum" imply "applied"? Not in *my* dictionary, and I hope not in yours. The implication that if, as a part of a rounded program, we provide training with *persons*, in the context of service to them—frequently the only condition under which certain phenomena can at all be studied—then we are by that very fact concerned with *application* solely, or even primarily, is decidedly a strange one. Yet we ourselves have been semantic dupes about this important point, and have let just this implication gain acceptance in some academic circles.

In fact, I detect something of this kind of confusion in our own program here in the title assigned to Eliot Rodnick's address tomorrow morning.[1] If the "applied" in the title is deliberate, then I am happily wrong, and I apologize for this error. If it is inadvertent, then we are dealing with just the unclarity I was talking about. Should not the title rather have been "Training for Research"? If it was intended that he deal with "applied" research, then I do not apologize for pointing out that in a balanced meeting program we should have had another address on "Training for Basic Research." Certainly our training is for *research*—whether basic or

[1] The title assigned in the program was "Training for Applied Research in the Mental Health Field."

applied. (The clearest discussion of this problem of what is basic and what is applied in clinical research [psychiatric and psychological] is to be found in GAP Report No. 25, *Collaborative Research in Psychiatry.*) We must get away from the naïve assumption that research which is done in test tubes or with animals, that is, investigation which is carried out in a context physically remote from the kind of subject to whom it is going to be applied, is by this mere fact of remoteness any more basic, or pure, or theoretical, than work done directly with the kind of subject to whom the findings will ultimately be applied. We have a term for this kind of primitive thinking—need we be guilty of it? What I am saying casts no reflection, of course, on either service work or applied research. I am merely trying to keep the issues clear. Just because one is working in an institution whose walls are of plaster, rather than ivory, and just because the activity takes place in the basement or on one of the intermediate floors, rather than in the attic, does that necessarily make the work less "pure"?

There is a further problem which relates to the standards for the setting and for the program. This issue I have already touched upon and shall not develop further except as I deal with it in a general suggestion which I shall make toward the end of my talk.

There are certain formal characteristics of the internship itself which are important and involve still other kinds of issues. I have the impression that the problems raised by these aspects have not been faced directly and sufficiently. It seems to me also that decisions in these respects have too frequently been made on the basis of expediency rather than principle. The aspects I have reference to are full-time versus part-time involvement, *in*ternship versus *ex*ternship, local facility versus distant facility. Let us consider them in that order.

There have been occasions when part-time rather than full-time internships have been defended as superior. I wonder if the acceptance of part-time internships is not a mistake. One of the major advantages of the internship type of training is the opportunity it affords the student for developing a sense of involvement, responsibility, and wholehearted devotion to an ongoing activity as well as feelings of participation in a complex group function. This is most difficult to achieve on a part-time basis. The same points hold for the part-year/full-year problem. Without going into a detailed defence of this point of view, I might state it as my present belief, that the optimal length of an internship is more, rather than less, than a year.

The internship-externship problem relates to whether the student lives *in* the institution or *out* of it. In this connection I should like to tell you a story about Adolf Meyer.

Sometime during the thirties Adolf Meyer came to the Worcester State Hospital for a visit. He had not been there since the time he had left it in 1901. I had the privilege of showing him around. During the course of our tour he told me how sorry he had been to leave Worcester where he had been very happy. In fact, he indicated that he considered the Worcester period to have been his most effective and productive period. He then told me the story of why he had left. It seems that the superintendent at that time, Doctor Quinby, wanted Meyer to live in town. Whether this was due to a pioneer attitude on the part of the superintendent to get his staff to live in the community and thus help break down the isolation of the state hospital, or whether it was because he needed Meyer's apartment space for something else, I did not get clearly. My suspicion would be the former because of the high level of support that Quinby gave Meyer and the quality of the staff which Quinby enabled Meyer to attract to Worcester during that period. Whatever the case, Meyer objected strenuously. He felt it most important to be with the patients and staff *all* of the time. He believed that living-in and the wards and the laboratories were all part of a 24-hour job, that much learning took place in the informal out-of-hour contacts, and that he would not be able to carry out his functions properly if he were not around full time. So Meyer left for New York.

I add to this an account of my own experience. My major responsibilities for the training of interns have been at two institutions, the Worcester State Hospital and the Neuropsychiatric Institute at Illinois. Disregarding the other differences between these institutions, I have always had the feeling that the Worcester interns got more out of their experience than did the NPI interns. I put this down largely to the fact that the Worcester students were *in*terns whereas the NPI students were *ex*terns. In fact, I have some corroboration for this in the fact that one of the five Illinois positions was for a period actually an *in*ternship. In comparing the experiences of those who filled this position with those who were externs, I was left with the same impression of greater gain by the interns.

The problem of local versus distant facilities is a different issue to deal with. The use of good facilities at a distance from university training centers raises many problems. It is important to face this issue directly, however. One must weigh the advantages of higher quality of the distant institution (when such is the case), and the great advantage usually offered in such an institution of the association of students from different university backgrounds, as against lesser quality, but much greater convenience, of the local institution. If expediency, based either on inconvenience for the university or the unwillingness of students to move to a distance for a year, determine the decisions, let us at least be clear that these are the reasons.

Now let us get on to a consideration of the relationship of the university and the internship center. With regard to the present state of integration, let me say right away that my detailed knowledge of the situation over the country is limited. What I have to say arises in part from my own experience and in part from what I have learned from talking with persons concerned with training in various parts of the country.

Sometime ago when I inquired about how much actual relationship there was between the universities and the internship centers, I received the impression that the situation was quite varied. Some universities maintained a periodic contact; others merely asked for a final report about the student; and still others did not seem interested even in this. What the situation is actually like at present, I do not know. What I have been talking about thus far is "*relationship*"—merely keeping in touch with each other, only the first and the very simplest step toward *integration*.

I am doubtful if there are many instances of detailed planning of the internship in the context of the university program. Certainly my own experiences in this respect afforded no evidence that such planning took place. The compliment implied in the lack of detailed interest in how our program fitted in with that of the university was flattering. I wonder, however, whether it *was* on the basis of an assumption by the university that our program was perfectly attuned with theirs which resulted in never more than one request—and that rarely—for a quarterly report on how the student was getting along. I also have certain limited data about integration based on the attitudes of our students. When the time arrived for them to consider re-turning to the university after their internship, separation anxiety (or was it *re-attachment* anxiety?) was a quite common phenomenon. Mainly, it appeared to be occasioned by the feeling that there was little more that they could learn at the university. The instructors had little further to offer; the younger (pre-internship) students seemed to talk a naïve, disembodied language which they could not believe they themselves had talked only a year earlier. They were therefore going back almost exclusively to work on their dissertations and they would much prefer being able to work on the dissertation at the internship center. It was at this period of individual and group evaluation of the year's experience that we would hear almost universally the demand for the extension of the internship. There was so little more to learn at the university and so much more to learn at the center! As for the integration to be achieved during this postinternship period, the students indicated that it had been already suggested to them in their pre-internship days, either explicitly or by implication, that it was *their* task to find the relationship between university theory and field experience. The good ideas about integrative seminars and other such suggestions for the fourth year, to be found in the '47 report and the Boulder Conference report, were apparently rarely implemented—at least in the case of the students with whom I had contact.

There are some aspects of the relationships between a university and the training center which deserve special consideration. These relate to the selection of students, the period when the internship comes, and the dissertation.

How much of a role does, or should, the internship center play in the selection of students for the total program? The problems here are many and I certainly do not wish to minimize them. It does, in some ways, however, point up the total problem, and might be used as a measure of the integration achieved. The issue is clear, however, and does not require elaboration.

The 1947 report and the Boulder Conference report accepted in general the desirability of a third-year internship. For this there were many reasons, mainly that in this way the double goal of the training might be best advanced. There was the further hope that some degree of integration in psychology as a whole would be achieved both by mixing the students trained in the field with the students trained in the laboratory, and the clinical students with the non-clinically oriented professors. The hope was that each would benefit from the mutual consideration of problems posed by the other. These arguments still seem sound. The achievement of this goal has, as you know, run into many difficulties. Some of the universities have solved these difficulties by placing the internship at the end of the program, *after* the student has met all of his regular Ph.D. requirements. Others have solved it in other ways. Many of these solutions have inevitably resulted in less, rather than in more, integration.

Some of the issues come to a focus most clearly in relation to the dissertation. A portion of what I have to say has relevance not only for the clinical student but for graduate students in psychology generally. However, I shall limit myself to the discussion of the problem as it relates to the clinical students.

There was some thought at one time that it might be possible for the student to get at least part of his dissertation work done during the internship. This (with rare exceptions) turned out to be impossible to achieve because of the amount of ground to be covered during the internship. Under the circumstances, what has generally happened is that the student goes back to the university after his internship and does his dissertation work during that year. In order to be sure of getting through in time he picks a "safe" dissertation, frequently a non-clinical one (because they are usually more easily packageable), and a problem not too infrequently handed to him by one of his instructors. How does this compare with what should ideally happen?

Of all the opportunities the Ph.D. program affords to test out a student, the dissertation is the best single device for indicating what kind of a person he is intellectually and in research ability. Isn't it therefore important to watch him through the various steps of the process of becoming an investigator—see him intrigued by a phenomenon, watch him learning how to put the proper question to nature, and then observe how he goes through the process of trying to get an answer to the question?

For the clinical student, is it not important, too, that this question should be asked in the place where he has most likely become intrigued with a problem, in the area in which his primary work lies? This area is full of unanswered questions which he has to face daily, an area where the difficulties of research and the need for more research are great.

By having the student go back to the university for his dissertation, what kind of attitude are we encouraging? Aren't we in a sense saying that research is not something to associate with the field setting, *that's* the place where service functions are carried out; the *university* is the place for theory and research. What does this do to hinder our efforts to build up this research area and the field stations as research centers?

By going even further and having the clinical student do his dissertation on a topic only remotely related to his area, what are we doing? Aren't we by implication discouraging the development of an attitude that the problems in this area are researchable problems, and even more than in the previous case associating not only clinical *settings* but the clinical *area* with service and non-research?

But when we go even further, and we have a clinical student do a non-clinical dissertation on a question which has never troubled *him* but which instead came out of the file-drawer of a professor who had some minor question which needed answering as part of a larger problem troubling *him*, what effect on the development of the investigative attitude of the student do we achieve?

What I'm saying is: Don't we have very definite responsibilities to our clinical graduate students? Should we divert them or make research assistants out of them in connection with their dissertations? Can't they do their research assisting, if this is necessary for earning, or even learning, on the side? As "dissertationers," should they not work in the area of their major interest and be independent through the *various* steps of the process, with only the most necessary guidance and help to which they are entitled?

May I, in a somewhat irrelevant aside, take this opportunity to leave another question with you about psychologists and research in the clinical field. (What I have to say goes beyond the clinical area, too, but again this is not for the present occasion.) Ought we not be concerned about the degree to which psychologists have become involved in methodology and research design as contrasted with substantial problems in research? It is, of course, important that thought be given to these aspects, and psychology has made a considerable contribution through such activities. But is it good for psychologists to be thought of almost entirely as critics, evaluators, designers of studies, and not as producers and investigators of ideas and substance—to be thought of as concerned almost solely with the "how," and as leaving to other disciplines, concern with the "what" and "why"?

These are some of the problems, some of the issues which I think need consideration and straightforward handling. It is in the context of this kind of a consideration that I should like to put before you the outline of a program of relationship between university and internship center which attempts to deal with some of the difficulties I have described. It is deliberately no more than a tentative sketch offered for discussion, and for development if it has promise.

The fundamental principles of the plan are that theory and practicum must be constantly associated and tied together whether in the university or in the field station, and that each type of activity—theory and practicum—starts with the very *beginning* of the program. I would suggest as axiomatic the statement: *The greater the degree of integration achieved between theory and practice, and between university and field center, the more effective the program.* We see an outstanding example of this trend in medical education in the Western Reserve experiment where there is an attempt to break down the traditional distinction between basic science years and clinical years and in which the program has been organized vertically rather than horizontally, with the opportunity for clinical contacts from the beginning.

What I am saying is that we must get away from the *layer*-cake principle on which most of our programs are based. (Some schools, I am afraid, actually work on *two* separate layer-cake programs.) I even believe that we must go beyond the marble-cake principle on which perhaps the most advanced among us base our programs. We must work toward achieving that ultimate level represented by the cake whose ingredients cannot at all be distinguished either in appearance or in taste, the one in which true fusion has been achieved. There does not seem to be a generic name for this kind of cake. (I offer the bakers the term "fuse-cake," gratis.) Sad to say that, taxonomically, the science of cakery appears to be behind even psychology!

The plan would essentially follow this pattern:

Integrated Program

Year	Theoretical Training		Practicum Training	
	Content	Provided by:	Content	Provided by:
I	"Core" theory	U	Lab.: observation, tests, psychodynamics	Uf
II	Advanced theory: personality, etc.	Uf	Clerkships	Fu
III	Theory: diagnosis, therapy, psychopathology, etc.	Fu	Internship I	F
IV	Dissertation, cross-discipline theory, etc.	Uf	Internship II	Fu

u U = University (upper case—major responsibility).
f F = Field (lower case—lesser responsibility).

Each year would have both its theory and practicum provided either by the university or the field center, but usually by *both.* In the first year there would be major emphasis on theoretical courses at the university, and at the same time the university would provide laboratory practice in observation and tests, and laboratory work in experimental psychodynamics or similar courses. In the second year, the university would provide additional advanced theory and the field would provide the clerkship with its associated theory. In the third year, the first internship year, the field stations would be required to provide theory related to the field work as well as the field work itself. I am recommending that the fourth year become a second internship year during which the dissertation work is carried out at the field center. During this year, *both* the university and the field station take the responsibility for the theoretical work connected with the dissertation and any other aspects of the training. Although during each year one of these agencies would carry a major responsibility, it is my thought that the other agency would also carry some degree of responsibility for the program.

The program places so much emphasis upon theory—whenever possible in the context of practice—because of a fundamental principle which is implicit in my whole discussion. This is the principle that our training programs at the doctoral level must be programs directed toward providing a *general* kind of professional psychological education, the only kind of foundation upon which later specialization can be soundly built.

What would be needed for implementing this program? We would obviously have to give up the notion of distant field centers. Local institutions will have to be developed to a level which a program of this kind calls for. This would permit the close interaction required between the university and the field center. Although there would be some loss here, some of the advantages of mixing students from different universities might still be maintained in those instances where there are several local universities in an area. Although there are many advantages to "captive" (in the good sense) centers, I think the gains are greater all around if there is not sole relationship with one university.

The personnel needs of both the university and the internship center that a program of this kind calls for require re-thinking. Because of relatively later involvement in training, the internship center is more likely to require building up mainly in quality of personnel to proper standards than is the university.

The professional relationships between the two institutions must become much closer than has until now generally been the case. They must become almost as one professionally, with the *major responsibility falling upon the university to achieve the unity,* since *it* is the degree-granting agency. Program planning must from the beginning be carried out in close association. It is important that the university people have free access to and whenever possible appointments at the internship center. The reverse must be true for the personnel from the clinical centers. (These appointments can be of various kinds and need not get involved in the complicated problems of permanent university tenure.) Their staff must be raised to the level of acceptance by the university. For *program* purposes, the staffs of the two institutions should be thought of as one as much as possible.

Let me try to sum up what I have been saying. It appears to me that psychology must now ask itself searchingly several questions about its programs in clinical psychology. These are:

1. How *psychology*-oriented are they? How well oriented are they to the trends in the field as a whole, to the general needs of psychology in the context of the needs of society generally?

2. How *student*-oriented are they? How well oriented are they to the needs of students rather than to those of the instructor and the institution? How well oriented are they to the individuality of the student so that training maintains a necessary flexibility?

3. How *broadly conceived* are they? How well are the programs training generalists well grounded in practice which is oriented to theory? How well are they providing a generalized training which is adaptable and on which later—post-doctoral—specialization can be based?

4. *How well do they develop self-teachers?*

5. *How well are they organized to achieve the double goal of developing persons to practice both a science and a profession?*

   a) How well do they develop practitioners who carry responsibility in relation to persons who come to them for help? How well do they develop practitioners who can deal with these persons sympathetically and with understanding?

   b) How well do the programs develop persons who can examine evidence critically, who are concerned with the advancement of knowledge, and who can carry on activities directed at the acquisition of this knowledge?

I have presented some of the issues which I think must be dealt with in trying to answer these questions. I have also presented a tentative program which I believe has possibilities for advancing us further toward the goals which are implied by these questions—goals which I think our presence here indicates we are all committed to achieve.

The program I have sketched is obviously not intended to prepare persons to be MMPI specialists on 42-year old schizophrenic women. It is even not intended to train medical psychologists or counseling psychologists or school psychologists or rehabilitation psychologists. It *is* intended to train *psychologists* (*clinical*), which all of these are. We might even make this parenthetical compromise with elegance to get the point across! (I don't, however, think that this compromise is necessary now that counseling psychology [APA, CCT, 1952] and school psychology [Cutts, 1955] have recognized their close relationship to clinical psychology, which is distinguished mainly because it became aware of its breadth and training needs earlier. Is it not desirable to use the most available [probably the *only* available] common term—*clinical psychology*—generically for all these areas of psychology concerned with the emphasis on the individual and his problems. It would be too bad if our personal identification needs stood in the way here. Usage would, I am sure, result before long in recognition of the broadened meaning intended.)

The greatest concession that such a program might make to specialization would be in permitting students who have clear-cut interests to have their clerkships or even their internships in those *good* institutions which come closest to the area of their interest—school or hospital or counseling center. This would permit them to obtain *on the side*, but *only* as a by-product, skills in dealing with these types of problems and techniques. The institution's training program itself would be directed *mainly* at the more general aspects of clinical psychology.

We are, of course, far from ready to carry out programs of this kind effectively. But now, after our first period of very serious, if fumbling, effort, aren't the signs fairly clear that this is the direction in which to turn our eyes and our efforts?

If you have detected some white heat in my less than sufficiently tactful remarks, you may be right. I hope a little more will be aroused by the discussion. With apologies to our chairman, I think what we need more of than flames is cool and collected self-evaluation while sitting on this moderately white-heated whatever-it-is. The situation calls for it—you and I and psychology can take it.

Discussion

The major problem raised by Dr. Shakow's paper—the integration of theory and practice, of the university and the field agency—elicited a good deal of discussion. Representatives both of universities and of field agencies agreed that, with the exception of a few programs, a satisfactory degree of integration had not yet been attained. Agency representatives complained that, too frequently, there was little or no communication between the university and the agency; that the university showed little interest in the teaching program of the agency or in the progress of the student during the internship; that the university seemed to consider theoretical training to be exclusively its own prerogative; that the university's bias in favor of "critical research" and elegance of experimental design tended to discourage interest and participation of students in research in the agency setting; that the university, in short, frequently made little or no effort to bridge the moat between the ivory tower and the field.

University representatives complained that agencies too frequently looked on interns as "cheap slave labor;" that service was emphasized to the exclusion of training or research; that the attitudes of agency personnel were too frequently anti-theoretical and tended to diminish the student's interest in his academic work. From the standpoints of all three parties involved—the university, the field agency, and the student—these criticisms indicated an unsatisfactory state of affairs. There was general agreement that closer integration must be established.

The achievement of this integration is a joint responsibility of the university and the field agency. The university must communicate to the agency the philosophy and objectives of its educational program and its responsibility for research training. The agency must communicate the nature of its service responsibilities, its training program, and its research interests. There must be a clear understanding that, insofar as the interns are concerned, training is the primary objective and the rendering of service by the intern must be incidental to his training. The acceptance of training responsibilities by an agency should involve a complete appraisal of its own structure, functions, and objectives as well as an understanding of the values, objectives, and methods of the university. The university must appreciate the fact that the relationship must provide satisfactions to the agency and must contribute to the discharge of the agency's primary functions.

Although the general tenor of the discussion was strongly in favor of closer integration between the university and the practicum agency, some reservations were voiced. The following statement was formulated to express this opinion:

Integration *per se* is not necessarily the main goal in university-agency relationships. The major goal should be providing good practicum training. In some instances, integration may be a way of providing good training by modifying orientations or raising standards in either the university or the agency. However, if good training is seen as the major goal, integration may, in some instances, detract from good training by failing to exploit the "different" points of view which may exist. Integration which aims at glossing over differences in equally respectable approaches to training may produce a harmonious local conventionalism with the consequent loss of the vigor which comes from different approaches. Often integration has the ulterior aim of "raising the standards" of the training agency. Where standards are low, or where the agency viewpoint is limited to technology, there can be little objection to integration. When, however, integration aims at unifying points of view to produce a locally conventional point of view, integration becomes suspect.

There was a time when graduate students were encouraged to spend a semester or a year at other universities. The assumption that intern agency and university programs should be "integrated" in order to avoid stresses on the student could hardly be reconciled with the commonly held assumption that the student should be exposed to a variety of points of view. Nor can one reconcile the integration notion with the obvious fact that students from some of our best universities could profit by an internship year at some of our best training agencies even though no "integration" was effected.

Such an attack on integration should not be construed as an attack on efforts to encourage communication between university and agency (in both directions) in order to accomplish better training for the student.

When the university operates the practicum agency, closer integration can be expected. Such an arrangement provides university staff members with an opportunity for practice with clients and a laboratory for clinical research. It ensures the placing of primary emphasis on training and encourages the maintenance of a research atmosphere. The research productivity of a number of university clinics and counseling centers is evidence of the value of an agency which is an integral part of the university.

Various methods of facilitating integration when the practicum training is offered in an independent agency were discussed. Consultant appointments on the agency staff for the university faculty and fuller utilization of faculty members not only as training consultants but for case, staff, and research consultations will increase mutual understanding. Equally important are university appointments for members of the agency staff. An opportunity to participate in the program of formal instruction, in discussions of the training program and in the periodic evaluation of interns will enhance the agency's interest in the integration of theoretical and practical training and will serve to reinforce the agency's commitment to its training function.

There was general agreement that the internship should provide a reasonable breadth of experience and that the primary criterion should be the quality of experience rather than the institutional setting in which the internship occurs. Diversity of experience may be achieved in a single agency if the clientele and functions are sufficiently varied, or by a rotating internship. A minimum of six months in any one agency, and not less than twenty hours per week, was considered desirable. It was suggested that agencies might be approved for training periods of different duration, depending upon the training potential of the agency.

The question of accreditation of practicum agencies was discussed at some length. While there was no objection to accreditation in principle, concern was expressed lest criteria for evaluating practicum agencies be crystallized prematurely. The discussion seemed to indicate that the amount of attention that has been given to this problem by various committees of the APA is not widely known. Accreditation was dealt with in some detail in the Shakow Report in 1947 and more briefly by the Boulder Conference in 1949, which recommended that "the APA take steps to study the problem and set up standards and procedures for evaluating internship training center." The Committee on Training in Clinical Psychology conducted a study which was published in 1950. With the dissolution of the CTCP, the Education and Training Board established a Committee on Practicum Training. Beginning in 1951, this committee organized a series of meetings with chief psychologists of a large number of agencies and with university representatives for discussion of criteria and procedures for accreditation. These meetings were held in different parts of the country, frequently in conjunction with meetings of the various regional associations. The committee began in 1951 to accumulate information on practicum agencies and by 1954 had made trial visits to 40 agencies in different parts of the country. These visits were guided by the criteria suggested by the CTCP Report and provided a fairly extensive basis for evaluation of these criteria. As a result of this experience, the committee revised the 1950 criteria and recommended that the E & T Board authorize the Committee on Evaluation to proceed with the accreditation of practicum agencies, which the E & T Board did during the current year. The Committee on Evaluation has formulated a plan of procedure, based on these revised criteria and will schedule visits to as many as possible of the 62 agencies which have currently requested accreditation.[2]

In spite of the study and experimentation that have gone into the present criteria, members of the Institute felt that further opportunity for discussion of criteria should be provided and were almost unanimous in the opinion that a conference on this subject should be scheduled in the near future.

Dr. Shakow's suggestion that the term "clinical psychologist" be extended to include counseling and school psychologists precipitated a heated discussion. One point of view stressed the medical connotation of the term "clinical." It was argued by some that clinical psychology should be synonymous with medical psychology; that training and practice should be restricted to a medical setting. This could include, as it does in medicine, concern with normal personality development and with the prevention of maladjustment. It would serve to designate the clinician engaged in public health activities as well as the individual working in a traditional clinical or hospital setting. It would have the advantage of maintaining the distinction between the clinical psychologist and counseling or school psychologists.

Recent surveys of opinion concerning reorganization of the divisional structure of the APA leave little doubt that the majority of members of the school, counseling, and clinical divisions wish to maintain their separate professional identities. Extension of the term "clinical" to include the other two fields is not likely to meet with approval in any of the divisions concerned.

On the other hand, as Dr. Raimy had pointed out in his paper, maintaining the distinctions among the areas of professional specialization does not require the maintenance of separate doctoral training programs. If a broader doctoral program were to be developed to provide basic professional training for the various special fields, it would be useful to have some term to designate this training, as the M.D. degree designates the completion of basic medical education. No generally satisfactory term was suggested during the discussion. The term "applied" was considered too broad, since it includes training, interests, and practice which lie outside the areas common to the counseling, school, and clinical fields. The term "professional," which is used in the title of American Board of Examiners in Professional Psychology, is almost synonymous with "applied" psychology but would probably be a somewhat more acceptable term.

[2] This program has proceeded and the initial list of approved agencies was published in the *American Psychologist* for December, 1956.

14. Seventeen Years Later: Clinical Psychology in the Light of the 1947 Committee on Training in Clinical Psychology Report

A decade after my period of direct and intensive preoccupation with the training of clinical psychologists, I was spontaneously roused to put down my reactions to the current scene. These were the thoughts of one who was no longer intimately involved with the current situation, seen in the context of the plans and hopes for clinical psychology held during its earlier period of development. The impending Chicago Conference on Professional Preparation of Clinical Psychologists also played a part in the decision to write this paper.

Psychology is admittedly an extremely difficult field; it has so many special burdens to bear. Rather than *being* a science, psychology is only *becoming* a science. Because of this developmental state and because of the nature of its phenomena, psychology depends on other disciplines for many of its advances; it so easily becomes bound up in metaphysical questions, and it has such trouble describing and measuring its variables with exactness. In addition, psychology is pestered above all other fields by amateur experts—for is not every man a psychologist?

In the light of such difficulties, the natural tendency of psychologists to escape into neurotic behavior or to slip into actions directed at obtaining immediate but secondary gains, rather than to deal frankly and humbly with primary problems, is understandable. The astute observer, however, is not fooled by these evasions, and it is not surprising when he becomes impatient with "poor dear psychology."

Faced as psychology now is by constantly growing demands to apply its rudimentary knowledge to the broad area of mental health, what from society's standpoint is the most desirable thing to do? What should psychologists in university training programs do? What should psychologists in the field do?

Having examined the complex issues repeatedly and from many different stances, and having considered the likely outcome of efforts of various kinds, I have been led to certain conclusions. I offer these as one person's view of the situation. Hopefully, it is an enlightened view since for over 30 years I was occupied and, for a considerable part of this span, preoccupied with the training of clinical psychologists *qua* psychologists. During the time of my deepest involvement, I participated in the writing of the 1947 Report, "Recommended Graduate Training Program in Clinical Psychology" (APA, CTCP, 1947). Although in the last decade my active engagement in this area has ceased, I have maintained a strong bond with clinical psychology. Perhaps because of this profound identification, I have been concerned about the present state of clinical psychology. I have had increasing misgivings about present trends in the field meeting the needs of psychology.

Reprinted with permission from the *American Psychologist,* vol. 20, 1965.

I state my conclusions baldly, and perhaps provocatively, from the very beginning. I expect that others holding different points of view will be as forthright—for only from a clear presentation of the many sides of the issues facing clinical psychology can suitable solutions arise.

These are my conclusions:

1. Psychology is immodest. It must become less assuming. This would allow it to become more accepting of itself and enable it to face the world with more assurance. Psychology must recognize that its principles are not those of physics nor its applications those of engineering. It must learn that permitting schismatic trends—whether these be splits within departments or substantial separations of training programs for different specialties—means evading the responsibilities of an undeveloped science.

2. Clinical psychology is *both* a basic and an applied area. A clinical psychologist is a psychologist with all that this identification implies.

3. Because of the undeveloped state of both psychology and clinical psychology, research is by far the most important responsibility of the clinical psychologist. However, an essential social function of the clinical psychologist does lie in the applied area—the practice of clinical psychology in institutions.

4. The university has primary responsibility for integrating training in both the basic and the applied areas. To assure adequate research in clinical psychology, a substantial part of training for research should be obtained in active, broadly based institutions. (These are, at least at present, most likely to be found in medical settings.) This training should be coupled with a systematic program of basic psychology. Training for applied clinical work should consist of a combination of a systematic program of basic psychology and substantial experience in clinical settings, and should be essentially of the same character as research training.

5. The private practice of clinical psychology is of minor importance. It should be restricted. It should be limited in every way possible to persons with considerable experience. However, since a substantial number of private practitioners are already in the field, psychology has a responsibility to upgrade the quality of their work.

Having stated my theses summarily, I shall now go on to examine the relationship of clinical psychology to psychology as a whole, focusing on the developments of the last two decades.

In October, 1944, at the request of the American Psychological Association and the American Association for Applied Psychology, a committee met at Vineland to consider the topic of "Graduate Internship Training in Psychology." The report of the Committee (APA & AAAP, 1945) recommended that the two associations implement a few experimental training programs in clinical psychology in which internships would be included as an integral part. These programs were to be supported, if possible, with foundation help, and would include fellowships to be awarded to students selected especially for the program. Some training in clinical psychology was available at that time, but it was scattered and unsystematic. The Committee members felt that the time had arrived for experimentation with systematically organized programs. The hope was that after several such programs had been in effect for some years, psychology would be in a better position to determine the future direction of clinical training and could then most profitably expand this training.

History, however, took the matter out of its hands. The years of the later '40s brought with them warborn demands for psychological services from the Veterans Administration and the Public Health Service, demands which these government agencies were ready to back up with hitherto unavailable support. And psychology then experienced what has been called a time of "breathless preoccupation with actual training [APA, 1947, p. 539]." The unusual opportunities offered psychology by both these federal organizations were, of course, beneficial in innumerable ways. But I have frequently felt that these developments were premature. Psychology was just then entering a period of slow and careful experimentation, experimentation that might have provided an opportunity to learn what was desirable and necessary in clinical training. Training institutions, whether universities or field centers, were far from ready to deal optimally with their problems. It was, therefore, a particularly inappropriate time to be overwhelmed with a superfluity of riches. Greed, coupled with feelings of inadequacy and insecurity, often led to making compensatory claims in which the more moderate psychologists were merely ready to take over the earth, but the more ambitious the heavens as well. (We were not alone in this, of course; some of our sister professions who were equally favored showed similar symptoms of grandiosity.) Had the pace of development been more leisurely, more favorable results might have been obtained. Certainly greater understanding of clinical psychology by non-clinical psychology faculty members would have been promoted. Instead, the engulfing character of the clinical influx contributed to the development of negative attitudes toward the clinical parvenus, attitudes which have continued seriously to plague psychology to this day.

It was against this background that the Committee on Training in Clinical Psychology (CTCP), appointed by the Board of Directors of APA, was occupied during the spring and summer of 1947 with the writing of a report which described a "Recommended Graduate Training Program in Clinical Psychology" (APA, CTCP, 1947). The Report was presented to and accepted by the Council of Representatives at the September, 1947, meeting and ordered published in the *American Psychologist* for December, 1947. It has since set a general pattern for clinical training programs. In the intervening period there have been two major conferences on training in clinical psychology—Boulder (Raimy, 1950) and Stanford (Strother, 1956). The Miami conference (Roe, 1959), although called to discuss general graduate training, tended to emphasize clinical training. In addition, there have been several minor conferences on related aspects of psychology. But in one way or another the essential points in the reports of these conferences have corroborated the general recommendations of the 1947 Report. As the report on the Boulder conference (Raimy, 1950)—the major grass-roots conference and the most important for the development of clinical psychology—stated, its deliberations "gave very considerable support to the policies that were specifically outlined or implied in the *1947 Report*" (p. 17).

The CTCP had assumed that training programs of the kind recommended in

1947 would naturally produce three types of persons: those who were identified with the teaching and research aspects of clinical psychology; those who were connected with institutional and community clinic practice but who in various ways continued to maintain an abiding interest and involvement in research; and a relatively limited number of persons who might, after considerable additional experience and training, enter into some form of private practice. The Committee had also expected—as expressed in the contemporaneous reports of the Policy and Planning Board and of other official committees—that, because of the uncertainties with which this third area in particular abounded, practice would be carried out mainly in group settings.

The Committee stressed especially the need for developing in clinical psychology a prototype of the "scientist-professional." The model was that of a person who, with a background of professional skills, maintained a strong interest in personality and psychopathology research.[1]

This principle of combined scientific and professional training, both explicit and implicit in the Report, was reiterated by the Boulder conference (Raimy, 1950). More recently it has perhaps been best expressed in Stuart Cook's (1958) thoughtful article.

The Report and the evaluation visits of the Committee which followed during this early period were intended to set a *general* pattern and provide a sample program for training centers. The Committee had presented an illustrative program and tried hard to get across the notion that: "Here is the *kind* of minimum program toward which we should strive. This is the *sort* of thing which training might be like." The Report was certainly not intended as a blueprint. (Perhaps the generality of the recommended program was not emphasized as effectively as it might have been, but one wonders if anything more persuasive *could* possibly have been said.)

During the period following the publication of the CTCP Report, many forces were unleashed. Let us successively examine the developments as they appeared in the universities, in the activities of the APA and its committees, and in the reactions of the students.

Although as I have indicated, the CTCP Report was intended to set a *general* pattern for training programs, only a few universities perceived it as intended. They were among the more secure universities, long accustomed to doctoral training and its problems, appreciating the fact that the responsibility for actual training was ultimately theirs. Some universities were quite negativistic; nobody was going to tell them how to run *their* departments! And some—the majority—looked at the Report

[1] The educational principle behind this formulation was similar to the assumption that guides the best and most effective medical training: If an institution educates students in an atmosphere of research and inquiry in the clinical setting, it is likely to imbue even those going into practice with the continuing attitude of inquiry necessary for the development of the field, as well as for producing the most competent researchers. A scientific area belongs ultimately to its investigators, not to its practitioners. No field can maintain its vitality, in fact its viability, without such a group. One of the most cogent criticisms that can be made of psychoanalysis at the present time is that it has neglected this indispensable rule for growth.

as Sinaitic, a second set of commandments handed down from on high.[2] (It actually took much self-control on the part of the Committee not to be seduced into the adoption of this tempting Jehovic role. The Committee members did not, however, deserve too much credit for this restraint; credit should go largely to the very understanding and tolerant superego provided by the APA Council and the Board of Directors which the members were able to introject.)

A special aspect of the negativistic attitude was reflected in the passivity of "experimentalists" in many university departments. As seasoned psychologists, they already knew many of the problems of graduate education in psychology, and had worked out ways for meeting them. Although their methods might not have been directly applicable, they could very well have taken the attitude of "big brothers," and provided the support and positive context in which any new program must be nurtured. In a few places such an encouraging attitude did prevail. But this was rare. In many places there was indifference. And in most places active antagonism was perhaps the most characteristic response.

Although the sudden wealth in the form of clinical fellowships and the initially comparatively high quality of clinical students played their parts in arousing the experimentalists, their sensitivities seemed to center around "purity." Elsewhere (Shakow, 1949c) I have spoken of this attitude[3] as the naïve division of the world into two categories: virgins and prostitutes. The experimentalists saw themselves safely within the first group, engirdled by their chastity belts daintily embroidered with the motto "unapplied." They found it difficult to appreciate that they actually lived in a complex world in which there existed a wide range of virtuous productive love relationships between the two extremes. These psychologists did not see that clinical activity was not necessarily prostitution. They did not see that it could encompass basic work carried out in a different kind of "laboratory," that in fact the "applied" aspect of the work was essential to establishing the validity of the phenomena studied, and that such validity was so often lacking in much existing laboratory-derived psychological data. They did not see that the combination of theory with field work might prove as valuable for the fundamental development of psychology as their own combination of theory with laboratory work. They not only sniped

[2] It was most discouraging for Committee members during their evaluation visits to be met by representatives of some of the departments under consideration with a checked-off list of the *exact* courses which the published Report gave only as *examples*, with the implication that *now* the department was obviously ready for approval. One can speculate about the background for this defensiveness. Was it due to the inexperience of departments in a new field? Was it due to a desire to get as rapidly as possible onto the bandwagon? Was it due to a recognition of social need, prompted by wartime experiences, and of the lack of proper personnel to carry out such programs? Was it based on some perseverative assumption of the simplicity of the task gained from previous experiences with training M.A. "psychometricians"? All of these, and probably other factors, undoubtedly played greater or lesser parts.

[3] Koch (1959), in his perceptive analysis of the recent history of psychology, has characterized an attitude related to the one here described as "scientism." I, myself, have considered the problem he refers to in the context of the peculiar self-consciousness of psychology (Shakow, 1953b).

at and failed to support clinical programs, but they frequently actually obstructed their development.

The splits which have taken place in some departments, the frequent threats of secession from the APA of some in the experimental area,[4] those from Division 3 in particular, and to some extent the development of the Psychonomic Society, may from one point of view be seen as congruent with this general "purity complex." This in the context of the growing trend to professionalization in *all* branches of psychology, including experimental (Tryon, 1963)!

Compensating for these developments, however, has been an enhanced theoretical concern with personality, both normal and abnormal, in departments of psychology. It is a rare department that has not been shaken up by the influx of students interested in personality, personality theory, and Freud. Even the few departments in which the development of clinical psychology resulted in an actual split have shown this trend in their experimental sections. And in association with this theoretical concern has certainly come a much greater interest in personality research.[5]

Looking back, the major factor that permitted the development of these forces in the universities was a lack of adequately trained and sufficiently secure persons in clinical psychology. Indeed the relative rarity of teachers highly competent in both the theoretical and research aspects of the field, as well as in clinical practice, remains a serious weakness. The lack was revealed in the failure of even the most sympathetic of university faculty—clinical and non-clinical—to appreciate the cost of an internship and the investment of individual teaching and supervision involved (Shakow, 1957). It resulted in a paucity of "proper" models for the students to identify with, models which in Frankfurter's (1962) terms not only lay the patterns of future professional standards but make it possible to "breathe in ethics" during graduate training. Despite its subtlety, this factor is perhaps the most important in the development of the attitudes of the psychologist—whether he be researcher, teacher, or private practitioner.

Adding to these difficulties—or perhaps merely another side of them, considering the relatively few competent teachers available—was the extremely large number of students taken on for training, and the precipitous pace at which this training was instituted in many universities.

Part of the problem, too, may have been the nature of the recruitment process. Selection and number of students are inevitably affected by the limited representation of psychology in high schools. Furthermore, during the writing of the 1947

[4] The irony of the situation is that we perseverate in this anachronistic use of "experimental" for certain limited aspects of psychology, particularly for the areas of sensation, perception, and physiological-comparative, in spite of the tremendous spread of the experimental approach through the whole range of psychology.

[5] Unfortunately, part of this interest has resulted in the escape into using college students as subjects. This type of research misses the great opportunities for theoretical development that acquaintance with the more profound phenomena of psychopathology and real field situations can provide. Further, this kind of "personality" research can so easily serve as a camouflage by taking the curse off being considered a "clinician," one different from researchers in other areas of psychology.

Report, it was assumed that Ph.D. candidates would remain of the same general kind as the colleagues of Committee members in their own graduate days. The question that now arises is: Have shifting educational policies changed the qualities of the students, or have the kinds of students themselves seeking graduate training changed? Any changes in the nature of the students may have had their reciprocal effects on the nature of the programs provided. Whatever the sequence, however, there appears to have been a disproportionate decline in the number of "rigorously" and "academically" oriented students, even if intellectual ability has remained constant.

Nevertheless, there has been an increase in skilled researchers and practitioners. Most have come from institutions where standards have been maintained and where at least a reasonably comfortable relationship exists between academic and clinical psychology. It must be admitted, however, that some have also come from centers where standards have not been of the highest level, and others from centers where the relationships were far from comfortable. Fortunately, exceptionally good people manage in one way or another to educate themselves!

With the passing of the years, and perhaps in the effort to deal with the academic problem we have just described, setting up clinical psychology training programs at the doctoral level in medical schools has been considered. Serious question must be raised about the wisdom of such a decision. Although medical schools and their associated hospitals are most valuable as training centers for clinical psychologists (even though subsequent work may be carried out in the community, the university, or other settings), they are best utilized as field training centers. In fact, for the present, good medical institutions offer the best kind of field training, because the patients who come to them are motivated by "suffering" and "need." I say this despite the fact that such a large number of psychiatrists are still insufficiently educated to working with colleagues, and tend to instill attitudes of second-class citizenship in their associates. I have dealt with this problem in detail elsewhere (Shakow, 1949c). The clientele who come to milquetoast university clinics are a far cry from the kind met with in medical centers. (This is to say nothing about the relatively less responsible way in which these university clinics are ordinarily conducted. Indeed some of the case material which has been used in some training institutions is a travesty on the term "clinical.")

Thus it seems reasonable to continue to insist on the principle emphasized in the 1947 Report: that clinical psychologists are psychologists first and clinicians second. This identification is particularly difficult to achieve in an environment where psychology is necessarily of minor importance. If for no other reason, then, the major, or perhaps better, the sole responsibility for the training and granting of doctoral degrees should lie with departments of psychology.

The difficulties of clinical training programs might have been eased had the APA, through its committees, strongly encouraged the implementation of the principles of the 1947 Report. The CTCP had followed its 1947 Report by a brief report on evaluated institutions in 1948 (APA, CTCP, 1948), and a more detailed consideration of the problem of evaluation in 1949 (APA, CTCP, 1949). The latter report, subsequent reports of CTCP after I left the Committee, and the Report of the Boulder conference, constantly reiterated the point that the Committee had never intended to establish "requirements." It had consistently presented a *model* of a program, leaving it to the universities and field training centers to design their own programs accordingly. The APA might have taken a firm stand on enforcing the *principles* behind the model while simultaneously permitting a range of experimentation in their implementation. However, evaluations based on flexible standards are admittedly the most difficult to make. There is always a tendency when faced with the difficulty of making a complex judgment to resort to easily formulated and relatively rigid "rules" and "regulations." And it is my impression—admittedly based on a limited knowledge of the developing situation—that there has been an increasing tendency to substitute the fulfillment of formal requirements for a sophisticated and careful upholding of the fundamental principles behind clinical training programs. Standards seem to have been generally lowered. This may be partially reflected in the shift from the 20 schools rated A or A—, recommended for full approval, and the 23 programs rated B or C for only one-year temporary approval in 1948 (see APA, CTCP, 1949), to the 55 given full approval and the seven given interim approval in 1963 (Ross, 1963).

As indicated earlier, the Committee had worked on the assumption that only a relatively small proportion of the trainees would enter private practice, and then only after considerable experience beyond their doctorate. And it had expected that group practice would predominate. Instead, a surprisingly large proportion of persons has entered the private practice of clinical psychology, particularly of psychotherapy, and almost entirely as single entrepreneurs.

E. Lowell Kelly (1961) estimated in 1960 that 17 per cent of Division 12 membership (about 350) were involved in private practice as their *primary* work setting. Albee (1963) estimated that 6 per cent of the total APA membership (about 1,200) is involved in the full-time private practice of clinical psychology, and he predicts the number will increase considerably.

With the extended concern with psychotherapy has come a proportionately decreased concern with psychodiagnosis and with the developing and perfecting of psychodiagnostic tools. Psychodiagnosis has gradually become infra dig. Meehl (1960) to the contrary, psychodiagnosis is an important function of the clinical psychologist.[6] If his tools now fall far short of the optimal, then it is certainly part of his task to continue to work upon them until they are improved. An attitude of resignation ill becomes a relatively new field, especially when this attitude can easily bolster rationalization for avoidance of less profitable or less prestigeful areas.[7]

[6] It should be pointed out that Meehl's data derive from adults, and even if there is some present justification for his point of view concerning adults, it does not follow that his strictures hold in the child area.

[7] There is a central problem here which needs careful thinking through. Assuming that psychologists are able to work out adequate psychodiagnostic devices, how are they to be used? If they are merely to be "integrated" into a psychiatrist's report, then the likelihood of serious work in this area is not very great. However, if the psychologist's diagnostic report is treated as the independent opinion of an expert to be considered in the context of several experts' opinions on a case—a procedure which is common in the best institutions—then the field is likely to attract workers. No professional person can with dignity accept the role of a technician who merely provides data for another person to "report."

What are the reasons for such a steadily growing concern with psychotherapy? In the public sphere there has emerged an increasing readiness, in this highly psychology-conscious period, to pay for services of a psychotherapeutic nature.[8] For professionals, the fleshpot has presented temptations. Many, perhaps too many, psychologists have tended to model themselves on those physicians in private practice, particularly psychiatrists, whose income levels are beyond rational toleration. The minority-group problem affects some psychologists who feel that in a culture where prejudices still play a role in preventing favorable employment or in obstructing promotion opportunities, the greatest security lies in being "one's own boss." Competition with and antagonism to the physician also probably play a role.[9] The universities contribute to the encouragement of private practice by the provision of opportunities to add to income through consultations. Moreover, in all areas of psychology changes in values are accompanying modifications of practice.

Because of increasing urbanization and the shortage of professionals, it is unlikely that this trend toward private practice will, in the ordinary course of events, be reversed. Are we really heading for the time when, as Albee (1963) says, "we may hear our APA Executive Officer testifying before the Congress against every piece of legislation that smacks of socialized psychology!" (p. 95)?

I have so far been considering past developments in the field of clinical psychology. However, as a result of the recent bills passed by Congress[10]—outgrowths of the work of the Joint Commission on Mental Illness and Health (1961) and the efforts of President Kennedy—the field of mental health has been handed new responsibilities which are of the greatest significance for psychology. Implicit in the legislation is the mandate that psychological principles be applied to groups (particularly the underpriviliged) which have heretofore received little consideration in mental health programs. To this end, psychologists will have to be most ingenious and unconventional in developing treatment and training techniques. (An interesting account of beginning efforts along this line will be found in Rioch, Elkes, Flint, Sweet, Newman, & Silber, 1965; see also Riessman & National Institute of Labor Education, 1964.) It is thus in relation to the major problems of training persons who can take the more traditional roles in society and of preparing

[8] A positive aspect of this concern, as Albee (1963) has pointed out, has been the general upward trend of salaries in all areas of psychology. The development of clinical psychological private practice has set a pattern and, in this respect, has had a helpful impact on the rest of the field.

[9] I have considered the general problem of the relations between psychology and psychiatry at length in a paper published some years ago (Shakow, 1949c). The issues are very complicated and paradoxical. There is a great deal of rationalization and defensiveness on both sides, all of which is ironical in the context of the inexhaustible amount of work for everybody to do! I might add that my own experience has been that for competent and mature psychologists the problem is not very significant. But the problem *is* serious for the younger worker. This prompts an even louder call for training in settings where supervision by the competent and mature is available.

[10] Pub. L. No. 129, 88th Cong., 1st Sess. (Sept. 24, 1963); Pub. L. No. 156, 88th Cong., 1st Sess. (Oct. 24, 1963); Pub. L. No. 164, 88th Cong., 1st Sess. (Oct. 31, 1963).

those who will be able to take on new roles that we must consider the future of clinical psychology.[11]

While this article was in preparation, the January 1964 issue of the *American Psychologist* brought the news that the APA had received a grant from the National Institute of Mental Health in support of a "Conference on Professional Preparation of Clinical Psychologists." Such a conference affords clinical psychology an unusual opportunity to discuss the major problems of training for old and new roles, to consider past errors of commission and omission, to examine how far and why achievement has fallen below initial aspiration, and to develop ways for upgrading performance.

Two points, relating to the general principles which seem to underlie the Conference, are important to consider.

First, a clear establishment of a true order of priorities—the putting of first things first. Obviously training for *competence* has top priority, whereas status problems, such as certification and licensure, which largely grow out of competitiveness with medicine, are of quite minor importance. (I hope, however, that time will be taken for a discussion of these problems to impress the conferees with how secondary they are, and how minimal are the criteria usually established. How much protection of the public is really involved?)

Second, the reexamination of the relationship of clinical psychology to other fields of psychology, and of its place within the discipline of psychology. Previous conferences have tended to take this problem for granted, but now an earnest effort should be made to solve it. It is unlikely that the problem can be solved through the establishment of a dual degree system.

In addition to these general issues, there are, besides, a whole series of specific points bearing on the future roles and contributions of clinical psychologists which the Conference needs to consider. These include:

1. Ways of training for research in clinical psychology. The role of the university, the role of the field center, and the relationship between the two types of institutions call for careful articulation. Concomitantly, the concept of research needs redefinition so it will encompass the most rigorous laboratory research and systematic naturalistic observation, whichever is appropriate. It should also allow for the contributions which can come from a serious attitude of inquiry leading to deliberate efforts to answer questions which arise during clinical operations.

2. Ways of training for the most effective application of clinical psychology to institutional and community settings. Here again the function of each of the training agencies and the integration of their work need elaboration.

3. Delineation of new and potentially likely areas for clinical research and practice and consideration of ways of training for them. This calls for much imaginative thinking. New methods of therapy, new methods of diagnosis, and particularly

[11] We might also note in passing the development of more accepting attitudes toward psychologists that is reflected in the Jenkins decision in relation to expert testimony (Hoch & Darley, 1962), and the agreements that the APA has been able to get from prepaid medical plans for payment for psychotherapy by psychologists. Clinical psychologists must become worthy of such developments.

preventive methods of education are becoming increasingly important and demanding of especial attention.

4. University training programs. The proper university setting for training in clinical psychology should be described and the importance of programs coming from unified departments and unified programs spelled out. The nature of the doctoral degree granted to clinical psychologists calls for special consideration. The place and nature of post-doctoral programs, especially such programs for psychotherapy training,[12] should be given equal consideration.

5. The composition, responsibilities, and standards of committees that evaluate the performance of institutions, both universities and field centers, and those that regulate the activities of individuals, such as the American Board of Examiners in Professional Psychology and state licensing and certification boards, should be reexamined.

6. Ways should be considered for continuously upgrading research and practice in the field. Periodic regional conferences to deal with the details of existing and potential training programs might be one area of effort in this direction.

7. Methods for limiting the private practice of psychology should be reviewed. This would involve setting more rigorous criteria—experiential, legal, and ethical.

The above presents a formidable agenda, but one which cannot be reduced if the Conference is to be a success.[13]

Underlying these basic considerations is the question: What kind of profession do we want? What we get depends to a great extent on whether we pay attention to our own inadequacies and are mainly concerned about getting the best training program, or whether we look elsewhere, using the natural tendency to project our difficulties. For one interested in psychodynamics, the situation is pathetic. Koch's defensive "scientism," accompanied as it is by a condescension to clinical psychology, is pervasive. At the same time, the inferiority feelings of clinical psychologists toward the "experimentalists," and their so ready acceptance of a relatively low status, is appalling, whether this is expressed by acceptance or defensive hostility.

[12] Until society is ready for a program of the kind proposed by Kubie (1954) and discussed in detail at the Gould House "Conference on an Ideal Program of Training for Psychotherapists" (cf. Report of Conference, 1963), psychology is faced with the serious obligations of developing competent psychotherapists from members of its own discipline and of overseeing their practice of this especially difficult art and science.

[13] Perhaps the best general preparation for the "Conference on Professional Preparation" would be to have a group of both clinical and non-clinical senior psychologists from training universities, clinical centers, and interested agencies meet prior to the Conference to rethink the whole problem of clinical training in the light of the experiences of the past two decades. With the goal of outlining programs of the highest quality, this committee should review carefully the present quality of students, the level of training, and the nature of the factors that play a role in the development of clinicians. The committee could then prepare a report which might serve as the central document to be discussed by the Conference. A report of this kind is needed to give focus and direction to a large conference. Without it the Conference is likely to flounder.

All material and suggestions in this article (and in the first paragraph of this footnote) were prepared before the appearance of a pre-Conference report in the March issue of this journal (see Zimet, 1965).

It is unnecessary to emphasize what this does to the self-image of the clinical psychologist as psychologist, and indirectly of psychology.

We will not have a generation of upstanding clinical psychologists until these symptoms disappear in psychology and until there are sufficient models of adequate teachers in all areas who clearly and effectively represent their own particular areas of interest.

So where do we end up?

If I were empowered to speak for clinical psychology, I would say this to the academic psychologists:

Come off it! Too many of you have helped to perpetrate a lot of nonsense on psychology and on clinical psychology. Part of the reason for this is to be found in your overreactive concern with premature experimental rigor which leads you to be particularly sensitive about possible identification with areas of psychology which by definition cannot (and should not) meet such standards. This need to be more *echt* than the *echt*est of scientists leads you to be particularly harsh on clinical psychology. In very considerable part this appears to be the basis for the induction of a reactive defensiveness in clinical psychologists and for the encouragement of separatist trends among them.

I would add that clinical psychology is important both because of the contribution it has made and is making to basic psychology, and because of the potential social significance of its practical contribution. I would say that I recognize that the private practice of clinical psychology is largely an escape, and that the rush into the practice of psychotherapy probably falls into the same category.

I would insist that clinical psychology be taught in the context of a total psychology—general, theoretical, physiological-comparative, child, social—centered on university departments that are representative of all of psychology, and that clinical psychology enjoy the active participation of the academicians. Further, I would stress that the universities themselves call upon the APA to maintain high standards of evaluation for clinical training.

And I would in turn say to the clinical psychologists: Working at the highest possible level of rigor, make yourselves competent in your field on the basis of both basic psychology and good field training. I would urge such clinical psychologists to stick to their guns, and admonish them that they have nothing to be defensive about. Rather I would say that they are dealing with an important phase of psychology which needs much cultivation. I would emphasize the research aspects of the field and suggest that clinical psychologists avoid escaping into either private practice or premature psychotherapy, whether to avoid the criticism of academic colleagues or to meet personal needs.

Even under the best of circumstances, achievement falls below aspiration level. Psychology must therefore try to develop programs which aim high if it is to reach a reasonably optimal level. Fortunately, a few powerful voices are being raised in our best universities and among our outstanding field centers about such problems as I have been dealing with here. Unless we heed these voices, we are likely to end up serving ourselves instead of serving others—concentrating on the "gimmies" rather than the "givethees"—the opposite of what a true discipline and a good profession calls for.

15. Thoughts Second and Sober on Education in Clinical Psychology

On April 13–14, 1967, the Judge Baker Guidance Center held its Fiftieth Anniversary Celebration. I was asked to be one of the speakers. Since I was especially concerned about a situation in clinical psychology that had developed at an important local university, I selected as my topic the problem of education in clinical psychology (in the context of professional training generally). In developing my major points I used material from some of my previous papers on this topic, particularly Nos. 13 and 21 (republished in this volume). This seemed justifiable on the grounds that this was intended to be my last major statement about training problems.

For purposes of a publication such as the present, there would appear less justification for such an overlap. However, in order to maintain the flow of the original presentation it seemed advisable not to omit these parts.[1]

I am deeply grateful to the Judge Baker group for inviting me to participate in this significant anniversary celebration. Let me add a small brick to your historical edifice. My association with the Judge Baker goes back, if not quite to the beginning of the period we are celebrating, to a period not very much later. In 1924, as a senior across the river, I took Richard Cabot's course in Social Ethics on "The Kingdom of Evils." In this course, Cabot brought in outstanding persons who would meet with the class to discuss the particular "Evil" that he represented. Among these was William Healy who talked with us about juvenile psychopathology.

I don't quite know what the relationship was between Cabot and Healy. Ideologically they must have had at least a few differences. I think of Healy as a Jamesian, interested in psychoanalysis and psychopathology, and having a point of view which enabled him to pioneer in setting up the first dynamically oriented child guidance clinic in Chicago in 1909 (Shakow, 1948a). Cabot, on the other hand, was a Roycean, rather dead set against psychopathology and psychoanalysis, and interested in the non-psychiatric side of medicine and social issues.[2] He *also* was a pioneer as seen in his initiative in setting up medical social work at the Massachusetts General Hospital in 1905 (Cabot, 1919).

However, Richard Cabot had as prodigious a superego as any two persons

Reprinted with permission from George E. Gardner, Director, Judge Baker Guidance Center, prior to publication.

[1] In the preparation of this paper I have cribbed unconscionably from previous papers on training in which I have had a part in writing (APA, CTCP, 1947; APA & AAAP, 1945; Shakow, 1946, 1947, 1948a, 1949c, 1957, 1965).

[2] I know of his attitudes with regard to psychoanalysis and psychopathology from a variety of sources, especially in relation to his views on the psychopathology emphasis in the theological training program set up at the Worcester State Hospital by Anton Boisen.

combined are entitled to. So if he felt the way I have described him, he would have been the very first to insist that a person with an opposite point of view be heard. Especially so if it involved the education of young people. Hence Healy in our course. Healy's talk had been preceded by a reading assignment which included a few of the little blue book case records, which, as I recall, the Judge Baker had been putting out at that time. Although I had known of Healy before, from my readings in other courses, it was a thrilling experience to come into such close contact with him.

I did have some further association with Drs. Healy and Bronner through Dr. Grace Kent in a year I spent at the Worcester State Hospital between my undergraduate and graduate work, but my main contacts with Healy came when my formal graduate days were over.

It was after I returned to Worcester in 1928 that I served on a committee which was responsible for Sam Hartwell's coming to the Worcester Child Guidance Clinic. Hartwell, after a long and successful career as a general practitioner in the Iowa countryside, had decided to provide himself with more formal training in psychiatry, which he had been practicing on an informal basis throughout his medical career. He took this training at Judge Baker. Instead of returning to his Iowa practice, he decided to stay in child psychiatry. Fortunately for us, the Directorship of the Clinic at Worcester was vacant in 1929 and, when Healy recommended him strongly, we took him on with enthusiasm. This provided another link with Judge Baker, for while he was at Worcester he reported on the "55 'bad' boys" (Hartwell, 1931) he had "fathered" at J.B.—a family which he increased many-fold at Worcester. The writing of this volume necessitated frequent trips to Boston. Throughout his period at Worcester he maintained regular contacts with his Boston alma mater; I was at times privileged to share these.

And then there have been the years of continuing friendly association with George Gardner at Judge Baker, in GAP, Ortho, and elsewhere. So when I have on occasion claimed a remote cousinship, perhaps I was not being too demanding!

When I last talked at Judge Baker my topic was on research. Today I am talking about education. I have some degree of embarrassment about selecting this topic since anybody who is at all acquainted with my writings should ask the obvious question: "Have you really anything new to say on this topic?" It was self-questioning of this kind which led to the hesitation. I suppose what finally led me to settle on this topic was the conclusion that much of what I have said in the past needed to be brought together, and that more common principles underlay the education of professional people generally than I had at one time been aware of. And what more appropriate place to talk about training than Judge Baker, which has had such a long and distinguished history in the education of professional persons connected with the mental health fields.

Educational Principles

As I was thinking of this talk, an excerpt came to mind from a letter written by Thoreau to Emerson over a century and a quarter ago, after a visit the former paid to Henry James, Sr. Thoreau wrote: "It makes humanity seem more erect and respectable . . . . I know of no one so patient and determined to have the good of you . . . ." [Sanborn, 1894, p. 95.]

I know of few better ways than this to introduce a discussion of the educational principles involved in the training of persons who are to work with other human beings. I plan to consider those principles which are common to all professional persons of this kind, those working in mental health, in particular, and especially those in clinical psychology. It is only in relation to the last, however, that I shall presume to outline a program of education as well.

In addition to substantive knowledge in his own special field, certain characteristics describe the psychosocially-oriented professional whose ultimate goal is to help people. Foremost among these is the recognition of the importance of attitudes in interpersonal relationships. Without the central acceptance of the all-importance of the attitudes of the client, patient, or anyone coming for help, the professional would find it difficult to function optimally. Integral to this, of course, the professional person must himself possess a warm but objective approach toward others.

Besides this characteristic, such professional persons should have developed in their approach to problems in their particular fields an apperceptive mass which is a combination of the following five principles that underlie the understanding of personality. (1) The *genetic* principle, which acknowledges the importance of antecedents in development, to account for present manifestations of personality. (2) The recognition of the *cryptic*, of unconscious and preconscious factors as crucial determiners of behavior. This point of view recognizes that behavior has, besides the obvious conscious motivation, further underlying motivations which are rarely perceptible to the actor, and frequently not even to the trained observer except with the use of special techniques. (3) The *dynamic* notion that behavior is drive-determined, that beneath behavior ultimately lie certain innate or acquired drives. (4) The general *psychobiological* principle that the personality is integral and indivisible, that there is a pervasive interrelationship between psyche and soma. This involves as well the acceptance of an organismic principle of total rather than segmental personality. (5) The *psychosocial* principle, which recognizes the integration of the individual and his environment as a unit, that drives and their derivatives are expressed in individual response within a social context, and that the social is of equal importance with the individual in the determination of behavior.

Implementation of the Program

I suppose I could just say that the obvious solution to the problem of implementing education for all groups is to follow the principle of the "three goods": Get good teachers to give good students good training. Unfortunately we cannot all quite agree on the definition of these "goods," so it becomes necessary to spell them out.

I shall in this section on the implementation of the program deliberately select the clinical psychologist for specific consideration. Many of the principles and techniques I shall consider are relevant for other professional groups, but I leave these open to your own selection and modification.

May I say from the very beginning that I shall be proposing a "druthers" program, and very clearly my own "druthers." I can afford to be independent and forthright since I am in the luxurious position of representing only myself. I believe that much of what I say will find sympathetic response among many psychologists, a little among fewer, and none, perhaps, among some—although I think the last is unlikely. Happily, a great deal of what I argue for has been achieved in some places during the last twenty years, the period during which so much thought and action has gone into training in clinical psychology.

One principle in the present era of education in clinical psychology has been most prominent. It is that the goal of such training is the development of a combined *scientist-professional.* This was first set forth in the 1947 report of the Committee on Training in Clinical Psychology's "Recommended Graduate Training Program in Clinical Psychology" (APA, CTCP, 1947). The model was that of a person who, while developing a background of professional skills, continued to maintain a strong interest in personality and psychopathology research.[3] This principle of combined scientific and professional training, both explicit and implicit in the Report, was reiterated by the training universities represented at the Boulder Conference (Raimy, 1950). More recently it has perhaps been best expressed in Stuart Cook's (1958) article, and in the report of the Chicago Conference (Hoch, Ross & Winder, 1966)[4] held in 1965.

The CTCP had assumed that training programs of the kind recommended would naturally produce three types of persons: those who were identified with the teaching and research aspects of clinical psychology; those who were connected with institutional and community clinic practice but who in various ways continued to maintain an abiding interest and involvement in research; and a relatively limited number of persons who might, after considerable additional experience and training, enter into some form of private practice. The Committee had also expected that, because of the uncertainties with which this third area in particular abounded, practice would be carried out mainly in group settings.

As for the content of the training programs, it was recognized that there was a need for preparing clinical psychologists with a combination of theoretical and applied knowledge in four major areas: diagnosis, therapy, prevention, and research.

What characteristics does a person fitted for this work possess? Obviously many combinations of qualities are variously suitable for the range of activities among which clinical psychologists will be able to choose. Some of these qualities, too, are

[3] The educational principle behind this formulation was the assumption that if an institution educates students in an atmosphere of research and inquiry in the clinical setting, it is likely to imbue even those going into practice with the continuing attitude of inquiry necessary for the development of the field as well as to produce the most competent researchers. A scientific area—indeed a profession—belongs ultimately to its investigators, not to its practitioners. No field can maintain its vitality, in fact its viability, without such a group. One of the most cogent criticisms that can be made of psychoanalysis at the present time is that it has neglected this indispensable rule for growth.

[4] I must say, however, that I agree heartily with Saul Rosenzweig's (1967) criticism of the Report as a whole in his "Topograph Bolder." The Report *does* lack the vigor and spirit of the Boulder Report.

those which become manifest and develop only during training. But, aside from superior scholastic ability, the potentials for resourcefulness, sensitivity, integrity, and acceptance of responsibility must be there. Some of the principles of selection which have been found successful for the Peace Corps (Stein, 1966) are relevant.[5]

My own experience has been that the best selective device for obtaining acceptable persons is the recommendation of college teachers who have proved themselves at the recommendation bar—those who are understanding of what it takes to work effectively in the clinical field and who have knowledge, objectivity, and sensitivity to personality.

Given the proper kind of person, what relevant *pre-professional* background experience and training may we expect of him? I shall first consider the non-academic, informal, experiential background of the person. Since it seems reasonable to expect the clinical psychologist to be interested in people and have a broad base of human contacts, he should have had experiences, particularly in his college years (summer holidays and other spare time), involving close relations with both ordinary and unusual persons in field, factory, institution, or laboratory. In addition to direct contact with people of various kinds, he should have had the indirect acquaintance with people that comes from immersion in great literature, because of the emphasis which such portrayals place on the molar aspects of behavior and the insights into human nature they give.

What formal educational background may we expect from the candidate who is entering the graduate program? Two distinct points of view are generally expressed. On the one hand, there is some demand that students come with a common, fairly defined background, especially in psychology, in order to make graduate instruction easier. On the other hand, some hold that, for the broad development of the field, to draw all the participants from the same mold would be undesirable. The solution probably lies somewhere between the two points of view. It seems to me that certain general requirements for the undergraduate program which the student could ordinarily be expected to meet can be laid down. But it is most important to constantly allow for exceptions.

The undergraduate program should be directed at providing a broad cultural and scientific base for specialized graduate study. In the context of a liberal arts background, the courses should help the student to attain a first insight into the structure and dynamics of human behavior, an understanding of the biological and social development of the individual, a preliminary acquaintance with the principles and methods of collecting and evaluating data, and an early contact with simpler case material. Although the undergraduate program must be recognized as *pre*-professional, some professional material might be introduced toward the end of the undergraduate period. Even though the professional and the more advanced courses in psychology should in general not be open to the undergraduate, we must ever keep in mind that the kinds of students we select have amazing potentialities for development and that as much as possible should be done to give them responsibilities early.

[5] Carl Rogers has a thoughtful article about this problem in the *Clinical Psychologist* for Winter 1967.

The basic principles which I consider important in the *professional education* itself are the following:

1. A clinical psychologist must first and foremost be a *psychologist* in the sense that he can be expected to have a point of view and a core of knowledge and training which is common to all psychologists.

2. The program of education for the doctorate in clinical psychology should be as rigorous and extensive as that for the traditional doctorate. In general this would represent *at least* a four-year program which combines academic and clinical training throughout, plus intensive clinical experiences in the form of an internship.

3. Preparation should be broad; it should be directed to research and professional goals, not to technical goals. Participants should receive the training in the four functions I have already mentioned: diagnosis, prevention, therapy, and research, with the special contributions of the psychologist in the last emphasized throughout. Although many will probably tend to specialize in one or another of these after obtaining the degree, I feel strongly that there should be training in each of these areas during the graduate period.

4. In order to meet the above requirements, the program calls specifically for study in seven major areas: (1) General psychology; (2) Psychodynamics of behavior; (3) Diagnostic methods; (4) Research methods; (5) Related disciplines; (6) Therapy; and (7) Prevention. Such a program should go far toward eliminating the possibility of turning out, as clinical psychologists, persons who are essentially technicians, persons who from the standpoint of the academic group have no real foundation in a discipline, and who from the standpoint of the clinical group have no well-rounded appreciation of the setting in which they function.

5. The program should concern itself mainly with basic courses and principles; it should not multiply courses in technique. The stress should be on fewer, well-integrated courses which subtly but inevitably leave the student with a solid foundation and on which he can build knowledge of techniques as he needs them. The relationship of the course material to personality theory should be constantly emphasized, and unless the whole program is oriented in this direction I doubt its final effectiveness.

6. The way the content is handled, that is, the quality of the teaching, is important. Courses should as much as possible involve active student participation, rather than merely requiring listening or even watching demonstrations. Individualized instruction, detailed personal supervision, and the encouragement of initiative and self-reliance must be recognized as important aspects of the teaching. The student should come in contact with a number of instructors representing a variety of points of view and types of experience.

Students should be presented with "models." The "models" I refer to are not theoretical models, but rather role models whom the students may emulate. Because of the considerable emphasis placed on courses in our universities and professional schools, one tends to pay less attention to the vehicles through which these courses are taught. In the end, it is amazing how much more permanent an impact teachers have on students by what they *do* in the context of what they say, rather than by what they just profess. The proper selection of professors who *do* can go a great way to achieving the aims of professional education.[6]

7. The specific program of instruction should be organized around a careful integration of theory and practice, of academic and field work, by persons representing both aspects. Just as there is great danger in the natural revolt against "academic" dominance of ending up with a "practical" program, so is there danger in the continued dominance of the academy. It is important to break down the barriers between the two types of approach and through their smooth integration impress the student with the fact that he is taking *one* course of training provided by *one* faculty.

8. Through all the years of graduate work, the student should have contact, both direct and indirect, with clinical material. This can be accomplished in the theoretical courses through the constant use of illustrative case material with which the instructor has had personal contact. The student should from the first year be provided with opportunities for actual contact with human material in naturalistic, test, and experimental situations that are provided in the settings of laboratory, clerkship, and internship. Throughout, an effort should be made to maintain and to build upon that most valuable quality, the naïve enthusiastic interest in human beings with which the student first enters the training program.

9. I have just made the point that the student should have contact with clinical material throughout the four years of training. Indeed, some of it might even come late in the undergraduate program, as I have suggested. Equally important is the need for the study of normal material. Opportunities should be provided to acquaint the student with the range of normal and borderline persons who never come to clinical facilities. Such training is essential to keep the student balanced in his interpretation and understanding of the abnormal.

10. The general atmosphere of the course of training should be such as to encourage his own increase of maturity, the continued growth of the desirable personality characteristics earlier considered. The environment should be "exciting" to the degree that the assumed "insatiable" interest in psychological problems that has brought him to this field is kept alive, the cooperative attitude strengthened, and the passivity usually associated with so much of traditional teaching kept at a minimum. The faculty must recognize its obligation to implant in students the attitude that graduate work is only the beginning of professional education.

11. The program should do everything possible to bring out the responsibilities inherent in professional relationships with patients or clients. There should be persistent efforts to have the student appreciate that his findings make a real difference to a particular person and to that person's immediate group.

12. A systematic plan should be laid to use representatives of related disciplines for teaching the trainee in clinical psychology, and opportunities for joint study with students in these disciplines should be provided. Through these approaches, the student learns to work closely and in cooperative fashion with those whose methods may be different but whose goals are quite similar. In these settings, he learns to acquire modesty about his own contribution, and to value the "team" approach to

[6] Cf. Eiseley's (1962) moving and profound essay on teaching in this connection.

the problems of service and research that he meets, problems which, because of their difficulty and complexity, often require a concentrated group attack. In the service aspect, he must learn that the team approach calls for the coordinated thinking of various specialists on the problems of a particular patient and that participation in such group activity involves not only immediate, but continuing, responsibility for the client, whether direct or delegated, on the part of all of the members of the team.

13. Throughout the course of training, there should be an emphasis on the research implications of the phenomena with which he is faced, so much so that the student is finally left with the set to constantly ask "how" and "why" and "what is the evidence" about the problems with which he is faced. There is probably no single more important task placed on the teaching staff than instilling this direction toward research.

14. In addition to the research implications of the data, he should become sensitive to their social implications; he must acquire the ability to see beyond the responsibilities he owes the individual patient to those he owes society. Some professions have developed codes which are admirable so far as they concern responsibility to the individual patient or client, but which pay relatively less attention to the other type of responsibility. It is our hope that psychologists will not only acquire more of that attitude toward individual clients or patients, that is, extend personal ethics beyond themselves, but develop a high degree of social responsibility as well—develop a "social" ethics.

In relation to the teaching of professional ethics, it is hard not to sympathize with Felix Frankfurter when he says in his discussion of his training at the Harvard Law School:

> There weren't any courses on ethics, but the place was permeated by ethical presuppositions and assumptions and standards. On the whole, to this day I am rather leery of explicit ethical instruction. It is something that you ought to breathe in. It was the quality of the feeling that dominated the place largely because of the dean, James Barr Ames. We had no course in ethics, but his course on the law of trusts and fiduciary relations was so much more compelling as a course in ethics than any formal course in ethics that I think ill of most courses in ethics [1962, p. 19].

15. And finally we return to the basic principle of the scientist-professional. To adequately achieve this goal calls for a relationship to be established between the *arts and science faculty* and the field centers. But here we touch on a needed rethinking of professional (as opposed to technical) education generally—and that I am afraid is a topic we must leave for another occasion.

Clinical psychology like the other behavioral fields is concerned with the observation of human beings. It therefore faces some very special problems. The importance of *variability* must be recognized. There is marked individual variability in the observed person and among observed persons, and there is equally great variability of both kinds within and across the observers themselves. Thus it is necessary to train and improve *the observer as instrument* in four major types of observation: objective observation, participant observation, subjective observation, and self-observation.

By *objective observation*, I refer to the observations made from the outside directed toward the careful description of the impact on the individual of internal and external forces—physical, psychological, and social—that are making him behave the way he does. These observations are "naturalistic," they are made from outside the situation which the client or patient is in. The observer here is not directly involved with the client.

The second kind of observation, *participant observation*, implies a much more intimate relationship between the observer and the observed. They are both members of the group. The observer has both to evaluate himself as a participant in the group, be able to make evaluations which are separated from those connected with his participation in the group, as well as evaluate what the effect of the act of observing has on the observed and the observation. The group may be just two people—the patient and the observer—as in the simplest form of this interaction, history-taking. Except for history-taking, it may be that situations of the participant-observer kind are relatively infrequent in many interrelationships with people. In other settings, they are much more frequent. Thus in mental health settings it is most strikingly found in psychotherapy, whether group or individual, in which the psychotherapist is both observer and therapist.

The third kind of observation is an especially important one for professional persons working with people. It involves *subjective observation*, the attempt to empathize with the client, to try to understand how the patient feels both about himself and what is troubling him.

The fourth kind of observation is that of *self-observation*, the understanding by the observer of his own feelings and attitudes, sort of asking himself what makes him tick. This would seem to be a vital tool for all persons trying to help others if they are to be sensitive to the psychological and social aspects of the troubles of others.

It is clear that what we are emphasizing throughout are techniques for learning by experiencing rather than learning from hearsay. Because of this real life learning, dangers are inherent in these techniques of, on the one hand, disturbing the validity of the observation and, on the other, of developing self-consciousness and exaggerated introspectiveness. Such dangers deserve careful consideration and concern.

I should like to put before you the outline of a program relating university and practicum center which attempts to incorporate some of the principles I have been discussing while at the same time dealing with some of the difficulties that exist at present in achieving integration. I deliberately offer no more than an outline.

The fundamental principle behind the plan is that theory and practicum be constantly associated and tied together whether in the university or in the field station, and that both, theory and practicum, start from the very *beginning* of the program, with emphasis on the three "earlys"—early experience with clinical material, especially of a developmental kind, early experience with normal persons, early involvement in research. I would suggest as axiomatic the statement: *The greater the degree of integration achieved between theory and practice, and between university and field center, the more effective the program.* We see an outstanding example of this trend in medical education in the Western Reserve experiment, where the traditional distinction between basic science years and clinical years has been broken, where the program has been organized vertically rather than horizontally, with the opportunity for clinical contacts from the first.

What I am saying is that we must get away from the *layer*-cake principle on which most of our programs are based. I even believe that we must go beyond the marble-cake principle on which perhaps the more advanced among us base our training programs. We must work toward achieving that ultimate level represented by a cake whose ingredients cannot at all be distinguished either in appearance or in taste, the one in which true fusion has been achieved.

The plan essentially follows a pattern where *each* year theory and practicum would be provided, either by the university or the field center, but usually by *both*.

Integrated Program

Year	Theoretical Training		Practicum Training	
	Content	Provided by:	Content	Provided by:
I	"Basic" theory	U*	Lab.: observation, tests, exp. psychodynamics	Uf Uf
II	Advanced theory	Uf	Clerkships	Fu
III	Theory: diagnosis, therapy, psychopathology, etc.	Fu	Internship I	F
IV	Dissertation, cross-discipline theory	Uf	Internship II Dissertation	Fu Fu

* The letters U and F indicate major responsibility on the part of the university and the field center, respectively.
The letters u and f indicate lesser responsibility on the part of the university and the field center, respectively.

In the *first year*, there would be major emphasis on basic theoretical courses at the university. These would include courses in general, physiological, comparative, developmental, and dynamic psychology. In the latter two, the practicum center would also carry some responsibility.

At the same time, the university would provide laboratory practice in the first of the four kinds of observation, namely, *naturalistic observation.* A preliminary and fairly extensive period of training devoted to naturalistic observation and description is fundamental to the work of the socially oriented professions which depend on descriptions of the complexities of behavior, feelings, and symptoms. It must come prior to actual diagnostic work, which is largely based on such procedures.

For this purpose, one-way screens, paired observers, and recording devices of both sound and visual types should be used in settings where individuals and groups are under observation in free and controlled situations. Constant checking of observer's reports against each other, against supervisor's observations, and against mechanical devices should be standard practice. It is important that a healthy respect for careful observation and report be developed in students who are going to work in a field where so much of the time the major instrument, in both respects, is the observer himself. With regard to reporting, both in this connection and in connection with diagnostic study, strictness and insistence on high standards of succinctness and accurate terminology are essential. The training should guard against the dangers that inhere in the too early acquisition of technical terms, for frequently such knowledge serves as a barrier to accurate observation.

This training in observation would be followed by work with the variety of diagnostic tests, starting with the more objective tests and working through to the preliminary work with projective tests. In addition, there would be a laboratory course in experimental psychodynamics. In all of this the field center would work with the university staff.

In the *second year*, the university would provide additional advanced instruction in history, theory and systems, and social psychology. The field center would cooperate with the university by providing the major part of the teaching of psychopathology. But the main task of the field center would be to provide clerkships where the students can get their first real contact with clients and patients.

It is also in this year that the student should have the opportunity for training in the second type of observation, *participant observation.* In this form of observation, the inadequacies of naturalistic observation are multiplied and reveal themselves in two particular ways: one in relation to the data, and the other in regard to the effect on what is observed itself. Like any reported observations, the data are bound by the capacity of the human observer as a reporting instrument. No matter how good human beings may be as conceptualizers, they are markedly handicapped sensorially, mnemonically, and expressively as observers and reporters. Put simply, they are limited in how much they can grasp, in how much they can remember of what they do grasp, and in how much and how well they can report even the slight amount they have grasped and remembered. The situation of participant-observation places an even greater stricture upon the data because one is then dependent upon a participant-observer whose participation is special and likely to be extensive. Distortions, both of omission and commission arising from this situation and the personality of the observer undoubtedly enter. It is for these reasons that techniques for training of the kind mentioned earlier need to be given special attention.

The clerkships afford the opportunity for training in the third type of observation as well: *subjective observation.* In this form of observation, we are concerned with the empathic insight into the nature of another person's difficulties and characteristics. It goes without saying that such insight is an important part of the armamentarium of the professional in the psychosocial field. To achieve the skill of "empathic understanding," in which the student can learn to alternate between the identification and objectivity that is simultaneously called for, is the goal of training in this area. For such purposes, exercises under expert guidance in role-playing and psychodrama can be most productive.

In the *third year*, the first internship year, the field station would presumably provide the theory relative to the field work (with some assist from the university), as well as the field work itself.

The internship year, after a few weeks of preliminary orientation, should provide training in clinical psychometrics, research, therapy, prevention, administration, teaching, the integration of psychology with other fields, and an opportunity for individual study. The important principle behind the internship is the full-time immersion in the clinical situation, where the clinical processes become part of the life of the intern. In a rich clinical environment with ample supervision and ample opportunity for independent work, the facilities for development are inexhaustible. The combination of a knowledgeable university staff with a theoretically as well as practically oriented clinical staff can provide at this point in the education of the clinical student that background of the clinical-theoretical which will stand him in good stead throughout the rest of his career.

In this environment, where the emphasis is on the individual patient rather than on problems or techniques, there are certain goals that one hopes the student will achieve related to *psychodiagnostic* procedures which might serve as an example of the principles common to the several areas of training. These include the following: In addition to acquiring skill, through repeated practice in the administration and understanding of a wide variety of tests, he will learn when tests are called for and when not, what tests and combinations of tests are required in specific problems, and the limitations as well as the strengths of these tools. Besides acquiring a sensitivity to the diagnostic and prognostic aspects of his test findings, he will also become sensitive to the therapeutic implications. In fact, one hopes that he will go further and develop a "therapeutic attitude" in his testing, will avoid probing and the carrying out of misplaced therapy, and, without violating the controls and in keeping with the spirit of good testing procedure, will leave the patient the better rather than the worse for the experience.

There are further related goals that one desires for the student: for example, the acquisition of some sense of balance between the extremes of rigorous pedantic exactness and slipshod guessing; the recognition that different problems lend themselves to differing degrees of control, that there are times and stages in the development of a problem when a rough negative correlation appears to obtain between psychological meaningfulness and degree of control; the knowledge that what is important—while working always for reasonably greater control—is to be honest about the degree of control obtained at the particular time, to admit ignorance and hypothesizing when such are the case; the attainment of enough security, on the one hand, not to escape into exactness about the insignificant, nor, on the other, into meaningless profundities, because he is overcome by the complexity and the difficulties of the significant. At the same time, the student should acquire modesty in the face of these difficulties and a sense of responsibility about his findings—an appreciation of the fact that his findings make a real difference to a particular individual and his immediate group—as well as a broader social, scientific responsibility. Also, the wisdom to be constantly sensitive about the research implications of his findings and his techniques, to be aware of the inadequacy of the methods, the data and the theory in the field, and therefore be on the lookout for significant problems and ways of attacking them in order to tie them up with the fundamental facts of psychology. And, furthermore, the skill to work closely and in integrated fashion with other disciplines whose essential goals are similar, and knowledge of the true value and meaning of the "team" approach to the problems which he meets, problems which require this cooperative attack, either in thinking through the problems or in action, because of their complexity.

These several principles are, of course, relevant for the other aspects of his training—therapy, prevention, and clinical research.

In this third year, too, the student would presumably become involved with the fourth type of observation: *self-evaluation.* An important aspect of the problem of the observer as instrument which arises particularly in dealing with motivational questions is the degree to which one's own biases, affects, and problems, frequently only different from the patient's in intensity, color the material provided by the patient. It has become obvious to those working in the clinical field that some kind of control of this source of error is necessary. Many in the behavioral sciences from their more extended experience with this type of material have accepted the principle of the need for self-evaluation as a prerequisite for their work. For most, short methods of self-evaluation may be sufficient; for others, self-evaluation of a psychoanalytic kind may be necessary. My own predilection is for some form of intensive psychoanalytic process (Shakow, 1940), although this may be postponed to the post-doctoral period. Whatever the form, training should include self-examination under the competent guidance of experienced persons. Some of us can perhaps adopt from social work practice a procedure that they have found effective in achieving partial self-knowledge. I refer to their use of intensive detailed case supervision of students. From a parallel contact with preceptors, similar gains may possibly be achieved. This self-evaluation might in some instances continue during the next year as well.

It is also during the latter part of this year, once the student feels comfortable in the clinical situation, that he can begin to think about his dissertation, the details of which I shall consider especially in connection with the *fourth year* of the program.

There was some thought at one time that it might be possible for the student to get part of his dissertation work done during the third-year internship. This (with rare exceptions) has turned out to be impossible to achieve because of the amount of ground to be covered during this period. Under the circumstances, what has generally happened is that the student returns to the university after his internship and does his dissertation work during that year. In order to be sure of getting through in time, he tends to pick a "safe" dissertation, frequently a non-clinical one (because they are usually more easily packageable), and a problem not too infrequently handed to him by one of his instructors. How does this compare with what should ideally happen?

Of all the opportunities the Ph.D. program affords to test out a student, the dissertation is the best single device for indicating what kind of a person he is intellectually and in research ability. Isn't it therefore important to watch him through the various steps of the process of becoming an investigator—see him intrigued by a phenomenon, watch him learning how to put the proper question to nature, and then observe how he goes through the process of trying to get an answer to the question?

For the clinical student, is it not important, too, that this question should be asked in the place where he has most likely become intrigued with a problem, in the area in which his primary work lies? This area is full of unanswered questions which he has to face daily, an area where the difficulties of research and the need for more research are great.

By having the student go back to the university for his dissertation, what kind of attitude are we encouraging? In a sense we are saying that research is not something to associate with the field setting, *that's* the place where service functions are carried out; the *university* is the place for theory and research! It hinders our efforts to build up this research area and the field stations as research centers.

By going even further and having the clinical student do his dissertation on a topic only remotely related to his area, aren't we by implication discouraging the development of an attitude that the problems in this area are researchable problems, and even more than in the previous case associating not only clinical *settings* but the clinical *area* with service and non-research?

But when we go even further, and we have a clinical student do a non-clinical dissertation on a question which has never troubled *him* but which came instead out of the file-drawer of a professor who had some minor question which needed answering as part of a larger problem troubling *him*, what effect on the development of the investigative attitude of the student do we achieve?

What I'm saying is: Don't we have very definite responsibilities to our clinical graduate students? Should we divert them or make research assistants out of them in connection with their dissertations? Can't they do their research assisting, if this is necessary for earning, or even learning, on the side? As "dissertationers" should they not work in the area of their major interest and be independent through the *various* steps of the process, with only the most necessary guidance and help to which they are entitled?

I am therefore recommending that the fourth year become a second internship year during which time the dissertation work would be carried out at the field center and be the central preoccupation of the student.

It is possible, too, that the kind of program I here recommend will develop persons who, while concerned about experimental design and rigor, still recognize the primacy of the substantive—persons who will avoid the "scientism" that Koch (1959) decries. Ought we not be concerned about the degree to which psychologists have become involved in methodology and research design as contrasted with substantial problems in research? It is, of course, important that thought be given to these aspects, and psychology has made a considerable contribution through such activities. But it does not seem good for psychologists to be thought of almost entirely as critics, evaluators, designers of studies, and very little as producers and investigators of ideas and substance, to be thought of as concerned almost solely with the "how," and as leaving to other disciplines concern with the "what" and "why." A program of the kind I have just mentioned could be a beginning in the right direction.

During this fourth year, then, *both* the university and the field station take co-operative and complementary responsibilities for the theoretical work connected with the *dissertation* and any other aspects of the training, a considerable part of which might consist of cross-discipline seminars.

The program I have outlined places so much emphasis upon theory—whenever possible in the context of practice—because of a fundamental principle which is implicit in my whole discussion. This is the principle that our training programs at the doctoral level must be programs directed toward providing a *general* kind of professional psychological education, the only kind of foundation upon which later specialization can be soundly built. It is based on a learning theory which accepts transfer and "learning sets" rather than one that emphasizes specific training.

What would be needed for implementing this program? We would obviously have to give up the notion of distant field centers. The best of these might be used for post-doctoral training, a trend which we are seeing. Local institutions will have to be developed to a level which a program of this kind calls for. This would permit the close interaction required between the university and the field center. There are many advantages to "captive" (in the good sense) centers, but, nevertheless, I think the gains are greater all around if there is not sole relationship with one university. Although there would be some loss here, some of the advantages of mixing students from different universities might still be maintained in those instances where there are several local universities in an area.

The professional relationships between the two institutions—university and field center—must become much closer than has until now generally been the case. They must become almost as one professionally, with the *major responsibility falling upon the university to achieve the unity*, since it remains the degree-granting agency. Program planning must from the beginning be carried out in close association. It is important that the university people have free access to and, whenever possible, have appointments at the internship center. The reverse must be true for the personnel from the clinical centers. (These appointments can be of various kinds and need not get involved in the complicated problems of permanent university tenure.) Their staffs must be raised to the level of acceptance by the university. For program purposes, the staffs of the two institutions should be thought of as nearly one as possible.

Accessory Problems

A few related problems call for consideration. One of these refers to the question of where the practicum education of the clinical psychologist should take place, another has to do with where his actual work should be carried out, and a third with where the specific educational program that I have described might be implemented.

For a long time psychology has been concerned about its relationships with other professions, particularly with psychiatry (Shakow, 1949). Because of this, there has been considerable questioning about the use of medical *settings for training*. In the early days of the present era of active clinical training which began with the end of the last World War, the prominence of the Veterans Administration training programs tended to tie psychology in closely with medically supervised settings. However, with the recent development of community-oriented mental health programs, following upon the acceptance of many of the recommendations of the Joint Commission's Report (1961), we have been hearing an increased call for independence from the medical. The argument is well presented in Albee's perhaps unnecessarily shrill "President's Messages" in the Fall, 1966, and in the Winter, 1967, numbers of *The Clinical Psychologist*, and his conference statement entitled "Psychological Center" prepared for the 1965 Conference on Professional Preparation of Clinical Psychologists (Albee, 1966).

I can agree wholeheartedly with Albee's (1966) position in his pre-conference paper on the undesirability of a separate degree training, the relative overemphasis on psychotherapy, and the importance of the measurement of behavior and of research.[7] I can also sympathize with his interest in replacing the medical model by an educational model in relation to mental health, his emphasis on meeting manpower needs through the training of bachelor-level personnel, and the need he describes for developing practicum facilities more closely associated with university departments of psychology. These all have their commendable aspects. With regard to the last three, I can only say we must by all means experiment with these approaches.

However, as I look back on some forty years of involvement with the training of clinical psychologists in medical settings, I am not impressed by Albee's discussion of the "sociology of professions," nor his descriptions of the dire results that come from violating its principles. I see the products of these training programs—and modesty forbids my mentioning names—playing pioneer and important roles in the development of a psychology making a significant contribution to society. And I can mention a few similar programs that have had equal, if not greater, success.

I might add that my own observations of efforts along the line of the recommendations made by Albee (1966) for "getting out from under the control of the medical model" leave me cold. Aside from the naïveté reflected in his proposals, many doubts may be raised as to whether the arrangements he suggests would provide the kinds of institutions which would result in quality training. And *that* is the one characteristic about which we must not compromise.

Actually Albee and I take opposite points of view on where training should take place. He says train psychologists in institutions controlled by psychologists. Because of their univocal character, the identifications with psychology will be strongly developed. The new psychologists will then be in a position to work anywhere—whether in medically controlled institutions or otherwise. I say train psychologists in the most adequate institutions (which, at least for the present, are, and probably for the near future will continue to be, predominantly medical) where competent and mature representatives of different disciplines are represented, and let the identifications develop. I have no concern about the identification of psychology students with psychologists under such circumstances! With this training they may

[7] However, I would insist that it be research "activity," not research "methodology."

pursue their profession anywhere—whether in academy, institution, or marketplace, in non-medical *or* in medical settings.

The crux of the matter lies, it seems to me, in the general orientation, and in the intolerance for others' approaches. I may be mistaken, but do I detect some power-need in the demands, an excess of missionary zeal, and a degree of arrogance about knowledge of the answers in a field where others, with equally good will, are struggling to find such answers?

I must say that I like so much better the modest spirit of what the CTCP said twenty years ago about this general problem:

> No group can become a profession overnight, a fact which clinical psychology is in the process of discovering. What really counts in the making of a profession—professional ideals and practices—cannot (un)fortunately be taught in courses. Proper technical training, professional certification and state certification, of course, play important roles. More important, however, are identification with a group having high ideals, and constant association in the actual work situation with persons having professional goals. It is in the work relationship that the student can learn to think of himself as a professional person. It is here that the student can gain an appreciation of how people meet such problems as maladjustment, illness, and handicaps, and in this context gain a feeling of responsibility about his work because he understands that his findings really make a difference in what happens to a particular individual and his family. It is here that he learns to carry, in addition to this responsibility for the individual, the broader social one which transcends the need of the individual patient. It is in this setting, too, that another important aspect of professional training, his relationship with other professions, is constantly brought to his attention. He learns the techniques and importance of the group attack on problems: how best to work with other professional groups for the benefit of the individual client and the frequent necessity for identifying himself with a group even broader than his own professional group, namely, the "team."
>
> If the student, after having achieved strong identification with psychology, learns to divest himself of his identification in order to become part of larger wholes for the benefit of a patient or a group, then he may be said to have achieved true professional growth. It is in this setting that ethical problems constantly arise and that the greatest learning in dealing with them naturally occurs [APA, CTCP, 1947, pp. 556–57].

In the relationships between psychiatry and psychology, which are both complicated and paradoxical, there is a great deal of rationalization and defensiveness on both sides. All of this is ironical in the context of the inexhaustible amount of work ahead for everybody! I might add that my own experiences have shown me that for competent and mature psychologists the problem is not at all significant. But the problem *is* serious for the younger worker, especially when he is placed in institutions where such competent and mature psychologists, to serve as models and with whom to develop the "strong identity" which the CTCP called for, are not available. This prompts an even louder call for training in settings where there *are* mature and competent representatives, not only of psychology, but of *all* the professions related to mental health. And this is what we mean by an institution of quality—one that is worthy of participating in the kind of educational program I have outlined.

Closely related to the question I have just considered is a trend in clinical psychology toward the *private practice* of psychotherapy. It had been the expectation of many of us involved in the education of clinical psychologists that only a relatively small proportion of the trainees would enter private practice, and then only after considerable experience beyond their doctorate. It had also been our hope that even then group practice would predominate. Instead, a relatively large proportion of persons, following the "medical model," has entered the private practice of clinical psychology, particularly of psychotherapy, and with relatively few exceptions as single entrepreneurs.

What are the reasons for such a steadily growing involvement in private practice? In the public sphere there has emerged an increasing readiness, in this highly psychology-conscious period, to pay for services, especially of a psychotherapeutic nature. For professionals, the fleshpot has presented temptations. Many, perhaps too many, psychologists have tended to model themselves on those physicians in private practice, particularly psychiatrists, whose income levels are beyond rational toleration. Competition with and antagonism to the physician also probably play a role. The universities contribute to the encouragement of private practice by the provision of opportunities to all faculty members to add to income through consultations. Moreover, in all areas of psychology changes in values are accompanying modifications of practice.

Because of increasing urbanization and the shortage of professionals, it is unlikely that this trend toward private practice will, in the ordinary course of events, be reversed. Methods for limiting the private practice of psychology by the setting of higher and more rigorous criteria, experientially, legally, and ethically seem called for. And at the same time there must come the development of increasing opportunities in community institutions which provide optimal working conditions and reasonable financial rewards.

Now to turn to the last of these related problems. Is there a likelihood that a program of the kind I have outlined can be *implemented*? For a brief period I had glimpsed such a possibility.

For in our Trust Territory in the Pacific, among Micronesia's two thousand islands, several of the larger inhabited islands seemed to offer a real hope in this direction. Despite the great neglect which has been characteristic of the American handling of this U.N. trust we had undertaken—which hopefully is beginning to change, as heralded in part by the coming of the Peace Corps to this area—the island of Nosmirc had, nevertheless, developed a great university. If you ask me how a great university could have grown up in a setting of such general neglect, all I can say is that I, too, find it most paradoxical. Not only is there this great university, but on a few nearby islands, particularly on the island of Notsob, there are a group of clinical facilities of a truly amazing quality. And what is equally unexpected is that the transportation system has been worked out to such perfection that there is almost instant transport from one island to another, so that for all practical purposes it is as if they were on the same campus. One would naturally ask: what better place to try such an integrated educational program in clinical psychology? This seemed equally obvious to a number of us. In this case, the advisability of such a step was buttressed by the fact that traditionally some of the greatest figures in the history of psychology, persons who represented a similar point of view, had been closely associated with this particular university.

Unfortunately, it was not to be. The university opted instead for the study of "pure personality."

This led to much soul-searching on our part. Were we wrong? Were we just antediluvians—being pushed around by an archaic *Zeitgeist*? Were we out of touch with the modern view which recognized the basic importance of the study of pure personality? Were we merely rationalizing when we argued that one of the most effective ways of contributing to the development of basic psychology was through the study of persons in real life stress situations?

When faced with samples of human behavior which are difficult to understand, one cannot avoid questions that come to mind about the other side as well. Did this option really represent an honest expression of full and single-minded devotion to the area of personality as a basic field for psychological investigation, even if it did have some of the quality of the "insight" shown by James' "broody hen"?

Or could this option have been tinged somewhat by the eternal "chastity" problem that plagues all new fields, particularly those that are on the borderline, about their standing with those they consider their *echt*er fellow-scientists? It does not take too much psychodynamic understanding to appreciate why persons involved with the field of personality, one so close to the clinical, find any contact with the "trafe" (the non-kosher) particularly abhorrent. However, in the end, it must be admitted that, since one is never really in a position to evaluate the complex motivations of others, or for that matter of oneself, we shall have to leave it to the Nosmircians to clarify the issues with their gods.

But naturally, for the persons enthusiastic about the kind of program I have outlined, there was great disappointment. Nevertheless, despite this failure in the "Far Pacific" I still have the faith that somewhere, sometime, somebody will try something of this kind.

Last Thoughts

I cannot close without a few further remarks. What will eventually happen to persons who receive the kind of training I have described? I am not at all concerned about their futures. Most will go on to post-doctoral training, some will not. Whatever they do, I feel comfortable that we have provided, or rather these persons have largely provided themselves, the kind of apperceptive mass and generalized approaches that constitute the best background to meet the myriad specific problems that they will face in the field—whether these lie in teaching, in practice, or in research. With the task- rather than ego-orientation, and with the generic rather than specific learning theory that imbue a program of this kind, such persons should be able to make their contributions no matter where they use their skills.

I have today presented you with one "druther." I trust that additional "druthers" will come forth.[8] It is only from constant experimentation with quality programs of different kinds that we will find those that best meet society's changing needs. I do believe, however, that, although I have directed my discussion mainly at clinical psychology, what I have said has important implications for all the mental health professions. In this period, particularly, when we are deluged with demands for service, each of our professions must, nevertheless, protect itself from being overwhelmed by the need to meet these truly urgent needs. We must rather strive with all our might to hold on to that characteristic which above all others describes the good profession—the maintenance of the *quality* basic to its development along lines which have *ultimate*, rather than immediate, social values in mind.

[8] One such additional "druther" is Saul Rosenzweig's so-called 3-6 program. In its "6" aspect, he presents a program which is in the spirit of the one I have proposed, although it includes what I postpone until the post-doctoral period.

16. Homo Scientius *et* Homo Professionalis—Sempervirens?

In late June, 1967, Fillmore Sanford wrote to me asking if I would review for *Contemporary Psychology* the Report of the Chicago Conference, *Professional Preparation of Clinical Psychologists*. I accepted this assignment but found that when I was through I had a review much longer than the one originally discussed. I called Sanford, advised him of the situation and of my reluctance to cut the review. He suggested that I send the paper to him and he would see what might be done. Unfortunately, his tragic death occurred at about this time so he never had an opportunity to react to the review. After some time I wrote to Gardner Lindzey who had taken over the editorship. He indicated that he would publish the review as it stood as part of a double-barreled review. It appeared in the May, 1968, issue of *Contemporary Psychology*.

To a Sierra Club Member, the Report of the Chicago Conference, *Professional Preparation of Clinical Psychologists* (Hoch, Ross, & Winder, 1966), unavoidably brings to mind the current battle over the California redwoods. Despite the clearly disparate motivations behind these two enterprises, the analogy remains apt because the pleasure principle is closely involved both in conservation and in clinical psychology training. Short-range needs for profit and local livelihood, and for psychological assistance, vie with the longer range needs for re-creation, and for the full use of the personal resources of both the helped and the helpers.

On the more technical side, my thoughts take this dendrological turn because of the dominance in the Report (as well as in all previous reports on clinical training) of the "scientist-professional" as the goal of training. This notion, most explicitly formulated in the 1947 CTCP Report (APA, CTCP, 1947), and developed further

Reprinted with permission from *Contemporary Psychology*, 1968, 13, 225–229, where it was published under the title *Troubled Clinical Waters*.

at the Boulder Conference in 1949 (Raimy, 1950), has a past that is, of course, longer than its history. It is an idea already implicit in the writings of William James and other "fathers."

What gives such viability to the notion of the combined practitioner-investigator as the model of a clinical psychologist? Clearly there are pressures against it: from the "personality" researchers, who prefer the laboratory to field, clinic, or consulting room, as well as from the "activists," who suffer unless they provide instant response to society's crying needs.

I believe that this viability has many causes but derives basically from the recognition by clinical psychologists that in the scientist-professional they have captured most adequately the underlying motivation—self-understanding through other-understanding by way of science—that led them to select psychology as a life-work. They see in the scientist-professional a person who, on the basis of systematic knowledge about persons obtained primarily in real life situations, has integrated this knowledge with psychological theory, and has then consistently maintained with regard to it the questioning attitude of the scientist. In this image he sees himself combining the idiographic and nomothetic approaches, both of which appeal to him.

A clearer definition of the scientist-professional perhaps comes from a deeper examination of the value systems that characterize him. They include a self-image of a psychologist identified both with his field and its history, and beyond that with science, whose major value Bronowski calls the "habit of truth." This habit expresses itself in the constant effort to guide his actions through inquiry into what is fact and verifiable, rather than to act on the basis of faith, wish, or precipitateness. Underlying and combined with this "hard-headedness" lies a sensitive, humanistic approach to the problems of persons and their societies. He recognizes, in the context of our overwhelming ignorance, the primacy of the need for building for the future well-being of persons and groups on a solid base of knowledge. Thus integral to his attitude is an implicit modesty, the acceptance of the need for experiment and the long-term view. He emphasizes principles, not techniques, ends rather than means; he keeps as close as possible to real situations while approaching their study with as much rigor as possible. Although he recognizes the legitimacy of the psychonomist's approach to psychological problems through the use of more segmental and more controllable laboratory approaches for his own area of interest, he, with dignity, insists on the importance of his own more molar approach. He also raises questions about the narrow and rigid boundaries within which the psychonomist attempts to confine psychology. In his molar approach, the scientist-professional exercises the utmost rigor compatible with maintaining the integrity of the situations he faces. The combination of the skilled acquisition of reality-based psychological understanding and the attitude of constant inquiry toward this knowledge is thus what defines the "scientist-professional."

Some forces—social, personal, and competitive—work against the full acceptance of this model. The social forces are of two major kinds. The first consists of the obvious social needs for service which the relatively short supply of psychologists makes even more pressing. This is compounded by the additional social pressure created by society's readiness to develop new and special institutions that offer almost unlimited opportunities for being at least minimally useful in meeting these needs. I refer to the programs described by Hobbs in his eloquent introductory address to the Conference. It is, however, not only the prerogative of a profession, but indeed its responsibility, to examine carefully, in the context of a sensitiveness to such needs, the ways in which it may *ultimately* be of the greatest service. A profession is not a "good profession" if it merely permits itself to be pushed around, even when this passivity results from the most laudable of purposes.

In addition to pressures that come from society, there are those that come from within psychology itself, through a form of exaggeration of the "scientific" contribution. This shows itself, for instance, in the notions of the more simplistic forms of behavior therapy—a "Look, Ma, no cavities!" kind of approach. This "nonies" method only serves to denigrate the more complex and realistic involvement of the professional in his day-by-day efforts, for the implications are both that the difficulties of professional clinical activity have been exaggerated and that almost anybody can do professional work. Nevertheless, I would encourage the utmost support of such laboratory-based, principle-oriented research with clinical problems. I should, of course, prefer to see it done by persons with some clinical background; happily, there appears to be a trend in this direction.

Besides these difficult social and intra-professional pressures that confront clinical psychology, there are personal pressures. They present another order of difficulty because they call for a very special self-examination by psychologists, especially when the scientist-professional model has been seriously accepted. I refer, for example, to the temptations of private practice. Except in occasional instances, it would seem that clinical psychology at its present stage of development must take a stand against the proliferation of private practitioners. This is so because such practice does not offer, except in the rare instance of a *most* unusual person or situation (in which case, rules do not hold), the possibilities for making the kinds of contribution which we may reasonably expect from a scientist-professional, basic contributions which society needs so badly at present.

Rival models may at first seem to offer real competition to the prepotency of the scientist-professional model. On closer examination, however, this turns out not to be so. Certainly the "sub-clinical psychologist," as Fred Wells used to refer to him, does not provide any competition. The Chicago Report solves the problem with regard to the important group of the sub-doctorally trained by suggesting that these technical workers should only carry professional responsibilities to the degree to which their personality, education, and experience make them competent. (There is no issue about the importance of developing such a group. I agree thoroughly that we have an obligation, together with other professions, to train such workers. Much thought and experimentation will have to be devoted to this problem.) Other models that have been suggested may at best be included in the scientist-professional model. In some cases, they really are not models for clinical psychology, as the Report declares in its discussion of the psychotherapist model. This does not in any way deny the essential place of psychotherapeutic training as part of the background of the scientist-professional clinical psychologist.

The scientist-professional model's strength lies in its basic appropriateness for a field such as psychology which is at an interface between science and the humanities. It also lies in its remarkable flexibility, since the truly fundamental value systems on which it is based can tolerate great diversity within its legitimate limits. In some respects, too, it offers an ideal opportunity for integrally achieving the values of the scientist and humanist in actual practice, a combination which is so important for most branches of psychology, but which some specialities can only realize by developing persons who only in parallel can be both good psychologists and good citizens. (I do not believe I am badly misreading history by emphasizing the ever-green quality of the scientist-professional.)

Aside from the continued acceptance of the scientist-professional model, perhaps the strongest emphasis in the Report is on the psychological center. Although the Report nods slightly toward the need for "complementary" experience (Hoch et al., 1966, p. 63), its acceptance of the center is overwhelmingly enthusiastic (". . . full endorsement given by the Conference to the establishment of the psychological service center as an ideal setting for training [Hoch et al., 1966, p. 85])." This response was apparently generated by the combination of Albee's ardent presentation of the arguments for such a center and the receptivity—indeed the marked affective readiness—of a great majority of the participants for what appeared to them to throw open *the* gates to independence.

The response to this call for a center under the direct and full supervision of a clinical psychology program is properly, "Let's try!" This provision of one setting for training which is completely under the psychologist's control has many attractive aspects. Whether such a system can be made to work should be tested to the limit. Its very establishment would offer a challenge to psychologists to make a center of this kind optimal for training. It should therefore only be made a responsibility of persons who are completely persuaded about its possibilities, persons who would do their utmost to make it successful. And if there are already existing operations of a high level of quality—I do not know of any but this may be due to my present remoteness from the training situation—they should be given the fullest support to enable them to work at full capacity. However, even while accepting the need to experiment with any reasonable new proposal, we must examine its basic character and potentialities for training with great care. And since my own background has been quite different, I am perhaps in a position to sketch the other side of the picture.

My experiences in evaluating training programs left me with the impression that psychological centers under department control used for training were "Milquetoast" operations. They were not effective, except for limited purposes. This seemed so to me because I saw them in the light of long experience in vital medical centers where training and research were closely interwoven into the fabric of a rich range of clinical operations. I believe that it will be a long time before psychological centers can truly reach acceptable levels for basic training, even if they cannot ever reach the levels that I refer to.

Meanwhile we should face the facts and be sure we are not deluding ourselves. This self-deception takes two forms: the first concerns the quality of the operation we are setting up; the second involves the motivations for setting up such independent operations. We must not rationalize nor accept shoddy quality in return for independence. In the final analysis, independence is not a cardinal value. Let us be honest, too, about the motives behind the drive for independence. Autonomy is a laudable—in fact, essential—ambition for any profession, so we need not be ashamed to indicate our wish for this openly.

The question of autonomy and independence is complicated and one into which we cannot here enter fully. I have enough knowledge of situations where such autonomy was not available to understand the conditions which give rise to the strong feelings about its absence. I have discussed some of these on a previous occasion (Shakow, 1949c). The immodesties of some members of the medical profession, particularly psychiatrists, with regard to their competences, both administrative and substantive, and their blindness about the social limitations of their code of ethics have often annoyed me, as well as it apparently has members of the Conference. However, we must be certain that it is not *merely* the power which comes with independence that we are really after.

More specifically, why do I tend to be negative about such centers? My observations of operations of this kind have, in general, indicated that they are limited in the range of clients, the significance of the problems represented, and the commitment of the clients. These difficulties are occasioned by both the absence of that force—illness—which drives persons to come to medical settings, and by the relatively limited resources of such centers for dealing with human problems. When a problem becomes "serious" or truly challenging, it is generally referred to another agency, or much more rarely to a senior person. This bypasses one of the greatest sources of growth for students, one that taxes them to the limits of their capacities. Then again, a fundamental rule, which is basic to the establishment of good clinical training facilities, is to set up an operation that meets a truly public need for service. Then one can build an effective training program on this base. If, on the other hand, one sets up the operation initially and primarily for training (and I seem to hear echoes of this in the Report), there is great doubt about its continued viability.

In the context of the zeal for the establishment of a psychological center, there is a concurrent tendency to underrate the medical center as a place for training. Aside from the independence aspect, which is based on many real but, I believe, more unreal, perceptions, what is usually offered for comparison is, unfortunately, some caricature of the "medical model." On the one hand, insufficient recognition is given to the strengths that still reside in the "disease" model. Its negative rather than its positive aspects tend to be emphasized. Or the medical operation selected for comparison is one obviously headed by a most limited person, rather than a top-level, public-spirited psychiatrist. More importantly, what is not recognized is that a substantial part of the medical model is increasingly constituted of prophylactic, preventive, and public health aspects. This latter quality, the growing trend toward the humanization of medicine, and the introduction of increasing amounts of behavioral science into the medical curriculum provide an even worthier opponent for a purely social-educational model to contend with (Cope, 1968; Cope & Zacharias, 1966). It is this newer medicine (and medicine is in the process of undergoing revolutionary changes which involves some extension into the social-educational model) that one ought to be thinking about, rather than the somewhat outmoded, purely pathological model.

In discussing the comparative richness of opportunities for training that the medical, as opposed to the psychological, center provides, I would like to comment particularly about their respective representations of disciplines. The psychological center calls for at best a variety of psychologists, with the "hopeful" representation of some other disciplines. But mainly it is conceived of as a group of psychologists, usually from one main area of psychology, working together. When one compares this with even the usual—let alone the optimal—medical setting, the representation of disciplines to which both the teacher *and* the student are exposed is indeed meager. In the medical setting, one has not only psychologist colleagues, but also representatives of many other disciplines, both medical and non-medical. I have written on a number of occasions (Shakow, 1938, 1942, 1946, 1957) about the immense resources of a good psychiatric hospital, so I shall not dilate upon them on this occasion. The superior opportunities for broad and basic training in such practicum placements over those in even the best of psychological centers are striking.

In addition, many advantages derive from a situation where a variety of superegos are represented. One check on the misjudgments that we all inevitably make in the complex clinical situation comes from the colleagues in one's own discipline. Another, quite different and perhaps more important, check comes from a person in a different discipline who approaches the same problem along his own road and by his own method. Such checks and counter-checks are particularly important in the uncertain clinical area. Further, the kind of learning that occurs when persons from different disciplines work together for a common goal is one of the most rewarding experiences I know of. And this is even more true for students from different disciplines when they receive overlapping parts of their training together, as well as have opportunities to mingle freely.

I find myself therefore taking a somewhat different view about the center in which major clinical training should take place than does the Report. The Report recommends a "captive" institution for training so that its graduates, having acquired a proper identification with psychology, can practice anywhere. I suggest training at the best kind of institution—and for the present these are likely to be medical institutions—after which the graduates will be in a position to practice anywhere. The best medical institutions are those having representatives of various disciplines—representatives who have appropriate autonomy because those responsible are competent persons. For that reason I have never had any fears about the identifications psychology students adopt. I have rarely known it to fail: where a person is competent, he is not troubled by autonomy problems; in fact he may have difficulties in resisting attempts of others to give him unreasonably excessive autonomy.

We have already dealt with the fundamental question about the relative importance of quality and independence. Naturally, where both can be had, the ideal situation exists. But I hasten to add that the choice may in most cases be artificial. For I believe we can achieve this autonomy, if we haven't already, in the quality institutions, even though they are medical institutions. (I will admit that I have known a few of these medical institutions of quality where for one reason or another such an achievement does not seem possible. These are of such high quality, however, that I would use them for at least complementary training.) Although I do not see this possibility immediately, I believe that in the not too distant future we will have a range of institutions. There will be those that are medically oriented and those that are socioeducationally oriented. But the majority will be some combination of the two, with predominance in one area or the other. These will offer the best facilities for training not only because of their wider range of problems, but because of the varieties of professions represented. Further, the leadership in them will be on the basis of the competence of the person for the job—not his professional associations. Although there will be some overlap in the areas covered by these institutions, mainly they will be complementary. And because of this, training in *both* these types of institutions would be the most desirable.

For the present, however, we must face our problems honestly, making sure that we do not sacrifice public service for personal or professional power, that the independence we seek is independence in the service of the ego, not independence in the service of the id!

It is of interest to view this Report in the context of previous reports. In general, the Report does not let us down. Many of the immediate training problems are dealt with more explicitly than in previous reports. This is to be expected, since we have had about twenty years of experience in which the problems have become more defined, and our failings to meet agreed-upon goals have manifested themselves.

The Report makes a clear statement about the differences between post-graduate and post-doctoral training. Above all, it not only emphasizes, as have previous reports, but emphasizes repeatedly three cardinal principles of clinical training—the integration of the academic and the practicum, the essential role of experienced clinicians as teachers, and the importance of research training and activity in appropriate clinical settings. It is also more explicit about the importance of psychologists working on the maximizing of human potential as well as on the remedying of disorder. The clarity with which the group distinguished between the content of training and the nature of the subsequent practice (Hoch et al., 1966, p. 68) is impressive. The closing reaffirmation of diversity in the context of a unified underlying model (Hoch et al., 1966, p. 74) is particularly gratifying.

Some of the discussion about the "internship," however, is rather puzzling. The suggestion that this part of the practicum experience come earlier may result from an omission in the Report of any substantial recognition of the importance of clerkship experience. The Boulder Report outlined a clear progression of practicum experience—from laboratory training in assessment devices, through clerkship experiences, to the internship experience. (I believe that the Conference slipped in not keeping to the Boulder Conference generic notion of practicum.) Under those circumstances there was no need for bringing the internship experience in earlier; indeed, it seemed more reasonable to postpone it to later in the program. If the clerkship experience—the less intense yet wider involvement with clients which provides such unusual opportunities for experience in so many of the new kinds of community setups—is not deemed an essential part of the practicum training, then there might be some justification for having the internship earlier. But this seems to me to be a loss. I agree, on the other hand, with the reluctance of the group to accept the internship at the fourth-year level, a step which would defeat the attempt to integrate the major field experience with the university experience.

Also puzzling is the statement that "the notion of a core curriculum is no longer viable" (Hoch et al., 1966, p. 52). Is this an editorial error? The Report actually goes on immediately to consider areas that belong in the core curriculum. And, more than puzzlement, annoyance is generated by the occasional semantic beguilements which creep into the Report, such as "chunks of knowledge" and "areas of subject matter" for "core curriculum." These semanticisms lead to claims of a "new" approach to the problems of training.

In comparing the Chicago Report with the Boulder Report, I must say that on the whole I find the earlier Report much more satisfying. (Is this because the clearer air of Boulder percolated through? Or is it my identification? Or can it be that, after all, I *am* objective?) The Boulder Report seems to be more complete and statesmanlike; more oriented to our own colleagues, to other professions and to the public; and more modest. In this Report, I detect a tinge of boastfulness or evangelism which the Boulder Report did not have. Such behavior is all right for a profession's boudoir, but isn't it better to keep it out of the ballroom?

My preference for the Boulder Report arises not only from its broader and more complete content, but also from its organization. The format of the two reports is quite different. The Boulder Report is unified, almost 200 of its 270 pages being devoted to Conference material; whereas somewhat less than 60 of the Chicago Report's 150 pages are of this kind. Although practically all of "The Issues" material and the "Appendix" material is relevant, a greater feeling of unity would probably have been produced if the material in the former had been relegated to the appendix as well. As it is, one feels the need to try to organize "bits" into a whole. Another problem is the difficulty in easily finding the resolutions in the present Report, which in the Boulder Report were usefully indented. An index would also have helped.

In examining the list of participants, I am troubled by what I consider a serious omission. At this late date in the organization of planning conferences, should we be neglecting the students? I suggest the advisability of involving them in future conferences. Innumerable experiences have impressed me with, on the one hand, how much we tend to underestimate the capacity of students, and, on the other, the great contribution that students can make to the development of programs.

Let me present a few examples. In the evaluation visits made in the earlier days of the CTCP, some of the most cogent suggestions and criticisms of programs came from the students at the universities visited. We always made it our business to interview a considerable number of students because we found their straightforwardness and honesty refreshing, and their comments most helpful. When I was at the University of Illinois Medical School, we had, in addition to a faculty curriculum committee, a student curriculum committee. On occasion, the faculty committee met with the student committee. The quality of the thinking and the recommendations made by the student committee were impressive. The students were frequently much more to the point than were the faculty. Not that the faculty committee was composed of old dodos. On the contrary, it had represented on it the heads of the most progressive departments and other faculty members who were doing the most serious thinking about medical education. But in the end, there is nothing like a good intelligent consumer to tell you what's wrong with what you are assumedly giving him!

In my remarks about the Chicago Conference, I may appear to be violating sound therapeutic principles by being too evaluative, too judgmental. I would plead guilty if I considered at all that I was speaking as a therapist. On the contrary, because of my continued concern about training, I identify with the patient or client. And one of the soundest principles for good prognosis for the patient, one which I believe all therapeutic schools would accept, is self- rather than projected blame.

The Conference had many productive aspects. It also provided a marvelous opportunity for group abreaction of the inevitable adolescent needs of the young profession we are, particularly that for independence. With some of this affect out, perhaps we can now more easily recognize that autonomy almost always comes with competence. Clinical psychology can now return to developing the most qualified, task-oriented clinical psychologists it can—clinical psychologists who recognize the immense needs of the field, a field in which there are many fellow-toilers from our own and other professions. Sometimes these persons work in overlapping areas; usually they have unique areas as well, in which they make their contributions. As competent professionals, clinical psychologists do not let themselves be pushed around either by society or by other professionals; neither do they do any pushing around themselves. While they do not settle for too little, their modesty, based on security, does not lead them to claim too much either.

As for the training programs themselves, can we in the final analysis go beyond the rule of "the four goods": Have good teachers (models who are mature, sensitive, with clear value systems) give good students (with the same potential qualities) good training (truly "scientist-professional") in good settings (where they are exposed intensively to a range of human problems, approached from a variety of standpoints)? Under such circumstances the unsatisfactory identifications and the "absence of excitement" in clinical programs about which the Report complains will vanish.

PART III

Liaison with other Professions

In this section on association with other helping professions, the first three papers deal with psychiatry, the next paper with a possible profession of psychotherapy, and the last two with medicine in both its training and practice aspects.

17. Psychology and Psychiatry: A Dialogue

As is the custom in the Division of Clinical and Abnormal Psychology of the American Psychological Association, the current president is called upon to deliver a presidential address. The present "dialogue" was delivered in part on such an occasion at the meeting in Boston, September 7, 1948, and subsequently published in the *American Journal of Orthopsychiatry*.

Part I

Persons: Psychologist *L* and Psychiatrist *T*
Place: The Psychologist's Study

T: It's nice to be able to get together, away from the hurly-burly of the clinic. Perhaps in the quiet of your study we can arrive at somewhat more insightful conclusions about the relationships between our professions than are ordinarily reached.

L: It's even possible, isn't it, that the privacy of the setting might permit us to consider some of the controversial problems that we would not as yet dare to discuss in public. We start off with a great advantage. We know that our own mutual regard is based on the fact that we respect each other's competence and that we have not hesitated to deal openly with differences as they have arisen. I am sure that here the same frankness will prevail, especially since we know that our fundamental goals are the same.

Reprinted with permission from the *American Journal of Orthopsychiatry*, vol. 19, 1949.

T: I have looked forward to this talk and am glad that we have finally got around to it. First let me say that I agree not only with your remarks but with their implications. There has been, on both sides, altogether too much heat and confusion of issues, too much blindness and recrimination, and too much readiness to generalize from unsubstantiated "I-heard-about-a's."

L: Or—shall we put the emphasis somewhat differently—too many considerations based on the conscious and unconscious needs of the two professions and their professors, rather than on the needs of the patient or the fundamental needs of society.

T: It is, of course, easy to separate these verbally, but isn't it rather difficult to achieve practically?

L: Suppose it is difficult! Isn't it clear that no real progress can be made while there is preoccupation with that facile indoor sport of preparing "little lists" of the other profession, or with Decaturish expressions of unyielding loyalty to one's *Fach*. In the last analysis, society is not interested in any profession or its representatives—it is interested only in having its problems dealt with by competent persons.

T: I'll admit that I don't see how any discussion of this kind can go on which is not guided by the central premise that meeting social needs through the most competent service is what has to be striven for. Aside from the questions of training and background that this point of view raises, there are, of course, a host of ethical problems.

L: Yes, and all the problems raised by the danger of closing off new methods of attack and new points of view that the adoption of such a stand is likely to encourage. I am reminded of the issues regarding medical licensure raised by William James some half century ago in his appearance before the Massachusetts legislature, an account of which you may have come across. I believe his statement at that time is quite pertinent to the present point and, because of its spirit, even has some relevance as general background for our discussion.

T: I don't immediately recall this particular Jamesian activity. What was it?

L: The story, as I remember it, runs something like this. The Massachusetts legislature, toward the end of the last century, had before it various bills for medical licensing. A clause in one of these bills required practitioners of the so-called "faith-cures" to pass the standard medical examinations and to have medical degrees. This was essentially an attempt to abolish mental healing, and James was aroused to protest this feature of the law. The details are in the second volume of James' *Letters*; it's somewhere on this shelf. Yes, here it is; let me read you some sections.

I assuredly hold no brief for any of these healers, and must confess that my intellect has been unable to assimilate their theories, so far as I have heard them given. But their *facts* are patent and startling; and anything that interferes with the multiplication of such facts, and with our freest opportunity of observing and studying them, will, I believe, be a public calamity. . . .

And whatever one may think of the narrowness of the mind-curers, their logical position is impregnable. They are proving by the most brilliant new results that the therapeutic relation may be what we can at present describe only as a relation of one person to another person; and they are consistent in resisting to the uttermost any legislation that would make "examinable" information the root of medical virtue, and hamper the free play of personal force and affinity by mechanically imposed conditions.

And I might add *this* from a letter to James J. Putnam written at that period, referring to his appearance before the legislature:

> . . . If you think I *enjoy* that sort of thing you are mistaken. I never did anything that required as much moral effort in my life. My vocation is to treat things in an all-around manner and not make *ex parte* pleas to influence (or seek to) a peculiar jury. *Aussi*, why do the medical brethren force an unoffending citizen like me into such a position? . . .

T: How about Putnam? What did he think about it? He was so much more in the midst of medical activities, and I'd like to know what he thought.

L: Well, here's this from a letter of Putnam to James:

> We have thought and talked a good deal about the subject of your speech in the course of the last week. . . . I think it is generally felt among the best doctors that your position was the liberal one, and that it would be a mistake to try to exact an examination of the mind-healers and Christian Scientists. On the other hand, I am afraid most of the doctors, even including myself, do not have any great feeling of fondness for them, and we are more in the way of seeing the fanatical spirit in which they proceed and the harm that they sometimes do than you are. Of course they do also good things which would remain otherwise not done, and that is the important point, and sincere fanatics are almost always, and in this case I think certainly, of real value [James, 1920, pp. 66–73].

I have brought up this ancient James incident so early in the discussion not so much because of its specific relevance, but rather because I believe even an extreme instance of this kind has general significance for the consideration of a multi-discipline approach to a problem. Besides, it raises issues that, in true Jamesian fashion, help to complicate our own set for our talk to an adequately realistic three-dimensional level. I am sure that we are both concerned that our discussion be neither oversimplified nor evasive, nor again, too theoretical. It seems to me important that from the beginning we be sufficiently aware of the fact that the acceptance of an interdisciplinary approach means the multiplication of real and difficult problems and requires a greater readiness to consider novel, and even heterodox, views.

T: I suppose what you're getting at is that it requires giving up the relative comfort that comes with the single-discipline, and particularly with the single-school, approach?

L: Yes, the multidiscipline approach complicates life considerably—and unavoidably. I can't help thinking in this connection of a current, though much less extreme instance than the one we have just considered. I refer to the attitudes expressed by some psychiatrists toward the so-called "non-directive" or "client-centered" therapy. I occasionally detect reactions that seem to stray rather far from the kind of goal we have here emphasized. Equal skepticism about various aspects of this program—quite irrelevant to our present discussion—is to be found among many psychologists, but one cannot help being troubled by the extreme attitudes of some psychiatrists. Especially in a field such as therapy, where we are all so ignorant and where the need for knowledge is so great, there is an obligation to encourage any sincere and consistent, even if, in our opinion, mistaken effort.

T: You *do* point out a real danger; one that a powerful professional group like medicine has to watch itself for constantly. Putnam's attitude in the incident you describe appears to me particularly courageous since he was a practicing physician and on the direct firing line. But I don't have to tell you that situations occasionally arise that make it difficult for even the best-adjusted person to remain socially oriented and not slip over into an affective identification with his own discipline! Tonight we have the great advantage of quiet isolation, an aid to careful reflection rarely available when a topic such as this is ordinarily considered!

L: I am rather interested in your mention of isolation. I take it you refer to the advantages that come with seclusion from one's colleagues. I, too, have been impressed with how differently the same person reacts to this problem when he is part of a group of persons of his own discipline as compared with his views when he speaks privately. One can't help rating Le Bon as a pretty good psychologist!

T: Well, let's make the most of this rare solitude and partial deprofessionalization! Doesn't the acuteness of the problems of the relationship between our two disciplines stem from the tremendous growth of their region of activity—the great present need for workers and the great present concern with training, in the areas of personality, of adjustment, and mental hygiene? Kubie (1947) has perhaps delineated the problems most persistently and with the greatest clarity. We see needs everywhere for work in diagnosis, in therapy, in prevention—in all of these, with the full range from normality through extreme pathology.

L: Isn't the acuteness emphasized by the fact that the techniques and the factual data for dealing with these problems, available in both psychiatry and psychology, are relatively sparse and on the whole quite primitive? I am sure, knowing you, that after conferences and staff meetings where you have delivered yourself of an opinion, you must frequently suffer from "post-oracular shudders," as I do. When I think of the tenuous body of data and study on which these glibly given opinions are often based, there would seem some justification for feeling guilty that these p.o.s. attacks are occasional rather than chronic!

T: What you say makes me think of Alan Gregg's (1948) recent statement to the effect that fifty more years' work by fine minds and devoted characters would make the present account of the limitations of psychiatry seem, I think he said in his "Greggorian" way, "hilarious and quaint if not unbelievable."

L: Well, it is in such a general setting of need that psychology says, "This is an area in which I can be of use, in which I have been of some help in the past, and in which I now want to help even more." And it is not psychology alone that is behind this request. To some extent, society encourages psychology to make this bid for participation on the basis of what it considers psychology's natural concern with a field that is so closely related to the understanding of normal human behavior, a field that is its by very definition. Historically, too, there are many reasons to justify this attitude. I might mention only a few. Thus, only recently the fiftieth anniversary of the establishment of the Witmer Clinic at the University of Pennsylvania was celebrated (Brotemarkle, 1947). Though the point of view of this clinic was limited and its development not in the main stream, it provides an example of pioneer interest on the part of psychologists in the area of personality adjustment (Shakow, 1948a). Then, too, from the early days of psychiatry's concern with problems outside the asylum, psychologists have in one way or another been associated in dealing with them (Shakow, 1945a). The bid now is for a recognized extension of its earlier role on such grounds as I have mentioned, but even more, on the basis of a growing competence on the part of that group of psychologists known as "clinical psychologists."

T: Would you tell me just *which* group that is? I must confess that I am often puzzled by what you psychologists mean when you talk about clinical psychology. Sometimes you seem clearly to mean the psychology that is practiced in medical or, more specifically, psychiatric institutions. Then again, I hear of clinical psychology in public schools, in reformatories, in industry—in places where there is no medical contact or, at least, where medical relationships are at a minimum. What *do* you really mean?

L: I can understand your puzzlement, since psychologists themselves are vague about the boundaries of this field and in some respects divided about its inclusiveness. Some hold that clinical psychology should be limited to psychology in medical settings; others hold that it involves a much broader area and includes all work where the problems of individual adjustment are the primary concern. When one comes right down to it, however, there is not so much difference of opinion as at first appears. Actually, there is more confusion about the issues that are involved than true difference of opinion about the range of activity. The difficulty seems to arise from not distinguishing clearly between the content of the *training* for the field, and the range of ultimate *practice* in the field. This confusion is to some extent found in the article by Pressey (1948) you asked me about the other day.

T: I was interested in his criticisms of the Committee on Training in Clinical Psychology. I wondered whether it implied the existence of quite marked differences of point of view among psychologists with regard to the nature of their training programs.

L: No, I don't think so. Mainly it was a criticism of procedure by American Psychological Association committees. For some situations the point Pressey makes is sound. I believe, however, that his criticism is irrelevant as far as the Training Committee report is concerned, since this was a "should" rather than a "what" report. Although there are several other questions that might be raised about the article, we are concerned here only with his criticism of the Committee for leaving out of consideration some areas in which clinical psychologists work. According to Pressey there are more psychologists working in schools and educational systems than in clinics and guidance centers, and for that reason training programs should be more prominently concerned with work in the educational area. Although Pressey's statistics are not fairly representative of the situation for the time they were compiled, and are certainly out-of-date now, the point he makes is nevertheless important and requires consideration quite outside the Committee's report.

T: In what way do you mean?

L: In this way: I don't know whether it would be universally accepted in the psychological group, but there are at least a substantial number of persons intimately concerned with training who hold a point of view that, stated boldly, runs something like this: Clinical psychology is the basic background for the practice of the greater part of professional psychology; the medical aspect of clinical psychology is the fundamental background for *all* clinical psychology. Some of us have even gone so far as to say that psychology derived from study in the medical setting is a not unimportant part of the training for general and social psychology! Why do we hold to this point of view? For various reasons: For one, suffering and illness open the personality to study as no other condition does, a point made long ago by Ernest Jones (Glover, 1934). For another, the exaggeration of the phenomena produced by nature enables much more clear-cut appreciation of the principles involved.

T: Would you accept as an additional reason the fact that the techniques of personality study used in the setting of illness are the most advanced and developed available, both in their individual aspects and in their coordinated approach by a variety of disciplines?

L: Yes, and an important reason, too. It is our belief that a study of a sufficient variety of sick persons, to which is added considerable contact with the range of normal persons, provides the best general groundwork for professional work in psychology. From the first comes particularly an appreciation of the tremendous range and complexity of the "id" factors, and from the latter particularly an appreciation of the "ego" factors—complementary knowledge that is indispensable to the full understanding of human beings. This holds especially for that branch of professional psychology known as clinical psychology, a type of psychology that is becoming more and more important in the educational field, in the industrial area, and in other work with the essentially normal, as well as directly in the medical-psychiatric setting. I want to emphasize that, at present, the former areas are as important as the last for the clinical psychologist; in the future they may well be even more important as a field in which he works. I understand that the Board of Examiners in Professional Psychology is receiving an increasing number of requests for diplomas in clinical psychology from persons who work exclusively in industry. In fact, it is impressive to hear how often psychologists who have received their training directly in the schools or in industry express the need for experience in the medical area. Without this experience they often consider themselves inadequate for dealing even with the relatively normal problems that they face. I realize that in what I have said I have skated around the problem of what is meant by clinical psychology. I shouldn't be surprised if you thought that I was trying to "weasel" out of defining the field.

T: I realize your difficulty, but I still think that it would help to have the field clearly defined. If we could say *this* is clinical psychology, *this* is psychiatry, *this* is abnormal psychology, *this* is social work, *this* is counseling, *this* is therapy, and so on, wouldn't we be in a much better position to consider the problems with which we are concerned?

L: Of course we would! And if we could say just what a "sick" person is, we'd solve a lot of our problems, too! But then again, would we, considering medicine's stake in the preventive aspects of disease? The more one thinks about the problem of definition of fields such as these, the more difficult the task becomes. Beyond making some very general statements about clinical psychology's concern with the psychological adjustment problems of the individual, it is obvious that no clear-cut defining boundaries can be laid down. In the end, in the interpenetrating fields in which we work, can we avoid falling back on the good will of the competent persons who are involved, on the mutual respect of disciplines qualified to do their respective and necessarily overlapping jobs? In the wise words of Bronson Crothers' Subcommittee (1932), it is important to avoid carrying "prestige" beyond the field where it was earned. At a much simpler level, don't you have a similar problem between pediatrics and child psychiatry?

T: Yes, one that has not been entirely solved. I find myself agreeing with what you say despite my strong need for clarity in the function of the disciplines.

L: I know just how you feel. How often I have struggled with the problem! Any number of definitions of clinical psychology have been offered, and they are all in some sense satisfactory and again in some other sense unsatisfactory. Taken by themselves they seem all right, but as clear definers and delineators of areas, they are utterly inadequate. This is true except in the case of definitions that are obviously too limiting, such as the one that holds clinical psychology to consist of the administration of intelligence tests, a definition on a par with the one that would define psychiatry as the custody and treatment of psychotic patients. There is great danger, too, in an era of great expansion and growth such as the present, of defining a field too narrowly and too rigidly. It is difficult to predict just what clinical psychology will be like ten years from now, and it would be regrettable to let our present ignorance or prejudice or compulsive need burden the natural development of the field.

T: What do you think of the effort on the part of some psychologists and psychiatrists to limit all clinical psychology to psychology carried out in psychiatric and other medical settings?

L: This is one of the narrowing influences I was referring to. What I said earlier holds. The *training* for clinical psychology might be, and I believe should be, heavily in the medical setting, but its application cannot by any means be limited to this area.

T: We have agreed that we must make social goals our final criterion. We imply by this, I suppose, that a discipline or a profession is unlike a business enterprise and that the activity must be oriented socially, rather than egocentrically—whether the "ego" be the discipline or the person. But, at the risk of sounding somewhat Socratic, what *are* these social goals?

L: Obviously, the betterment of the individual, the person with a problem who is immediately at hand; but more important, are we not most concerned with the ultimate betterment of large numbers of individuals?

T: Yes, but who is to be the "betterer?" As you pointed out a little while ago, society has some difficulty in recognizing quickly who is competent to accomplish this task. It must have short cuts to identification of the competent, a task which it accomplishes through licensing and similar procedures. Doesn't this throw back upon the disciplines involved the burden of working out among themselves the criteria for competent persons, the fields of overlap, and so on?

L: With just such a recognition of the needs in the field, Miller (1947), Kubie (1947), and others have come forth with interesting plans for the development in this area of a type of composite competent person—a combination of a psychiatrist and a psychologist, as it were.

T: Even granted the desirability of such a program, there doesn't seem to be much likelihood that it can be achieved in the very near future, does there? For this reason isn't it important to work out the problems which we have indicated in the light of the general patterns of *present* training?

L: Yes, but isn't there another vital aspect to this problem—the complexity of the field?

T: I was just coming to this point. There *is* so much complexity that a combined attack by more than one discipline is unavoidable. Psychiatrists, you will agree, are the group essentially responsible to society for treatment in the area of personality maladjustment. For that reason they have an implicit, if not explicit, delegated right to ask: What is the basis of competence on which you psychologists make your claim for participation in this associated attack on the problem? It has been a rather generally accepted principle in medicine—we need not argue its merits here—that it is better for society in the long run to struggle along with a small group of competently trained persons, than to spread training thinly over a larger number. Thus, since the major limiting factor in the organization of more medical schools is the shortage of competent teachers, even though there may be a need for more medical personnel, few additional schools are being established. A similar attitude is being taken by many psychiatrists at the present time about the problem we are now discussing.

L: Yes, but such a responsibility carries with it the associated duty to be constantly alert as to how the task can *best* be carried out!

T: I'll accept that with all its implications! Psychiatrists recognize that society's problems in the field related to personality maladjustment are not being taken care of adequately and, considering the various limiting factors, are not likely to be so taken care of in the future, at least by psychiatry alone (Rennie & Woodward, 1948). The question arises whether adequate care can be achieved by calling to a greater extent on non-medical groups, among them, psychologists. As you know, there are various shades of opinion among psychiatrists about this matter, particularly with regard to the participation of psychologists. At one extreme, there are those who hold that permitting psychologists to work in this field will result in more harm than good; and at the other extreme, there is a group that says that psychologists, given proper standards of selection and training, can play a very important role in taking care of needs in this field.

L: Psychologists have not been kept entirely uninformed of the range of opinion that is represented among psychiatrists!

T: I am, of course, merely describing the situation—not identifying myself for the moment. The problem of the selection of persons for clinical psychological training is one of the points about which psychiatrists are concerned. It is unnecessary to say that they are even more deeply concerned about the principles that should be used in the selection of psychiatrists; for this purpose assessment studies are under way. We have the impression, and you can check me on its accuracy, that a number of students go into clinical psychology who, for one reason or another, have not been able to get into medical school. A number of these are likely to be persons who are much attracted by the unlimited opportunities for the expressions of the power motive afforded by medicine and psychiatry—persons who are overcome by the "doc"-white coat-stethoscope-Svengali pattern—and, not being able to reach their destination by the usual path, enter clinical psychology as a substitute way of reaching these goals.

L: The images you provoke of projecting stethoscopes and dangling stop watches! You offer the quick-witted symbolist something to work with!

T: To use your terms, for these people the stop watch *is* an acceptable substitute. I am not saying that the same needs do not play a considerable role in the students who are accepted in the medical school. I remember reading one of Frederic Wells' (1936) articles in which he points out the dangers that a field with status, such as medicine, runs, in attracting to it persons who need considerable ego support, persons who might use this support in the exploitation of others. This is, I believe, an insufficiently recognized danger. Medicine has, however, developed certain important techniques for attenuating and controlling these drives. The delegation of increasingly serious responsibility and the pressure for making important decisions are two of these devices. We wonder how far psychology has gone in the same direction.

L: I agree that the problem of selection that you mention exists, but I am doubtful if it is as serious as you indicate. Insofar as it does exist, it carries with it a related difficulty, namely, what dangers for the profession of psychology lie in the recruitment of persons who are fundamentally disappointees of another profession? It is unnecessary to say that backdoor medicos and psychiatrists are certainly not the goals of our selection program!

T: What principles *are* you using in your selection?

L: We're approaching the problem from various angles, and with an experimental point of view. Universities are being encouraged to be quite liberal in their selection of persons with differing backgrounds. The American Psychological Association is also encouraging universities to experiment and not to set up inflexible requirements in the way of prerequisites for entrance to graduate work in clinical psychology. Until dependable data come from the intensive assessment and validation studies now in progress, psychology will have to depend on what is the best present-day "armchair" opinion. Generally, we are trying to select persons with a reasonable balance among humanitarian, scientific, economic, and prestige needs and with a fundamental interest in the problems of clinical psychology. There is an effort to avoid extremes, especially as these are expressed in mercenary and power needs. Psychology is concerned, too, with avoiding the extremes of the other drives—humanitarian needs that lead to intrusive "do-gooding," or scientific drives so rigidly impersonal that they inevitably lead to undue pressures on the individual patient. Although there are some disadvantages in a flexible system of this kind, we feel that with the field so undefined at present, experimentation is important. It would seem unwise to "fix" clinical psychology by the selection of a particular kind of person. With an attitude of this kind, one that above all considers each applicant on his merits, I do not think that we shall, in the future, be too much burdened by the problem of medical rejectees that you raise. I might mention, in passing, that reports coming from the universities about the quality of students now enrolled in clinical training programs are quite encouraging.

T: You know that the psychiatric group has done a lot of thinking about ways of dealing with the problem of inadequate psychiatric care. They have considered the possibility of making general practitioners more aware of psychiatric problems. A good example of this is the Minnesota experiment (Witmer, 1947) in the post-graduate education of general practitioners by a group of psychiatrists. Some hold that the way to solve the difficulties that are created by the immense territory to be covered, besides extending the training of general practitioners, is to improve the training of medical students, to give them much more awareness of the psychiatric problems they will face in practice. Although such efforts are commendable and highly important, I believe it is generally recognized that these programs can be of only limited value. This is true because of the shortages of physicians to take care of even the physical difficulties; and psychiatric care requires so much more time! The type of training we are discussing can be of value in sensitizing the medical practitioner to factors other than the physical, to the necessity for referring persons to proper agencies early, and to some extent, to aid in prevention. The major task cannot be solved in this way. There is, besides the groups I have mentioned, another group of psychiatrists who have worked closely with social workers and who are anxious to bring into the field more persons with that type of training. Among these are a few psychiatrists, usually those who have had little or no field contact with competent psychologists, who, as you know, are opposed to drawing in psychologists further.

L: Yes, that's an interesting attitude, one which I won't deny is sometimes justified from personal experience. More frequently, I am afraid, it involves considerable rationalization. How about, for a few minutes, exploring further the point you make about the social workers?

T: Sure. Of all the groups who have been concerned with the problems of personality adjustment and mental hygiene, I think you will agree with me when I say that social workers have given the most thought to problems of training, and have prepared themselves most adequately for what they consider their range of activity. Their frank recognition of a service function, filling a role which, if not handmaidenish—"ancillary," if you want to be fancy—is what the social workers themselves have called "adjunctive," has made it much easier for the psychiatrist to accept them. This role has been explicitly described at various times, and I am sure you are acquainted with the accounts (Ginsburg, 1947; GAP, 1948a). In all of these, you find depicted a role that, though considerably more independent than the traditional nurse's function in the medical setting, is still quite acceptable to the psychiatrist, even at a formal explicit level.

L: I suppose a further factor in this acceptance is the sharp distinction made formally by social workers between case work and therapy.

T: Yes, and there is a third factor, one whose actual influence is hard to evaluate but one that, at least unconsciously, must play a considerable part. I refer to the almost exclusively female constitution of the social work profession.

L: I admire you for being able to work around to this point so quickly! Besides making the situation less threatening to the psychiatrist, this fact would presumably result in a greater general readiness on the part of the social worker to accept a lesser role in the professional setting—at least insofar as the formal professional structure of the clinic is concerned.

T: I suppose that an examination of actual clinic practice would reveal quite a different actual picture. It would, I am sure, be quite shocking to many of us psychiatrists if we permitted ourselves to become consciously aware of what a large part of clinic procedure and clinic policy is determined by these females! What will happen with the increasing number of men going into the field of psychiatric social work is hard to predict. Some inkling of possible developments was given by the war experience when a fair number of male social workers became part of the military clinic teams. One hears reports that there were many more problems in these situations than ordinarily occur in civilian settings. When the number of male social workers increases appreciably, will the women begin to identify with the men in their own profession rather than with psychiatrists, as at present?

L: But this is speculation about depth problems and about an indeterminate future! Although the psychiatric social work situation may be relatively more defined than that of psychology, I am interested to find you agreeing that it is not so clear and stable as many people tend to assume. Not all social workers—in fact, not all psychiatrists—see definitely the distinction between case work and therapy (Lowrey, 1948), and there are an increasing number of social workers who carry on "therapy," called such right out by all.

T: We might mention also the beginning of an interest in the private practice of social work, although this trend does not seem to be very active.

L: What I think is more important is that social workers are now beginning to think in terms of research, and not merely in terms of service or practice. If this trend develops, and it will require a considerable change in both training and fundamental attitude to become effective, we will see an increasing contact with sociology and a growing interest in the theoretical aspects of the problem. This will require the development of a fundamental body of theory of their own, one that is not so largely determined by the psychiatric group as is the case now in the social work teaching program. We are hearing of more and more social workers who are interested in obtaining a doctoral degree. If such a development becomes at all prominent, some of the problems that have arisen in relation to psychology will probably develop in relation to social work. But even though the social work situation is relevant, it is, of course, not the direct issues with which we are concerned. The discussion arose, I believe, from the question you raised about competence.

T: Yes, at the present moment we are concerned with the fundamental competence of the *psychologist* in this area. What about it?

L: Psychology has, especially in recent years, recognized increasingly the need for developing competent people. Although the definition of competence has been the concern of psychology off and on for at least thirty years, no really effective methods for implementing the goals were developed until this decade. Departments of psychology in the universities had been carrying a fairly adequate program of training for general psychology. There was some degree of recognition of the unsystematic and inadequate training being offered in clinical psychology. This involved facing the fact that most of the people in this area were receiving training on their own, in the practical setting rather than under the auspices of the university. Once the widespread need for clinical psychologists was recognized, it was not difficult to obtain general acceptance of the notion that there must be a radical change in the nature of the training for this aspect of psychology.

T: I should say that you have then been quite fortunate in psychology. It took Flexner's Bulletin Number Four (1910) to blast the situation open in the medical field and to make the medical profession and the public aware of the inadequacy of the training being offered by the medical schools.

L: I don't mean to imply that the going has been entirely smooth. While there has been gratifying support, and both helpful criticisms and wise cautions, from many who may be taken to represent the more traditional academic approaches to psychology, there have also been less helpful criticism and lack of understanding from those with an unquenchable nostalgia for the "psychology of 1860–1910." You know, in psychology, as in other fields, there are still a few proponents of that simple typology which divides persons into two classes: virgins and prostitutes. Safely engirdled by their chastity-belts, daintily embroidered with the motto "unapplied," they find it impossible to appreciate a complexly organized world in which there exists a wide range of virtuous, productive love relationship between these extremes. Aside from very few exceptions of this sort, strongly positive attitudes were shown by university departments to the general recommendations on clinical psychology made by the American Psychological Association and its committees. The two reports you know about (APA, CTCP, 1947; APA & AAAP, 1945), which recommend a doctoral program of four years of training at the graduate level, one year of which is to be spent in the field, have met a recognized need.

T: I like the inclusion of a year's internship as an integral part of the program. That's an intriguing notion, too, that of placing the internship in the third year. I am glad that psychology is experimenting with a pattern different from the medical one. It will be interesting to see what effect this placement has on departments of psychology as well as on students.

L: But all around, the internship area is one where psychologists have a lot to learn from both psychiatrists and social workers.

T: I can see why. I don't believe that many psychologists have a real notion of how costly a good internship is. Having been mainly concerned with didactic instruction that can be carried out satisfactorily in groups, few psychologists are aware of the time and effort that go into the close supervisory relationship that is the essence of the internship experience.

L: I wouldn't put it so extremely! They have come near to this problem in the properly supervised thesis relationship. I will admit, however, that the doctoral thesis relationship does not ordinarily involve the close day-by-day contact of the internship and that, in general, what you say is true. For the present, I suppose, we'll have to admit that the internship has been accepted largely on principle, without realization of its full meaning. Constant progress is, however, being made toward wider appreciation of its significance, and I look forward to even more development of internship programs when the Committee on Training undertakes, as I understand it will soon, the problem of evaluation of internship centers.

T: Would you refresh my memory on just which major areas of training are covered in the four-year program?

L: There are six: fundamental general psychology, psychodynamics of behavior, work in several related disciplines, diagnosis, therapy, and research. Although the general pattern of training is laid down for the universities, a special effort has been made not to be too specific about the content, in order to avoid "setting" the course too rigidly and to permit a flexibility of atmosphere that would encourage variety, especially an atmosphere favorable to the development of research workers.

T: In some respects we are faced with the same kind of problem in psychiatry that you apparently have in determining your relationship to general psychology. We have insisted on the notion that a psychiatrist should first have a general medical training, and then, on this basic foundation, build his psychiatric knowledge. It is true that some of us have regretted the amount of time spent on some aspects of medical training, aspects that, those holding to this view have felt, played little or no role in the future effectiveness of the psychiatrist. But medical training has, nevertheless, been accepted as the basic preparation. The arguments for this type of training are that it develops a sense of responsibility and provides a background that cannot be equaled by other forms of preparation.

L: It is rather interesting to note how much was made of the point about responsibility by the psychiatrists in the National Research Council panel discussing the relationships of the two professions (NRC, 1921). You remember how Salmon, in particular, came back to this point repeatedly.

T: I was much impressed with the document which you let me see, and I was struck with the similarity of some of our problems today to those considered by this group of psychiatrists and psychologists over a quarter of a century ago. With regard to the comment that you have just made, actually, what the psychiatrists said seemed to me not to involve the training aspect so much, except by implication. Didn't they emphasize rather the tremendous feeling of responsibility that the psychiatrist, because of his medical training, feels for his patient? Psychiatry, they held, could not give up this final responsibility for the patient. There has, of course, been some discussion about whether another form of training would provide this same result.

L: As you say, there are analogies in the two training situations. Psychologists have a situation similar to the one you just described relating to medical background for psychiatry. Since, in the past, some good clinical psychologists have been drawn from those who took their training in traditional academic psychology, it has been argued that this type of psychology is the best background for a clinical psychologist.

The Committee on Training has accepted this notion in part, but apparently not for the reason given. It has recognized the contribution that a good background training in general and experimental psychology provides, and has therefore taken the strong stand that a clinical psychologist is primarily a psychologist. But it has taken the equally strong stand that it is not the traditional training of psychologists for the Ph.D. that is the proper training for the clinical psychologist, but rather that there are certain specialized areas of training that the *clinical* psychologist needs in his formal program in addition to the basic training that *all* psychologists should have. It has apparently not been willing to accept the argument that what was done through necessity at one time, and by chance turned out to be fairly satisfactory in some instances, should therefore be established as a policy.

T: You were talking about the six different parts of the training program. With relatively few exceptions, psychiatrists in general would accept all but a few aspects of such a program as quite satisfactory. [Pause.] I paused because I suddenly realized how patronizing this last statement of mine might have sounded. I don't need to assure you that no such intention existed. I am afraid that I may have automatically adopted the tone of some of my colleagues, a tone, I know, that must be quite hard for you to listen to, for it makes *me* uncomfortable when I hear it. I am sure that most psychologists can take such displays in their stride toward their goal, accepting it as one type of temporary unpleasantness that inevitably stems from a confused status situation. To get back to what I was going to say before this digression on condescension! No question can, of course, be raised about the basic general training and the training in psychodynamics of behavior, although there is a feeling among psychiatrists that they should perhaps play some role in the teaching of psychodynamics, just as many of them recognize the need for having psychologists play a role in some aspects of their own training. You ought to realize that there is considerable agreement about this need for drawing psychologists into the training of psychiatrists. Though the points made by Glover (1934) in the article you have already referred to about academic psychological courses for medical students and psychiatrists were sound—

L: Sound, but pretty harsh!

T: Yes, quite harsh, but don't you think deservedly so? I believe, however, that psychiatrists recognize the marked changes in emphasis that have taken place in psychology, when compared with the academic psychology of a quarter of a century ago that he so severely criticized. I even think that with the extension of clinical psychological facilities to medical settings, GAP, in its next report, will have some basis for modifying the reservations of its recent Report on Medical Education (GAP, 1948b) about psychology courses in undergraduate medical education. With regard to diagnosis, there is also little problem. The days when psychiatrists were sensitive about psychologists' using the term "diagnosis" are substantially gone. Woodworth's concern with the problem in his communication to the 1921 NRC group of psychiatrists and psychologists sounded more "dated" than almost anything else in the document (NRC, 1921). Despite his conciliatory suggestions of "measurement" for "diagnosis," and so on, it is of interest that *his* statement was the one that aroused the most opposition among the psychiatrists present. However, we must keep in mind Huston's (1948) point about the various factors that are involved in diagnosis in the psychiatric setting—namely, that it includes much more than the diagnostic material ordinarily provided by the psychologist.

L: Yes, and we must keep in mind also that it doesn't mean mere pigeonholing, but involves rather the breadth of content that is included in the Training Committee Report's discussion of this point (APA, CTCP, 1947).

T: Whatever the case, the contribution of the psychologist in this area is generally acknowledged. In research, psychiatrists have recognized the more adequate general preparation of psychologists; and it is interesting to note how frequently in clinics the research is, by common consent, turned over to the psychologist, or at least made a major part of his responsibility.

L: Although this is very flattering to the psychologist, I have been somewhat puzzled by the readiness of many psychiatrists to say to the psychologist: "Research is your area." In the first place, psychologists don't deserve the implied compliment. A good deal is lacking both in the quality and in the amount of research that has been turned out by psychologists in this field. But aside from these considerations, since research is really the most important lack in this field, and distinctly the area in which the greatest contribution is called for, it appears strange that so many psychiatrists are ready to relinquish this activity. For satisfactory progress to occur, it is imperative that research workers from *all* relevant disciplines be available. In part, the reaction of psychiatrists is understandable on the basis of the inadequacy of the research training of most of them, and in part by reason of the primary clinical interest of the psychiatrist in the patient. Some part, I suppose, must also be attributed to private practice, which has a great attraction for the individual psychiatrist; and private practice is apparently a setting that is little conducive to research, or shall we put it more bluntly, conducive to little research.

T: I must admit that this attitude is somewhat puzzling to me, too. In fact, it is more than puzzling, it is deplorable; as is deplorable the whole trend of emphasis on private practice. It means, first, a reduction in the number of persons who will contribute substantially to advance in the field. Further, it involves preoccupation with the needs of those who can afford treatment, a difficult test for social integrity to weather, as Laski (1948) has pointed out in his discussion of American lawyers. I suppose this attitude toward research grows naturally out of the feeling of being overwhelmed by the immediate pressing needs, and the responsibility for meeting the needs, that the psychiatrist feels especially, and that the psychologist is generally in the luxurious position of being able to disregard. The other factors that you mentioned are, of course, important too.

L: Doesn't it mean that society must find some way of making research more attractive financially, as well as in other ways, in order to reduce the sacrifices demanded by a research career?

T: Yes, emphatically. But psychiatry must recognize more fully its own responsibilities in this direction. It must develop more research interest and provide more research training. In any case, with some exceptions, psychiatrists are apparently ready to depend for a considerable part of the research in the field on the psychologist. Some of the research can, of course, be independent, but the greater part will have to be collaborative research with psychiatry, and to some extent with other disciplines, especially on problems having somatic aspects. I'd like now to turn to another aspect of your training program—therapy—and see what we can make of it. However, I'm sure we'd get deeply involved, and the hour is pretty late. I want very much to continue this discussion and quite soon. Are you free tomorrow evening, and may I come over then?

L: I feel the same way as you do about how much there is still left to consider. I *am* free. Shall we say tomorrow at the same time?

Part II

L: I suppose we've both been thinking about what we were saying last night and as usual have all kinds of second thoughts infinitely better than our first ones. Shall we leave these, however, to come out during the course of our discussion? I'd like to get to the topic you raised when we quit—therapy.

T: That suits me. I was going to say last night that of all the aspects of your training program, the part about which most questions would arise among psychiatrists is, of course, that relating to therapy. This is the area in which the greatest conflict exists. One has here all the problems that stem from traditional medical control of the field—the natural insistence by the physician that treating the sick person is his prerogative.

L: I recognize the central nature of this problem in the relationship of the two professions. Some have held that this crucial question could be solved by defining the "sick" person. It is my belief, however, that a satisfactory definition cannot really be formulated; and even if formulated, it would not be too helpful. Obviously, the medical man is, by the very nature of his work, bound to pass over from the problem of treating disease to the problem of preventing disease, and once he does that, he necessarily leaves the realm of dealing with the sick person. When you broaden "sickness" to include "potential sickness" you cover a rather wide territory!

T: To say nothing of the problems lying in the immense borderline area between health and disease. Let's not even *raise* the question which has been asked by some, whether psychological sickness is of the same order as physical sickness.

L: From the psychologist's side the problem, though different, is also great. The psychologist is interested in the functioning of the normal organism. He is naturally interested in the variations in behavior—not only the natural biological variations, but also the more extreme ones that border on the pathological. In the final analysis, can we put it any differently than this: Psychologists work from the normal end of the distribution toward the middle, and psychiatrists work from the pathological end toward the middle. There is bound to be a very considerable area of overlap (to a slight degree extending even to the other extreme), an area of overlap where definition *is* not, and *cannot* be, clear. Is not our major concern with the development of adequately prepared professional people who have a care for the needs of the person studied, who are sensitive to the range of problems in their own field and to the problems of colleagues in other fields, who are appreciative of social needs, and who above all possess essential good will? Under such circumstances couldn't we depend on specific problems being taken care of satisfactorily as they arise?

T: I have come to the same general position myself, a position with which some of my colleagues do not, however, agree. I am wondering about the obstacles on either side to carrying out a mature program of this kind. Obviously we are plunked right down in the middle of the problem of control. Before we get on to a discussion of the handicaps on the psychologist's side, I'd like to have your views of what might be possible handicaps to its achievement on the psychiatrist's side.

L: Since you ask me, perhaps I'd put it this way: The advantages of medical training for a considerable portion of the activity of the psychiatrist are enormous and cannot be questioned. I see some possible disadvantages in the somatically permeated environment of the ordinary medical school for developing alertness to psychological problems. There is, too, the possibility that the selective program of medical schools may work against choosing psychologically sensitive persons. Some question also arises with regard to the effects of the relative overemphasis on cure at the expense of prevention in the standard medical school training. There is one aspect, however, that has impressed me particularly, an aspect on which I should like to get *your* attitude. I have in mind the relative narrowness of the point of view of the physician—his tremendous in-group identification, contrasted with his general insensitivity to the broader social connotations of a field that runs into social factors at almost every turn, to say nothing of every step. I say this though I am not unmindful of the tremendous pressures on the physician to keep up with extraordinarily fast-changing technical developments as well as to take care of his ordinarily heavy day-by-day work.

T: Some of these problems have been recognized by physicians themselves. I mentioned the Flexner report earlier—the report that resulted in much-needed changes in the direction of making medical education more "scientific" and rigorous by bringing the laboratory and the medical sciences into training. There is a question in the minds of many who are concerned with medical education today as to whether after these forty years, now that the type of training called for in the Flexner report is well entrenched, there is not a need for another revolutionary step, one that will concern itself with balancing the present program with an emphasis on the humanitarian and social aspects. Some medical schools are at present working on just that question. The in-group feeling that you speak of is one important facet of the problem.

L: This feeling is only in its infancy in psychology, and we possibly have the power to control its development, if such control is called for.

T: It is amazing how important this factor is in medicine, and how much it is emphasized throughout the training. The Hippocratic oath is a symbolic, but nevertheless clear, reflection of its importance.

L: Indeed it is. The tremendous medical concern for identification with one's professional colleagues, the guild characteristic which has so often been pointed out, has appeared to me, looking at it from the outside, to result in weaknesses as well as in obvious strengths. One suspects that the attitude is, both consciously and unconsciously, in large part an outgrowth of the primary emphasis that is placed on a kind of "familiocentrism," on loyalty to teacher and fellow-worker, in the Hippocratic oath. The code is a noble one and has served medicine well for some twenty centuries, but some advances in ethical thinking and psychological insight have been made since this code was first advanced, to say nothing of the fundamental changes in the structure of our society that have occurred. It seems to me that implicit in the oath lies some degree of ethical limitedness and psychological immaturity that is anachronistic in a culture so broad-minded and, at the same time, so specialized as ours, and one wonders sometimes whether the code should not reflect these advances.

T: But isn't it true, as Sigerist (1939) points out, that each successive generation of physicians interprets Hippocrates' words to cover the ideals of its own period?

L: Yes, but I wonder whether a more explicit formulation of the generation's goals would not be desirable, and indeed necessary. Binger's book (1945), in fact, all the publications of the Committee on Medicine and the Changing Order of the New York Academy of Medicine (Allen, 1946), as well as the recent William Menninger volumes (1948a,b), are an evidence for this need. In any event, psychology as a profession can learn an incalculable amount from medicine, but it has the advantage of being largely "tradition-unbound" so that it can set up its own ethical goals. Can we say it any better than the way the Training Committee has put it in its Report? Let me read what they say: "If the student, after having achieved strong identification with psychology, learns to divest himself of this identification in order to become part of larger wholes for the benefit of a patient or a group, then he may be said to have achieved true professional growth." Psychology or, to go further, as Conant (1948) has suggested, all the sciences, could use an Hippocratic oath. If psychology attempts to develop such a code, I trust it will take cognizance of some of the points we have just made.

T: I must admit that there is a good deal to what you say, but we must not forget that the Hippocratic oath carries certain kinds of controls—in fact a long, long tradition of controls. This is a factor of utmost importance when it comes to the extremely serious responsibilities placed on one who deals with persons abased by illness. What do you psychologists have in mind in relation to control? Or have you not given the matter much thought? Excuse the barb!

L: I *deserve* a little jab for touching a medical man in so personal a spot as his oath! Your question is decidedly pertinent. Yes, we *have* given the problem some thought and even some *action.* I must admit, however, considering the importance of the topic, that what we have done seems insignificant. We recognize that this aspect of the training of the psychologist has in the past been relatively neglected—neglected because it was not particularly relevant to a large part of the work he was doing. Considerable emphasis, in contrast, has been placed on another kind of control, the kind of control that a scientist generally develops toward the collecting and handling of his data. Psychology, recognizing the greatly increased sources of error that are involved in its data when compared with those in the more exact sciences, has been particularly concerned with training in this respect. Such controls, as you know, are of a high order.

T: However, are they not of a quite different nature from those that arise in relationships with people, especially sick people?

L: Of course, in many respects. It is this different kind of responsibility that the psychologist must develop a good deal more of now, at the same time retaining that which comes with being trained as a scientist. Just as you do in medicine and in psychiatry, we recognize four major types of control: inner personal, internal professional, external professional, and external legal ones. With respect to the first —the inner personal controls—the controls that in the final analysis are the crucial ones, our first task is to select the right kind of people; that is, persons with good minds whose motivation, as we have discussed earlier, is fundamentally humanitarian and scientific. Persons of this kind, in constant contact with a group of selected teachers with whom they can identify, teachers exemplifying these ideals and representing a self-respecting, dignified profession that is making a distinct and sound contribution, are in the best possible setting for developing these inner controls.

T: How about the other types of controls?

L: The three other kinds of control can at best merely serve as reinforcing agents for the first type. Considerable attention in psychological circles has in recent years been devoted to the development of intraprofessional controls, of which I can mention only a few. A formal professional code of ethics is being developed by a committee under Dr. Edward Tolman (Proceedings, 1947), an American Board of Examiners in Professional Psychology has been established (APA, CABEPP, 1946. See also *American Psychologist*, 1948, *3*, 480, 499–500.) and is now actively engaged in certifying diplomates who are required to meet ethical and competence standards of the level of those set up by the specialty boards in medicine; membership standards in the American Psychological Association and particularly in its Division of Clinical and Abnormal Psychology have been clarified, and carry with them some informal certifying aspects; post-graduate courses of various kinds are being established in order to provide contact with new developments and aid in the maintenance of competence in old techniques. Besides these intraprofessional controls, directed at the individual psychologist, there are numerous controls that indirectly affect him through the establishment and maintenance of standards growing out of the evaluation programs of universities and field centers, carried out by the American Psychological Association and its committees.

T: I hope the psychologists have learned what has been impressed on psychiatrists so much—the fact that setting up elaborate machinery for control is not enough, that it is necessary to maintain constant vigilance to see that the devices work effectively, and that when they don't, they must be modified.

L: I believe that psychologists *are* becoming aware of this danger. There is one problem of intraprofessional control, one particularly pertinent to our discussion, that we have *not* solved. I refer to the problem of controlling members of our profession in how they express themselves about relationships with other professions! One wishes sometimes that there were ways of controlling the bright, impatient youngsters with ideas—many of them sound and meritorious—who, despite their limited experience, know exactly how related professions, as well as the one they are on the verge of commencing to enter, should be conducted. And they don't hesitate to give a full two-semester course on the subject, in an unwittingly arrogant fashion!

The same holds for oldsters who for one reason or another, mostly another, don't like the members of a related profession and manage to find a channel for expressing their feelings. And while we are compiling the list, we may as well cover the complete range and add those in the middle years who appropriate to themselves and psychology the full cloak of psychological science and then accuse related disciplines of scientific nakedness. I know that incidents of this kind have served to interfere with the smooth development of relations between our professions. However, since these are obviously personal expressions of opinion, there is serious doubt if any attempt should, or can, be made to control them professionally.

T: I could point to similar instances on psychiatry's side. But in one respect, aren't such incidents valuable since they serve as tests of the strength of the principles we evolved at the beginning of our discussion?

L: Yes, we may take that comfort from them. And perhaps they serve another purpose, too—an abreactive one. But so much for intraprofessional controls. The external legal controls I had reference to are connected with active efforts in various parts of the country to set up state standards for certifying persons for the practice of psychology and are exemplified in the already-established Connecticut (Heiser, 1945; Miles, 1946) and Virginia (Finger, 1946) laws.

T: You also mentioned external professional controls. How do you conceive of these in psychology?

L: The external professional controls I had in mind are the most complicated. They involve the interrelationships of the various professions concerned with the area of our interest, especially the interrelationships between psychology and psychiatry. They are concerned also with the problems raised by group, as contrasted with individual, practice. If we examine the practice of psychology, at least the practice of clinical psychology, we find that, just as in psychiatry, three types of practice are current: group institutional practice, group private practice, and individual private practice. By far the greatest field of activity for the psychologist is in the first—group institutional practice. In this type of practice I have reference, of course, to what has been called the "team" approach.

T: Hail! I am surprised that we have only at this late hour come to the consideration of a topic that is on everybody's lips nowadays.

L: Yes, it *is* surprising, and I sense some of the feeling that lies behind your "Hail!" I am sure that we have been equally annoyed with some of the talk that has currently gone on about the "team." There has been so much football field in it! In fact, it takes considerable strength of mind not to dwell, as a defense against these "old Siwash" appeals, on the images they evoke of attractive exposed limbs in attitudes of supplication for a thundering triple "Team!"

T: Beyond this slightly mawkish aspect, which we can forget, I have been impressed with the many differences in interpretation of what the team approach means and the varieties of forms it takes.

L: Hasn't a committee of the American Orthopsychiatric Association been working on this problem during the last year or so?

T: Yes, the Committee on Membership Study. Pending their report, you might be interested in what is essentially my own analysis of the team approach as I have seen it in a variety of actual clinic settings. Although it is necessarily based on rather limited observation, I don't believe that the Committee's, or anyone else's, analysis is likely to be substantially different in pattern from mine. No matter how the principle works out in practice, the fundamental philosophy behind the team approach is the notion that the area in which we are interested, that of personality maladjustment, is very complex. To have the opinions of experts from various disciplines on a problem is therefore helpful, and often necessary. This may involve either having opinions based on the actual study by each discipline of each patient or, more commonly, actual study by one or two of the disciplines only, and having the other(s) available for consultation during the course of contact with the patient or at the final evaluation. As I see it, there are five major types of team relationships, or associations between the professions, where so-called coordinated services are available. The first may be called the *contiguous* type of relationship.

L: "Contiguous" in what sense?

T: In the sense of mere close geographical presence of the different disciplines involved; that is, each is available when needed. The disciplines may be fairly equal in status, but the functions are quite separate and there is no attempt at unification. The second has a *collateral* type of organization. In this form, the various services are merely operative at the same time. Again there is no coordination in any true sense, as in joint evaluation conferences. In this case, however, although there is the same kind of separation as in the contiguous service, the relationship of psychology and social work to psychiatry is very definitely subsidiary and both report to it. A third kind is the *ancillary* type of relationship, a relationship most characteristic of the earliest types of clinics. Here there is a definite connection between the services, but the relationship of the other two to psychiatry is clearly subservient, although intimate. Generally, in this type, each patient is seen for direct study by each of the disciplines, and then the material is synthesized by the psychiatrist at a staff conference.

L: Then the major difference between the last two, I take it, is in the degree to which the services are drawn together?

T: Yes. The fourth may be called the *articulative* type. Here the connection again is fairly close, but the parts, essentially equal in standing, remain clearly distinguishable. Each of the disciplines maintains its own characteristics and an identity which is different from that of the others. Each has its separate skill which is combined either in the actual study of the individual patient or in the various evaluation conferences. Usually only two, sometimes all three, of the disciplines make actual studies of the same patient. The fifth might be called the *integrative* type. In this organization the different disciplines are indistinguishable, since they all carry out essentially the same function. They all have a common skill—with few exceptions, this is therapy—and they do virtually the same kind of work, the assignment being determined by the qualifications of the staff member for handling that particular problem. In a sense, there is complete unity and the status is equal. Perfect examples of this kind of setup are rare, and the most advanced existing types of clinic organizations usually fall somewhere between the articulative and integrative. In these most advanced settings, a large part of the function, for instance, therapy, is similar, but each of the disciplines maintains its particular skills for use on occasions where they are necessary. Thus, ordinarily, only two of the disciplines would be concerned with the actual study of a particular patient, but all three might be involved in the evaluation.

L: This analysis is quite enlightening. I must say I had never thought this problem through systematically. I had the feeling that the old notion of a team, one in which each discipline had a different job to do that it contributed to the pool in the consideration of each case, didn't describe the actual clinics with which I had contact. I took it for granted, however, that the usual arrangement was of this general kind, but that I had been associated with rather unusual settings. Would it be fair to conclude from what you have said that the essence of true team activity is the *coordinated thinking* devoted to a case, thinking contributed by persons with differing points of view growing out of different training, rather than the specific and detailed study of each case by each discipline's specialized techniques (Shakow, 1948b).

T: Yes—and well put!

L: In your discussion you haven't considered the problem of administration, have you? How do you see it from that point of view?

T: I suppose we would agree that administration is essentially of two kinds: The first, we might say, is of an executive type. This involves care for what could be designated as the autonomic and spinal functions of an organization, the functions that are quite unimportant when they work smoothly and invisibly, but which become all-important when they are disturbed. The other is a professional type of administration, one that involves the care of what might be thought of as the cortical and higher affective functions of an organization. The first type of administration could ideally be in anyone's hands, that is, in the hands of any one of the three disciplines we are mainly concerned with; it might even be in the hands of an outsider, such as a businessman. The choice of person would depend on the interests and peculiar abilities of those available in the particular situation; to some extent, it would depend on whom you can get to be the "goat." The second type of administration is of course highly dependent on the nature of the agency, that is, what problems of final synthesis of the professional contributions are involved.

L: The statement of the joint Committee of the two APA's (APA, CCP, 1946) puts this latter point quite adequately, doesn't it?

T: Yes. I'd say the nearer the agency is to dealing with medical problems, the more desirable is it that a medical person be the administrator. If the agency is fundamentally psychological in character, then it is more desirable that a psychologist be in charge; if the agency is educational, an educator; if the agency is of a social service type, then it is desirable that a social worker be the administrator. Thus, in relation to a state hospital, there is little question that a medical person, a psychiatrist, should be the administrator. In the case of a state school, because of the importance of the problem of education in the training of the feebleminded, a question may arise. But in general the feeling is, and correctly so, that the medical problems are primary and that a medical person, again a psychiatrist, should be the administrator. In the case of the industrial school, that is, a school for delinquents, since both the social and the psychiatric aspects are equally important, there would seem to be good ground for placing a psychiatrically oriented sociologist or criminologist, or a sociologically sophisticated psychiatrist, at the head of the organization.

L: I suppose that in the case of a special school, say for the retarded, there is little doubt about the desirability of a specially trained educator or psychologist serving at its head?

T: Yes, I should say so. Despite the fact that all of these agencies deal in differing degrees with problems of maladjustment, it is obvious that the head need not be a psychiatrist in every case, a point of view that is held by some persons. Although it is important to keep the "professional-administrative" and the "professional-professional" functions separate, in reality this is very difficult to do. The former, for mature professional people, should be relatively unimportant. In fact, the wiser the person, the more ready is he to give up these responsibilities. We must, however, recognize the great part that administrators can play in the determination of policy and in the direction of the group toward the institution's goal. It is for this reason that there is considerable concern about the professional administration of agencies.

L: Isn't this concern with administration to some extent a reflection of an especially strong characteristic of our American culture, one in which presidents and deans and directors play such a great role?

T: I suppose that this general characteristic comes out here, too. There is one point, that we have considered implicitly, which I should like to bring out in the open. Though unimportant in itself, it unfortunately is a source for considerable debate—in fact, it has become a focal point for controversy. I refer to those grand old complexes of terms: supervision-direction-guidance-advice, on the one hand, and collaboration-association-cooperation, on the other.

L: "Complex" is a very appropriate characterization! Innocent words in themselves, they certainly become charged words in this setting. Where status is so heavily involved, there is grave doubt as to whether any formal public statement about the issue will in the near future be acceptable to both groups. The problem arises, of course, mainly in relation to therapy. The situations included in this area are so varied in the degree of "sickness" involved, the skills of the respective persons have such a range, both absolute and differential, and the affective factors are so great, that, speaking privately as we are, I can say what I feel, namely, that a little psychiatric understanding is called for. And the psychiatric understanding, it seems to me, should, in this case, come mainly from the psychiatrist, through not insisting always on the power-status words. In the field of therapy, all but a few psychologists would admit that at the present stage of knowledge, and in relation to the greater part of the range of cases (especially as they shade away from the simpler guidance problems), they ought to work under the supervision of the psychiatrist. This view would be taken in all cases, because of the responsibility delegated to the psychiatrist as physician for the health of persons and, in most cases, because of the greater skill of the psychiatrist in this area. But is it psychologically insightful for psychiatrists on *every* occasion to collect the status pound-of-flesh from a discipline that is in the process of establishing itself professionally and for that reason is understandably sensitive about such factors as status? In this instance, the choice of words seems to mean more symbolically to the psychologist than to the psychiatrist, and the latter can therefore afford to make concessions, except, of course, in those instances where important issues are involved. The psychologist in the field would voluntarily recognize the need for supervision in areas where it is indicated. The controls we have talked about would, in the main, take care of problems that might arise.

T: I, myself, am in favor of just such a step if the psychologists would show in their professional activity a real acceptance of the responsibilities for competence that are involved. I'll admit that I am disturbed that some psychiatrists should insist, on purely formal grounds, on the kind of status relationship you have described. Leadership should be established, at least in the main, on the basis of *personal* competence—membership in a select group can only provide a small proportion of the justification for being a director or a supervisor. The problem is, of course, made particularly difficult by the really enormous range of competence represented by present practitioners in both our disciplines. When the discrepancy in competence between the psychiatrist as director and other members of the staff, in favor of the latter, is great—a situation which I know does not occur rarely—the problem is made embarrassingly obvious. I am sure that the increase of the number of competent people resulting from our respective training programs will substantially reduce the extent of the problem.

L: To return, after this long digression, to the question of control—that which is supplied by the external professional group of which the psychologist may be a part. It is this team setting, this working together of groups made up of different professions, that acts as a strong, outside control on the activities of the psychologist, just as it acts in the same way on the activities of the other members of the team. In the case of private practice, the situation is somewhat different. In private *group* practice, the situation is theoretically similar to institutional group practice. Actually, there is a considerable reduction in the control exercised on all the members of the group, both because of the reduction in the institutional controls and the increase in the monetary pressures. In any case, this type of organization still retains a number of satisfactory restricting characteristics and raises relatively few questions. The great problem, in the case of the psychologist, arises with respect to *individual* private practice. Although this type of practice has a strong tradition in medicine, though a less extensive one in psychiatry, cannot a question about its desirability be raised in psychiatry? If group practice is necessary in the institutional setting, why is it any less necessary in individual practice?

T: It is rather interesting that the Committee on Medicine and the Changing Order (1947), recognizing the complexity of modern medicine and the trend toward specialization, comes out so wholeheartedly for group practice in general medicine. They point out its advantages in encouraging the maintenance of both ethical and technical standards and are aware of the dangers lying in practice on one's own. Implicitly they recognize the fact that everybody's superego needs repeated bolstering and nourishment and that group practice provides a support to inner control that is not provided by licensing or malpractice provisions.

L: I, too, have watched with interest this trend in general medicine. But to get back to the psychologist. For him the question is exceedingly important. The medical man has various controls and sanctions which come from a profession with a long tradition of private practice, considerable experience with licensing, and, most important of all, having legal and social sanctions for the treatment of persons. Psychologists have little background of this kind and actually do not have legal or even social sanctions for the treatment of sick people. It is because of this that there should be considerable reluctance on the part of all concerned to permit psychologists, at least in the present stage of the development of the profession, to practice independently. The psychological group generally is rather negative toward completely independent private practice by psychologists in the area touching on the therapeutic. In fact, official psychological groups have recommended strongly the desirability of group practice (APA, PPB, 1947) and have indicated that wherever private practice takes place, contact should be established with a psychiatrist, or at least some medical person. The latter raises a problem that involves a danger—a problem which we ought perhaps not to go into at the present time. I refer to the care that the psychologist has to exercise in establishing relationships with medical men in a way that does not involve the bypassing of the psychiatrist.

T: What you have said seems very definitely to be leading in the right direction, but you know that certain psychiatrists have raised a question about the desirability of a psychologist's doing *any* private therapeutic work. They point out that even though a person may be working in association with a psychiatrist in the treatment of a case, the general busyness of everybody prevents actual close follow-up of the work and that, therefore, dangers are inherent in the practice. Considered from all aspects, the problem is not so easy to solve as it would seem at first, even *with* the establishment of quite careful controls.

L: I am aware of these reservations, but not everything can be legislated, can it? Doesn't a good part of any problem of this kind have to be worked out in the give-and-take relationships of the field? May I turn now to a related point that is of the greatest importance. All along, we seem to have been talking as if psychologists believed that therapy was their outstanding function. Actually, most psychologists do not believe this at all. Although they have some interest in this activity, they feel a certain amount of social pressure on them in this respect, pressure that comes from various sources.

T: How do psychologists react to this pressure?

L: Generally, I believe, there is a tendency among psychologists to resist it. They feel rather that of the four major functions that a psychologist can be said to be concerned with: diagnosis, therapy, prevention, and research, their most important contribution lies in research—research in the areas that their training makes them competent to undertake. And it is for this reason primarily that they are interested in therapy. The report of a number of teachers who have been responsible for the training of clinical psychologists is of interest in this respect. They say that many of their students—particularly the better ones—after having had an opportunity to carry on ordinary therapeutic work for a time, express a dissatisfaction with such activity and indicate a preference for research, either in therapy or in other aspects of the clinical field. Psychologists, however, believe that not only can therapeutic experience be of great help in improving diagnostic skill and making it more effective, but it can be of inestimable help in making research in almost any branch of this field more meaningful. We know that there is probably no better entree into an appreciation of the complexities of human motivation than the therapeutic relationship. A research worker or a diagnostician in this area is seriously handicapped if he has not had such experience, as well as some form of personal analytic experience, as background. Certain regions of the personality remain closed to him otherwise, and there is a kind of "thinness" about his research projects. Indeed, psychologists have on occasion been criticized by psychiatrists for the exaggerated use of statistics and a preoccupation with the study of segmental function—frequently with justification. Both these tendencies stem in considerable part, I believe, from limited clinical, especially limited therapeutic, contact. Besides the area of general research there is the area of research in therapy itself. There appears to be some reason for believing that the psychologist will have to bear a substantial part of the burden for research in the future. Because of these various considerations, psychologists have been calling for training in therapy, and asking psychiatrists and psychoanalysts, and to some extent social workers, to help in this training.

T: What do you think of the recent action of the American Psychoanalytic Association with regard to non-medical therapists (Hendrick, 1947)?

L: What I have just been saying makes me feel that the Association is in error in the step it has taken of limiting greatly, and in some respects practically eliminating almost entirely, the training of psychologists in therapy.

T: The psychoanalysts *have* reacted strongly to this problem, largely, I suppose, for fear that psychologists would enter the private practice of psychoanalysis.

L: But in taking the stand in the negative way it has, the official psychoanalytic group has, I believe, done a disservice to the whole area of mental health. They have in effect, if not literally, also cut off a large number of psychologists who need psychoanalytic training in order to do more effective teaching and diagnostic work, but more important than these, more effective research in both the general personality field and in the therapeutic area. If the present trend toward private practice by psychoanalysts continues, it is rather unlikely that many of the persons who are now receiving psychoanalytic training will contribute in any fundamental way to the development of either psychoanalytic theory or psychoanalytic therapeutic research. Psychoanalytic institutes would, it seems to me, make an important contribution if they would set aside a fair number of their training openings each year for psychologists and representatives of other basic disciplines whose interests are primarily in research and teaching. In this latter respect, I might mention a fact that Donald Marquis has pointed out, namely, that the psychoanalysts could have, through analyzed psychologists, an unusual opportunity to present psychoanalytic principles correctly to an astounding number of college students each year. For it is the instructors who teach college classes in psychology who have the first contact with students in this general area. It is not only with regard to psychoanalysis that this problem of research enters. In the whole psychiatric field, it becomes more obvious daily that altogether too few persons with this type of training plan to devote themselves to research.

T: The situation, I understand, is generally bad in medicine, where research workers are becoming scarce because of the seductions of private practice. In the psychiatric field, this trend seems even more marked at present than in the general medical field.

L: Because of their academic background and their fundamental interest in research, psychologists provide a good nucleus for a group interested in attacking the research problems in the field. This is a major reason for discouraging them from being drawn into the practice of therapy. From the social point of view, it would appear to be a good investment for the other professions involved to contribute some of their time to the training of the psychologist, in order to give him as full-bodied a background for research as is possible. Psychologists themselves are recognizing increasingly that their training in the past has been too limited and too removed from clinical contact to provide the best preparation for research in this area. We recognize that even with the best of training not everybody can become a research worker. However, with the programs of training that psychologists are working out at present, and planning for the future, that is, programs that emphasize research, and with their outgrowth from an academic discipline having a tradition of research, it seems likely that at least a larger proportion of persons devoting themselves to this aspect will come from psychology than from either psychiatry or social work. Anything that can be done to improve the quality of the training for research and to raise the status of the research worker is a task for which all disciplines have a responsibility. It is most important that all possible effort be made to increase the number of research workers from all disciplines, since many of the problems to be met call for a multidiscipline attack.

T: The backwardness of the state hospital, in my opinion, may in large part be accounted for by the preferred status of the administrator over the clinician. Some change in this policy toward equalizing the status has been coming about in recent years, with noticeable improvement in conditions. I agree with you that a major need at the present time is to improve the status and satisfactions of research workers, both medical and non-medical, in order to attract competent persons from all disciplines into this most important work.

T: Well, we've done a lot of talking and covered a lot of ground. What would you say is the upshot of it all?

L: I'll speak only of the implications of what we've said, for the psychologist. It seems to me that what has come out of our discussion is a need for psychologists to realize that full recognition in the field can be achieved only by hard work and significant contribution, and not through any special rights. This would seem to call for less claim based merely on promises or on privilege, or on underprivilege, or even on having completed a full term of apprenticeship as a minority; and more claim based on actual accomplishment. Although the situation may in some respects resemble the political scene, in which colonial peoples and minorities are increasingly calling for equality, there is one fundamental difference. In the political situation, independent status may be justified as an inherent right, the capacity for self-government being irrelevant. In the professional realm, recognition can be justified only on the basis of competence; only the opportunity to manifest this competence may be called for as a right.

T: May I break in here and say that your point about minorities has relevance for the psychiatrist, too. He is in a particularly difficult situation. On the one hand, we are asking him not to let the frustrations of his own minority status in the medical group act either as an unconscious determinant of overidentification with the dominant group, or as a basis for displaced aggression against other minority groups. On the other hand, we are asking psychiatry to go in the other direction and exercise the mature privileges of its age. Having celebrated its centennial in 1944, whereas clinical psychology reached semicentennial estate only in 1946, psychiatry has sufficient seniority to permit it to assume the role of the understanding, and perhaps analyzed, older sibling, rather than that of the rivalrous threatened one; the role of the sibling who is appreciative of his adolescent brother's wish and need to grow up and who provides him with every legitimate opportunity to achieve maturity, accepting as natural, the unavoidable missteps in the process, and not too critically, the avoidable ones.

L: I must say that this is the attitude I had been hoping for from psychiatry. I saw a basis for this hope in the great advances that have come in recent years in the quality of the recruits it has attracted, in the improvement of its status and standards, but especially in the preoccupation with social goals of some groups of psychiatrists.

T: What you say is quite true, but with respect to the issue we have been discussing, I am afraid that the problems are so involved that we shall have to wait a while longer. There is still need on the part of some of the psychiatric group to learn to transcend the boundaries of its own profession, to do more of the "divesting" of which you spoke so hopefully earlier as a goal for psychologists. But I think it is coming in psychiatry.

L: I agree, and I think there is progress in this direction, too, in psychology, though we have still a good deal of infantilism to overcome.

T: Before I go, I want to thank you for these evenings. They have been helpful in clarifying my own thinking. You know, as we have been talking, I have been wondering whether most of what we have said under the protection of privacy does not need saying publicly, and whether we are not underestimating the maturity of our colleagues if we think they are not quite ready for it. I believe that there is a growing appreciation by both our professions that in a society so disturbed as ours, dealing as we do with an area so focal to the pathology, there is a kind of *noblesse oblige* to set a pattern of cooperation for social goals, cooperation that is minimally impeded by irrelevant personal motivations. We ought not to underestimate this trend.

18. "One Hundred Years of American Psychiatry" A Special Review

To celebrate the hundredth anniversary of American psychiatry, the American Psychiatric Association put out a magnificent volume entitled *One Hundred Years of American Psychiatry*. The review which appears below was published in the *Psychological Bulletin* in response to a request for it from the editor.

Hall, J. K., Zilboorg, G., Bunker, H. A. (Eds.) *One Hundred Years of American Psychiatry*. New York: Columbia University Press, 1944. Pp. xxvi + 649, numerous illustrations.

In those halcyon post-war days when even librarians shall have succumbed to the pressure of streamlined living and replaced the complex Dewey "classification" with a simple chronological classification, the library browser's attention will be drawn immediately to this robust Adonis of a volume standing out so prominently among the war-starved runts of 1944. He will be impressed with its structure: the half-rag specially water-marked paper, the wide margins, the attractive type, the gravure illustrations (of persons and institutions important in the history of psychiatry), the specially designed emblem and the generally outstanding printing job.[1] His surmise that the responsiblity for the production of the volume must have been a true bibliophile's will gain considerable support from such items as the account of the pains taken to unearth the signature of Dr. Samuel White, one of the original thirteen founders.

Even the more careful and sophisticated reader will agree with the casual browser that the work, except for the few typographical errors which have eluded the proofreaders, meets the highest standards of bookmaking and comes close to the limit of realistic bibliophilic aspiration for a volume of this nature. In some ways, however, so high an achievement in form places an unfair burden on the contributors, for, both consciously and unconsciously, it sets the reviewer to expecting from them at least equal achievement in content. A set of this kind is particularly difficult to avoid in the case of a work by psychiatrists, since they above all others may be expected to see beyond externals.

The volume consists of two introductory statements and fifteen chapters (the latter varying in length from fifteen to ninety-four pages) contributed by thirteen different authors.

In presenting the volume, Gregory Zilboorg, who appears to have been the managing editor and coordinator, describes the goal as the achievement of "a historical synthesis of a century of American psychiatric evolution . . . a survey of

Reprinted with permission from the *Psychological Bulletin*, vol. 42, 1945.

[1] The volume was actually designated by the American Institute of Graphic Arts as one of its selections for the month of July, 1944.

psychiatry as a growing cultural force ...." Psychiatry is treated "within the frame of reference which a synthesis, not a symposium, imposes ...." He elaborates further with a statement to the effect that uniformity of perspective rather than uniformity of opinion was aspired to by the authors of the several chapters. J. K. Hall, in the introduction, considers the American geographical and historical setting in which the American Psychiatric Association (then the Association of Medical Superintendents of American Institutions for the Insane) was founded in 1844 and describes the conditions of the inception and production of the volume.

The first chapter, by R. H. Shryock, presents the beginnings of psychiatric history in this country from colonial days to the founding of the Association. H. E. Sigerist follows with the story of psychiatry in the various European countries during the middle of the nineteenth century. This serves as a backdrop against which Winfred Overholser depicts the founding of the Association and the personalities of its thirteen founders. The longest chapter (94 pages), on "*The History of American Hospitals*," by Dr. Samuel H. Hamilton, follows. The next three chapters: "*A Century of Psychiatric Research*," by J. C. Whitehorn, "*American Psychiatric Literature during the Past One Hundred Years*" (77 pages), by H. A. Bunker, and "*The History of Psychiatric Therapies*" (51 pages), by William Malamud, form an interrelated group. Albert Deutsch then presents "*The History of Mental Hygiene*." Another related group is formed by the three chapters on "*Military Psychiatry*," the first and last by Albert Deutsch, on the Civil War and the World War II periods respectively, and the second by Edward A. Strecker on the World War I period. The last four are relatively independent chapters: "*A Century of Psychology in its Relationship to Psychiatry*," by T. V. Moore, "*American Psychiatry as a Specialty*," by H. A. Bunker, "*Legal Aspects of Psychiatry*" (78 pages), by Gregory Zilboorg, and "*The Influence of Psychiatry on Anthropology in America during the Past One Hundred Years*," by Clyde Kluckhohn. Except for those whose length is indicated in parentheses, the articles run from approximately fifteen to forty pages.

The intrinsic difficulty of the task of reviewing this multi-authored volume can be lessened to some extent by first considering briefly the individual contributions which are of relatively less importance to the psychologist, by then considering at greater length those which are especially pertinent for him, and by following it finally with a consideration of the volume as a whole.

The two background chapters provide the appropriate screen against which to see the developments of psychiatry in the last one hundred years. (One wishes that the Sigerist chapter were a little fuller.) Overholser provides a good start on this with his portraits of the founders. Hamilton's chatty chapter is full of interesting and important facts about the development of institutional psychiatry from its beginnings in the workhouse and almshouse through the lunatic asylum and lunatic hospital to its present status as represented in the state and private hospitals. He discusses the various aspects of psychiatric administration and provides several valuable statistical tables. The presentation, however, suffers somewhat from insufficient organization. It is a little strange, too, to find in a chapter on "American Mental Hospitals" no mention of Bryan at Worcester and Read at Elgin, two superintendents who have done so much in the recent period to raise the standards and set the goals of state hospitals. (In fact it is surprising that Bryan's name does not appear at all in the volume except for Bunker's listing of his book on *Administrative Psychiatry*. Present-day administrators do not fare well at the hands of these psychiatric historians even when their influence, direct and indirect, on research, therapy, and administrative procedures has been great.)

The chapters on literature (Bunker), therapy (Malamud), and legal aspects (Zilboorg) are the highlights of the volume. It is difficult to choose among them—they are all of such excellent quality. Each may, however, be singled out for its particular strength: the Bunker article for its careful, smooth scholarship and its accurate tracing of an important point of view; the Malamud article for its effective organization and clear presentation of a difficult topic; and the Zilboorg article for its lively and detailed presentation of a fundamental social psychological problem.

It appears to a psychologist that Bunker's article misses the part played by the more strictly psychological journals such as the *Psychological Bulletin*, the *Journal of Abnormal Psychology*, the *Psychological Clinic* and the *American Journal of Psychology* in helping to spread psychiatric notions. (He lists the first three as "psychiatric" journals!). When it is considered that the first American psychological journal was founded in 1887, 43 years after the founding of the first psychiatric journal, the contribution seems considerable. Actually he himself has many references to articles in psychological journals. Thus, of the series of some half-dozen articles by Adolf Meyer appearing during the period 1903 to 1911, referred to by Bunker as "a group of articles which collectively considered, form without any doubt, in their path-breaking character and their enormous influence upon American psychiatry, the most original and the greatest single contribution to American literature,"[2] three were published in psychological journals (*American Journal of Psychology* and *Psychological Bulletin*). This minor flaw is, of course, negligible when compared with the detailed and thorough portrayal of the development of the functional as opposed to the anatomical point of view, as well as of other aspects of psychiatric progress reflected in the literature.

The article by Malamud lucidly and succinctly presents the evolution of therapeutic notions in American psychiatry. His account impresses one with the important part played in this development by laymen such as Dix, Tuke, and Beers, persons who could see the problem either from the very outside or from the very inside. The reader cannot help feeling that an important lesson is here to be learned, one which has important implications for the current controversy with respect to medical care, particularly in relation to the position taken by some medical groups that such care is a strictly medical problem.

Zilboorg's chapter on legal aspects traces the successive advances and retreats in the battles between enlightened psychiatrists holding for the existence of a pathology of feeling without a pathology of intellect ("the irresistible impulse"), against unenlightened law which insists on pathology of intellect as the criterion of

[2] If not explicitly, at least implicitly, the volume is dedicated to Adolf Meyer. His is the only portrait of a living person included, and after Freud, his name occurs most frequently in the index. The evidence for his great influence permeates almost every chapter.

insanity. The essay very properly revolves mainly about Isaac Ray, a striking instance of the man much ahead of his time.

The chapter by Deutsch on mental hygiene sets forth in very adequate fashion the development of this important aspect of psychiatry as related to other social developments of the period.

The three chapters on military psychiatry should be made required reading for recent critics of the "I-heard-of-a-case" school (the graduate department of Stanley Cobb's "I-know-a-case" school) who make wide-sweeping criticisms on the basis of isolated instances and minor imperfections. The Strecker chapter strikes one as being somewhat too detailed for this type of volume, but the three articles together certainly impress the reader with the great strides made by psychiatry in dealing with military problems, despite the great handicaps with which it has had to contend.

"*Psychiatry as a Speciality*" (Bunker) is an interesting chapter, but its purpose, at least to the psychologist, is somewhat obscure; implicitly or explicitly its contents are to be found in other chapters.

The chapter on anthropology by Kluckhohn really belongs with the three superior chapters mentioned earlier. The only reason for not having included it with the others is its quite different content. From a dynamic psychological standpoint, it is the most sophisticated of all the chapters, in fact the only one which really probes below the surface. Besides being excellently documented in the region of overlap of anthropology and psychiatry, a thorough grasp of the relationship between the two is revealed. It recognizes the debt which anthropology owes to psychiatry, but at the same time delineates anthropology's own field of activity and point of view, both of which it expects to have recognized in its relations with psychiatry. The important part which Sapir has played in the association of the two disciplines is duly recognized and emphasized.

We may now turn to a consideration of the two chapters which are of special importance for psychologists, viz., Whitehorn's on research and Moore's on psychology.

Although by the ordinary standards of journal articles Whitehorn's chapter is an adequate sketch of the high points of psychiatric research, in the present setting it is disappointing. The author has missed an unusual opportunity to carry through the difficult task of which he is capable, viz., to indicate, at this strategic stage of the development of psychiatry, the meaning and direction of psychopathological research in America, both past and present, to evaluate this research and to point out the promising lines for future development. (It was particularly important not to miss this opportunity because of the narrow evaluational article by Myerson in the anniversary issue of the *American Journal of Psychiatry*.) Such an exposition would necessarily have resulted in one of the longest articles in the series; instead we have one of the shortest. Aside from its brevity, it is rather poorly systematized, only superficially evaluative, and in its discussion of research developments mainly organized around the very inadequate and secondary classification of geography, rather than that of concept. A striking instance of the incompleteness of the production is the omission of even the mention of Charles B. Dunlap's work in pathology, work which Bunker, in the very next article in the volume, calls "one of the outstanding contributions to American psychiatric literature" and representing the major work of "one of the most thorough, scrupulous and rigorously scientific workers whom American psychiatry has known."

Under such circumstances it is not surprising that the minor contribution which psychology has made is not recognized. As an instance, let us take the case of McLean Hospital. Whitehorn points out that perhaps the most definite reply to Weir Mitchell's severe criticism (at the semi-centennial meeting of the Association) of the contemporary state of psychiatry was to be found in an account by Hurd "of the provision made for intensive laboratory research in the basic medical sciences of pathology, physiology and biochemistry" at McLean Hospital. The fact "that the major emphasis of this pioneering enterprise was put upon physiology and biochemistry—the study of the living, rather than of tissues post-mortem" was "an interesting indication of the direction of thought." The conscious or unconscious change of "physiological psychology" in Hurd's text to "physiology" in Whitehorn's is a little hard for the psychologist to take! If anything is clear from Hurd's article (1895–96), G. Stanley Hall's article (1894–95), Cowles' presidential address (1895–96), Hoch's (1895–96) report on Kraepelin,[3] Cowles' enthusiastic reception of the *American Journal of Psychology* because of its concern with the "new psychology" and its promise of "concrete application" to the alienist's clinical needs (Cowles, 1887–88), and Cowles' article in Hurd (Hurd, 1916), it is that physiological *psychology* was involved. It was physiological *psychology* in which Cowles was so much interested and toward which he had been directed by Stanley Hall under whom he had taken psychology and with whom, when the latter was medical superintendent (!) of Bay View Hospital for the Insane (Meyer, 1924–25), Cowles had worked.[4]

If Whitehorn's chapter is disappointing, then Moore's is nothing less than distressing, particularly so to the psychologist since it is the one which for him is most important and with which, in this setting, he most naturally identifies. Instead of meeting his expectation, based on the author's standing and peculiar fitness for the task by reason of his expertness in both disciplines, that it will be among the best chapters, he is reluctantly forced to conclude that it is the poorest in the volume. The bases for this judgment are various and lie in the nature of the tone and style, as well as the content.

With respect to style, one can find neither a clear conception of the task involved in the writing of such a chapter nor a unifying principle of organization. There is a tendency to repetitiousness, irrelevancies of a reminiscent and historical nature (cf. pages 468 and 457), and loose writing (e.g., a list of 83 persons is referred to as a table of "several" psychologists, p. 448). In a volume which is on the whole singularly clear of typographical and similar errors, Thurstone's initials are given as

[3] August Hoch was appointed to be in charge of the McLean laboratories. As part of his preparation he went to study the Wundt-Kraepelin techniques in Kraepelin's laboratory (cf. Hall, 1894-95).

[4] Bay View appears to have been a hospital connected with the Johns Hopkins University Medical School.

"E. L." (p. 449), Harrell is referred to as "Howell" (p. 462) and "psychology" is written for physiology (p. 446). I mention these minor defects not because of their intrinsic importance but because they reflect the more important contentual carelessness which is so frequent.

The combination of a very definite positive view, viz., neoscholasticism, and very definite negative views, viz., anti-sensationalism, anti-behaviorism, and anti-"social service psychiatry" carry Moore into *ad hominem* arguments, extreme statements, and irrelevant criticisms of different schools, criticisms not at all related to the problem of the relations of psychology and psychiatry (cf. the criticism of gestalt psychology, pp. 465–66).

Thus his positive philosophical approach leads him to identify Adolf Meyer with (perhaps unawaredly) "reviving some of the fundamental concepts of scholastic philosophy" (pp. 455–56, 458). His negative attitude to behaviorism leads to the gratuitous assumption that "Psychobiology . . . had its origin in the hopelessness of the behaviorism of John B. Watson and of the experimental psychology of Knight Dunlap," because, after conducting a course in psychology in collaboration with Watson and Dunlap for one year, Meyer conducted the course alone thereafter (p. 455)! It is, of course, possible that the assumption is correct, but Moore offers not the least bit of evidence for this. In fact, certain data available to us make the assumption quite unlikely, at least as it applies to Watson. On one occasion, for instance, Meyer speaks of Watson's work as one of several contemporaneous developments fostering "a wholly unprecedented burst of dynamic interest in man . . . and in the study of the functioning of the human organism as a personality (Meyer, 1932, p. 246)." Further, Watson, in his autobiography (Murchison, 1936, p. 279), expresses his gratefulness to Meyer for coming over to Watson's laboratory each week with his whole staff for the purpose of discussing the manuscript of *Psychology from the Standpoint of the Behaviorist*. To look at the matter from another side, it is a questionable compliment to Meyer to imply that psychobiology was conceived on the rebound!

His antagonistic attitude to "social-service psychiatry" leads Moore to talk about a "tendency [which] has arisen to eliminate the psychologist from the child guidance clinic and to get rid of all psychometrics (p. 474)." Those well acquainted with the prevailing situation would be surprised at this statement. Actually, when a comparison is made between the data in the table which he has constructed, based on the 1940 Directory, and a similar table found in the 1936 Directory, it will be seen that the trend for New York, the state about which he is most concerned, is actually in the direction of an increase in the employment of psychologists for community clinics. Moore seems to be unacquainted with the New York situation, where many of the psychiatric clinics are sent out from the state hospitals almost exclusively to check on their own adult patients who have been released into the community. For such a purpose, only a psychiatrist and a social worker would, except rarely, be necessary.

Moore has misinterpreted, too, the Witmer statement (p. 476) with respect to the dropping out of routine psychological examinations in child guidance clinics. Such a policy does not mean, as Moore thinks, the elimination of the psychologist.

Rather does it mean that the psychologist is taking on other, broader, functions, just as are the other members of the clinic team whose routine physical examinations and routine family investigations are also being reduced. The trend is one to be welcomed rather than deplored, as Moore would discover if he were to consult the numerous psychologists now concerned with improving the status of clinical psychology. We must also note the several extreme statements in this context, for example, references to psychologists being "eliminated," "ousted," considered "superfluous," and the reference to a tendency to "get rid of all psychometrics."

In addition to pointing out these inaccuracies, two other points should be made with respect to the general tone of the article. I refer to its unwitting arrogance and its lack of dignity. Evidence for the former may be found in what seems to be an underlying assumption of the article, viz., that the term "relationship" in the title refers only to the influence which psychology has had on psychiatry. The considerably greater influence which psychiatry has had on psychology, particularly the influence of Freud and of psychoanalysis, is never even considered. The closing sections, those which discuss the place of the psychologist in the child guidance clinic and the conflict between psychology and psychiatry in the 1916–20 period, are rather picayune. The reader cannot avoid making the obvious but painful comparison of Moore's article on psychology with the modest, dignified, and mature presentation of Kluckhohn on anthropology. In the latter case, the reader is left with the feeling that the author knows just where the stand should be taken in a relationship between two disciplines, each of which has its own contribution to make. In the case of psychology, he is left wondering what all the lamentation is about and with his respect for it anything but enhanced. One could go on with other instances of these more formal inadequacies but it is necessary to turn now to the fundamental aspects of the contribution, viz., its content.

What may one reasonably expect to find in an article on the relationship of two such disciplines as psychology and psychiatry? Essentially the following: A consideration of the intellectual influences, in the sense of ideas, methods, points of view, and the "propagandist" influences, in the sense of aid of a non-professional kind such as promotive, of one discipline on the other, whether they be direct or indirect, definite or presumptive. One might expect, in addition, a discussion of the working relationships of the disciplines in the past and an evaluation of the outlook in this respect for the future.

Of these various aspects, Moore limits himself almost entirely to the intellectual influence of psychology on psychiatry and he does this in such a way that it is generally difficult to tell whether the influence is direct or indirect, definite or merely presumptive. He mentions not at all the propagandist contributions of psychology, as seen, for instance, in Hall's influence through the founding of journals and the support of various movements, and James' influence in the founding of the mental hygiene movement, which is even greater than Deutsch, in the chapter on "Mental Hygiene," has indicated. He touches on the relations of the two fields but never in a manner which would indicate that the true interpenetrative complexity of the relationship has been recognized.

Early in the paper Moore presents a list of 83 psychologists (actually of those included, two, Rorschach and Rosanoff were *not* psychologists in any technical sense or in the sense in which he uses the term) "whose names were looked for in 93 textbooks of psychiatry appearing in the United States from 1861 to 1942," and gives the number of times a reference to their work was found. There are no explicit conclusions drawn from the list in the body of the article, but the implication, on the basis of the discussion which precedes it, is that very little psychological material gets into psychiatric texts. That this is true I would not dispute, but I am disturbed about the method used to arrive at the conclusion. In the first place, the list is motley and strange, containing the names of persons who, however important their contribution to other fields, have done very little related to psychopathology, for example, Hartshorne, Ogden, Otis, Washburn. Then it omits the names of persons who with much more reason should have been included, such as, among Americans: Bronner, Doll, Franz, G. H. Kent, Landis, Sidis, F. L. Wells, Witmer.[5] (His Europeans are more adequately selected.)

But assuming that the list contained only appropriate names, the compilation of such a list is in itself naïve and at best pseudo-objective. Influence, as any historian of ideas knows, is frequently most difficult to trace. The fact that a name is not mentioned in a book is no criterion that the author was not influenced by the person involved. This is true for two reasons: (1) textbook writers, especially the older textbook writers and even more especially non-academic textbook writers, are not accustomed to giving credit or references. (Until recently this was also generally true of elementary textbooks in psychology.) Particularly in psychiatry, where the textbooks are largely concerned with nosology, the theoretical and experimental suppositions are at most implicit. (2) Influence is so often indirect and unconscious that it needs a Lowes or a Boring to unearth it. Thus, supposing Herbart had been included in Moore's list, and it could be shown that Herbart influenced Griesinger profoundly, and that Griesinger in turn influenced the writers of early American textbooks, Herbart might not at all be mentioned by the latter but actually his influence might have been considerable. Historical research unfortunately (or fortunately) needs more than the turning over of the "preparing of a table" to a "statistical assistant (p. 448 n.)."[6]

But, again, the list is, after all, a minor matter. Any student of the subject knows that the influence of conventional American psychology on psychiatry has not been very great. It is, therefore, particularly disturbing to find that the few major influences have been omitted. G. Stanley Hall is not mentioned at all (except in

[5] The name of H. Gruender is included in the list. Since the name aroused no associations, psychological or otherwise, the APA yearbook, the *Psychological Register*, Hunt's *Personality and the Behavior Disorders* and several histories of psychology were searched but no reference could be found. Finally, a reference was found in *Minerva* (1930) which indicated him to be Professor of Psychology at St. Louis University, and in the *Psychological Abstracts* for 1932 an abstract of a book of his on experimental psychology was found. The excerpt given there provides a cue as to why he did not influence psychiatry.

[6] I do not wish to raise a question as to the accuracy of the statistical work in the table, since I have not attempted to check it. However, casual examination of the first standard psychiatric text which comes to hand (Strecker and Ebaugh, 4th ed., 1935) records the name of Kuhlmann in the index—a name which is given a zero frequency in the table.

the list), although there are seven references to him by the other, non-psychologist, contributors. Hall, the propagandist, who gave Freud his first academic hearing, who gave courses in Freudian psychology beginning in 1908, and whose pressure for its consideration remained life-long; Hall, who influenced Cowles in establishing the psychological laboratory at McLean Hospital which had as directors following Hoch, Franz, Wells and Lundholm; Hall, who stimulated Adolf Meyer (1932, p. 241), by his early interest in child study, to write his first paper on a psychiatric topic—*Mental Abnormalities in Children during Primary Education*—and who did so much to make the country child-conscious; Hall, whose students Goddard and Huey (also Meyer's students at the Worcester State Hospital) did the early pioneer work on feeblemindedness;[7] Hall, whose bravery in handling the problem of sex did so much to break down the first barriers, thus greatly facilitating the later child guidance handling of this and related problems; Hall, whose student Terman achieved so much in the development of the Binet method in the United States and whose student Gesell did so much for other aspects of developmental psychology; Hall, whose journals regularly published material of psychopathological interest; Hall, the ramifications of whose psychological influence are most pervasive in fields related to psychopathology—it is this man who is entirely omitted in the consideration of the influence of psychology on psychiatry.

William James is another major influence whom Moore does not mention except in his list. In the latter, it is indicated that text references to him have been found fourteen times, the second highest after Binet who has a score of fifteen. Despite this obvious hint, James is not considered and the many aspects of his influence on psychopathology, among which were his wide influence through his *Principles* and *Varieties*, and his deep and lasting interest in exceptional mental states (on which he delivered a Lowell Lecture Series), are missed. His high evaluation of these special conditions led him to state, during the height of the psychophysical period in psychology, that these phenomena threw more light on human nature than did the work of the psychophysical laboratories. James' propagandizing influence, viz., his mental hygiene interests already mentioned, and his influence through students such as Healy, Sidis, Thorndike, Yerkes, and Woodworth are forgotten. No recognition is given to the indirect, but nevertheless important, effects of the "humanization not only of psychology but of philosophy through William James' espousal of the characteristically American concepts of pragmatism, instrumentalism, and the humanization of religious experience (Meyer, 1932, p. 245)," of which Adolf Meyer speaks.[8]

Boris Sidis, who, at least until 1908 when he took his medical degree, was distinctly a psychologist, is not even mentioned in Moore's list. He thus misses the influence which Sidis, and therefore indirectly William James, had on William A. White with whom the latter worked on dissociated states at the New York State Pathological Institute. White himself says of this association:

[7] Cf. H. H. Goddard, 1943. Hall recommended Goddard for the Vineland position.

[8] Cf. also Coriat's statement that the interest in psychotherapy in the Boston area was probably originally stimulated by James (*Psychoanalytic Review*, 1945, 32, 2).

It was an exceedingly interesting, valuable, and I believe crucial experience for me personally. Almost without knowing it I absorbed the rudiments of what was subsequently to be the doctrine of the unconscious and accepted in my attitude toward these problems the principle of determinism in the pychological field [1933, pp. 20–21].

Several times (cf. especially pp. 448, 477) Moore refers to a body of experimental data which is available for application to psychiatry. Nowhere, however, does he actually indicate what it is or what its possible applications are. He apparently has reference to the type of data which is so ably presented in the volumes edited by Hunt on "Personality and the Behavior Disorders," but insofar as the article itself indicates, these data are illusory. His concluding paragraph says:

When we look back over the relations of psychology and psychiatry in the past hundred years, what a marvelous growth has taken place in each science! Benjamin Rush, just before the dawn of the hundred years we have reviewed, turned to psychology as he found it, but there was little to find. In the years that have elapsed psychology has grown. There is a large body of experimental empirical research in the field of psychology that has never been evaluated for psychiatry; there are methods and techniques that have been developed in psychology that would open up vast tracts of the *terra incognita* of psychiatry. Only when psychiatry is based on a sound and broadly adequate psychology can it make the progress that physiology has made possible for medicine.

It is to be regretted that Moore has nowhere in the article revealed the actual nature of this body of knowledge or actually described any of these Columbian techniques!

I have considered the specific chapters at lesser or greater length. What is the impact of the work taken as a whole?

In presenting the volume, Zilboorg says that it "will have to be looked upon and stand as a whole," and emphasizes that what was intended was a "synthesis, not a symposium." It is somewhat difficult to appreciate the distinction which he draws between these terms. They would appear to arise from two different universes of discourse and it is doubtful if they can be contrasted in this manner. The symposium, whether in the form of conversation, panel discussion, or round-table, may or may not result in a synthesis depending on the amount of "putting together" of ideas which is achieved.

But terms aside, how successful is the result attained? From several statements which Zilboorg makes, and which are clearly corroborated by the internal evidence, one gathers that the various authors wrote their articles quite independently and that actually, except for dividing up the topics and perhaps discussing a general point of view, little effort was directed toward integration. It would otherwise be hard to explain the amount of duplication and repetition which occurs. The degree of synthesis which *is* attained seems more or less fortuitously derived from a point of view held in common by several of the contributors rather than from any systematic and deliberate attempt to achieve it.

For many reasons, one wishes that there had been less democracy in the process; or to put it more accurately, less *laissez-faire* and more true democracy. It would seem that each author could have been left with "complete freedom of judgment and opinion" and his own "trend and even bias" and still a synthesis achieved beyond one which consists only of "uniformity of perspective." In a collaborative enterprise of this kind, in fairness to those other important partners in the undertaking, the readers, group acceptance of mutual self-criticism during the process of preparation of the articles would seem to be essential. A final integrating article by the coordinating editor would also have helped. Such a closing chapter would have resulted in a much more complete unification than has been achieved by mere arrangement. It is rather strange and peculiarly unsatisfying from the "closure" standpoint to read through a volume devoted to a hundred years of psychiatry only to end up with a final chapter on anthropology. This very fact would imply that such a goal was never in the true sense envisioned. It is difficult to avoid suspecting that the talk of synthesis involves at least some element of rationalization. Although it is true that the impressionistic technique employed in the organization of the volume partially achieves results of the kind intended, the question arises as to whether a synthesis of mere perspective was not too cheap a price to settle for; the volume as a whole deserved a higher level of synthesis.

The shortcomings pointed out in *One Hundred Years of American Psychiatry* should by no means be permitted to divert the reader's attention from the many valuable contributions which the volume makes to the true understanding of the development and place of this related discipline. Some of these have already been discussed; space, unfortunately, does not permit the enumeration and elaboration of the others.

There is one point of paramount importance to psychology which must, however, be mentioned. As the reader progresses through the volume a question arises which becomes increasingly persistent in its demand for an answer: Where is the evidence for the oft-repeated assertion that psychology is the basic science for psychiatry, in the manner in which physiology is for medicine? One must admit that there is little to be found in this volume, and it seems to be generally true that the psychology contributed by the academies has had little influence on the development of psychiatry. An attempt to inquire into the reasons why this plausible hypothesis has not been corroborated goes beyond the compass of a review. However, it is a question which psychology must find the answer to both for its own development as well as for the development of an important section of psychiatry.

19. Some Aspects of Mid-century Psychiatry: Experimental Psychology

In the spring of 1951, Roy Grinker invited me to participate in the dedication of the Institute for Psychosomatic and Psychiatric Research and Training of the Michael Reese Hospital. The Dedication Conference was held on June 1, 1951, and the proceedings were subsequently published.

I have been asked to consider the relations of experimental psychology to psychiatry. Although the term "experimental psychology" has been widely accepted as "the psychology of the generalized, human, normal, adult mind as revealed in the psychological laboratory" (Boring, 1950), such a narrow definition is now not justified, considering the breadth of modern psychology and the methodological ferment which characterizes it. I shall, therefore, deal rather with what I judge to be included within the spirit of the term, and trespass beyond the literal meaning by defining "experimental psychology" to be that psychology which is *oriented* to the laboratory and its controls, but which may be concerned with phenomena in non-laboratory situations where the attempt is made to achieve control of conditions. The "mind" may be animal as well as human, child as well as adult, aberrant as well as normal. The ensuing discussion will, I trust, provide the contextual body for this skeletal definition.

The statement has on occasion been made that psychology is the basic science for psychiatry in the sense in which physiology is for medicine. Although theoretically this may be justified, and a reasonable hope for the future, evidence is not lacking for denying the actuality of such a status for psychology. Even traditional psychologists would, I believe, agree that psychology has not reached its promise of some half-century ago and has not achieved a codification of principles sufficiently broad to enable it to serve as a sufficient foundation for any applied science or technology of *general* human behavior. (Its success in relation to certain specialized areas of human engineering based on knowledge in the fields of sensation and perception is, of course, outside our area of interest [Stevens, 1951]).

Why is this so? The possible factors are many but this condition would seem to stem largely from the direction which psychology took in the second half of the nineteenth century on its release from philosophy—the direction pioneered by Fechner, Helmholtz, and Wundt of a laboratory psychology modeled on physics and physiology, set up in the university tradition, and expecting to achieve sudden identification with the quantitative experimental sciences. Because of these special influences and the peculiar interests of the persons involved, psychology concerned itself with the microscopic and the segmental, especially with the fields of sensation and perception. Total life situations were almost entirely avoided, particularly in

Reprinted with permission from R. R. Grinker (Ed.) *Mid-century Psychiatry*, 1953 (Charles C. Thomas).

the area of the affective and motivational. Human-being-sensitive William James' natural reaction was to raise doubts about the contributions deriving from this approach and to insist that there were "more nutritious objects of attention" for the psychologist.

It is intriguing to speculate on what might have happened if instead of this laboratory approach, the French tradition of the hospital had become dominant, and experimental psychology had taken its start from experience there. Would psychology have a different face today? It took a "lonesome" person like Freud, working in the consulting-room by himself, to serve as a major force in counteracting this trend, a counteraction which did not, however, affect experimental psychology in any fundamental way until almost three-quarters of a century after its beginnings. Actually, as Bernfeld (1944) has pointed out, Freud, through Brücke, was trained in the doctrines of the school of Helmholtz and Du Bois-Reymond, also fundamental influences on the early experimental psychology. Why did Freud and Wundt (by 24 years the older, it must be recognized), both brought up in physiology and medicine of a not-too-different kind, go such different ways in their psychology? Can it be that Freud, finding the academic path closed to him, was forced into extensive contact with patients, to become in the process the father of dynamic psychology, whereas Wundt could remain on in the academic setting of the laboratory, to become the father of experimental psychology? In the consulting-room, Freud, despite, or perhaps because of, his scientific training was ready to deal with phenomena in the "intuitive" field heretofore the realm of the literary psychologist (Kris, 1950).[1]

As Boring (1950) indicates, general experimental psychology has had three historic phases in which the dominant problems were successively: (1) sensation and perception; (2) learning; and (3) motivation. Would experimental psychology be in a more advanced state today if these stages had been reversed? Or did the *Zeitgeist* just not permit such an order; especially a *Zeitgeist* aided by such powerful forces as Helmholtz and Du Bois-Reymond! The possibility, of course, exists that the particular kind of experimental stage through which psychology passed in the latter part of the nineteenth and the early part of the twentieth century, a stage of a segmental, physical-physiologically oriented type, was a necessary step in the historical process of its development. Who can say? But certainly, the degree to which meaning and motivation were partialled out in the psychological study of the period, and the great preoccupation with what was "pure," unfortunately resulted in a poverty, insofar as human and motivational problems are concerned, that only a tremendous intellectual revolution, such as is represented in Freudianism, could overcome.[2]

[1] What influence "act psychology" had on Freud, who had taken several courses under Brentano (Merlan, 1945, 1949) in 1874–76, is difficult to evaluate.

[2] This happened despite the influence of such persons as G. S. Hall, a most important figure in the psychology of the early part of this century. His advocacy of psychoanalysis apparently had little effect upon psychology. Freud's influence on psychology was at first indirect and largely exerted from without, through its effect upon the social scene generally, and upon psychiatry particularly.

It should be pointed out that the intense "schoolism" in psychology of two and three decades ago is no longer a prominent feature of the present. The McDougall-Watson controversies of this earlier period have no counterpart now. Instead we find much more emphasis on experiments that have significance for various points of view, and considerable reinterpretation of fundamental approaches, so that common factors, as well as differentiating aspects, are brought out. Disagreements among psychologists still exist, of course, but these are resulting increasingly in attempts to reach understanding and to set up experimental tests of hypotheses.

It appears true, despite these advances, that psychology is a self-conscious discipline. Because of its peculiar place in the hierarchy of the sciences, situated as it is between biology and the more strictly social sciences, and because of its not too remote separation from philosophy, psychology has been preoccupied with problems of methodology, and with self-examination generally, as reflected in its auto-historical interest. An unfriendly critic could probably make a case for the neurotic character of some of this self-preoccupation. He could point, for instance, to its exaggerated doubts, to the concern with techniques rather than with content, to the too-ready imitation of the pattern and language of the physical sciences. As against these characteristics, however, one may point to the signs of developing maturity contained in this pattern and to decided gains resulting from the process of self-examination. The "neurosis," may I hopefully diagnose, appears mainly to derive from natural adolescent needs and conflicts, rather than from adult deviant needs.

Against this background, let us see what the preoccupations of the psychology of the recent past have been that may be of general or specific interest to psychiatry. In considering this topic, it will be most profitable to devote the time to the area of methods, attitudes, and approaches—that is, to an examination of how psychology views its field and attacks its problems—and merely mention in passing specific studies from some relevant areas of psychology. The former area is especially important since psychiatry has many of the same methodological problems to solve. I shall consider this topic from two points of view: the attitudes with which a study is *approached*, affecting necessarily the way it is carried out; and the methods that are used *after* a study is completed. Since it will be impossible to mention more than a limited number of specific studies, I shall consider them at appropriate places under method.

What kinds of questions are of special concern to psychologists in approaching their material? Some prominent ones are: (1) What is the primary subject matter of psychology? (2) What is psychology's unit of study? (3) How should psychological studies be organized?

Throughout the history of psychology, different views have been held as to the nature of its fundamental subject matter. In the earlier years, the range accepted for study was quite narrow. This century has seen a progressive expansion of what is included in systematic and experimental psychological investigation, so that at present the range of study is much broader, from simple sensory and motor processes through complicated social situations. Thus even so conservative a volume as the recent *Handbook of Experimental Psychology* (Stevens, 1951), has the following major sections: physiological mechanisms, growth and development, maturation, learning and adjustment, sensory processes, human performance.

The trend, to take but one example, is seen in the changing attitude toward unconsciously determined behavior. Although a notion of the unconscious is already to be found in Herbart and Helmholtz, experimental psychologists for a long time refused to deal with this area. Only after Freudian views had affected psychology through various avenues was the construct of the unconscious as explanatory of a wide range of behavior accepted as legitimate material for study.

One of the troublesome problems relating to subject matter has been that of the "single case." Allport (1937) has expressed the conflict succinctly in asking the question: Should scientific law be taken to refer to "any uniformity that is observed in the natural order" or should it be considered to involve only statements of "invariable association common to an entire class of subjects?" If prediction in science must by definition involve prediction across individuals, then it is clear that the single case cannot be considered proper subject matter. However, there have been some stout representatives of the point of view that the *individual* may have his own laws. If we accept Kluckhohn's and Murray's (1948, p. 35) neat characterization of an individual's personality characteristics, namely, that each person is in some respects like all other persons, in other respects like some other persons, and in still other respects like no other person, then laws in psychological science have to take account of phenomena at all of these levels: (1) universal; (2) type; and (3) individual. It is in relation only to the last that controversy arises.

The distinction between the nomothetic and the idiographic (Allport, 1937) is only a more elaborate way of stating this fundamental problem. The nomothetic view calls for a discipline with uniform general laws, whereas the idiographic calls for a discipline interested in particular events or particular individuals. Under certain limited circumstances, prediction is certainly possible for the individual, such prediction being made on entirely empirical bases, involving no "intuitive" acts. Psychology would, therefore, appear to gain from using both of these approaches.

Accepting some agreement on the subject matter of psychology, the complexity which faces the investigator when he is about to attack a problem is generally overwhelming. Within the organism numerous questions such as that of the latent as opposed to the manifest, the purely psychological as opposed to the physiological, the historical as opposed to the contemporary, confront him. When problems in the organism are further complicated by the variations outside, in the culture and the environment, variations that are created by a multiplicity of interactions, it is obvious that effective systematic study at any one time must be placed within set limits.

The experimental psychology of the past *did* set itself certain limits. It solved the problem of complexity, as in the case of structuralism, by chopping up its subjects, or, as in the case of behaviorism, by highly oversimplifying the situation through what one critic (Bentley, 1941) has aptly characterized as a "glorification of the skin" at the expense of the brain and central nervous system. Such solutions, however, have been unsatisfying to many twentieth-century psychologists, psychologists who held that these methods of attack evaded the issue by destroying the very subject matter with which they were concerned. In the reaction to such approaches there has been much talk of dealing with the "organism as a whole." It must be admitted that sometimes this talk has been quite loose and naïve, being merely a reaction to the elementarism of the earlier period. At other times, however, it has stemmed from rigorously developed theory.

We are faced here with the dichotomy that has been set up between one approach characterized by such terms as segmental, elementaristic, atomistic, associationistic, and molecular, and the other for which such terms as total, organismic, field, and molar are employed. Although the contexts in which the different terms in each of these categories are used sometimes have different shades of meaning, for our present purposes we can consider them synonymous. We are necessarily concerned here with a problem of degree, for the extremes of these positions can experimentally be nothing but absurd. The fundamental philosophies of the proponents of each are clear. The major point at issue is whether even simple processes can be fully described or validly explained if dealt with in isolation from other processes. If psychology is heading in any direction, in the recent past it seems to have been traveling definitely in the direction of the *total* approach.

It is of interest to note the difference between what is happening in psychology and in other sciences. The trend in physics, as indicated by Born (1950), is in the direction of atomistics. One should, however, bear in mind that physics is a science that has shifted from the remarkably experimentally controlled one- or two-variable situation to the highly *disorganized* complex situation that calls for an actuarial approach. However, a science much closer to psychology, namely, physiology, seems also to be heading in the direction of atomistics, witness Adrian's (1950) statement, "..... physiologists have always been eager to learn .... from the physical sciences in the way of new ideas and instruments and at present these seem to lead to the study of the cell rather than to that of the organism." The question is essentially that raised so clearly by Warren Weaver (1948) in his article on "*Science and Complexity*": How is science to handle the problems of "organized complexity...... problems which involve dealing simultaneously with a sizable number of factors which are interrelated into an organic whole,"—the kinds of problems which are so characteristic of psychology?

I shall consider some of the suggestions that have been made by psychologists in recent years to handle this problem. These proposals reflect psychology's attempts to come to grips with the fundamental questions relating to method of attack necessitated by the nature of its data.

With the development of notions such as those I have described, it is not surprising that controversies over heredity *or* environment, and organism *or* environment have lost some of their force. The trend has been to accept a psychology that deals with phenomena which involve these forces in *interaction*, even if in inexplicable interaction, rather than to attempt the operationally difficult, if not impossible, task of disentangling the contribution of each. Field theory has taken on an increasingly important role in psychology (Lewin, 1936), as it has in biology (Weiss, 1939).

On the basis of the acceptance of the principle that complexity should be left relatively undisturbed and that closer contact should be established with the original phenomena, more and more attempts are being made to bring into the laboratory as nearly lifelike situations as possible.

This is to be seen particularly in the social psychological sphere, where studies of leadership and group life (Lippitt, 1940), the effects of frustration on social relations of young children (Wright, 1942), and studies in group dynamics (Lewin, 1935b) have, by setting up controls such as matched groups and systematically varied conditions, brought complex functions into the laboratory for investigation.

Another approach that goes even further in this direction is that represented in *psychological ecology*. This method takes advantage of actual field situations for the study of psychological phenomena. Since the approach is naturalistic rather than experimental in character, the problem of the refinement of the investigator as instrument is especially important. An example of this type of study is to be found in the researches of Barker (Barker & Wright, 1949) and his group at Kansas. A small community, "Midwest, U.S.A.," has been selected as a natural habitat in which to study normal childhood development. One aspect of this study is to follow a child around for a day making a systematic record of his behavior which by various coding devices is made available for analysis (Barker & Wright, 1951). Another example is to be found in Brunswik's (1947) studies of perception in which a person is observed in his daily environment to see how he actually deals with perceptual problems. In some respects, the psychoanalytic situation partakes of the ecological in the surrogate sense that it is a relatively free situation in which the subject verbally (and non-verbally) reproduces both his present and past outer and inner experiences and interactions. The studies of counselling and psychotherapy of the Rogers group (Rogers, Raskin, Seeman, Sheerer, Stock, Haigh, Hoffman & Carr, 1949), in which recorded interviews are made available for systematic analysis, also meet in some respects the requirements for ecological study.[3]

One other aspect of the problem of achieving "wholeness" and recognizing complexity might be mentioned. I refer to the increasing consideration that is being given to the place of the "*intervening variable*." This concept was proposed originally by Tolman (1938), who developed a molar approach after a growing dissatisfaction with the segmental stimulus-response point of view. It has now been adopted also by those more closely identified with the latter point of view, as the complexity of even rote learning is receiving increased recognition. Emphasis is here placed upon the fact that variables exist between the stimulus and the response which play an important role in determining the response that is finally made. Whether thought of in terms of past learning, "the apperceptive mass," drives, or in some other fashion, the growing awareness of the importance of such "unobservable constructs"[4] and the efforts to define them by their effects, are playing a considerable role in theoretical formulations in psychology.

Having faced up to the complexity of the data in these ways and in others that

[3] Cf. Darling (1951) for an interesting discussion of the ecological approach to the social sciences.

[4] Cf. MacCorquodale and Meehl (1948) on the distinction between hypothetical constructs and intervening variables. Tolman (1949) apparently now prefers to make the intervening variables parts of more general hypothesized models.

we cannot take the time to consider, the task is then one of reducing the material to manipulable units. This reduction must not, however, sacrifice the fundamental nature of the material as did some manipulations of the past. Various methods have been suggested to achieve this end, of which I shall consider a few.

One proposal emphasizes a preference for one area rather than another because of greater importance. Lewin (1926), for instance, asked the question: Should psychology study the homogeneity of the factors that *produce* effects which may be quite varied, that is, the *genotypical;* or, should it, rather, study the homogeneity of *end results*, arising perhaps from a variety of factors, that is, the *phenotypical?* Concretely, for example, is it the symptomatic or characteristic aggression, or the underlying cause of the aggression, whatever its manifestations, that deserves primary investigative consideration? Lewin was critical of psychology for having generally overemphasized the phenotypical and neglected the genotypical. Although Lewin was primarily interested in the cross-sectional approach rather than the longitudinal one of psychoanalysis, a sympathetic relationship between the two systems may be seen in the mutual primary concern with the genotypical in personality.

A quite different proposal for achieving limitation is that of the deliberate reduction in the field encompassed. We see this most clearly delineated in Hull's (1943) attempt to provide a model for system-making in the field of learning by the use of the hypothetico-deductive method. He sets up a "miniature system" in which he isolates from the variety of psychological phenomena in the field of learning a few interrelated variables in the field of rote learning, and attempts to give a logically rigorous, systematic account of these in great detail. These miniature systems have played a prominent role in the development of the physical sciences. The hope is that psychology can, after detailed application of such systems in small areas, bring them together into larger and larger systematic units. For the development of such a system, a sufficient number of quantitative experiments must be carried out so that functional relationships can be defined with some assurance and the interrelationships expressed in mathematical terms (Hilgard, 1948). Such attempts are now mainly limited to several subareas of learning, a field where some of the most systematic work in psychology has been done. Several other limited fields also offer possibilities in this direction.

Still another way of approaching the problem of limitation is that taken by the animal psychologists. These investigators, having accepted the principles of evolutionary progression, hold that at least in the present stage of psychology it is important and even essential to study psychological phenomena in simpler organisms. Infrahuman animals, they argue, provide, in addition to relative simplicity of mechanism, a short life span, and the possibility of knowing the life history as well as of controlling environmental situations with a great degree of rigor. From this method of attack, to mention only some of the more directly relevant studies for psychiatry, have come such investigations as those of Liddell (1944) on experimental neuroses in sheep and other animals, Maier (Maier & Klee, 1945) on "abnormal fixations" in rats, Jacobsen (Jacobsen, Wolfe & Jackson, 1935) on learning in monkeys with prefrontal lobectomy (studies that provided the rationale for the prefrontal lobotomy work of Moniz), Harlow's (1949) studies of learning and "learning sets" (studies devoted to the important problem of how animals learn how to learn), and Levy's (1934) work with dogs. Some animal psychologists recognize the dangers of extrapolating from animal to human subjects because of the importance of cultural influences and the markedly disproportionate cortical development in the human; others do not see the risk as so great, even while admitting marked disjunctions in evolutionary progression.

Another expression of the attempt to simplify the subject matter of psychology—a step, in fact, which goes beyond the mere limitation of the presenting field—is that seen in the points of view of psychologists like Skinner (1938). Without committing himself on the relationship between physiological and psychological phenomena, he holds that it is not necessary to concern oneself with physiological phenomena in order to understand the psychological data; psychological data, he says, should be dealt with in their own right. At the present stage of psychology, this is a defensible point of view which has the advantage of avoiding the neurological tautologizing which has been so prevalent in the psychological (and psychiatric) fields for many years.[5]

Although this point of view is held by a substantial group of psychologists, it should be pointed out, however, that there is another group, mainly physiological psychologists, who are strongly of the opinion that the concurrent study of physiological processes with the psychological is most important. In fact, some of them, mainly on philosophical grounds, hold the view that the physiological processes are primary and that "all psychological explanation must move in the direction of physiology" (Pratt, 1939). A similar point of view is put forth on theoretical grounds by Krech and Tolman. Krech (1949; 1950a,b) argues that hypothetical constructs cannot be psychological and that in model-building, molar neurological events should be used. Tolman (1949) appears to have retreated from his earlier position (Tolman, 1932) of opposition to neurological constructs and recommends the use of what he calls "pseudo-brain models," by which he means models comprehensive enough to meet psychological theoretical needs and not bound by present neurological knowledge. Hebb's (1949) recently proposed theory of behavior, based largely on neurological constructs, is an important contribution to the psychoneurological point of view. The majority of physiological psychologists, however, go about their *experimental* business, using *both* psychological (behavioral) and physiological concepts, apparently making the implicit assumption that they are dealing with phenomena at two different levels of emergence.

A characteristic of the recent period, too, has been an increased interest in studies of a longitudinal nature, especially with emphasis on the genetic (Jones, 1943; Macfarlane, 1938). It is also true, however, that certain groups (particularly the Lewinian), without denying the importance of the genetic, have systematically taken a point of view that emphasizes the importance of studying the dynamics of

[5] Rapaport (1951), with a very different point of view from Skinner's, also recommends staying within the psychological realm, at least for the present. He proposes a psychological conceptual model based on psychoanalysis as being most inclusive of the observed phenomena.

the existing situation, and therefore, have preferred a cross-sectional approach (Lewin, 1935a). This has, of course, served as another way of reducing complexity.

We have considered rather briefly some of the problems connected with subject matter and with the definition of units of study. We may now turn to the problems involved in actually setting up a project.

In psychology, *experimental design* has become a matter of increased concern during recent years, largely through the influence of R. A. Fisher (1937). Because psychologists have been persistently troubled about how to handle with rigor the complex problems which they have to face, they have been much intrigued with the possibilities lying in the methods used by Fisher and others for planning and evaluating agricultural experiments. His procedures seemed to provide a way of reducing the expenditure of both the time and energy required in carrying through long series of single experiments on single relationships through the adoption of designs which permitted a systematic attack on many variables at once, especially when supported by the statistics appropriate to such designs.

Closely related to this interest in experimental design is the growing recognition of the importance of *preliminary conceptualization* or *hypothesis-testing* in experimental work. In the early part of the century, as a reaction to the then prevalent philosophical speculation and introspection, a marked antagonism to hypothesis and theory developed, resulting in a predominance of studies emphasizing "facts" and the accumulation of data for subsequent analysis. This probably reflected the similar trends in the physical sciences of that period (Brunswik, 1951). Recent years have seen a definite retreat from this point of view, and increasing emphasis placed upon theory and hypothesis as a basic guide for both experimentation and observation.

Another prominent recent development has been "operationism," the principle that concepts of science are to be defined in terms of the operations by which they are observed. Growing out of Bridgman's (1928) original formulation for physics, and developed for psychology largely by Stevens (1939), it has achieved recognition as a tool to be used *before* actual experimentation but *after* a scientific proposition has been made. It serves as a device for determining whether what has been said is empirically meaningful, thus aiding the experimenter to avoid pseudo-problems, problems for which no observational test can be provided. The possible misuse of the principle as an inhibitor of wider generalization, as well as other criticisms have been raised (Israel & Goldstein, 1944). Instead of the exaggerated emphasis placed upon it at first, such cautions have led to operationism's falling into its proper role in the psychological scene as a device for increasing methodological rigor.

These are some of the problems faced before undertaking a psychological study. Two other developments during recent years, statistical analysis and factorial analysis, relate particularly to ways of viewing already collected data.

Because of the persistent cautions that experimental psychologists have about their complicated material, there has been particular receptivity to the controls provided by *statistics*. We have already seen the interest in the factors entering into the design and control of conditions under which experiments are conducted.

Since the control ordinarily attained at this stage is only partial, psychologists recognize the need for using statistics to provide additional controls *after* the data are collected. This is achieved through partialling out factors not controlled before and during the experiment. In this area the *null hypothesis* has assumed considerable importance. The basic assumption is made that the experimental results under consideration arise from chance. It is then the obligation of the experimenter to disprove this hypothesis through the use of tests of significance and to show the degree of confidence which may be placed in the obtained results, that is, the degree to which they are *not* the result of chance. Aside from measures of sampling error, which are involved in the hypothesis, psychologists have used extensively other statistics describing the central tendencies and variation of groups, the interrelationships between groups and among factors, as represented in the various kinds of correlation coefficients, and other procedures which modern statistics provide both for describing large and small samples, and for determining the dependability of differences.

Psychiatrists have at times been critical of this preoccupation with statistics by psychologists. This criticism has been justified on those occasions when statistics have been inappropriately used in certain clinical settings, when the stones of means and standard deviations have been substituted for the bread of clinical understanding. However, psychiatrists have sometimes shown a tendency to dismiss *any* statistical manipulation of material on general grounds. Such lack of regard for one of the really potent tools of science is a handicap to the development of psychiatry. Fortunately, this is beginning to be recognized. One of the contributions which psychology can perhaps make is a demonstration of the applicability of statistics to problems in the psychiatric setting.

Whereas statistics are used in order to deal with the inadequate controls of the experimental situation, *factor analysis* is used essentially to deal with the inadequately formulated concepts of the original experiment. It is a method whereby a set of intercorrelated performances are analyzed into independently variable factors. Thurstone (1947), one of the major leaders in this field, has pointed out that factor analysis is a powerful, but very definitely an *exploratory*, technique. It can be of great value in pointing up potentially profitable avenues to investigate. Factorial mathematical manipulation has, however, at times been substituted for preliminary rigorous psychological thinking-through of a problem. When used with carefully collected data, and with some systematic preliminary psychological hypothesization, it may in complex settings provide the basis for psychological insights not easily obtainable without its use. In the field of psychiatry, it has special appropriateness for the establishment of syndromes. Some attempts (Degan, 1952; Moore, 1933) in this direction have already been made, but these have not been successful because of incompleteness of the original data and lack of rigor in their collection.

Given this kind of present-day psychology, a psychology that is concerned more and more with dealing with molar units in as controlled and quantitative a way as possible, what can we expect in the future, especially of that part which has the greatest relevance for psychiatry? The general goal can be no other than, in Adrian's (1946) words, to bring "the mind within the compass of natural science." My own impression is that this will be achieved in a somewhat different way from that expected and hoped for by the founders of experimental psychology.

Psychology will probably increasingly model itself more directly on its nearer neighbor to the right, biology, rather than on its more remote neighbor in that direction, physics. At the same time it will recognize more fully its similarities to its neighbors on the left, the social sciences. In this way psychology will more adequately establish the proper balance between its capacities and its functions as a member of a scientific community that is so constantly faced with problems of ordered complexity.

I shall discuss the ways in which this trend will express itself under four headings: One relates to the unit of study, a second, to the conditions of study, a third, to interrelationships in study, and the fourth, to the place of theory in study. In the course of the discussion, I shall also consider some special areas of investigation.

Let us take the first: *units of study*. I believe that the trend for the future will be a continuation of the interest in molar behavior, attempts being made to deal with larger and larger units of reaction. Instead of trying to simplify the organism by segmentalization, the organism will be permitted to react as a totality. "Simplicity" and analyzability will be achieved rather through improvement of the techniques of observation, through improved conceptual selection and analysis, and through improvements in statistical analysis. This is not to say that molecular study will not be continued as appropriate, and used fruitfully. In fact, it is very likely that molar study of the kind described will provide the basis for more reasonably oriented molecular study. What I am saying is that the psychologist will attack "cognitive-conative-affective" units, from which aspects of psychological behavior of interest to the experimenter will be partialled out for analysis. In this connection, too, I believe that the intensively studied individual case, for use in the determination of both general and idiosyncratic laws, will play a substantial role. It is indeed strange that nowhere in the literature is there to be found an adequately documented long-term individual record that would lend itself to systematic hypothesis-testing.

As another reflection of this point of view, we can expect that more studies will derive from real-life situations. The ecological approach will provide data to be worked over by successive selective analyses from the total context of such threateningly detailed studies. To achieve this, techniques for making situations objective, such as films and specially trained observers, will be used to an increased degree. Is this not a return to a stage similar to the naturalistic era in biology? In a sense, it is just that. The naturalistic stage was glossed over in psychology. A reasonable case may be made for the proposition that psychology has sorely missed an intensive period of direct preoccupation with the bare facts of life, a gain to be obtained only from such an approach.

In association with the field studies, I would expect a further growth in the use of closer-to-life problems brought into the laboratory for more controlled study. In fact, the hope is that there will be a constant shuttling forth to the field to search for situations providing the relevant conditions not to be obtained in the laboratory, and back to the laboratory to test out the field findings under more controlled conditions.

In relation to the second point, the conditions to be set up for the study of psychological phenomena, we can expect to see a development of greater objectivity in many directions.

We may anticipate an increased "*candorization*" of psychology, that is, the transformation of much more of what are now private and non-communicated data into public data, open for general examination. The range of phenomena transferred from the former category to the latter should be considerable. We have already seen a trend in this direction as relates to the study of the process of psychotherapy (Rogers et al., 1949). This will be strengthened in the direction of adding to sound recordings other revealing devices. Whether the implicit and the presently cryptic in behavior can be entirely brought to the public level is questionable, but that procedures and technical aids directed at constricting the private area considerably can be developed, is quite likely. Already available, although little used, are such techniques as the sound-film (Shakow, 1949b), which make possible the recording of complicated behavior that can be made available for repeated individual and team study, and for systematic successive hypothesis-testing.

It seems inevitable that the clinical area will be placed under greater control, and even experimental attack. Experimental design will be improved and the statistical understanding of problems of a clinical nature will be increased. Such experimentation, I expect, will, however, be more productive than present and past experimentation because many more psychologists will enter this area of study *after* a substantial experience period in the clinical setting. Under such circumstances we can expect that experimentation and observation both in the laboratory and in the field will be more sophisticated.

An increasing trend toward *quantification* is to be expected, a quantification which will be appropriate, growing out of experience with complex psychological problems, rather than the naïve kind from which psychology has sometimes suffered in the past. Statistics and mathematical treatment of data appropriate to the complexity of the situation and especially appropriate to the individual are beginning to be developed and these should supplement other types of measurement. The application of various special correlational techniques such as "Q technique" (Stephenson, 1950), probability sequence analysis (Miller & Frick, 1949), and content analysis (Schutz, 1951) are several promising developments in this area.

In connection with my earlier discussion of ecological studies, I should expect that the techniques of observation and the perfecting of the psychologist himself as a major instrument of investigation will show many advances. Considerable thought has in recent years been given to problems of this nature. We can expect studies of the experimenter himself to determine his capacities for accurate report, his biases, and his other limitations. We can look forward to programs of systematic training developed to improve his span of apprehension and to refine him generally as an instrument. In this context, the place of psychoanalysis as a refining device must be thoroughly examined, since its usefulness for this purpose is still controversial.

Apropos of the point about the individual case which I made earlier in the discussion of molar trends, it is to be expected that psychologists here and also in the ecological sphere, will pay increasing attention to prediction. Just as prediction plays the leading role in astronomy, which is not an experimental science, so psychology, hampered so frequently from achieving satisfactory experimental control, should place more emphasis upon prediction for the validation of its findings. A beginning in this direction has already been made, particularly in the industrial field and even in some of the clinical activities of psychologists, but it is hoped that this area will see consistent expansion. From recorded predictions, and the bases for them, made as explicit as possible for subsequent check, a contribution of considerable magnitude, supplementary to experimental studies, may be made to the understanding of personality.

In the third area, that of the interrelationships of psychology, the reference is mainly to the nature of the collaboration with psychiatry and other disciplines, but I should like also to mention team collaboration within psychology.

Since the major problems in this area appear to go beyond the compass of a single discipline, perhaps all but exceptionally talented and exceptionally prepared individuals can make their most effective contribution through joint effort. Here the logic of Weaver's (1948) "mixed team" approach becomes obvious, and I should expect the future to show an increase in the amount of both intradisciplinary studies of the kind exemplified by the Murray group (Murray, 1938), and interdisciplinary studies of which the Worcester (Hoskins, 1946) and Columbia-Greystone Associates (Mettler, 1949) projects are relatively recent examples. The best interdisciplinary studies, however, are likely to be those organized around concepts common to the fields involved. Through such joint research activities we can expect the development of the most effective communication between the disciplines interested in this area. Psychology, lying as it does, in the hierarchy of the sciences concerned with this problem, between physiology on the one hand and psychiatry on the other, is in some ways located at a strategic position to advance the process.

A necessary caution needs, however, to be expressed with respect to interdisciplinary activity. I have reference to the danger of achieving what Frankfurter (Whitehead, 1949) has called a "cross-sterilization" of the sciences rather than their cross-fertilization. This is especially to be feared in situations where sciences of different degrees of development, quantification, control, and status come into contact. Such deleterious effects are sometimes reflected in collaborative research projects where psychologists and psychiatrists, because of the lure of the exact and the simple, are drawn away from research on the less controllable and more qualitative psychological aspects of the problem to preoccupation with primarily biochemical and physiological material, the more quantitative fields of their collaborators. We might keep in mind what has at various times been suggested as a definition for maturity: the ability to tolerate uncertainty. In the fields of psychiatry and psychology, the investigator has so many opportunities to exercise this blessed quality, that it is not strange if slips are more than occasional.

In the fourth area, that of the place of theory in study, one can expect an increasing trend in the setting up of theoretical models to serve both as bases for the codification of existing knowledge and as guides to further research. These can be expected to range from theoretical systems which deal in detail with small areas of study, for example, Hull's (1943) model for rote learning, to more ambitious attempts to deal with broad areas of science, such as is represented by the general theory of action (Parsons & Shils, 1951).

I can only say a few words about the areas which I consider likely in the future to draw the particular interest of psychologists in the field of psychiatry.

One such area of considerable importance for psychiatry is the systematic study of normal persons. Psychology has during recent years shown a growing interest in the abnormal, neglecting somewhat the intensive study of the normal person, except as he is used for control purposes. Several investigations of normal subjects, of which those by Roe (1953) and Macfarlane (1950) are examples, have impressed psychologists with the importance of giving the same detailed attention to the developmental and environmental factors in the personality study of normal subjects that has been devoted to disturbed subjects. The frequency with which pathological findings are to be found in persons making good and even outstanding adjustment leads to the obvious need for studying the stabilizing process. A larger number of psychologists having become acquainted with important personality factors and concepts through experience with the aberrant, a more adequate study of normal subjects now seems possible. The growing interest of psychiatry in mental hygiene and prevention should make such studies of direct value to psychiatry.

Two other areas of major interest to psychologists will, I believe, be research in psychoanalytic and other dynamic concepts, and in psychotherapy. With respect to psychoanalysis, it is to be expected that as intimate contact of psychologists with this field grows (and such contact has been steadily increasing in recent years) more and more experimentation on the theoretical postulates of psychoanalysis will be undertaken. With respect to psychotherapy generally, it is to be expected that the relationship between the psychotherapeutic and the learning process will be systematically explored further; explored, I trust, on the basis of more thorough understanding and first-hand acquaintance with the complexities of psychotherapy. The impression cannot be avoided that many of the formulations offered thus far have been made on the basis of acquaintance with oversimplified forms of the therapeutic process.

Other areas of interest will perhaps be those of psychosomatics and somatopsychics, which call especially for collaborative set-ups. Still another area is that of nosology, where the proper use of factorial techniques based on adequate clinical data may result in a contribution of some importance. It is to be hoped, however, that the experimental psychologist's *major* concern in all of these areas will be to use the facilities for fundamental research on the problems of personality.

I have tried in broad outline to draw a picture of experimental psychology's methods and content, especially of the areas in psychology most relevant to psychiatry. As I look back on what I have written, I am impressed with how much more attention has gone to the consideration of method than to that of content.

The reason for this, I suppose, lies in part in the fact that in an essay of this kind, the presentation of contentual material requires too much unfair singling out of particular studies. Further, some difficulty arises in presenting even the selected studies in enough detail to carry sufficient meaning. Mainly, however, the emphasis stems from recognizing that at the present time even the best of studies in psychology are merely "gropings" toward the significant. The major significances at the present time seem rather to lie in the delineation of important areas for study, the asking of the proper questions, and the development of appropriate methods for attacking them.

It is customary to refer to the *youth* of experimental psychology, to talk of its infancy, or, when the optimist has the floor, its adolescence. Actually, is this true? Experimental psychology may be youthful in its *performance*, but is this also true of its *age*? We must recognize that experimental psychology is getting close to its century-mark. If we take that famous October morning in 1850, when Fechner, lying in bed, was struck with the solution to the problem of providing a scientific foundation for his philosophy—a solution which involved a quantitative relationship between bodily energy and mental intensity—as the birthdate of experimental psychology, then the century-mark *has* already been passed. With psychology's accomplishments during this period, we need merely compare those of chemistry which is only 50 years older, of organic chemistry which is 20 years older, or of biochemistry which is only half as old.

So it does not seem to be a matter of the passage of years (nor of more gifted personnel, I am ready to contend!). I have sometimes toyed with the notion that the various sciences have their own tempos of development, just as have the various biological species. Maturity in different species, as we know, is reached at quite different periods, the time for its achievement being roughly correlated with the complexity of the species. Psychology's developmental tempo (and that of the social sciences generally) is perhaps analogous to that of man, if the tempo of the physical sciences is taken to be that of the dog, let us say. On some such scale, then, what takes developmentally a month for physics would take a year for psychology, a year would take a decade and a decade a century. Comparing their respective spirals, the form which perhaps characterizes best the path of progress,[6] the slope of the spiral for physics would be steep, while that for psychology would be quite gradual. If there is anything to this notion of differences in developmental tempo, then we should perhaps be somewhat less critical of the slow progress of experimental psychology. The impatience of a James in the 1890's (Perry, 1935, p. 114), which led him to confront Fechner's accomplishments with little Peterkin's pragmatic, "But what good came of it at last?," and the impatience of a Broad (1949, p. 476), in the 30's, which led him to remark that psychology "has never got beyond the stage of medieval physics," should be less cause for concern. For, by our new time scale, these came respectively only three and seven years after the founding of experimental psychology! Although we can appreciate the impatience of these eminent critics, as well as that of a society which has such pressing need for dependable knowledge in this area, we must be prepared for progress to be slow.

Fechner founded experimental psychology by contributing a revolutionary notion —that of placing the *mind* under quantitative experimental study. The persons who

[6] Could we call this the "helical theory" of progress?

associated themselves with this enterprise did not quite realize where they were heading, nor how complicated a task they had undertaken. But persons who have successively taken up the battle, have continued working toward this goal stubbornly. Slowly and deliberately they have held to experimental rigor, even at the cost of psychological meaningfulness, to quantification at the cost of richness of quality, to impersonality at the cost of personality.

There have been psychologists, on the other hand, who recognized some limitations in this approach and who pressed for broadening activity at the cost of some temporary reduction in rigor. These have served as gadflies to the plodding oxen, not without a modicum of effect. Other social sciences that had no pretensions to being experimental or quantitative, having reached a stage of readiness for psychological enrichment, turned to psychologies which also had no such pretensions. Compare, for instance, the considerable absorption of psychoanalytic principles by cultural anthropology with the minimal effect upon it of experimental psychology.

Of course, in history's telescopic eyes, the fundamental point of view represented by this group of slow experimentalists may be correct, and in the end the wait may have been worthwhile. What one wants to be sure of, though, is that travel is along a *spiral* and not in a *circle*! Certainly, as one examines the work of at least some of the psychologists in this group, the latter appears to be the case.

Here the historian, who views development in the longer sweep, can be of help. As I pointed out earlier, Boring sees the history of experimental psychology as consisting of three phases in which sensation and perception, learning, and motivation were successively dominant. He has even gone so far as to say that: "The student of the history of psychology would not be promoting an absurdity if he placed on the horizon of his imagination three landmarks to represent the beginning of these three phases: Fechner's *Elemente der Psychophysik* of 1860, Ebbinghaus' *Ueber das Gedächtnis* of 1885, and Freud's *Die Traumdeutung* of 1900" (Boring, 1950, p. 741).

Certain developments in psychology in recent years have great importance for the understanding of these phases. As outlined by Boring, they were *successive* phases, separate and independent developments with little overlap among them. What we are seeing now is the growing recognition of the importance of the motivation phase and of the interrelationships among the three areas. The period when learning was considered as merely cognitive and motor, and perception as merely cognitive, is rapidly passing. Instead, recent years have evidenced a growing dissatisfaction with the studies of learning in humans as being *too* cognitive, a turning to learning in animals because of the possibility for studying in them really important motivating factors, and finally the penetration into the field of human learning of motivational factors, as seen in the concern with "emotional learning," and the interest in psychotherapy as learning (Dollard & Miller, 1950; Mowrer, 1950). Even more recently we see the invasion of the perceptual field by motivational problems (Bruner & Krech, 1950). Thus the early segmentalization into separate fields which grew out of a need for control, and which so dehumanized psychology, is now being replaced by a decidedly more integrated attack upon the organism.

We see, then, that even in slow-tempoed psychology there are signs of progress. The methodological activity which I considered in some detail earlier is still another sign. But the tempo of progress must be speeded up. Physics, having acted the hamster in recent years, rather than sticking to its canine tempo, has made such a speed-up mandatory for the social sciences. Weaver's suggestions for dealing with the problems of "organized complexity" by the use of the mixed team approach and modern computational devices have possibilities which must be exploited, as should those proposals I have mentioned as coming from within psychology itself. Above all, however, what an inevitably *adolescent* psychology needs is development by *mature individual* psychologists. This development should, of course, take place along the line of their own predilections, but accompanied by a recognition of the fact that at this stage of psychology's progress no promising methods, experimental, naturalistic, statistical, or other, and no theories or frames of reference can be disregarded. What is needed is a greater tolerance for a wide range of approaches and a greater freedom from the rituals of science (Allport, 1940).

Ralph Barton Perry (1938), writing some ten years ago *In the Spirit of William James*, said of him:

> Had he known the psychology of today, he would have said, "The tent of psychology should be large enough to provide a place for the Bohemian and clinical speculations of a Freud, or the rigorous physiological methods of a Lashley, or the bold theoretical generalizations of a Köhler, or the useful statistical technique of a Spearman. Only time will tell which of these, or whether any of these, will yield the master hypothesis which will give to psychology that explanatory and predictive power, that control of the forces of nature, which has been achieved by the older sciences."

Some of us may take slight exception to the "Bohemian"; for the rest, can't we go along?

20. Ideal Program of Training for Psychotherapists: Patterns of Institutional Sponsorship

I was invited to participate in the "Conference on an Ideal Program of Training for Psychotherapists" held at Gould House at Ardsley-on-the-Hudson in 1963. The persons mainly responsible were Robert Holt and Lawrence Kubie. My assignment was to consider the patterns of institutional sponsorship for an ideal training program. The report of the Conference is to be published by the International Universities Press in 1969.

Introduction

In considering the institutional auspices under which an ideal training program in psychotherapy should be established, a major problem of strategy arises. Does one

Reprinted with permission from R. R. Holt (Ed.), *New Horizons for Psychotherapy*, 1969 (International Universities Press).

immediately set up an "ideal" program, or does one initiate the program with an interim stage? Since my own predilection is for the latter, my suggestions will be oriented along such lines. It seems best, however, to consider first the nature of the ideal institutional arrangement and then, knowing what we are aiming at, examine the conditions desirable for the interim arrangement. I shall be recommending an autonomous institute in a university as the best institutional arrangement.

Before going into either the interim or ideal arrangement, however, I should like to emphasize certain preliminary conditions that are essential to the success of the program. These relate to the underlying attitudes of the planners and of the institution, and the general qualifications of the institution.

The major point about the planners is that they must be deeply convinced of the importance of the program. They must have a readiness to see it through despite the variety of problems and irritations which are bound to arise in any novel enterprise—but particularly so in a delicate operation of this kind.

It is likewise most important that the administration of the university as a whole, and that of its relevant parts, be strongly committed to such a program. The deans and department heads involved, as well as the general university administration, must be convinced of the desirability of carrying through an experimental psychotherapeutic training program of the level we are considering.

It is also important that the university chosen as a setting have at least high-quality medical and social work schools, and a graduate school that is particularly strong in psychology and in the social sciences.

The basic goal of the program is to train top-level psychotherapists who might serve not only as psychotherapists themselves, but also as leaders and teachers in the development of the large body of psychotherapists which the community will need in the future.

As part of the expectations which such a program might arouse, it is important to keep clear that what is planned here is *not* a psychoanalytic institute, although it would be very desirable if a university-connected psychoanalytic institute were available on the campus. The psychotherapeutic program itself is of course not intended to meet the same kinds of needs. Neither should this program be thought of as attempting to meet the same professional needs as psychiatry, social work, or clinical psychology. Although it is likely that candidates for our program will either come from these fields or be persons who might ordinarily have entered one of them, the program itself should be clearly separate. While it may also provide a training background similar to that of the other groups, the program should aim at the development of what is essentially a new profession having its own major goals and philosophy.

The Ideal Program

In considering the "ideal program," I plan to discuss problems relating to the general institutional arrangements, fundamental pedagogic principles, the general nature of the faculty and of the students, and then to consider certain relevant general issues.

Institution

As I stated previously, I strongly recommend that the institutional arrangement itself be an autonomous institute within a university. Let us examine the advantages of this arrangement. In describing the advantages of a university, I am not unaware of the inadequacies of many such settings. I am far from considering universities small utopias. But of the many institutions in our culture which might be considered suitable, good universities would in general appear to be the optimal places for such an arrangement.

The semi-protected environment of the university, wherein the goal pattern is consonant with the values of a life oriented to teaching, research, and scholarship, seems most likely to offer the community support for one's superego that all of us, with rare exceptions, need. This includes an atmosphere of constant competition for ideas, both within one's field and with other fields. The stimulation comes from pressures of colleagues and from student pressures which carry over from their contact with other departments. Such external review necessitates constant self-review, thus providing the controls which any profession must have if it is to develop optimally.

The university standards—those which cross departments—have both explicit and implicit effects on the standards of a particular department or school. They result in the provision of models of instructors who must meet these standards, whether as clinical teachers, as basic core teachers, researchers, or scholars. The students therefore have a variety of models with whom to identify, a variety rarely found in independent institutes.

Organizationally, I would recommend that the psychotherapy program be under the auspices of an autonomous institute of psychotherapy. This should not be a "department," but actually an autonomous *institute* with its own administrative structure, and considerable freedom in establishing relationships with other institutes and departments. The most relevant of these would be with graduate departments of psychology, sociology, and anthropology, with the medical school—particularly with departments of psychiatry and pediatrics—with schools of social work, and with other relevant professional schools. (The details of the autonomy will, of course, have to be spelled out in each case.) The institute of psychotherapy could then be an important center of intercourse between those who are primarily clinically oriented and those who are primarily theoretically oriented. The most effective teaching of psychotherapy takes place in an environment of this kind, an environment where these two kinds of activity are given equal prominence. An additional benefit of this scheme would be that it ensures that those with a major interest in practice will receive the necessary complementary training in theory.

In addition to the existing clinical resources of the university, the institute of psychotherapy should have its own clinical facilities for the care of out-patients, and perhaps even for occasional in-patients. These patients would come directly, by referral from outside sources, or by transfer from other facilities of the university. Except for what it needs for its own research purposes, I do not believe the institute of psychotherapy should attempt to duplicate the science laboratories of the university for teaching purposes. Arrangements should be made with other parts of the university for the use of its general resources.

The program, I believe, should start off as a four-year program using four full rather than four academic years. It is important that the program culminate in a degree which might very well be that of *Doctor of Psychotherapy*. Although there may be a tendency to extend the program further, I believe it would be a mistake to attempt to put everything into this doctoral program. If further training is necessary, it should be carried out at a post-doctoral level.

The detailed content of the program is of course being presented by some of the other participants at this meeting. I do not, however, believe that a research dissertation is a necessary part of the requirements. I think that the presentation of an intensive psychotherapy case well worked-up might replace the dissertation for some students. When a research dissertation is required it should be on some aspect of research in psychotherapy.

Before going on to discuss questions relating to faculty and students, I would be neglectful of my responsibility if I did not review other possible types of institutional arrangement which have seemed to me less satisfactory than the one I have recommended. The other major possibilities are: (1) independent organization (or institute); (2) present arrangement within department with increased emphasis on psychotherapy; (3) committee arrangement using already existing facilities; (4) summer school/field work ("squatter") arrangement.

Let us briefly consider each.

1. The independent organization. For a variety of reasons, such an arrangement does not seem promising. The great amount of administrative machinery, the breadth of representation, the variety of facilities, and the immense amount of money required to initiate and maintain an educational program of this kind, make this a very unlikely possibility. Certainly experience with psychoanalytic institutes, which have more justification for independence and much narrower goals, does not make one optimistic.

2. Use of present training facilities in existing departments of psychiatry and psychology and in schools of social work, but with greater emphasis on psychotherapy. Such arrangements would not be in harmony with the goals which we have set for this "ideal" program. It is hard to see how an independent profession with its particular goals and philosophy could be developed under such circumstances. Additionally, the problems in training for psychiatry, social work, and psychology are already complicated enough without adding this extra burden to these departments.

3. A committee arrangement like that of the Committee on Human Development of the University of Chicago. This system calls for the appointment of an advisory committee for each student composed of faculty representatives from each of the relevant departments. The student, with the advice of his committee, selects the courses and work he requires for completing his degree. When working optimally, a system of this kind does have the advantage of individualizing the programs. It loses, however, the tremendous advantages that would come from participation in a

group enterprise directed at the development of a new profession. Besides not being congruent with our primary goals, it has also been my experience that as this system has worked at Chicago, it has not been very successful.

4. The summer school/field work arrangement (the "squatter" system). This arrangement would follow that used by such schools as the Smith College School of Social Work. Here, a campus that is not ordinarily used in the summer is taken over during this period for intensive didactic work, the rest of the year being spent in field work placements. Although this scheme has certain advantages, such a program does not seem to provide the desirable constant interaction between formal teaching and seminars, on the one hand, and clinical work, on the other. Neither does it provide the constant interaction of students which is so large a part of the educational process.

While it is true that a proper program of this kind could not be made to function unless the institutional arrangements are optimal, at best, institutional arrangements are facilitative. They can help a good program to prosper, but they are not the essentials of a good program. In the end, a good program will come from good teachers, who give good students the kind of good education that will start them off in their careers as good psychotherapists. I wish to consider now some of the more formal aspects of problems related to these "goods."

Pedagogic Principles

First and foremost of these formal considerations is the question of atmosphere. In the area of psychotherapy, this question centers largely around the recognition of the importance of *attitudes* in both therapist and patient. Of central importance in this atmosphere is the fostering of the development of a warm but objective approach toward patients.

Equally important is the integration into the therapeutic approach of a working acceptance of a combination of these five principles underlying the understanding of personality: (1) the *genetic* principle, acknowledging the importance of antecedents in the genetic series in accounting for present manifestations of personality; (2) the recognition of the *cryptic*, of unconscious and preconscious factors as crucial determiners of behavior—that behavior has underlying motivations which are rarely perceptible to the actor and most frequently not even to the trained observer, except with the use of special techniques; (3) the *dynamic* notion that behavior is drive-determined—that underneath behavior ultimately lie certain innate or early developed drives; (4) the general *psychobiological* assumption that the personality is integral and indivisible—that there is a pervasive interrelationship between psyche and soma—involving the acceptance of an organismic principle of total rather than segmental personality; (5) the *psychosocial* principle recognizing the integration of the individual and his environment as a unit—that drives and their derivatives are expressed in individual response in a social context, and that the social is of equal importance with the individual in the determination of behavior.

In this general context we must constantly be aware of certain more specific fundamental pedagogic principles. It must be recognized that knowledge essential to the practice of psychotherapy cannot be obtained solely from books, lectures, or other strictly academic devices. Thus, instead of a multiplication of courses, the students should, insofar as possible, be encouraged to learn as much as possible for themselves. Patient material should be used as frequently as possible in training, whether this be in the form of analysis of case material or demonstration of cases. The building of an apperceptive mass of experience which gives concrete meaning to general principles can be attained only through volume of experience with actual clinical problems. The program should provide the student with a broad base for later specialization by throwing him into full-time contact with human clinical material, contact of an increasing intensity in which the unfolding of psychological processes are longitudinally followed.

A major function of the training is thus to provide practical experience of gradually increasing complexity under close and competent supervision. Nevertheless, a fundamental aim of the process of instruction must also be the gradual development in the student of a sense of a responsibility and self-reliance in handling clinical problems. The whole program should be organized to provide the student with increasing responsibilities commensurate with his growth in ability to accept them. This requires constant knowledge by the supervisor of the state of the student's progress. At the start of the program, the supervision should be close and the supervisor should assure himself of the ability of the student to handle even simple procedures. As the student shows increasing competence, the supervision should be proportionately reduced and greater responsibility placed on him.

Another pedagogic principle is that psychotherapy should be started early in the program, with appropriate supervision at each stage. Psychotherapy should thus be thought of as being central from the very beginning. It should not be put off as a final reward to be given the student during the latter part of his training.

During the whole process of training—in lectures, seminars, supervisory hours—the student must be made aware of the inadequacy of knowledge in the area of psychotherapy, and of the vital need for an attitude of inquiry and research. This is most concretely aided by actual student participation in ongoing research projects.

Faculty

The faculty should be representative of the different disciplines centrally involved in psychotherapy. Also included should be other specialists, such as biologists and persons from the humanities, who might very well come from other parts of the university on joint appointments. The full-time members of the faculty should practice psychotherapy from a quarter- to half-time, preferably with patients in the university or institute clinics, rather than in private practice. They should be in a position to make their case material available for teaching purposes.

Aside from their competence as practitioners, teachers, and researchers (some combination of these qualities), it is important that the faculty of this kind of an institute represent an attitude of boldness, associated with just the proper dash of caution—an attitude which would enable them to tackle the problems in this borderline area with the freedom that involvement in a new area calls for.

Students

Students should be selected on the basis of maturity or potentiality for maturity. In order that they be ready for this highly demanding full-time experience, for the present I would require that they have their bachelor's degrees. I do not think that we are quite ready to start at the high-school level or even at the two-year college level, although these are not impossibilities. Experience with highly motivated, highly competent youngsters such as the Ford Merit Scholars, Westinghouse winners, and with the Peace Corps, would lead one to believe that it is neither necessary nor wise to postpone training pending a graduate professional degree. It is important, however, to obtain people who are relatively mature. Although we know that this maturity is not necessarily perfectly correlated with chronological age, there is a higher level of relationship in our own particular field of interest. There should be no problem of obtaining needed fellowship support for such students.

The ability to carry out effectively the combination of functions called for depends upon the psychotherapist being the right kind of person. Initially this would mean a person who has a relevant informal experience background into which has been integrated the proper formal education. While students may come mainly from the social sciences, selection criteria should be sufficiently flexible to admit promising persons with quite different educational backgrounds. This means the criteria should be directed more at personality qualifications, at educability, than at specific contentual background.

What characteristics does the "right kind" of person possess? As yet, we do not know definitely. But it is generally agreed that the personality qualifications represented by a reasonably well-adjusted and attractive personality are especially important. Until dependable research data are available, the following supplemental list, which includes the kind of specific attributes experienced observers believe clinical work requires, may be useful for selection purposes: superior intellectual ability and judgment, originality, resourcefulness, and versatility, interest in persons as individuals rather than as material for manipulation—a regard for the integrity of other persons, insight into own personality characteristics, sense of humor, sensitivity to the complexities of motivation, tolerance, industry, ability to tolerate pressure, tact and cooperativeness, integrity, self-control and stability, discriminating sense of ethical values.

The list is formidable, indeed almost "frightening" to potential teachers who dare not measure *themselves* by such criteria. In the present state of our knowledge, nevertheless, it represents the kind of selection *goals* toward which we must work. Characteristics of this type seem a necessary foundation for work in a field which requires so much in the way of maturity, sensitivity, and knowledge.

How are we to obtain such persons for training? Problems of both recruitment and selection are involved. The problems of recruitment are more difficult than they are in such major professional fields as medicine and law, and even in the relatively newer fields of psychiatry, social work, and clinical psychology. The former fields are well-established and known to youngsters from quite early years, while the latter are becoming better known. For the present, the major recruiting effort will have to be made at the college level through teachers of psychology, the social sciences, and vocational advisors. In coming years, growing general acquaintance with the field, and the multiplication of courses in psychology and the social sciences at the secondary level, are likely to lead the student to think of psychotherapy as a lifework. A first rough self-selection might then come in the secondary schools.

General

May I add a few general comments about programs of this kind?

First, if there is a possibility of getting two or even three programs started, I should like to see them experiment with varied ways of trying to meet the needs of the field. As we do not know the answers to education in this area, any seriously thought-through program deserves a test.

A major consideration is the question of how to make psychotherapy central throughout training without at the same time making it vocational. The faculty will have to spend a good part of its time on problems of this kind during the formative years of the program in their efforts to build a true philosophy of psychotherapy that includes the attitude of constant inquiry.

The last general consideration I wish to touch upon is that of identification. The problem of identification will be difficult in the early stages in view of the multidisciplinary faculty and the absence of one special group with whom to identify. In time, however, if the quality of the program is maintained, such problems will gradually disappear.

Interim Program

For the present, we can lay plans for the ideal program while we are already working within the confines of an interim program. We can achieve many aspects of the ideal program during this period by being practical in accepting compromises, but not by compromising on essentials.

The interim program must provide the opportunity for long-term planning. Since we have agreed that the institute of psychotherapy should be established in a university, it is important from the very beginning to make temporary use of existing facilities while building the new ones. This means both personnel and physical resources. In this context it is important to utilize the most sympathetic persons in the various parts of the university in the planning of the long-range as well as the interim program.

My own guess is that the best approach would be to choose the core staff of the ultimate institute approximately a year before an interim program is adopted to allow for them to be together during the planning phase of the operation. I would not make this period too long because I think the program loses out greatly in being delayed. After this first year of planning, a *small* group of highly selected students should be recruited with whom to initiate an experimental interim program. During this stage it is probably wisest to take on students who already have some background in one of the three mental health professions, although later there can be experimentation with less advanced groups. During this stage, too, the clinical facilities of the neighboring departments will have to be relied upon.

For this interim period, the faculty should be kept small. There should be a possibility for constant conferences among the members of the faculty, and students should be brought into meetings that consider the strengths and weaknesses of the various aspects of the training.

So much will depend on the personnel during this interim period that the greatest efforts should be expended at obtaining not only dedicated, but also administratively able persons. The role of the dean of the institute of psychotherapy is particularly important. The amount of "negotiation" which this project entails is so immense that these points cannot be overemphasized.

Concluding Remarks

I have presented briefly a general statement about the institutional auspices under which an ideal training program in psychotherapy might be carried out. The preferred institutional arrangement—an autonomous institute within a university—was discussed and some of the major disadvantages of other types of organization were examined. Recognizing the somewhat auxiliary nature of institutional arrangements, I have considered some of the more formal facets of the teaching program as represented in some aspects of institutional atmosphere and in certain pedagogic principles. Briefly, I have considered the general nature of the faculty members and students that should be recruited for such a program.

With this image in mind of where we might very well be headed, I discussed some of the problems to be dealt with during the interim period, for I have argued that the ideal program might be more successful if a period of experimentation with existing resources were first gone through.

21. Comments on Behavioral Science in Medicine

In May, 1966, Oliver Cope and Douglas Bond, acting for a steering committee, invited me to participate in a "Study of Behavioral Science in Medicine" to be held for a two-week period in the fall of 1966. It was planned as a sequel to the Endicott House Conference of July, 1965, (Oliver Cope and Jerrold Zacharias, *Medical Education Reconsidered* [Philadelphia: Lippincott, 1966]). A report of the study, published early in 1968 by Oliver Cope (*Man, Mind and Medicine: The Doctor's Education*), includes the paper I sent to the Conference at Swampscott after a week's attendance. The following is a later version of that paper.

Interpretations of the Task of the Conference

The major goal of the Conference had obviously been construed differently by various members of the group. It appeared to me that at one time or another these four goals were expressed:

1. socialization and humanization of the physician;
2. the behavioral sciences as basic disciplines necessary for the full teaching of medicine;
3. the medical school as a part of the broader university setting and the place of the behavioral sciences in the combined set-up; and
4. the narrower proposition of Judge Bazelon relating to the adequate preparation of the medically trained psychiatrist to deal with important social issues.

Let me elaborate somewhat on each of the above.

The argument for the socialization and humanization of the physician in training arises from recent developments. Advances in medicine have tended to direct the students' energies to areas deriving their prestige largely from laboratory work. The recent advances in neurophysiology, in molecular biology, and in other basic sciences have had the effect of emphasizing process rather than the person. This has resulted in a kind of impersonalization of the physician as physician. Many medical men who come into direct clinical contact with patients believe that it is necessary to inject into medicine a more social, a more personal, and a generally more human approach. This attitude is what is generally reflected in Walter Goodman's recent article in the *New York Times Magazine* (Oct. 12, 1966) and the earlier books of Carter, Greenberg, Lasagna, and Cross.

Those who held that the Conference was directed toward the consideration of the behavioral sciences and their place in the basic medical curriculum presented a somewhat different argument. They indicated that in earlier years there had been

Reprinted with permission from O. Cope, *Man, Mind and Medicine: The Doctor's Education,* 1968 (Lippincott).

a recognition of the importance of the physical sciences, particularly chemistry, and, in more recent times, of biology, as represented by biochemistry, molecular biology, and related fields in medicine. They saw now a need to recognize the present and growing potential contribution of the behavioral sciences to medicine. This includes not only the biotropic aspects, such as physiological psychology and individual psychology generally, but also the sociotropic aspects, including social psychology, sociology, and anthropology. For some, the medical curriculum should also include certain aspects of political science, economics, and history.

The third group largely emphasized an underlying issue. They argued that before discussing either one of the two topics just mentioned, it was important to redefine the position of the medical school in the total university setting. They maintained that the medical school has tended to become a quite independent and separate, as well as isolated, institution and that it is important for medicine to return to the university of which it is a part. Their belief was that only in such a broadened setting could the behavioral sciences adequately be integrated into the medical program.

It is in this same general context that Judge Bazelon's concern was presented. He has been much disturbed by the repeated experiences he has had in calling upon psychiatrists for help in dealing with the problems that come before him. He has found psychiatrists inadequately prepared to deal with the social issues involved. Not only are they limited in knowledge in this respect, but he feels that, in addition, they tend to report their findings in a jargonist fashion and are defensive about making available, in a clear and forthright manner, the information they have about patients. Although it is possible that the point was never explicitly made, I believe that implicit to what he was saying was the need for medicine to have a much greater social orientation, with the further implication that psychiatry particularly would benefit from such an approach.

The discussion at first seemed to be largely centered on determining what the specific topic of the Conference was actually to be. Although this was not decided, I believe I am accurately reflecting the state of opinion at the time I left. In the course of the meeting, two additional, and secondary, notions developed regarding what people expected to accomplish at the Conference.

It may have been the difficulties in reaching some consensus on the fundamental purpose which led to the development of an attitude which accepted a much less ambitious goal. This goal was that at the least the members of the Conference could mutually educate one another and go away with considerable gain in planning medical education programs for having attended this Conference. This mutual education could be of two major kinds: (1) being thrown together, anti-psychiatrist and psychiatrist would be afforded opportunities to discuss frankly their attitudes toward each other and the failings they saw in each other; (2) another major group of contenders, the psychoanalytically oriented among the psychiatrists and those non-psychoanalytically oriented (these included both organic and socially oriented psychiatrists), could confront one another in a similar manner. Although these two controversies are somewhat intertwined, in general they can be separated as I have described them. There were, in addition, a few less important issues.

The Humanizing of the Physician

My own interpretation of the major goal of the Conference was to contribute to the consideration of ways of achieving greater humanization of the physician by way of his medical education. I am therefore limiting my discussion to some aspects of this problem to which I feel my own background of experience in training psychologists, psychiatrists, and medical students can contribute.

In addition to a substantive knowledge of basic medicine, certain characteristics describe the psychosocially oriented physician. Foremost among these is the recognition of the importance of *attitudes* in interpersonal relationships. Without the central acceptance of the all-importance of the patient and *his* attitudes, integral to which is a warm but objective approach toward patients by the physician himself, a physician would find it difficult to function optimally.

Besides this characteristic, the physician should have developed, in his approach to professional problems, an apperceptive mass which combines the following five principles that underlie the understanding of personality: (1) The *genetic* principle, which acknowledges the importance of earlier experiences in the development of the person to account for present manifestations of personality. (2) The recognition of the *cryptic*, of unconscious and preconscious factors as crucial determiners of behavior. This point of view recognizes that behavior has, besides the obvious conscious motivations, further underlying motivations which are rarely perceptible to the actor, and frequently not even to the trained observer except with the use of special techniques. (3) The *dynamic* notion that behavior is drive-determined, that beneath behavior ultimately lie certain innate or acquired impelling forces. (4) The general *psychobiological* principle that the personality is integral and indivisible, that there is a pervasive interrelationship between psyche and soma. This involves the acceptance of an organismic principle of total rather than segmental personality. (5) The *psychosocial* principle, which recognizes the integration of the individual and his environment as a unit, that drives and their derivatives are expressed in individual response within a social context, and that the social is of equal importance with the individual in the determination of behavior.

Principles of Teaching

With these general principles as the broad goals of the teaching program, I shall consider briefly some specific aspects of the teaching program that fall more into my own area of competence.

What kinds of material and what kinds of techniques shall we use? We can agree that as much of the teaching as is possible should use case material and should come from *direct* contact with patients. It is necessary to present this material at the appropriate level of simplicity for the student's current state of knowledge. This calls for a proper combination of simplicity and complexity. Thus, when cases are presented there ought to be a special effort made to keep the material relatively simple and, especially in the earlier period, to emphasize the *therapeutic* aspects of a problem, not merely the presentation of the data. (Too often in the teaching of psychiatry in medical school the case is presented as too difficult to deal with therapeutically and the student is left with a feeling of therapeutic nihilism.) In addition, the material should be "real," not fabricated for the occasion. Students are quite sensitive to the presentation of what they recognize to be sham material. As far as possible, too, the material should occur in a service setting where something useful is being done for the patient. This is, of course, related to the previous point. Moreover, in the earlier years of medical training there should be a serious effort to select problems relevant to the medical field. The new medical student has waited a long time to come face-to-face with medical problems and is strongly oriented in this direction. It is therefore wise to take advantage of his interest.

As for the kinds of techniques to be taught, I shall consider later the need for training the students in four kinds of observation techniques. Three of these have to do with patients and one revolves around the observer himself.

It is important that as much of the teaching as possible take place in a setting of responsibility and involvement with the patient where the student does as much of the actual work himself as is feasible at his stage of development. (Most teachers tend to underestimate their students, and therefore fail to take advantage of their full capacities.) It should be carried out in an atmosphere of warm concern for the patient. Yet a student must have an opportunity to make errors and correct them. Therefore, at least in part, he should have the possibility for working with situations which at first do not carry with them danger for the patient. He should also have opportunities to teach, for teaching is a most effective method of learning. This would presumably mean, in the earlier years of the medical program, the teaching of persons like nurses and technicians and, in the later years, perhaps teaching of medical students of less advanced status. One general principle can perhaps be laid down: the teaching relating to cases should come as early as possible in his program, and during its course the emphasis should be on graduating the difficulty of the material with which the student is faced.

Although there may be occasions when the student should be placed entirely on his own, ordinarily he should work independently under preceptorial guidance appropriate to the stage of his development.

Training in the Four Kinds of Observation

The behavioral sciences, insofar as they are concerned with the observation of human beings by other human beings, face some very special problems. Important among these is that of *variability*. Not only is there marked intraindividual and interindividual variability in the observed, but there is equally great variability of both kinds in the observer as instrument. We must recognize that there are different kinds of observation which contribute to this variability and must consider ways in which we can help to reduce, or at least understand, it.[1] The goal of training in observation is, of course, to extend into the human range the "habit of truth" which Bronowski (1956) speaks about and which has been so effective in the physical and biological realms.

After discussing the different kinds of observation, I shall continue with the consideration of how to train and improve the observer as instrument. Four major types of observation are involved: objective observation, participant observation, subjective observations, and self-observation.

In *objective observation*, we deal with the observations made from the outside directed toward the careful description of the impact on the individual of internal and external forces—physical, psychological, and social—that are making him behave the way he does. These observations are "naturalistic," they are made from outside the situation which the patient is in. The observer here is not directly involved with the patient.

The second kind of observation, *participant observation*, implies a much more intimate relationship between the observer and the observed. They are both members of the group. The observer has both to evaluate himself as a participant in the group and be able to make evaluations which are "objective"—separate from those connected with his participation in the group. He needs, as well, to evaluate what effect the act of observing has on the observed and the observation. The group may consist of just two people—the patient and the student—as in the simplest form of this interaction, history-taking. Except for history-taking, it may be that situations of the truly participant-observer type are relatively less frequent in ordinary medical relationships than they are in psychiatry. In mental health settings it is most strikingly found in psychotherapy where the psychotherapist is both observer and therapist. Some therapeutic situations in medicine are more likely to be of this kind.

The third kind of observation is an especially important one for medicine. It involves *subjective observation*, the attempt to empathize with the patient, to try to understand how the patient feels both about himself and his illness.

The fourth kind of observation is that of *self-observation*, the understanding by the observer of his own feelings and attitudes, sort of asking himself what makes him tick. This would seem to be vital in the practice of medicine if one is to be sensitive to the psychological and social aspects of the illness of others.

It is clear that what we are emphasizing throughout are techniques for learning by experiencing, rather than learning from hearsay. Because of this real-life learning, dangers are inherent in these techniques of, on the one hand, disturbing the validity of the observation and, on the other, of developing self-consciousness and

[1] In passing, I might indicate that I have been particularly impressed with this problem of variability of response because of my long time concern with schizophrenics in whom variability is so pronounced. This is another area where we can learn from the pathological to which Douglas Bond has referred in the course of our present Conference. I would go along with him particularly in the point he made about working with the pathological but always with a window onto the normal. To rephrase Bond in literary terms, what we want is "a room with a view."

exaggerated introspectiveness. Such dangers deserve careful consideration and correction.

Four Kinds of Observation—Implementation

Before actually beginning to work with diagnostic problems, students should have a preliminary and fairly extensive period of training devoted to *naturalistic observation* and description, procedures on which diagnosis is so integrally based. Because so much of medicine depends on the description of the complexities of behavior, feelings, and symptoms, a portion of the time of the first year should be spent in training students in careful observation and report. Insofar as possible, these observations should be carried out on physically sick people. For purposes of training, one-way screens and paired observers (and, on occasion, recording devices) should be used in settings where individuals and groups are under observation in free and controlled situations. Constant checking of observers' reports against each other, against supervisors' observations, and even against mechanical devices (such as tape recorders) should be part of the practice. It is important that a healthy respect for careful observation and report be developed in students who are going to work in a field where a good share of the time the major instrument, in both respects, is the observer himself. With regard to reporting, both in this connection and in connection with diagnostic study, strictness and insistence on high standards of succinctness and accurate terminology are essential. A further argument for early training in observation is suggested by Wenckebach's statement, "*Das Wissen verdrängt das Sehen*," which points up the dangers that inhere in the early acquisition of technical terms and how frequently such knowledge serves as a barrier to accurate observation of the conditions with which the student is concerned.

In *participant-observation*, the inadequacies of naturalistic observation are multiplied and reveal themselves in two particular ways: one in relation to the data, and the other in regard to the effect on what is observed.

Like any reported observations, the data are bound by the capacity of the human observer as a reporting instrument. No matter how good human beings may be as conceptualizers, they are markedly handicapped sensorially, mnemonically, and expressively as observers and reporters. Put simply, they are limited in how much they can grasp, in how much they can remember of what they do grasp, and in how much and how well they can report even the slight amount they have grasped and remembered. The situation of participant-observation places an even greater stricture upon the data because one is dependent upon a participant-observer whose participation is special and likely to be extensive. Distortions, both of omission and commission, arising from this situation, as well as the personality of the observer, undoubtedly enter. It is for these reasons that techniques for training of the type mentioned earlier in settings of this particular sort need to be given special attention.

With regard to *subjective observation*, we are concerned with the empathic insight into the nature of another person's difficulties and characteristics. It goes without saying that such insight is an important part of the physician's armamentarium. How to achieve the skill of "empathic understanding," in which the student can learn to alternate between the opposite demands of identification and objectivity that are called for, is the goal of training in this area. For such purposes, exercises in role-playing and psychodrama under expert guidance can be most productive, such as exercises in which one student is asked to play the part of a person with a particular form of illness and another the part of the attending physician. In this way the student is more likely to gain an appreciation of the "feeling" that comes with different illnesses.

An important aspect of the problem of the observer as instrument, one which arises particularly in dealing with motivational questions, is the degree to which one's own biases, affects, and problems, frequently only different from the patient's in intensity, color the material provided by the patient. It has become obvious to those working in the clinical field that some kind of control of this source of error is necessary. Many in the behavioral sciences, from their more extended experience with this type of material, have accepted the principle of the need for *self-evaluation* as a prerequisite for their work. For this, many have undergone psychoanalysis.

Physicians in general would also be helped by some kind of self-evaluation. For most, short methods of self-evaluation are preferable. Whatever the form, training should include self-examination under the competent guidance of experienced persons. Physicians can perhaps adopt from social work practice a procedure that has been found effective in achieving at least partial self-knowledge. I refer to their use of intensive detailed case supervision of students. From a parallel contact with preceptors, similar gains may possibly be achieved.

More General Questions

Two questions of a more general nature are also relevant in this discussion of the humanizing of the physician. Although significantly related to the whole field of medical education, a discussion of the questions of models and of ethics seems peculiarly appropriate in the context of a discussion of the behavioral sciences.

The "models" with which I am here concerned are not theoretical models but rather teachers whom the student may emulate. Because of the considerable emphasis placed on courses in our universities and professional schools, one tends to pay less attention to the vehicles through which these courses are taught. In the end, it is amazing how much more permanent an impact teachers have on students by what they *do* in the context of what they say, rather than by what they merely say. And how much more impact they have when they encourage the student to do, than if they merely set the example. The proper selection of professors who *do* in both these ways can go a long way to achieving the aims with which this Conference is concerned.

In relation to the teaching of medical ethics, the same general principles hold. It is hard not to sympathize with Felix Frankfurter when he says in his discussion of his training at the Harvard Law School:

> There weren't any courses on ethics, but the place was permeated by ethical presuppositions and assumptions and standards. On the whole, to this day I am rather

leery of explicit ethical instruction. It is something that you ought to breathe in. It was the quality of the feeling that dominated the place largely because of the dean, James Barr Ames. We had no course in ethics, but his course on the law of trusts and fiduciary relations was so much more compelling as a course in ethics than any formal course in ethics that I think ill of most courses in ethics [1962, p. 19].

Fortunately, a good deal of medical ethics becomes part of the student's heritage in the same way.

Unfinished Business

I have assumed that this Swampscott Conference has selected the "Humanizing of the Physician's Training" as its major topic and come to some reasonable closure on it. There is one other important and broader problem relating to the behavioral sciences (raised by various conferees) still left for consideration. It can perhaps be dealt with by a conference which considers the medical school as part of the total university (the problem placed before us so cogently in the discussion at this Conference by Ralph Wedgwood.) Behavioral science could in this context be considered in both its aspects as a basic science for medicine, as well as in its applied aspects.

Many of us felt that although this wider topic is of paramount importance, the group of conferees assembled at Swampscott was not necessarily the most appropriate to consider it. Such a conference, we felt, would have to have a different membership—not only the particular persons and the fields represented at Swampscott, but others connected with university education generally and from other areas of the behavioral sciences as well.

Such a conference dealing with the medical school in the university and society, and of the behavioral sciences in both, could, I believe, make a substantial contribution to the understanding of the broader problem of which the one to which our particular Conference devoted its major attention was only a part.

22. Psychology for the General Practitioner

In 1947 I was invited to two conferences dealing with medicine and its relationships with other professions. The first was the Third Clinical Conference of the Chicago Medical Society, held on March 16, 1947. The second was the Second Annual Coordinating Conference of the Western State Psychiatric Institute and Clinic, Pittsburgh, Pennsylvania, held on April 10, 1947. The paper I presented at both was substantially this one.

Although in recent years psychology, particularly clinical psychology, has been contributing to certain aspects of psychiatry and medicine, actually its potential

Reprinted with permission from *Postgraduate Medicine*, vol. 3, 1948.

contributions have been tapped to only a moderate extent because of the early stage of development of clinical psychology itself as well as the limited view taken of the areas of contact.

Since the relationships with psychiatry, which are fairly intimate, have been relatively well defined, I shall not concern myself with these. Rather it is the purpose of this paper to explore the regions of contact of psychology with general medicine and the non-psychiatric specialties as they exist in private practice, the clinic, and education, with respect to three major aspects of psychologic function; namely, clinical study, both diagnostic and therapeutic, teaching, and research.

It might be said, in introduction, that psychology is attacking with considerable seriousness the problem of adequate preparation of persons for these functions in connection with activities to be considered. Because of the rapid extension of psychology to various aspects of applied and professional fields in recent years (in connection with industry and education as well as with medicine), several programs have developed which attempt to assure the competence of persons practicing psychology. Within the psychologic group itself, various official committees of the American Psychological Association have concerned themselves with the problem. On the basis of their recommendations, graduate work in the universities is being reorganized to meet the needs of professional, in contrast with academic, activity.

In the last few months, an American Board of Examiners in Professional Psychology, similar to the medical speciality boards, has been organized. It consists of nine members whose duty it will be to screen persons according to certain ethical and personality, as well as technical, qualifications; and to examine and certify these as specialized psychologists.

For clinical psychology, the tentative pre-examination requirements call for a four-year post-baccalaureate training program, one year of which shall consist of an internship in a recognized neuropsychiatric training center leading to the Ph.D. degree, and an additional four years of experience in acceptable centers. The general plan is for the examination to consist of at least a detailed practical section involving the handling of patients, but it may also include a written section. Membership in the American Psychological Association, which serves as a preliminary screening, is also a requirement.

Steps are also in progress for the certification of universities and training centers which take part in this program. Outside of the psychologic group itself, governmental agencies, for example, certain states, Connecticut and Virginia, have passed bills certifying psychologists. Several other states are considering bills of this kind.

Psychology is in the early stages of becoming a profession after a long period served as an academic discipline. It is going through the natural disturbances and difficulties which attend a growth process of this kind—a process well known both to medicine in general and to its specialties. Psychology is interested in taking advantage of the experiences of other disciplines in order to achieve its status with the very least cost and pain to society, and in establishing itself in such a manner that it can as rapidly as possible be of service to related fields, whether it be medicine or industry, but particularly medicine, since the nature of its goals is so much more similar.

I shall start first with the discussion of problems relating to general or specialized nonpsychiatric, private practice, and then consider the problems associated with hospitals and medical education.

The relationship between the professions of medicine and psychology which grows out of the needs of the individual patient who comes to the physician is of the same kind as is found in calling upon any specialist as consultant in a case. Patient problems are frequently such as to require specialized technics and bodies of knowledge not ordinarily available to the general or specialist physician. Under such circumstances, he calls upon the radiologist, or surgeon, or other medical specialist.

Until recently, because of the emphasis on the traditional aspects of medicine, such consultations have been limited almost entirely to the medical specialties. However, with a recognition of the broader connotations of disease, especially with the recognition of the importance of personality and social factors in disease, a call is arising for consultation with many related disciplines which are not in the immediate medical fold. The development of this trend for medicine as a whole in respect to the field of psychology is indirect and an outgrowth of previous developments in several specialties of medicine—pediatrics, to some extent neurology, but notably psychiatry. In the latter the "team" approach of psychiatry, psychology, and social work has reached extensive application and is standard practice.

Although a large area of contact regarding psychological problems involves essentially relationships between the general physician and the psychiatrist or the neurologist (who may in turn call in the psychologist to help on special aspects), there are many occasions, and a not inconsiderable zone, where the contacts may eventually very well be directly between the physician and the psychologist. With the growing sophistication about the psychological aspects of disease which the general physician is acquiring because of the fostering by psychiatry, this area is constantly expanding.

There is frequently, of course, some difficulty in drawing the line between these areas of contact, since the first analysis of a situation may turn out to be quite different from what develops subsequently. Such misjudgments are not serious if there is awareness by all involved of the kind of expertness which is called for. Since in so many respects, the family physician is in a peculiarly favorable position to catch problems in their incipient stages, he has naturally to be sensitive about the variety of specialized resources available to him and to select from them.

In the area now under discussion, the major procedure available to the psychologist is the psychologic test. It is a far cry from the series of situations first set up by Alfred Binet in 1904 to serve as a test of intelligence, to the approximately 5,000 different kinds of tests now available. Binet, I am sure, had not the slightest notion of the flood of development and application in all sorts of psychological fields which the intelligence scale that he proposed would eventually release.

Some notion of this development is obtained from a recent report which the secretary of the American Psychological Association compiled for Dr. Walter Dill Scott, President Emeritus of Northwestern University, one of the veteran psychologists in this country. Dr. Scott, in the process of revising *Nelson's Encyclopedia*, had occasion to become interested in the status achieved by the psychological testing field. The report indicated that during 1944 some 60 million standardized tests were administered to 20 million people. Of these, some 25 million had been given to approximately 4 million persons in the armed services. These figures are frightening as well as impressive!

What are the peculiar characteristics of psychological tests? Their purpose is to obtain systematic samples of certain types of verbal, motor, perceptual abilities and aptitudes, samples of levels of achievement, and of affective and personality characteristics, in the setting of standardized, relatively controlled situations. They have the advantage of involving little or no subjective selection in securing the data. Further, the standardized scoring systems based on standardized material, methods, and norms built up from samples of the general population permit organization of the data relatively free from subjective factors.

On what kind of problem can the psychologist be of help to the physician? I can best indicate this by listing some examples from among the many concrete problems which may arise in the general course of practice (I am, of course, omitting those types of cases which are strikingly psychiatric or neurologic and would come to the psychologist through these specialists):

A hydrocephalic child about the normality of whose intellectual development the family is much concerned; a person with cerebral palsy whose capacities must be evaluated in order to plan for his educational and vocational future; a person with a head injury in whom it is important to distinguish between functional and organic factors; an unresponsive child in whom it is necessary to determine whether intellectual retardation is the basis for this type of behavior; a physically handicapped child or adult with marked inferiority feelings who is obviously not taking advantage of his capacities and for whom the objective test results can be used as a much more effective device for overcoming self-depreciation than can mere encouragement.

Other examples include: an obviously retarded child whose level of retardation can be established in order to lay out a practical program of activity in relation to his capacity insofar as it involves his health, education in tool subjects (3 R's), habits, and vocation; a retarded (or even normal) child who has demanding and over-ambitious parents for whom objective tests are more convincing than lecturing, to get them to set up reasonable aspirations for the youngster; a hypothyroid child undergoing treatment who can be examined before and at various stages after treatment to determine the psychological effects of the medication; a child or adult with speech disability involving delayed speech, or articulatory difficulty (stammering), or rhythmic disorder (stuttering), where an analysis of the nature of the difficulty and a plan for treatment has to be made; a patient with hearing difficulty or visual defect who requires an evaluation of capacities and aptitudes in order to lay out a vocational program; a case of school retardation with difficulty in learning to read, to rule out low intellectual level, and, intellectual normality being determined, to outline a remedial reading program. Still other problems are: a case of epilepsy of long standing to determine the degree of deterioration existing and what vocational possibilities are left; any one of the many problems arising from the senescent process, for example, a 70-year old patient whose memory is failing (is his memory difficulty of pathologic degree and are his other psychologic functions, such as his judgment, up to the level of the normal person his age?); or the case of a couple who are ready to adopt an infant (how normal is the infant developmentally in its psychologic functioning, how good a "bet" is it generally?).

I have deliberately presented a sampling of unrelated and varied material which represents the type of case that the physician may at one time or another naturally come across, either in private practice or in the clinic, in order to indicate the range of problems on which the psychologist may be of aid by providing data about the psychologic functioning of the patient. He can, through the use of psychologic devices, with varying degrees of completeness and assurance, depending on the problem and the conditions of the examination, provide answers to questions which fall into four major fields: the intellectual aspects of the personality, the emotion-activity aspects of the personality, certain aspects of diagnosis, and certain aspects of disposition (treatment and the laying out of a program).

In the intellectual sphere such questions are: At which intellectual level is the patient functioning? What relationship does this level have to his optimal level? What specific intellectual abilities or disabilities does he have?

With respect to the emotion-activity aspects of his personality, questions may be: What are the patient's traits and his characteristics? What are his latent trends? What are his dominant preoccupations? How much do these characteristics aid or hinder the achievement of his intellectual and other capacities?

With respect to diagnosis, such questions are: What kind and what degree of disturbance does he manifest in intellectual functions generally, and in specific functions such as memory, reasoning, or association? What evidences of change in function, that is, improvement or deterioration, does he show as compared with what he showed at an earlier period, for example, following a course of therapy or a long illness.

With respect to disposition, the questions may be: What educational recommendations are indicated? What vocational recommendations can be made? What are the prognostic possibilities of the use of his capacities in a vocation, or in education, or in life generally?

In relation to some of these questions of disposition the psychologist can, in addition to helping diagnostically, be of aid in carrying through the remedial and therapeutic program indicated. This is especially true in the case of problems involving special disabilities and difficulties of a general personality nature growing out of and associated with these.

There is still another area in the private practice of medicine which deserves consideration. I refer to the psychologic aspects of the general, rather than the specific, problem of illness. Because of its great overlap with the same topic as it relates to the hospital, I shall postpone its discussion until later.

The problems which we have just considered, those of a diagnostic and therapeutic nature arising out of the situation of the individual patient, exist with some minor variations in the general hospital or clinic setting. In almost every department of the hospital, on one occasion or another, questions arise in which the psychologist may be of aid.

In some departments, such as pediatrics, these problems are naturally likely to occur more frequently than in others. They may arise from the attitudes toward defect or the personality characteristics associated with defect, whether it be in relation to body build such as obesity, in the sensory field of a visual or auditory type, in the motor field, such as an orthopedic or speech handicap, or in the cosmetic field, in the form of nasal, skin or dental deformity. They may relate to the capacities as affected by these and other conditions, both acute and chronic, or may involve planning programs of therapy and disposition. In any or all of these aspects, the technics at the command of the psychologist enable him to make a contribution both in the general hospital and clinic or in the special hospital or institution.

Unfortunately, the present setting does not permit an exposition of major samples of the devices on which the type of assistance mentioned in our discussion thus far is based. I have in mind such tests as the Stanford-Binet, the Wechsler-Bellevue, the Gesell Developmental Scales, the Rorschach Ink-Blot, the Thematic Apperception Test, the Wells Memory Test, and many others. It is important that physicians who call a specialist such as a psychologist for consultation have at least a general acquaintance with the nature of the technics he employs and their uses and limitations. It is the physician, because of his overall acquaintance with the situation, who should be in a position to evaluate the specialized findings in the light of the general picture.

I cannot leave this part of my presentation, however, without saying a few words about the availability of the type of resources which I have described. With some exceptions, psychologic service is usually to be found in connection with institutions, either in general or special hospitals and clinics, or in university centers. There is some development of an independent practice arising in association with physicians, particularly psychiatrists, and in some instances entirely independently. Since there is a growing demand for services of this kind, there is the considerable likelihood of an increasing development of extra-institutional psychologic service. Except in certain special areas, such as vocational guidance, it is desirable that patients come to the psychologist on a referral basis. Otherwise one runs the usual dangers which arise when the patient is his own diagnostician.

We may now turn to another, quite different, aspect of the relationship between medicine and psychology—that which grows out of the general problems of illness, whether seen in the office or the hospital, rather than out of the specific problems of the individual patient which we have just considered. I have reference here to what may be termed the social psychology of illness.

A few preliminary words about certain developments which have occurred in engineering education may not be out of place. For a long time engineering schools turned out competently trained engineers—persons who were abreast of the latest developments in technology and its related sciences. These men went into industry and did a capable job as engineers. But increasingly it became evident to the administrators of such schools that their graduates did not remain long at the level of working with machines. More and more these men were the group from which industry drew upon for its managers. And in the process of managing they found that there was one factor which had been entirely neglected in their engineering training; namely, the management of the *human* rather than the inanimate machine.

Outstanding schools—the Massachusetts Institute of Technology is an example—recognized this difficulty and attempted its remedy by setting up departments variously called Human Engineering, Industrial Relations, Human Relations, etc. These departments were responsible for providing students with training in the understanding of personality and interpersonal relations parallel with standard engineering training in order to enable them to deal with the equally difficult, and sometimes much more important, human problems of industry.

Medicine, having made the same quick and striking technical advances in its own field as has engineering, has in some ways been slower in attacking the human problems systematically. The reasons for this are not entirely clear, but it is perhaps partly due to the fact that medical men have been dealing so directly and intimately with human machines, rather than with inanimate machines as has engineering. On the one hand, they were compelled to handle these problems in an immediate, individual, empirical, rule-of-thumb way. On the other hand, being so close to the problem they were not so aware of its broader implications.

The change which finally came in medicine came, in one sense, in an extreme fashion. It arose largely out of psychiatry, through the development of psychosomatics, a movement which emphasized strongly the primacy of the personality and the importance of psychologic factors in their influence on bodily function and disease. In this development, what seems to me a natural step was on the whole rather neglected. I have reference to that field which might be termed "somatopsychics," the field in which the psychologic factors which grow out of and are associated with *physical* disease, whether general to illness or specific to a particular disease, are considered.

It is in this area that the psychologist, because of the technics which he has available, such as tests, opinion polls, job analysis, interviews, and experimental set-ups, the technics which are peculiarly fitted to deal with problems involved, can be of considerable aid in its systematic general study. Besides the experience in the use of these approaches and in experimental design generally, he has a deep and direct interest in problems of this kind since they are definitely of a psychologic nature.

Whereas in the psychosomatic field the psychologist's major contribution, because of the strong somatic components involved, is as an associate and assistant to the psychiatrist, in the somatopsychic field a large portion of the psychologic questions are more nearly pure and separable from the somatic problems and can be studied as such in a general medical setting. Although a certain amount of preliminary work has been carried out on problems of this nature, as indicated in the excellent survey of the field by Barker and his associates, published recently by the Social Science Research Council (Barker, et al., 1946), the fundamental problems have barely been touched.

What *are* some of the problems which would bear systematic investigation from this point of view?

The first is closely connected with that of preventive medicine—how to get the patient to the doctor early. What factors play a role to delay the seeking of medical help? There are certain objective factors, such as expense, but it is probable that a considerable portion of even these obvious factors and the greater part of another group, essentially subjective factors, involve attitudes built up in the person by various influences and play the more significant role. From the point of view of public health and individual therapy, a problem of the first magnitude is involved here and calls, first, for the analysis of the obstacles to seeking help and then for experimentation with technics which are effective in achieving early medical contacts.

Having got the patient to the doctor, what part does the setting—the organization of the reception room, the examining room, etc., have on the attitude of the patient toward the treatment? Does the patient develop an attitude of confidence in the treatment if he is ushered into a room with complicated apparatus, whose walls are covered with strange and impressive instruments, or is it more conducive to optimal receptivity to therapy if he comes to an ordinary "lived-in" office? What individual differences, and also what type differences, exist in this respect?

How about the technics of obtaining a history? What should the interview method be like? Should it be of the active direct question-and-answer type or of the passive kind which depends largely on spontaneous productions by the patient in response to a few preliminary questions by the doctor?

Which is the most effective and least threatening way in which a physical examination can be carried out?

How much should one tell a patient about diagnostic and therapeutic technics? How much should he be told before surgical and before test procedures? How important is it to keep him informed of the timing of procedures? How much should he be told about prognosis? How (in what manner and with what degree of authority) should he be told whatever he is told? The importance of these problems does not require underlining for medical people. Obviously, patients nowadays do not come uninformed to their physicians. An amazing amount of medical information and misinformation is disseminated through newspapers, radio, books, and other ways. And like the young medical student who finds himself having the symptoms of the various diseases he reads about, when the patient finally brings himself around to seeing the doctor, he has certain notions of what is wrong with him. What effect does the knowledge, complete or incomplete, true or false, with which patients come to the doctor have on the speed and effectiveness of treatment? *Is* it true, as has so often been argued, that a little knowledge of medicine is dangerous?

An example of disagreement as to what constitutes good procedure in this respect is found in the instance of Benmosché's book published in 1940, *A Surgeon Explains to the Layman*, wherein he describes the methods followed in various common operations. He explains that he belongs to the school which believes that "it can do nothing but good to have a thorough understanding of yourself. We fear what we don't understand, and so most people are terrified by the simplest operation." Another surgeon, reviewing the book, dismissed it, taking the diametrically opposite stand, saying, "The reviewer is one of the group which believes the average patient should know as little as possible."

Beverly (1936) reports an interesting example of attitudes as they are brought into the treatment situation. He studied cardiac and diabetic children at the Children's Memorial Hospital in Chicago. In reply to a question, "Why do children get sick?" about 90 per cent replied with answers meaning "because they are bad." With such an attitude, it is easy to see how treatment could be interpreted as punishment with possible effects on the successful progress of treatment.

How much help is it to know what the goal of treatment is, what its various steps are intended to accomplish? I am reminded here of the story told by one of the psychologists who worked with the Air Corps during the war. A group of aviators were sent on an extended mission which involved their stopping and reporting at various far-separated stations, finally returning to their base. They were not told the purpose of the trip. Another group were given the same task but were explained the purpose of the trip. It was found that the latter group showed much less fatigue at the end of the trip than did the first. How much importance do factors of this kind have in the therapeutic process?

What are the best ways of administering painful procedures? What factors play a role in setting up anticipatory fears? What factors play a role in increasing or decreasing these fears and the actual pains? We hear, for instance, more and more about the deleterious effects on the infant of extensive anesthetic administration to the mother before and during delivery. If this is so, how can psychologic methods for the reduction of pain, such as hypnosis, be adapted to such purposes?

Which factors play a role in convalescence? We know that there is a wide range of difference among patients in the speed with which they recuperate from the same illness or surgical procedure. What psychologic factors play a role to aid or hinder physiologic recovery? How much is indulgence of the patient during the convalescence process desirable? What part do certain procedures such as family visits play in convalescence? How much and how early should self-help be encouraged?

There is a need for more fundamental research in the whole psychology of physical illness. Even casual observation of sick people impresses one with the frequency with which regressive and infantile behavior is found among them. In some ways the illness situation appears to present fundamentally the educational problem that one has with the young and immature—how to get maximum growth and development without overloading the personality, that is, the determination of how much support to give and how much responsibility to expect at any particular time. A great deal of what has been learned in child psychology can be adapted to the problems created by illness—whether acute or chronic.

These are, of course, not new questions for physicians. They have dealt with them in one way or another. To a rare few, most of these problems essentially do not exist—they just naturally take care of themselves. Most physicians, I am sure, have wrestled with them when not overwhelmed by technical medical problems, and they have worked out rough empirical methods to take care of some. For the vast majority, the problems are serious and still left unanswered. They fall mainly into that part of medical practice which has been subsumed under the "art" of medicine. Whether it will ever be possible to take over all of the "art" into the "science" of medicine is doubtful. But it is true in this aspect of medicine, just as in the physiological aspects of medicine, that the area which is "art" can be reduced in extent.

One dares say this despite the acceptance of the fact that patients are individuals, and physicians are individuals, and both have their psychologic idiosyncrasies as they do their physiologic idiosyncrasies. Although each patient has his own peculiar needs, there is a much greater area of common needs, just as there are physiologic commonalities which can be determined, and without which there would be no science of medicine.

I am not trying to suggest ways of making professional medical life more complex than it already is. I realize that technical developments in medicine come so fast that there is probably no professional field which demands so much plasticity on the part of its practitioners and requires them so constantly to remain in a learning situation. The physician *has* to keep up with these advances and it is understandable if there is some tendency with respect to the general psychologic handling of patients to leave well enough alone and continue with the more or less effective methods which each has worked out empirically for himself.

May I point out, however, that the technical advances made in medicine, particularly in recent years, have come from controlled systematic investigations of phenomena. Frequently, it is true, these grew out of the clinical insights of individuals, but when they did they were put to a general test and then made available to medicine as a whole. This same approach is necessary for the psychologic phenomena of illness as it is for psychologic phenomena generally and for the physical phenomena of disease, and it is to be expected that development will be in this direction.

In addition to the type of research just considered, which has its obvious connotations for both private practice and the hospital setting, there is a type of research having several different aspects and more directly connected with the hospital, in which the psychologist can make a considerable contribution.

I am referring to research in the social psychologic problems of the hospital as an institution. This involves, on the one hand, problems of personnel selection at all levels—from physicians and administrators down to orderlies and maids—and, on the other, an analysis of the hospital situation as it involves interrelationships within and among the several classes of the personnel and interpersonal relationships among individual employees, particularly as these ultimately affect the therapeutic efficacy of the institution. (I might emphasize that above all other kinds the psychiatric hospital needs this type of study, for it is in such institutions that therapy is so much determined by the custodial aspects of hospitalization, aspects in which the human factor has always played such a great role.)

With regard to personnel selection, as has been found by industrial organizations, some advances have already been made which may be of immediate practical significance. It might be pointed out, however, that even in the broader field of the general hospital organization several studies carried out in industry by the Harvard and Massachusetts Institute of Technology industrial relations groups have already shown their great possibilities for the improvement of efficiency.

In the general hospital situation, too, arise problems of instruction to which the psychologist can contribute. In the first place there is the basic instruction in psychology which nursing and occupational therapy students should receive in the actual hospital situation. For these groups, aside from a general acquaintance with psychologic test technics which all workers in the hospital setting should have, there should be instruction in basic psychologic principles. These courses, however, should not be of a general type but should be directly connected to the problems of the profession concerned. They should, for instance in the case of nursing, deal with the applications of psychologic principles to nursing problems; the course should be on the "Psychology of Nursing" rather than on "Psychology for Nurses." Such courses necessarily require instructors who are acquainted with the specific problems of the field as well as with the principles of psychology.

Toward the members of the medical staff, too, the psychologist has certain teaching responsibilities: to keep the staff informed about the nature of his technics, their applications, and potential significance in relation to the specific problems in their respective fields.

There is one other important aspect of medicine in which the psychologist has played little or no part but which has decided possibilities for the future. I am referring to his relationship to medical education, particularly his relation to undergraduate medical education.

His contribution in this sphere would appear to be of three kinds: (1) teaching of medical students; (2) diagnostic work in relation to student health; and (3) research in relation to selection.

Although it would be difficult to arrange for in the present medical curriculum, I believe that in time, as medical curricula become modified because of the growing recognition of the importance of psychologic factors in disease, the psychologic preparation of the medical student will include a basic course in scientific psychology, paralleling the basic course in physiology. This will take its place in relation to the other courses on the pathology of psychic and psychosomatic processes very much as physiology does in relation to somatic pathology. Such a course would presumably come in the first year. In the third and fourth years of the curriculum, demonstrations and clerkships in psychological procedures might be introduced as part of the psychosomatic and psychiatric parts of the program.

Another, and quite different aspect of the teaching process which might receive consideration, relates to the general nature of the curriculum and the methods of teaching. Although psychology itself still has a good deal to learn about the learning process, a considerable body of data about educational principles has accumulated which it seems to me the medical schools could apply with considerable profit. The medical school program is an unusually heavy one and involves for both the student and the instructor an extraordinary expenditure of energy. Some of this energy, I am sure, could be saved for more effective use if these principles would be adapted to the actual medical teaching situations. This should, of course, be preceded by a searching investigation of the nature and efficacy of present-day procedures.

In relation to selection for entrance, medical schools have, in the past, experimented with the more simple psychologic devices, devices which on the whole have not been too successful. It is encouraging to see more sophisticated efforts in this direction being started in various places. Because of the great expense involved in medical training, it is important that all support be given to research along any promising line such as this. In relation to the even more difficult problem of selection for a specialty, much less has been done.

Here, again, there are beginnings of experimentation with the more complicated personality devices, studies aimed at correlation of the findings with success in various professional activities. A systematic attack of this kind in the various medical specialities might result in a contribution of no little significance. In connection with either selection problem, it is important to realize that what is needed is good hard systematic work on the problem; psychology cannot through magic supply the answer to adequate personality evaluation. Clinical psychology, though young, is sufficiently grown-up to hold psychologic magicians in ill-repute, just as medical magicians are held in medicine.

With the increasing development of post-graduate medical teaching, especially teaching which is more sensitized to the psychologic aspects of disease, it is natural that here, too, the psychologist will be called upon more. We can expect that opportunities will be afforded him to present clinical demonstrations and didactic lectures on psychologic technics and advances as parts of graduate clinical conferences and refresher courses.

If I have emphasized the contributions which psychology can make to medicine in relation to private and hospital practice and medical education and have said nothing explicitly about the gains which come to psychology from these contacts, it is because of the restrictions imposed by the topic. The broadening of psychology, both theoretically and practically, which would follow from the need for dealing with the range of problems which medicine presents would, of course, be marked. What is important, however, is not the question of gains for the one discipline or the other, but rather the values which accrue to the individual and society from a common attack on that most important of problems—man's knowledge of himself, whether in health or disease.

PART IV

Relationship with Psychoanalysis

Part of my early interest in psychology derived from early exposure to psychoanalysis (see introductory paragraphs of Chapter 25, pp. 281–2). This interest has continued through to the present. It has not been an interest in psychoanalysts as colleagues or psychoanalysis as a profession, but rather with psychoanalysis as an important school in psychology (cf. Shakow and Rapaport, *Influence of Freud on American Psychology*, 1964). The next four papers deal with a psychologist's relations to psychoanalysis in these respects—particularly as analysand and researcher.

23. One Psychologist as Analysand

At the request of Gordon Allport, editor of the *Journal of Abnormal and Social Psychology*, I participated in the "Symposium of Psychoanalysis as Seen by Analyzed Psychologists." The symposium was originally published by the journal in 1940 and was republished in 1953 by the American Psychological Association as a book.

One's previous psychological background necessarily plays a considerable role in finally determining whether or not an analysis is undertaken. In my own case, I had been exposed to psychoanalytic concepts for a number of years before actually commencing analysis. I had entered psychology with the usual fundamental basis for its study—the desire to understand behavior (perhaps unconsciously more the desire to understand myself?)—and continued through a rather conventional, if not deep-rooted, change to a concern with psychophysics because of the lure of the exact. The interest in personality continued, however, with an attempt to apply more stringent methods to its study. This endeavor brought me into the field of the abnormal and into contact with phenomena for which too frequently only the psychoanalysts had explanations—strange ones sometimes—to offer.

Reprinted with permission from the *Journal of Abnormal and Social Psychology*, vol. 35, 1940.

I can see reflected in myself the pattern of reaction to psychoanalysis which was true of psychiatrists as well as of psychologists ten or more years ago. (What I am about to say is less true at present because of the degree to which psychoanalytic thought has permeated both fields, leading to the greater exposure of the novice to psychoanalytic notions.) Although distinct stages can be differentiated, they tend to merge into one another imperceptibly. First came the state of complete denial in which no consideration at all was given to psychoanalysis; it was fantastic—a system which the person with scientific and logical ideals had merely to dismiss. This stage was followed by a period of combativeness, of refutation, in which the attempt was made to build up a counter-system and counter-arguments. At the same time, with more exposure to the problems of personality came the discovery that the more obvious mechanisms, such as projection, rationalization, etc., had already been partially accepted. I was further impressed by the fact that it was the analysts who had comprehensive theories to offer for complex behavior and that other schools were relatively sterile in suggestions. Increasing contact with the concepts, through both persons and books, together with an increasing recognition of the fact that psychoanalytic terms such as "castration complex" were not to be taken entirely literally, naturally resulted in the gradual disappearance of the extreme negative attitude. Finally, I was led to a more general conscious acceptance and use of psychoanalytic concepts and theories—but always with a certain amount of reservation.

With a continuing interest in psychopathology and constant contact with psychiatry, I was, perhaps more than the psychologist in the academic field, in a better position to evaluate the comparative contributions of the analysts and other groups of psychiatrists to the understanding of psychopathological phenomena. The favorable impression made on me by the psychoanalysts was in part due, not so much to what the analysts themselves had to offer, but rather to how little the others had. Although the analytic interpretation of a situation did not necessarily seem valid, it at least presented something to chew on, whereas the contributions of others offered little even to bite into; the latter were either mere descriptions of the phenomena without any attempt to account for them or unspecific explanations in terms of constitutional defect, poor habit systems, and the like. When one wanted to know why it was that the patient showed this peculiar type of repetitive behavior, it was not satisfying to be told that he was "constitutionally weak" or suffered from "poor training." In such instances, rash explanations appeared to have more scientific validity in the final analysis than the conservatively vague ones which were either meaningless terms or tautologies disguised as knowledge. At least something was offered to work with, some hypothesis, no matter how improbable.

Against such a background the opportunity for analysis arose. It is very difficult for those not seriously ill to disentangle the multifarious factors which make one undertake an analysis. Particularly is this true in the case of relatively well-adjusted people who are professionally interested in some phase of psychological work. On first considering an analysis, the explanation one offers is: "I am going to undertake a 'didactic' analysis for the purpose of being better able to deal with the problems of my work." If the camouflage of "pure" didactic analysis is not seen through immediately, it is the rare person who does not see through it very shortly after starting. I did recognize from very near the start that, although in part the analysis would be didactic, it would also be therapeutic. In addition, I planned to satisfy my curiosity about this elaborate procedure, and expected to gain considerable understanding of the theories and concepts. With less openness, I hoped also to overcome those "few" handicaps to maturity which I suspected I had. No matter how critical one plans to be and how little conscious expectation of gain exists, one cannot, I believe, prevent those odd upsurges of hope for the occurrence of some miracle of personality transformation. In more sober moments, I hoped, with respect to these therapeutic aspects, to achieve some additional modicum of maturity; but in more fantastic moments I had hopes of even achieving the limits of those Jamesian energies for which evidence is found in dream life but which unfortunately seldom come to fruition in waking life. Thus it happened that though on principle I was opposed to unnecessary therapy, the possible values to be derived from an analysis persuaded me to undertake the treatment.

When the decision in the affirmative was made, there arose subtle problems involving attitudes toward the analysis against which I had to guard myself. It is rather natural for any person who has made such a decision to feel a certain amount of resentment about having had to admit that he could profit from an analysis. In the case of the psychologist, this reaction is perhaps unusually strong. There is a tendency at first to adopt the set: "Show me what your rather strange system can do that mine can't!" Under the best of circumstances, it is very difficult not to fall into such an attitude occasionally. Experience was to indicate, as might be expected, that as I rid myself of this feeling, the treatment became more productive. I advanced a good deal faster, too, by accepting the analytic process as a game with distinct rules, about the validity of which there was no point in arguing.

I entered into the treatment with a general attitude which was essentially this: "I am going to play the game insofar as I can according to the rules." More specifically, I adopted early in the analysis the view that criticism should be at a minimum, especially in the earlier stages (a period, unfortunately, where criticism is most difficult to keep out). Interpretations should be accepted to see where they would lead. The aim should be to follow implicitly the rules of free association and recognize that the task for the analysand is to give the analyst an opportunity to sample behavior and attitudes. I resolved to leave, therefore, until the completion of the analysis the real sizing-up. Although these were difficult sets to keep and shifts occurred not infrequently, such conditions appeared to be essential if I was to make any real progress.

I ran the risk—a risk which should not be minimized—of having my judgment so biased at the completion of the analysis that I would be in no position to make the evaluation. I can only say that my experience, and apparently the experience of others with psychological training, has been that so radical a shift does not actually occur to any marked degree if a reasonable period is allowed to elapse after the analysis.

The evaluation of the analytic process necessarily goes on *during* the analysis as well as after. It is a particularly rigid person, however, whose evaluation remains the same at these various stages. Changes of view, especially with regard to specific aspects of the process, take place constantly, and it is only in retrospect that one feels able to judge the analytic experience with any degree of objectivity.

In the attempt to make the present appraisal systematically, I found myself distinguishing sharply between the analytic process and analytic theories. It is with the former that one is more naturally concerned in an evalution such as the present. The latter lie in most respects outside the scope of this paper. Free association, dream-analysis, and interpretation are the aspects of the process which come to mind first, but there are also such topics as resistance, transference, activity-passivity which come up for consideration.

Although the psychologist may be well acquainted with the theory and nature of *free association*, I do not believe it possible for him really to understand the process until he has subjected himself to a long series of sessions of the psychoanalytic kind. Continuous and repeated periods of free association were to me a revelation. In no better way, it seems to me, can the psychologist be impressed with that which is most essential for him to know, viz., what is tritely referred to as the "complexity of the human mind" and the complications of the thinking process. The tremendous effect which years of organization of thinking within the individual have had in eliminating from ordinary awareness the devious bypaths, the strange and impossible associations, which occur in connection with any topic, are not known to us until we have learned really to free-associate. One is then struck not only by the richness of the associations but also by the abundance of the limitations which scientific training and convention have apparently placed on freedom of mental activity—perhaps better, on mental license. The cognitive Tartar under the Russian is, at least to the psychologist, just as fascinating a creature as the affective-conative one which has been given so much attention by the psychoanalyst. The danger lies in the possibility that the wealth of material will awe and discourage the psychologist by its complexity.

What is made of the free associations by the analyst is another matter. He interferes little with the associations if they flow freely and are not of the superficial type that the analysand can with experience attain some facility in providing. The analyst is sometimes, in the view of the analysand, altogether too prone to accept mere contiguity of associations as implying some kind of causal relationship. Yet the honest analysand (as are to a considerable degree all analysands who continue in analysis) recognizes, on the other hand, that succeeding associations frequently *do* tend to bring together and integrate apparently unrelated points. Such a contiguity may make a series of isolated incidents "click" into a pattern, resulting in what is termed "insight."

With respect to *dream analysis*, one faces a problem similar to that of free association, for we are here dealing essentially with the free association of the sleeping state. Whatever degree of acceptance he may give to the symbolism, it seems to me a considerable advantage to the psychologist to be placed in a situation in which he has to give attention to psychological phenomena such as dreams, about which he is, strangely enough, ordinarily not concerned.

The problem of *interpretation* is intimately related to the two topics just discussed.

The analyst, although he may occasionally throw in an interpretation, generally waits for the associations and interpretations to come from the subject. In my own case, interpretations which were "accepted" led to the insight experience, so that I then went beyond the "as if" attitude. As for those which were not accepted, time frequently made many seem more probable. Whether this change was due to my being worn down by becoming accustomed to the notion or whether with additional material the interpretation took on more reasonableness was sometimes difficult to say. I like to believe that it was the latter.

Another question is that involving "wrong" or approximate interpretations. I got the impression that the analyst frequently made a guess just to get things going. Despite this touch of sophism about the procedure, wrong interpretations frequently justified themselves since they started associations along quite different and occasionally profitable lines. In this connection the sometimes eagerly sought opportunity to be critical of the analyst was afforded. To the psychologist it is revealing to follow the process of taking advantage of opportunities to express hostility. I was also struck by the fact that a part of analysis is dependent not upon *what* is said but on the fact that *anything at all* is said. I sometimes felt that analysis could go quite a way with a generalized list of themes dealing with fundamental human motives, to be associated to by the analysand. Personal reference, during at least part of the process, does not seem very important. At these times, mere talking about the general topic and the chance to consider its various ramifications seem of more consequence.

Generalized, rather than specific, interpretation also plays a role. A statement such as, "There seems to be a center of disturbance about your relations with children," may offer a good wedge for forcing an entrance into a body of data of great significance.

The problem of *resistance*, its development and resolution, was, now that I look back on it, a fascinating one. In the beginning there was the problem of adjusting myself to the possibilities of anybody's being able to tell me (a psychologist!) about myself. The signs of resistance and the ways which one finds of weaseling out of the resistance were of particular interest. I used to be struck with the utter unreasonableness of the relief I would experience when a session had gone by without my having mentioned a point which had been troubling me before the session, but which, without my breaking the rules and requirements of the analysis, had not come out during that hour. I learned considerable, too, about the psychology of the interview from this, as from other parts of the analysis.

The *transference* relationship has a number of aspects which were enlightening to me and which I believe could be equally so even to the experimentalist who works on problems in which personal relations are at a minimum. The degree to which one becomes involved with other persons or identifies oneself with them was impressive because I saw the numerous possibilities for the subtle appearance of biases of one kind or another. I did not find the transference relationship so overwhelming an experience as it is ordinarily described, but that it is deep cannot be denied.

It is in relation to transference as well as to *activity* and *passivity* that the personality of the analyst plays a considerable role. As to the relative merits of activity or passivity, it is difficult to decide. My feeling toward passivity on the part of the analyst, while actually in a session was likely to be: "Why doesn't he say something?" (Frequently, the analyst's talking offered a partial rationalization for not following up a train of thought which seemed to be leading in a rather unpleasant direction!) I was more likely to be disturbed by the purely passive approach, but I felt much more certain of the interpretation when it arose from my own undirected associations. Under the latter circumstances, however, the analytic process ran the danger of becoming too long-drawn out and aroused antagonism because so little seemed accomplished. An active attitude, on the other hand, though much less smooth and more likely to lead into blind alleys (which may not be serious), kept the analysis moving at a faster tempo. When I could be relatively objective about the interpretations—that is, able to accept the fact that a certain proportion of these were guesses, instead of spending my time arguing with the analyst—then the active process seemed to work out best.

In considering the analytic process as a whole, I am now impressed with the tremendous part which *time* (both the period covered and the number of analytic hours) played in whatever was gained. I believe that this was one of the most effective features of analysis. The process of attrition seemed to have a favorable therapeutic effect, if only in making commonplace the discussion and consideration of problems ordinarily avoided. This observation seems to hold true also for problems which are not of special personal significance. (There are some dangers and some delays because of this occupation with non-personal problems, but the gains are probably greater than the losses.) The frequency with which interpretations once rejected were, after a time, in some degree accepted has already been mentioned.

At intervals I reacted to the analysis with considerable discouragement, very much as one does toward all pursuits of a verbal-theoretical kind in which progress is for a long time not evident. I had the feeling of being a participant in an endless game of manipulating words, where "nothing is what it seems." I asked myself: "What is all this leading to? Is this process any more than a form of verbal gymnastics, remote from reality and getting nowhere?" These periods, which recurred, lasted for longer or shorter times. Most of them may be of no special meaning for the analysis itself, representing rather a natural reaction to the seemingly inevitable dull, stagnant periods of the treatment. I have thought it likely, however, that some of these do have significance for the process, that is, they are necessary stages through which one *has* to go in order to loosen up the associations. Such loosening is accomplished indirectly through the affective response generated in the analysand by the apparent waste of time. From this concern about wastefulness arises much of the antagonism toward the analyst, and in the process productive material not infrequently results.

The *scientific validity* of the analytic process is rather difficult to judge. It appears to me a distinct mistake to dismiss the process cavalierly as having no scientific validity. In considering the problem, one must first distinguish between investigations in which generalizations are to be based on a few readings from each of a sample of diverse individuals and those in which they are to be based on many readings from a sample of one.[1] For our present purposes, it is unnecessary to discuss analysis insofar as it involves generalizations about people as a whole. Let us consider rather the analytic process in relation to a particular analysand.

I have become more and more impressed with the reasonableness of looking upon analysis as an experiment on one subject from whom many repeated sessions are available—something in the nature of running a rat through a maze 300 or more times. Of necessity, the problem of control is complicated, because only part of the stimuli are determined by the actual setting. Indeed, the reports of the subject regarding outside stimuli and his response to them form the basis on which a great part of the behavior has to be judged—a circumstance which of necessity brings in all the problems of *Aussage*, with its irrelevancies and inadequacies. At first there is an accumulation of a seemingly limitless variety of response (in this way quite different from the laboratory experiment which attempts to study one variable at a time, while the others are controlled). With repeated sessions, however, as one becomes impressed with the repetitive nature of certain patterns of behavior, congruence emerges. There comes a time when the analyst seems justified in generalizing about the analysand, to the effect that the latter reacts so and so because of so and so—even though he, the analyst, has not himself set the situation. The process has some resemblance to the naturalist's approach, in the sense that the situation is set for the investigator and that he sits around and observes day after day, describing as accurately as he can what goes on and expecting that the subject of his study will get into a variety of situations, both in and out of the analytic session, so that he can generalize about the latter's behavior. Occasionally, if the analyst is an experimentally-minded naturalist, he may introduce some change in the setting by making an interpretation and observing the effects. He then watches not only the immediate response but also its effect on subsequent behavior as presented and reported by the subject.

Essentially, the difference between the laboratory and the psychoanalytic approaches, with respect to scientific method, lies in the factor of selection. The experimentalist selects *beforehand*—he investigates a particular variable, and either controls or shuts his eyes to the others. The analyst takes whatever comes to hand, trusting to his acumen to be able to select *afterwards*. The analytic approach comes closer to being a statistical method than does the experimental—the analyst being the partialling formula.

If an experimentalist is studying problems of personality in a group of ten subjects simultaneously, definite information on a few variables may become available in a month. From the analytic study, at the end of the same period, much less in the way of definite observations on a great number of variables from the same number of subjects may become available. At the end of the year the experimentalist might with ingenious experiment have collected observations on a very considerable number of characteristics from these subjects, while the analyst would have his data from the same number. The former would probably have more data of an

[1] Allport (1937) has ably presented the case for the latter.

objective kind (which for some purposes might be more important), but the latter would probably have the more pertinent data for understanding the personality, no matter how ingenious the former may have been. Selection, *a posteriori*, however, which results in any close approach to the experiment in objectivity, is so much more difficult that it is probably a method which relatively few have the wisdom and skill to practice.

Although there is nothing essential to the analytic process which prevents its meeting the conditions of scientific investigation, there arise numerous difficulties—perhaps because of the complexity of the subject matter with which it deals—which do not occur with equal prominence in other methods of study. I have indicated the importance of repetition as a basis for generalization with regard to characteristics of personality. The problem remains, however, as to what really constitutes repetition in behavior. Does it mean the doing of exactly the same thing on several occasions? How far is one permitted to go in conceptualizing, in finding symbolic similarities in items of behavior? It is with respect to this point that a great deal of the criticism of psychoanalysis has occurred—and with considerable justification. Analysts have through the years compromised, progressing finally from fixed symbolization to a more fluid type, determined by the specific case. Obviously, a constancy hypothesis is even more untenable in the field of molar behavior than in that of sensation and, obviously also, everything can't mean everything else, for in that case valid generalization would become impossible. The problem is exceedingly difficult because it becomes a matter of drawing a line, and knowing *where* to draw lines seems to be the most difficult of all tasks. Where *does* one draw the line with regard to this important problem of symbolization?

Because of the great variety of response encompassed in analysis, the problem is here relatively more important than in any other field. The only conclusion to which one can come is that the rules of scientific validity must hold. Being a dahlia-fancier and being afraid to ask one's boss for a raise *may* have the same underlying significance if, repeatedly, one appears in associations when the other does; if the affect from one seems transferable to the other; if the disappearance of one is followed by the disappearance of the other, etc. It becomes a question of the accumulation of evidence to the point where a committee of unbiased experts is ready to accept the generalization advanced.

The answer to the question of the scientific validity of psychoanalysis depends also on the answer we give to the question of the nature of hypothesis in science. Every interpretation or generalization in analysis is an hypothesis. In analysis, as in science generally, there are two kinds of hypotheses: (1) those based on numerous facts and readily acceptable, and (2) those based on relatively few facts and advanced rather to clarify issues, to direct attention in one direction or another. It is mainly the latter type of hypothesis which gives rise to the controversy which Boring (1929) reluctantly concluded to be the material from which scientific truth is obtained. In the analytic process, although the analyst generally believes that he is dealing with the first type of hypothesis, very frequently he is really dealing with the second. It is this confusion which may perhaps account for a considerable amount of the antagonism to psychoanalysis. If the analyst were more modest, a good deal of unnecessary misunderstanding could be avoided.

In the analysis itself it both does and does not matter. If the analyst is a good analyst, he does not push his interpretations beyond the "readiness" of the analysand to accept them, and thus he essentially meets the objection. It is also true, however, that although in an impersonal situation this conservatism might be sufficient, it does not hold when dealing with material of personal importance to the analysand. Objectivity is then difficult to attain, and interpretations are likely to be taken by the analysand, not as hypotheses, but as facts from which important reactions result. Whether it works out one way or another in practice, it is difficult to see anything essentially unscientific about the procedure.

With the *language* of analysis, the psychologist need not be too much concerned. He can accept as much or as little of it as he wishes, for he can translate most of what he cannot accept into his own terms. It is usual, too, for the analyst to prefer that the analysand keep away from technical terms, since it encourages retreat behind labels.

When I draw up the profit and loss account of my analysis, what do I find? I realize, of course, that the analysis has *not* been completed—but there is some solace in the belief that the "completely analyzed" person does not exist.

What are the gains? I should say that they fall into two categories: I have improved as a person and have inevitably been improved as a psychologist. (It is a source of gratification that distinguishing sharply between these elements is difficult!)

On the psychological side there seems to have been a sensitization to the tremendous amount of mental activity which goes on below the surface and a growth in the appreciation of its true meaning because of direct contact with it. I have become aware of the innumerable sands which help make the mountains of our conduct, but of which we are ordinarily little conscious. I have become more sensitive to the minute, to the nuances of individual social relationship, more likely to tighten the brake on a tendency to generalize readily from gross and explicit manifestations of conduct. Analysis has increased an interest in fields of psychology likely to be avoided when one's primary concern is with making psychology quantitative.

It has had considerable value, too, in helping to overcome any overemphasis of that "nervousness" which James has pointed out as coming with scientific training, and to loosen up the rigidity in thought and methodology that scientific training develops in all but the unusual investigator. I am referring to psychoanalysis' encouragement of the freest of associations—the *bête noire* of the ordinary teacher of science. The latter usually goes too far in pushing the neophyte over into being a technician. Analysis to some extent breaks through this training in the direction of encouraging originality. On the basis of a sound training of the former kind, psychoanalysis should do a great deal toward developing more productivity in the investigator. In this respect it is probably preferable for the analysand to have his academic training *before* analysis, rather than after; that is, if the training is such as to leave him with some degree of plasticity.

To the experimentally-inclined person, analysis is of great value in offering leads for investigation. Numerous problems for experimental investigation, such as anxiety, the defense mechanisms, the abreactive process, the memory process in connection with affect-laden material, suggest themselves as challenges to his investigative ingenuity.

Personally, I learned a great deal about myself—and it would seem reasonable that the psychologist should have as his first rule the knowing of himself. The discipline of the process is great and of considerable value for this reason. The necessity for "telling everything" and for keeping unpleasant appointments resulted in my learning to face myself and others to a greater degree than before—a process invaluable for ego development. The necessity for being persistent in the face of failure, too, was of value. (There is, however, another side to this picture. The analysis may become a habit, a form of escape, as seen in those who continue analysis interminably.) The process was a maturing one. When I was through, I was generally able to consider *any* behavior, whether my own or somebody else's, with relative objectivity—or at least with a greater amount than previously. There was a release of normal aggression, resulting in an ability to handle social relations with increased poise and assurance.

The miracles which I had secretly hoped for may not have been achieved, but I have evidence of some self-improvement, some essential growth in maturity. How much of this alteration is due to the truth of analytic theory, how much to the process itself, and how much to the personality of the analyst, it is difficult to determine. All three probably play their roles, although I am inclined to believe that it is the process itself which is most important.

There is in analysis another great value which comes while one is actually in it. This lies in the opportunity it affords for catharsis in relation to current problems. One is impressed with the value of having somebody to go to at regular intervals just to "get things off one's chest." There is the possible disadvantage of releasing pent-up tensions which might perhaps be productively harnessed, but in my experience tensions of this kind rarely lend themselves to conversion into constructive activity.

It would seem that the above account indicates almost all profit. For most psychologists I believe this conclusion to be valid if the investment of time and money required is not excessive.

24. Training in Clinical Psychology—a Note on Trends

This paper is related to the preceding paper, the issues being viewed here in the impersonal and broader context of training.

Fundamental to the current discussions of the problem of training in clinical psychology must be a recognition of the roles to be played in the process by the

Reprinted with permission from the *Journal of Consulting Psychology*, vol. 9, 1945.

varying approaches now prevailing in clinical and abnormal psychology. An examination of these reveals that in relation to the two major emphases represented, that concerned primarily with the individual subject and that concerned with groups of subjects, at least four main trends can be differentiated.

The first may be characterized as advocating a *dynamic* approach to the problems in the field. The group representing this point of view is primarily interested in the understanding of the genetic development of motivation and personality organization, both in their structural and contentual aspects. It sees the problems of clinical psychology as one of research on the individual case directed at obtaining data about the individual both for generalizations about him and about the group of which he is a member. It frequently uses these data for therapeutic purposes. The affiliations of this group are largely with a dynamic psychology, psychiatry, and psychoanalysis.

The second may be characterized as a *diagnostic* approach to clinical problems. The group representing this point of view is primarily concerned with the use of test devices which investigate the structural aspects of personality, for example, in relation to intelligence and other capacities, aptitudes, and skills. Its interest is in the light which these devices throw on the person's adjustment with a view toward making recommendations for disposition which are usually carried out by others. The affiliations of this group are mainly with educational and vocational workers.

The third may be characterized as the *diagnostic-therapeutic* approach. This group has certain affinities with each of the two former groups but differs from them in several respects. Although it has an interest in the use of tests for the understanding of the presenting problems, it is mainly interested in the therapeutic implications of test results for the individual person. In contrast with the first group, there is here not so fundamental or systematic an attack on the problems of human motivation nor is the therapy involved generally of such a searching and extended type. Its major interests are in diagnosis and certain specific types of therapy. Two subgroups may here be distinguished: One of these accepts the principle of the psychiatrist-psychologist-social worker triad as the most desirable clinic organization; the other takes the view that this type of organization is not essential and that other affiliations may be equally satisfactory, for example, those of psychologists with teachers, pediatricians, or social workers.

The fourth may be characterized as the *experimental* approach. Its major interest is the study of clinical material from the experimental point of view. Here, also, two subgroups may be distinguished. The main concern of one is with problems involving the cross-sectional structural characteristics of the deviant organism under varying conditions; the main concern of the other is with problems of a more dynamic kind, mainly cross-sectional but to some extent also longitudinal. Neither is interested in therapy per se—in fact, both generally take the view that therapy is not intrinsically a field for the psychologist. They are not interested in test devices as they relate to the individual case. Their concern is rather with the establishment of laws about types of deviants, very much as certain groups of workers in normal psychology are interested in establishing laws about normal people. The individual deviant subject is considered by them merely as a means to such an end.

The above descriptions have attempted no more than to epitomize the essential nature of these differing points of view. In practice, obviously, there exists no such sharp distinctiveness—the overlapping among them is considerable and the shifts in emphasis with the passage of time pronounced.

All of these points of view should be reflected in a program of preparation for clinical psychology since they all have a contribution to make. An examination of the field, however, reveals that certain of these trends are gaining ground faster than others and we must therefore anticipate corresponding changes of emphasis in the nature of the preparation which the clinical psychologist will be expected to undertake.

The major change which seems to be taking place lies in the increasingly greater attention which is being given to what has been termed the "dynamic" approach. Psychologists, in the past, have been rather slow in occupying themselves with this field—a field which to the layman is definitely that of the psychologist and to psychologists themselves becoming increasingly so. The historical factors, deliberate and accidental, personal and impersonal, which have deflected the interest of psychologists from the complicated problems of motivation and personality development need not be gone into here. But that there has been such a lack of interest until fairly recent years cannot be denied. Psychoanalytic psychology, slowly boring its way through the rather resistant skin of a non-personal psychology organized largely on a physical model, has finally been able to reach deep enough to meet burgeoning long-repressed inner yearnings. The juncture of the two has resulted in the recent remarkable growth of interest in personality dynamics and genetics. It is reasonable to suppose that no field of psychology will be more influenced by this development than will be clinical psychology.

If I am not wrong in the evaluation of this trend, it seems desirable for psychology to place more emphasis than it has on the aspects of the program of preparation for clinical psychology which the trend represents. In this connection, the increasing concern of psychologists with the problems of psychoanalysis and its techniques should be encouraged. There is perhaps no better introduction to the complexities of human motivation than through some form of psychoanalysis. For this reason, serious thought should be given to the desirability of encouraging persons about to enter clinical psychology to undergo a psychoanalysis. The pros and cons of this problem for psychologists are perhaps best stated in the symposium of analyzed psychologists edited by Gordon Allport (1940). If a psychoanalysis is deemed advisable as part of a program for clinical psychologists, special care will have to be taken to select analysts who are relatively free from doctrinairism and who have an interest in psychological theory as well as in therapy. Although a Freudian type of analysis, because of its relative completeness, is perhaps generally preferable to other types of analysis, any detailed self-examination under competent guidance might serve as well for most candidates. In this connection, even Freudian psychoanalysts are beginning to recognize the desirability of broadening the base of psychoanalytic training to include non-Freudian approaches. It is understood, of course, that the purpose in proposing such a step is not to advocate the acceptance of a particular theoretical point of view; rather, it is to suggest the consideration of a technique which many have found valuable for the acquisition of insight into the complexities of personality dynamics.

Whatever the reaction may be to the last suggestion, it is clear to those who have given thought to the subject of trends in clinical psychology that no program of preparing clinical psychologists can be considered adequate which does not recognize the need for providing the student with a background which takes cognizance of the various points of view described. The relative emphasis will for the present presumably have to depend upon the personal philosophy of the instructor and upon his sensitivity to growing trends in a rapidly developing field.

Psychoanalysis and Social Science

For the twentieth anniversary of the Chicago Institute for Psychoanalysis, a *Symposium* was held on October 11, 1952. I was asked to discuss the paper by Talcott Parsons on "Psychoanalysis and Social Science." I used the occasion to consider the need for training social scientists (particularly psychologists) in psychoanalysis. Sometime in 1961 I was approached by Roy Grinker, Chairman of the Program Committee of the Academy of Psychoanalysis, and asked if I would participate in their winter meeting by contributing to their symposium on psychoanalytic education. I prepared the following paper which was later published (J. H. Masserman, Ed. *Psychoanalytic Education*, 1962, Grune & Stratton) in somewhat abbreviated form.

Since the latter talk included much of what I had said in the first, I am omitting that article. It may be found in F. Alexander & H. Ross, Eds. *Twenty Years of Psychoanalysis*, 1953, W. W. Norton, pp. 216–226.

25. Psychoanalytic Education of Behavioral and Social Scientists for Research

When I was about 15 I was a member of a nature study-hiking-discussion group at a settlement on the Lower East Side of New York. At one of the meetings the head worker, who was especially fond of our group, told us about a revolution in ways of thinking about man which had resulted from the work of "Yungenfreud." I was much intrigued, and after the meeting made a beeline for the Seward Park Public

Reprinted from J. H. Masserman (Ed.), *Science and Psychoanalysis* (vol. 5, *Psychoanalytic Education*) 1962, by permission of the publisher, Grune & Stratton.

Library to get some books by this author. But a search in the card catalogue under "Y" yielded nothing. I was finally, with some loss of pride, reduced to asking the librarian whether they had any books by Yungenfreud. Luckily for me she was—to use old-fashioned, but appropriate, terms from introspective psychology—of an analytic rather than synthetic type. She was thus able to disentangle the "Freud" from the gestalt and refer me to the proper shelf.[1] In some way, I don't quite know how, Jung sort of got lost in the shuffle. This is perhaps not surprising since "Dreams," "Psychopathology" and "Wit" were enough to occupy any youngster!

From that time on, even though William James soon became my permanent hero, I have had a deep interest in Freudian theory. This was true in college and in the year immediately after college which I spent at Worcester. There in the middle 20's I had long and searching discussions about psychoanalysis with an initially negative Lewis Hill, who was then Assistant Superintendent. Through Raymond Willoughby, the only analytically active person in Worcester at the time, Hill became increasingly involved in psychoanalysis, undergoing his first analysis with Willoughby. After graduate work, I returned to Worcester, and it was during this period that I had a personal analysis with Zinn, and later a control analysis with Roheim. During these periods at Worcester, and later in Chicago and Washington, I have retained close contact with psychoanalysis, though I have never had any institute training.

I have been little more than an onlooker so far as the formal organizational aspects of psychoanalysis are concerned. I have, however, been much involved with psychoanalytic theory, its relationship to general psychological theory, and its application to personality. In the last several years before his death I was associated with David Rapaport in the writing of a monograph on the impact of Freud on psychology. Through the years I have tried to keep abreast of psychoanalysis and the advances and natural changes that any system of ideas must undergo.

I have spoken personally because I want to be able to talk frankly—and I shall. I will attempt to be tactful, but I will *not* be "politic." If I were, I might better stop now. I take for granted that this group is accustomed to listen to heterodox opinions. I am concerned, however, about the different way in which such opinions are usually examined by *groups*, as contrasted with the way they are examined by *individuals*. All I ask is that insofar as you can, you divest yourselves of your group membership on this occasion and listen to this only temporarily one-sided personal conversation. I assume that you understand that I speak for myself alone—neither for my colleagues nor for the institution with which I am associated.

A good deal of what I shall have to say, both explicitly and implicitly, revolves around the future of psychoanalysis. One of my recent great disappointments came from reading *Psychoanalytic Education in the United States*, (Lewin & Ross, 1960) where I had expected to find some thoughtful opinions about this question. I was most sorry to find that Lewin and Ross had apparently deliberately limited the definition of their task so as to exclude a critical overview of psychoanalysis and

[1] I have distinguished company in this type of "telescopic" misunderstanding. Faulkner, I understand, did not disentangle the constituents of "damyankee" until he reached adult years.

education for psychoanalysis. This is a pity, since they could have contributed so much to the discussion of these important questions. Although I may not go along with all of the strictures contained in Paul Bergman's (1961) review of the volume in *Contemporary Psychology*, I find myself reluctantly agreeing with him.

Some nine years ago the Chicago Institute for Psychoanalysis celebrated its twentieth anniversary with a scientific meeting. At that time, Alan Gregg (1953) talked on "The Place of Psychoanalysis in Medicine." Using for his text a question raised for another area by Thomas Nixon Carver, he asked pertinently: "Can psychoanalysis survive prosperity?"

At this same meeting I discussed certain aspects of the relation of psychoanalysis to the social and behavioral sciences. I used as a text the following statement: ". . . psychoanalysis appears to be entering a new era of security and maturity growing out of the recognition of the significant contribution it has made to many fields. Psychoanalysis is at a point where its choice of direction for the future can be deliberate and determined by the objective needs of the situation" (Shakow, 1953a, p. 216). You recognize in the statement, at least by implication, the same question which Dr. Gregg had asked.

The intervening nine years have only served to strengthen these views. Despite some very important theoretical advances in ego psychology and in the systematic presentation of psychoanalytic theory, both of which are so prominently associated with the name of David Rapaport—whose death is a grievous blow to both psychology and psychoanalysis—the present situation in psychoanalysis strikes me as calling even more for the kind of program which I suggested in 1952. There is a more widespread negative attitude about psychoanalytic therapy and practice than there was at that time, and, except for ego theory, and increasing questioning of various aspects of psychoanalytic theory. In considerable part these reactions are due to the relative absence of research and scholarly activity around psychoanalysis proper. The excuses offered for this absence during the middle period of psychoanalysis are now less justified and much less acceptable. Psychoanalysis is approximately 60 years old, if we accept the date Jones labels as the period when Freud emerged from isolation to organize the "Psychological Wednesday Society" in 1902, and cannot so easily get by with excuses. We must also recognize that psychoanalysis is, with rare exceptions, attracting persons different in kind from the restless souls with questioning minds who were attracted to it in the early days. Most disturbing, perhaps, are the increasing evidences of dissatisfaction and disenchantment on the part of persons who are fundamentally sympathetic to psychoanalysis.

It is necessary for psychoanalysis to take account of this situation and to deal with justified criticisms. Isn't it time to take stock rather than to retreat into the highly vulnerable, if seemingly self-sufficient and impregnable, private shelters which the institutes so frequently represent? At one time, when psychiatry departments were not so strongly analytic, there was at least this arena in which psychoanalytic ideas underwent some degree of testing. But psychoanalysis' prosperity has resulted in the loss in exposure to the aids to vigorous development which an adverse environment so frequently provides.

Before going on to my central theme, I wish to deal briefly with a subject which is *not* part of my topic. I feel I must, however, mention it. I refer to the training of social and behavioral scientists in psychoanalysis for *psychotherapeutic or psychoanalytic practice*, although I believe that persons in these disciplines have a more important function than psychotherapy to fulfill in relation to psychoanalysis.

I think it only fair to state that my position on this topic is probably quite different from that of most of you. My fundamental attitude is that training for psychotherapy—whether psychoanalytic or other—should not be determined by a person's discipline. Many years of observation in this area have led me to believe that so far as psychotherapy is concerned, the order of importance of the three factors which are integrally involved are: first, the personal qualities of the therapist; second, the nature of the patient and his problem; and third, the nature and adequacy of the therapist's training. I do not include *Fach* among the important factors.

In fact, in relation to medicine as professional background for psychotherapeutic training, I have often wondered whether the conventional training in this profession does not sometimes serve as a hindrance rather than as an aid to optimal preparation for psychotherapy. The training in dealing with patients and acting as healer of physical ailments certainly has its helpful aspects, but there is some danger in this process of making the student less sensitive to the subtleties of psychological relationship and to social factors. The long experience of medicine in inculcating ethical principles affords an advantage over the experience existing in other, younger fields. Nevertheless, it is important to recognize that ethics is not a medical monopoly and that its major mainstay lies in the character of the practitioner. Given the proper selection principles—both external and self-selection—and proper safeguards in the form of internal and external superego controls (Shakow, 1949c), this problem is "reasonably" well cared for.

The test with regard to this professional question for anyone is, I suppose, to examine the criteria one has used in the actual situation of having to recommend a psychotherapist for a person for whom one has personal regard. In such a situation, I have found myself making my recommendations largely on the basis of the personal qualities of the therapist and the general competence of his training. I have paid little attention to whether he was a psychiatrist, a psychologist, or a social worker. If you examine your own conduct, I wonder whether many of you will not find that your experiences are not too dissimilar.

When I speak of personal qualities (I include particularly those qualities of personality which we designate as honesty, integrity, and fundamental human sympathy), I cannot think where these qualities are more important than in carrying out the functions undertaken in the field of psychoanalysis. I do not wish to minimize the value of training *background*, however. I cannot say that I am entirely satisfied with the training given *either* to psychologists *or* to physicians. I would feel most comfortable if we had persons—properly selected, of course—who had gone through a training program of the kind recommended by Lawrence Kubie (1954).

It may have been unwise to introduce my major topic by raising this controversial issue. I did not, however, feel that we would keep the issues of training therapists and training researchers properly separated if my views on this matter were not out in the open.

Let us now turn to the central theme—the education, for research and scholarly purposes, of social and behavioral scientists in psychoanalysis.

Besides such personal background as I have described earlier, I am using as a basis for my talk the reactions, coming from long-time contact, of a number of behavioral and social scientists who have received different degrees of training at institutes recognized by the American Psychoanalytic Association. In addition, I have recently sent out a questionnaire to as complete a list as I could compile of persons in these disciplines in this country who have received such training. The questionnaire was designed to obtain a full reaction to the educational program in which they participated: the personal analysis, the theory and technique seminars, the case seminars, and the supervised cases. They were also asked to describe the personal and professional effects of participation in the program and to make recommendations for an optimal program. The respondents were guaranteed absolute anonymity for themselves and for their institutes. The response has been excellent—thus far I have returns from 45 of the approximately 55 persons written to. Since the results are only partially analyzed, and since I plan to report these results in some detail in a separate paper, I shall during the course of this presentation merely mention a few of the most pertinent trends. On the basis of this varied background material, I have some degree of confidence in the objectivity of what I shall say.

The major task which seems to me to lie before psychoanalysis is the consolidation of psychoanalytic contributions about personality within the scientific framework. The achievement of this goal requires that psychoanalysis do as other sciences do: make its propositions explicit, identify and make public the data on which its predictions are made, and test these predictions by relevant methods. While we are setting this task before psychoanalysis, we must at the same time recognize the difficulties that psychoanalysis, perhaps even more than other behavioral sciences, has to overcome: the difficulties created by the markedly heterogeneous universe from which samples of behavior are drawn, the biased samples from which subjects are drawn, the difficulties of translating concepts into testable hypotheses, the difficulties in repeating observations, and the especially difficult problem of the effect of the observer upon the observed. The latter problem is perhaps more prominent in psychoanalytic work than in any other field, for in no other area is the dependence upon the individual observer as instrument so great, the processes investigated so clandestine, and the identification of the investigator with his theory so profound.

The delay in psychoanalysis' becoming a part of the family of sciences is not entirely due to the intrinsic difficulties of the field. There have been certain important, if extrinsic, factors involved in this delay. One of these has been the marked opposition of both medicine and psychology to psychoanalytic data and hypotheses. Others stem from the fact that psychoanalysis is a therapeutic device as well as an investigative method leading to a body of theory. Although this relationship of therapy and theory has many advantages, the relationship also carries with it some disadvantages. One such disadvantage is a tendency for the practical to take precedence over investigation or theory development. A result of this emphasis on therapy has been the almost total limitation of participation in the field to persons with medical training. Such a limitation tends to exclude classes of persons whose fundamental interests are more apt to be on the investigative and theoretical side.

I shall make nine major points about the importance and organization of psychoanalytic education for research. They may be considered as theses that I am ready to defend. Let me first list them together and then consider each in some detail.

1. Even though psychoanalysis is a closely intertwined combination of theory of personality (including a body of observations), method of investigation, and form of therapy, the three aspects appear to me to have this order of importance: first, theory; second, method; and third, therapy. A fourth aspect—that of a "movement" —I don't consider of equal value.

2. Psychoanalysis is a part of psychology. It has peculiarly strategic and close associations to the social sciences, to the biological sciences, to the humanities, and to medicine—in fact, to any field involving human psychological function.

3. In order to remain viable—to maintain and develop itself—psychoanalysis must much more strongly than heretofore be supported by continuing research and scholarship.

4. The most promising additional group to draw upon for scholarly and research activity in psychoanalysis is the behavioral/social science group.

5. Persons selected for this purpose must be given the best psychoanalytic education possible. This involves the acceptance of several principles:

   a) Such education is best carried out at an institute associated with a *university* —that institution of our society created to encourage scholarly and research endeavors.
   b) The university setting should provide the psychoanalytic institute with independent status to establish particularly close relationships with *both* the graduate and the medical school.
   c) In order to progress, psychoanalysis must continually experiment with new patterns of education.
   d) New programs are best developed, not by general adoption, but rather through pilot projects.
   e) The actual content of the programs should be limited primarily by the needs of the students.

Now let us consider each separately.

Thesis 1—The theory of psychoanalysis is the most important of its four fundamental aspects.

The point about the multiple character of psychoanalysis has been developed by Benjamin (1950) and others in the process of clarifying the issues connected with the "objective" study of psychoanalysis. With respect to theory, for the purposes of the present paper, there is no call for distinguishing sharply between the empirically derived data leading to theory (what I have called the "body of observations") and the theory itself. I am including under "theory" the range from these data through the special clinical theory to the general metapsychological theory. With regard to method, the problem is somewhat more complicated than it is for psychoanalysis as therapy. Although originally the psychoanalytic interview—the retrospective historical approach—was the only way to attack the study of psychoanalytic theory, over the years three other major approaches to such study have been originated: the developmental prospective, the experimental (using animal or human subjects), and the cross-cultural. Though these three later methods are important, nevertheless the psychoanalytic interview for the present remains primary, and the other methods largely complementary. I myself have argued strongly for the use of the interview, under certain controlled conditions, as an objective approach to research in psychoanalytic theory (Shakow, 1960).

Psychoanalysis as therapy is gradually being less extensively used in conventional form. With the growing recognition of the need for fitting a special kind of therapy to a particular patient's needs, and with the growing interpenetration of psychoanalytic theories into other forms of therapy, there is good reason for using the lengthy process of psychoanalysis more sparingly, and for purposes—training is an example—where it remains of the greatest importance. It appears to me that the psychoanalytic method, which can be used both as a method of therapy and as a method of investigation, will with time be increasingly used for the latter purpose, and less as a method of therapy. But psychoanalytic therapy will always remain important for providing the rich data on which its theory must in large part be based.

Thesis 2—Psychoanalysis is a part of psychology.

Psychology is a very broad field, and as is true of any discipline, is not the possession of any person or group of persons, organized or unorganized, whether in the academy or in the consulting room. The place of origin, place of domicile, vocation, etc., of the contributor are irrelevant to his participation. The content he contributes is the primary factor. I am pressing this obvious point in order to make clear that I do not consider psychoanalysis a medical discipline.[2] To insist on its medical character seems to me a parochial way of looking at psychoanalysis and is the result of giving too much importance to certain historical events which Rapaport and I have considered in detail elsewhere (Shakow & Rapaport, 1964). It is of interest in this connection to examine the four "greats" of psychology as Boring (1950) lists them in the second edition of his *History*: Helmholtz, Darwin, James, and Freud. Three of these had medical degrees and one some medical training. But is not this fact quite irrelevant? For the most part it seems to reflect the educational culture of their time. There is, of course, a psychoanalytic theory of neurosis. But is this not part of that field of psychology—abnormal psychology—which is particularly closely related to medicine?

[2] In this context, Jones' chapter on lay analysis (1957, pp. 309–23) is particularly pertinent.

Academic psychology, now one hundred years old, in its battle to free itself from philosophy, has necessarily had its own share of vicissitudes and prevailing and countervailing prejudices. Eventually, I hope we will have a psychology which is delineated entirely by the content relevant to the area, and the interrelationships among the different aspects of this content, rather than by temporary irrelevant political issues.

Thesis 3—Psychoanalysis needs research and scholarly support in order to remain viable.

Psychoanalysis has to plan ahead in two major interrelated areas: the training of psychoanalytic therapists, and the development of psychoanalysis through research. Relatively much more effort will, I believe, have to be directed to the latter goal than has been the case in the past. This is so for two reasons. First, because therapeutic activity is much more likely to draw support. Besides requiring less nurture, therapeutic activity is further encouraged by considerable outside pressure to meet immediate needs in this area. Second, because the research and scholarly goal is the more important for the advancement of the field.

I therefore make a plea not only for greater recognition by institutes of the importance of research in psychoanalysis, but for emphasis on educational programs that are oriented toward the development of persons who can contribute effectively to research. This will necessarily involve institutes in giving to research a status and a proportion of staff time and resources that has not been true in the past. Compare that which is being done in the institutes in the way of research and scholarship in psychoanalysis with that in any area of medicine or psychology. Suppose medical schools over the country no longer had basic science faculties, merely faculties consisting of medical practitioners who devoted a part of their time to teaching. How long could medical schools prevent themselves from becoming vocational schools, perhaps not as bad as those in the era before Flexner's Bulletin 4, but still vocational rather than professional schools, to say nothing of centers of research and scholarship?

Thesis 4—The most promising additional group upon which to draw for research and scholarly support is the behavioral/social science group.

It appears to many who examine the present scene, including myself, that if research and scholarly aims are to be accomplished, a change in certain policies of psychoanalytic institutes—particularly policies relating to the recruitment of students—is called for.

Psychoanalysis too rarely attracts from medicine itself persons with a research outlook and motivation. In addition, as I pointed out earlier, psychoanalysis has, because of its therapeutic emphasis, almost entirely cut itself off from recruiting non-medically trained persons. In fact, such persons have generally had to break down quite formidable barriers in order to be able to obtain analytic training.

When one considers the predominant social science aspects of psychoanalysis, one wonders if psychoanalysis should not more actively seek out young behavioral and social scientists for training, to supplement its medically trained recruits. Psychoanalysis has a great need for such scientists as have shown promise in their own specialties and who are strongly motivated to continue in the investigative area related to psychoanalysis or even in psychoanalysis itself. (The need of social and behavioral science for psychoanalysis does not require emphasis and is, I trust, implicit in everything I say.)

There are many reasons why a revision or recruiting policy seems called for. In fact, it appears to me the only reasonably practical way to achieve the goal I have outlined. The constriction of the population from which psychoanalysis has permitted itself to draw has led not only to an artificial limitation of the number of research workers, but has also resulted in a narrowing of the range of the field. One cannot help but believe that such effects have hindered markedly the scientific advance of psychoanalysis.

Both of these points are perhaps obvious, but I should like to develop at least the second briefly. Alan Gregg (1941) some twenty years ago commented in relation to medicine in general that the problem of the recruitment of persons for research was particularly difficult. (It does not seem that the situation is substantially better now.) The student at the end of his training period has open to him not only a research career but also a career of practice which offers substantially greater financial rewards. In the particular branch of medicine of greatest interest to us, psychiatry, a field where the training investment is even greater, the attraction of practice is inevitably greater. For the non-medical student, such conflict is markedly less. And what is perhaps even more important, these students, especially the ablest of the group, have already gone through a process of selecting a field of interest which does a great deal to ensure a life devoted to scholarship or academic research. I would, of course, include in this class persons with medical training who see their primary contribution lying in research and scholarship. If such students are brought up in environments where the behavior supports for the research values are available, the number in this category will increase with the years. The importance of such an outcome for the continued development of psychoanalysis cannot be exaggerated. I have, on another occasion, discussed what I considered the deplorable tendency among many psychiatrists to delegate research to other disciplines (Shakow, 1949c).

I should point out that the American Psychoanalytic Association has in the last few years recognized the importance of training social and behavioral scientists for research. The Committee on Training Standards in Relation to Training for Research (Report of Committee, 1957) has been working actively on this problem, to which it has given serious and thoughtful consideration. Although this represents a substantial step forward, it nevertheless reflects a philosophy quite different in scope from the one put forth in this paper.

Thesis 5—Students who are to contribute along research or scholarly lines must be given the best psychoanalytic education possible.

Sub-thesis (a): In our society the institutional setting that can most appropriately provide such an education is the university.

For historical reasons, during the early days of psychoanalysis, the psychoanalytic institute had considerable justification for its independent status. But I raise the question whether we have not for some time been in a period where there are so many disadvantages to the private institute and so many advantages to association with a university that the time for a change has arrived.

What are the handicaps of the independent institute?

Certainly any independent psychoanalytic institute with a serious interest in research, but carrying a heavy burden of therapy training programs, has to struggle with many problems in the present type of setting. There is serious question as to whether such institutions can provide the superego supports so necessary for perseverance in research.

Another handicap of the independent institute is its hothouse atmosphere where lack of serious criticism is inevitable. In an environment where everybody holds essentially the same point of view, self-deception is easy. Counterfeit conceptual currency can pass easily from one person to another, since for mutual self-protection there is tacit agreement not to examine the currency too carefully. This *quid pro quo* tolerance can in the end become highly destructive of fundamental values.

The part-time nature of the operation cannot help but result in an overemphasis on the "practical." In an institution where private practice is the dominant model provided by the instructors, the influence on the ego ideals of the students must also be in this direction. In addition, a situation that calls so generally for the recouping of financial commitments made at great personal cost must inevitably direct the attention of the students away from scholarly pursuits.

What, in contrast, are the advantages of the university setting? In describing the advantages of the university I am not unaware of the inadequacies of many university settings. I am far from considering universities small utopias. But of the many institutions in our culture which might be considered suitable, good universities would in general appear to be the optimal places for such an arrangement. In the semi-protected environment of the university—where the goals are organized in a pattern more consonant with the values of a life oriented to teaching, research, and scholarship—one is more likely to get the community support for one's superego that practically all of us need.

The university provides an atmosphere of constant competition for ideas, both within one's own field and with other fields. This comes both from the pressures by colleagues and from the pressures of students which carry over from their contact with other departments having these values. Such external review necessitates constant self-review and provides the controls which any discipline must have if it is to develop optimally. The university standards—those which cross departments

—have both explicit and implicit effects on the standards of a particular department or school.

The university also provides models of instructors who must meet university standards, whether as clinical teachers, as basic teachers, researchers, or scholars. The students therefore have a variety of models with whom to identify, a variety rarely found in independent institutes.

If psychoanalysis hopes to achieve status as a member of the disciplines involved in achieving knowledge about man, it must take its place in the university. While it keeps itself outside this setting and restricts its activities as it has in the past, it cannot help but develop an image—for itself and for others—of not being a member of the family of sciences.

For these reasons, among others, we must consider whether ultimately a much closer relationship of institutes and universities is not called for if we are interested in meeting the research needs of psychoanalysis. Such a step would not only have reciprocal benefits for psychoanalysis and the university fields, but would also result in an increase in the number of medically trained as well as non-medically trained investigators.

Sub-thesis (b): The psychoanalytic institute should be an independent institute in the university setting associated with both the graduate school and the medical school.

Even if it is granted that the psychoanalytic institute should be part of the university, a serious question arises about the particular place in the university where the institute should be located. Whitehorn (1952), in the appropriately entitled "Academic Lecture" at the 1952 meeting of the American Psychiatric Association, has presented some major arguments for associating the institute with the university. But Whitehorn would go only part way—associate the institute with the university as part of a Department of Psychiatry. This point of view I do not share. As you know, there have actually been two instances of institutes and one of a training center being made part of the medical school setting. In each case these have been made a part of the clinics of the Department of Psychiatry. Though this is a desirable step forward and has undoubtedly led to an improvement in the situation, I do not believe that this arrangement is optimal. Psychoanalysis has a much broader function to fulfill. Essentially the form of organization here described results from what I consider too narrow a definition of psychoanalysis. This definition, I believe, sells psychoanalysis short by considering psychoanalysis as merely an adjunct to psychiatry.

Further, as I see it, this form of arrangement is not truly "university-connected." It is "department of psychiatry-connected." My own view has been that the optimal arrangement would be an *autonomous* institute intimately related to the graduate school and the medical school. (The details of the autonomy will of course have to be spelled out.) The psychoanalytic institute could then be an important center of intercourse between those who are primarily clinically oriented and those who are primarily theoretically oriented. Effective teaching of psychoanalysis takes place only in an environment of this kind, an environment where both kinds of activity are given equal prominence. An additional benefit of this scheme would be the opportunity it affords those with a major interest in one area to receive complementary training in the other.

It is, of course, possible to consider establishing two quite different kinds of institutes. One type would be an organization set up specifically for practitioners, either like the present type and quite independent of the university, or similar to the newer type associated with departments of psychiatry. The other kind would be for theoretically—oriented potential researchers and scholars and associated with the graduate school. I doubt, however, that this is a desirable arrangement. There is much to be gained by the theory-oriented from constant contact with those who are clinic- or field-oriented and vice versa. Medical schools discovered this a long time ago, and I do not see any trend toward changing their arrangement. In fact, the trend is in the contrary direction—to integrate the field and theory orientations and to bring them closer together.

It would be ungracious, in this context, not to recognize the great amount of teaching which persons associated with the institutes are carrying out in medical schools and, to some extent, in graduate departments. Though this activity is important, it does not of course meet the much broader problem with which I am concerning myself in this paper.

Sub-thesis (c): In order to develop optimally, psychoanalysis must experiment with new educational patterns.[3]

I merely want to make the obvious point here that every field must constantly be reexamining its educational content and educational techniques in order to achieve most effectively. Attendance at some of the conferences of the American Association of Medical Colleges has impressed me with the amount of thinking that is going on in medical schools about the most effective ways of achieving medical educational goals. A number of these schools are trying new and sometimes quite radical educational patterns. It seems to me that psychoanalysis must also open itself up to this kind of experimentation.

Sub-thesis (d): New programs are best developed through pilot projects.

I think it would be a grave mistake to adopt all at once a program such as I suggest, on a wide basis. There must be an initial period of testing. A few pilot programs should be established for trying out such notions as I have advanced. These programs must obviously be set up in places where there are both a good medical school and a good graduate school which is strong in psychology and the social sciences. Because of the reluctance of universities to set up independent institutes on their campuses (although the number appears to be steadily increasing), and because the suggestion here is that the institute have considerable autonomy and especially close relations with two quite separate parts of the university, it is most important that the administration of the university as a whole, and that of the medical school and the graduate school in particular, be strongly committed to such a program. I shall not at this point discuss the receptiveness of academic institutions to such a plan, since the first step must be taken by the field of psychoanalysis.

[3] Among others, the papers of Balint (1948, 1954) and Szasz (1958) are relevant.

It is particularly important to emphasize the need for commitment to such a program on the part of psychoanalysis. In the questionnaire I have referred to, a number of respondents have indicated that there existed clear evidence of ambivalence regarding their training on the part of the institute with which they were associated.

Given such a setting and arrangement, who should be the *students?* I shall not discuss the group which psychoanalysis has traditionally trained any further than to say they must also be included.

The social and behavioral scientists should be persons of quality who have clearly indicated from their past history that their primary concern is for research, teaching, and scholarly pursuit in the area of the social and behavioral sciences, and that they are clearly committed to careers of this kind. The combination of the obvious criteria for such a status, with the selective procedures which the institutes themselves must necessarily introduce, should ensure obtaining students of this description.

What about the *instructors?* They should be highly selected for competence in their specialities, whether theory or clinical work, and for their ability as teachers. They should be friendly toward research, and have a willingness to make their experience, and sometimes even their data, available for research purposes. In addition to psychoanalysts, the institute should have a considerable proportion of instructors from the behavioral and social sciences—specialists in their own areas who have gone through psychoanalytic training and are interested in research and scholarly work in this area. Most of the faculty will be at least half-time and many full-time. Under such circumstances it would be possible to establish a closer relationship between instructors and students—in some cases a kind of apprenticeship relationship.

Hopefully, a good portion of the faculty would be devoting some of its energies to research. For the best way to teach research is not to teach about research, but to *do* research in which the students get involved. And still more hopefully, this research would be on psychoanalysis and psychoanalytically oriented topics. Long observation of the psychiatric scene has impressed me with how much of the research of psychiatrists is in fields other than psychiatry itself.

What shall we say about the *educational program* to be provided for behavioral and social science students? I do not believe that any of us is prepared to be very specific at this time. Of one general point I am, however, convinced: the program must involve a combination of theory and clinical work. A personal analysis is a *sine qua non*, and some form of supervised analytic work is almost as essential. Of course, a considerable part of the present program of training is also valuable. In any case, experimentation and individualization are necessary.

We might for the present assume that, in general, the program in this institute would contain the same five major groups of experience as is contained in the present program: personal analysis, theory courses, methods courses, case seminars, and supervised cases. To these should be added a sixth important area, that of *research* in psychoanalysis, including related fields. This entire program would be open to all of the students, with a recognition of the need for setting certain program prerequisites—both general prerequisites based on needed basic experience in the field, and individual prerequisites based on a particular student's goals. If the program were to be limited to theoretical seminars, as it has been in some institutes, there would of course be little reason for this talk. Any graduate department can arrange to give theoretical courses in areas relevant to its mission. It is because psychoanalysis cannot *really* be understood unless there is an opportunity to work with clinical material and to interact with persons expert in handling clinical material that the present program has been suggested.

In this context, it would be of interest to you to know that there is general agreement in the questionnaire responses I have received from behavioral scientists trained in approved psychoanalytic institutes about the relative value of the five categories now represented. The educational value of the five categories was ranked from the highest to the lowest: personal analysis, supervised cases, case seminars, methods courses, theory. It is a little difficult to tell whether the lower value placed upon methods and theory courses, particularly the low value placed on theory, is due to the generally poor quality of the teaching in this area or to the essentially better learning contacts provided by the case-oriented experiences. The respondents did, however, complain generally about the theory courses, commenting unfavorably about them in comparison with graduate school courses. My own guess is that the evaluation is based on poorer teaching, since there seemed to be such universal agreement in the opposite direction about the teaching of one person who had given theory courses in several institutes. His theory courses were often evaluated as having as great or sometimes greater value than any other parts of the program aside from the personal analysis.

Some development of these general points about curriculum can be made with regard to range of content. The questionnaire replies indicate that too often the scope has not been based on the candidate's needs, but rather on extrinsic considerations. These appeared to grow either out of the fear that the student might sometime "practice" psychoanalysis, or the *fach*-symbolic emotional investment in the control case. Instances were given of acceptance by physician-students of the participation by non-medical students in the theory courses and even in the case seminars. They apparently feared, however, that they would lose their distinction if those who were not physicians were given supervised cases as well.

We must assume that in the new setting we have just described this problem would be minimal. There could not exist an attitude on the part of the instructors that non-medical students could have everything but supervised cases, either for the reasons given earlier, or because insufficient supervisory time was available for even the medically trained students.

The institute should provide an atmosphere in which it is possible to establish one's respective professional identity with pride and equanimity and to maintain this identification without constant threat. We must recognize the highly charged atmosphere of the analytic institute—an atmosphere where strong needs are constantly being brought to the surface, where education is taking place at an advanced age with concomitant neglect of family and ordinary satisfactions, and where financial commitments are a constant source of concern. Such a situation encourages instabilities and defensive behavior which is not helped by ambivalences introduced by the instructors. It is important throughout, as I have said, that the instructors achieve a state of non-ambivalence and that they be stable about their roles and goals. Under these circumstances, the medically trained students would find it easier to avoid the kind of feelings or fears I have just mentioned.

The program I have outlined, then, is one which recognizes that only an integration of clinical and theoretical training in a scholarly atmosphere can provide the optimal background for the education of social and behavioral scientists, and for potential researchers with medical backgrounds. Although for the effective execution of such a program the university setting I have described seems at present optimal, I do not necessarily see this as the pattern for all institutes. My expectation is that there will be a place for a variety of other organizational patterns—in association, for instance, with strong clinical centers, or with research institutes such as the intramural program of the National Institute of Mental Health. I am most doubtful, however, about the future usefulness of maintaining a considerable proportion of institutes in their present dominant pattern.

Summary

What shall I say briefly in summary? Except for the theses which I have stated twice (and therefore do not need to present again) the rest of what I have had to say really revolved around an attitude—an attitude which may have only been implicit but which I shall now try to make explicit. I am not thinking of organized psychoanalysis but of organized *society*. Psychoanalysis is part of the social body of knowledge. Psychoanalysis can no longer keep its resources isolated, it must get into the center of intellectual activity, make its contribution and be contributed to as other fields of knowledge are doing and have in the past. If changes in psychoanalysis result from this intercourse, this is only what is to be expected and they are to be welcomed. More specifically, two ethical issues underlie this attitude.

The first is this: When society has invested heavily in the education and concentration of talent in a field, the group so privileged has an obligation to contribute its knowledge to the general body of knowledge.

The other is this: In a period where in so much of our daily life we are surrounded and constantly bombarded by irrationalities—at the international, the national, and the individual levels—it would appear to be an unavoidable obligation on the part of that group whose members have presumably gone through the most searching, formalized examination of their own irrationalities to set a pattern for rational conduct. (You see I am old-fashioned in my psychoanalytic views.) At the very least, within its own realm it ought to be able to face problems objectively. If this group can't, which can? *Noblesse* does *oblige*. And to the argument which might be advanced about the puniness of such efforts against the overwhelming odds, there are several answers. One is that ethics does not consider odds. The other is that there must not be any underrating of the importance of the effective power of that group which is most closely identified with one of the great revolutions in human thinking

—a revolution which has provided man with the means of facing up to himself honestly and with courage. If such values are frittered away in preoccupation with petty internecine battles or in the satisfaction of selfish needs, then the group is not worthy of its heritage. Society cannot afford to leave the responsibility for such an important area to such a group.

Freud's (1926) own opinion on this issue is well-known to you. His gloomy view thirty or more years ago of the "future of analysis if it does not succeed in creating an abode for itself outside of medicine," (letter to Ferenczi, May 13, 1928: Jones, 1957, p. 319–320), a view reiterated again only a year before his death (letter to Schnier, July 5, 1938: Jones, 1957, p. 323) has at least in part been prophetically correct.

In its worry about the relatively minor problem of lay analysis, psychoanalysis has run the risk of throwing out the baby with the bath. One never knows about history because there are no controls. But let us even accept the argument that it was historically desirable for psychoanalysis to take the direction favored so strongly by the American group (IPA, 1927). Let be what has been—we can't help that. But is it not time now to examine objectively the future of psychoanalysis as a discipline and decide where it is—better, *has*—to go? At the *present* time this is largely up to you.

26. Ethics for a Scientific Age: Some Moral Aspects of Psychoanalysis

In the course of completing the monograph "The Influence of Freud on American Psychology" David Rapaport and I had been working on, ethical issues seemed to call for attention, especially in relation to psychotherapy. After Rapaport's death, I considered including a chapter on ethics in the monograph, but decided finally to publish it separately. This paper was read at the Third Annual Conference of the Council of Psychoanalytic Psychotherapy on February 14, 1965, and published in the Fall 1965 issue of *The Psychoanalytic Review.*

To these times which so persistently face us with crucial moral issues, psychoanalysis has much to contribute. It is thus appropriate now to reexamine this system of psychology in the context of morality. Aside from having ethical ties to important areas within psychology proper, such as psychotherapy and ego psychology, the psychoanalytic system embodies principles that carry with them clear implications for moral conduct.

Reprinted from *The Psychoanalytic Review*, vol. 52, no. 3, Fall 1965, through the courtesy of the editors and the publisher, National Psychological Association for Psychoanalysis, Inc., New York, N.Y.

I use the term morality not to express "nobility and rectitude," but to approximate Dewey's (1922) use of the term as the strength to make choices. It also conveys the sense of "inherent strength" which Erikson (1964, p. 113) talks about in *Insight and Responsibility*. I suppose that I am too old-fashioned to go further on the road which Erikson takes when he makes a sharp distinction between morality as based on threats to be forestalled and ethics as based on ideals to be striven for (p. 222). Although I see some rationale for his distinguishing between these terms, I am afraid that too much is lost in the process. For instance, it is somewhat precious to talk of "ethical indignation." "Moral indignation," on the contrary, is a most important weapon in our social armamentarium, a weapon that needs more exercise than it has recently been getting. So I trust that you will go along with me when I use "ethical" and "moral" more or less synonymously in what I shall be saying.

Three types of arguments have been offered concerning the relationship of ethical considerations to psychoanalysis. The first argument denies moral implications altogether, the second considers them integral and positive, and the third finds the implications integral, but negative.

The first, the denial of moral implications, is Freud's own original argument (Freud, 1932, pp. 216–249; Hartmann, 1960, p. 87). It states that psychoanalysis, as a scientific system, makes no pretense of offering a code of morality, but asks to be judged solely by the scientific criterion of truth. Bertrand Russell put the general problem this way in *A History of Western Philosophy*:

> The pursuit of truth, when it is whole-hearted, must ignore moral considerations; we cannot know in advance that the truth will turn out to be what is thought edifying in a given society . . . One of the defects of all philosophers since Plato is that their inquiries into ethics proceed on the assumption that they already know the conclusions to be reached [Russell, 1945, pp. 78–79].

The second argument—that moral considerations are integral—is offered in one form or another by such psychoanalysts as Flugel (1951, 1955) and Brierley (1951). According to this argument, psychoanalysis cannot avoid moral implications; it is involved in a scientific area that is close to the origins and problems of morality and importantly related to ethics. Such authors postulate a positive contribution of psychoanalysis to morality. It is clear from empirical studies (Parloff, Goldstein, & Iflund, 1960; Rosenthal, 1955), on the one hand, and from philosophical considerations, on the other, that psychotherapists cannot avoid transmitting values during the psychotherapeutic process. For example, Reid (1955), although strongly sympathetic to psychoanalysis, maintains that psychoanalysis encourages enervation through the belief that choices are determined by early childhood or other antecedent events. He points out that the problem of reconciling psychic determinism with a sense of responsibility for one's own choices and their consequences, is more than an exercise in school metaphysics. Although such enervation may occur at only one stage in the process of psychoanalysis, Reid's criticism remains a valid one. Solutions growing naturally out of Freudian psychology, such as those offered by Flugel and Brierley, will be discussed later.

The third argument emphasizes the negative contributions of psychoanalysis to morality. While it bears some relation to the point Reid makes from within the psychoanalytic framework, the argument leads to the abandonment of this framework. LaPiere and Mowrer, who are not at all sympathetic to psychoanalysis, are among those holding this view. LaPiere (1960), in *The Freudian Ethic*, contrasts the Freudian and Protestant ethics, the Freudian coming out much the worse. Mowrer defines the core of *The Crisis in Psychiatry and Religion* as the contrast between psychoanalysis' biological values of "adult genital sexuality" and "unencumbered assertiveness," and religion's social view of man as a "child of God" (Mowrer, 1961, p. iv). Both Mowrer and LaPiere center extended arguments on Freud's presumed advocacy of the proposition that society rather than the patient is to blame for neurosis. Such a proposition seems to be contrary to the well-known prognostic rule which holds that accepting responsibility is much more conducive to recovering health than rejecting responsibility. LaPiere and Mowrer are deeply concerned that psychoanalysis may have deleterious cultural effects. In fact, they become so apprehensive that LaPiere occasionally becomes rather snide in his criticism (p. 52) and Mowrer is often led into making quite extreme and questionable statements. For example, Mowrer holds that the increasing number of churchgoers refutes the Freudian stand on religion and indicates the imminent demise of psychoanalysis. He is carried into making numerous exaggerations and "digs" such as:

> Our mental hospitals are now, alas, full of persons who have had this new form of treatment [psychoanalysis] and not profited from it [p. 83]. . . . barely two decades after Freud's death, the signs of confusion and disintegration he launched in the movement are rampant [pp. 122–123]. . . . Freud's aims and motivations were not messianic but demonic [p. 131].

And he even goes so far as to quote Anna Russell's "Psychiatric Folksong" (p. 49) as catching the spirit of a particular psychoanalytic doctrine. This folksong is another of the general type of Dunlap's and Titchener's off-color parodies on psychoanalysis. Since psychoanalysis by its very nature invites these efforts more than most fields, such manipulations are of the order of taking candy away from a baby.

Mowrer's arguments deserve extensive examination. He is one of the most vehement opponents of Freudism; his point of view represents that of many others in both the theological and psychological fields. For example, Köhler (1958), in "The Obsessions of Normal People" discusses the "smog," largely created by psychoanalysis, that has descended on modern man. Köhler is disturbed by the feeling of irresponsibility psychiatry engenders and the negative pall it spreads. "Death instinct, anxiety, inferiority complex, frustration, aggression—what a vocabulary!" he writes. Never, he continues, will the psychoanalysts and the psychoanalytic psychologists mention cheer, joy, happiness, hope, or fortitude!

Although Mowrer presented his general argument in 1950 in *Learning Theory and Personality Dynamics* and stated it again somewhat more vehemently in 1960 in *Learning Theory and the Symbolic Processes*, the 1961 *Crisis* volume gives it perhaps the clearest expression. By this time, Mowrer is not quite so "understanding" of Freud as he was earlier (Freud, 1940 [1938]). No more does he refer to *An Outline of Psychoanalysis* or to the "Splitting of the Ego in the Defensive Process" (Freud, 1938) as marking a new direction in Freud's thinking. Yet even in his more tolerant days, Mowrer did not appreciate the early and long history of psychoanalytic concepts (Shakow, 1949a).

Nevertheless, criticism of Mowrer is difficult, since so much of what he says calls for hearty agreement. Basing my discussion primarily on the *Crisis* volume, I will first consider these positive aspects.

Mowrer's statements about the professionalization of psychiatry and clinical psychology, the "big business" aspects of psychoanalysis and the misguided tendency of certain groups in organized religion to accept Freudian notions are undoubtedly legitimate. It is indeed difficult to understand how orthodox religion and Freudian notions can be reconciled, unless one possesses the ability to reconcile irreconcilables, or to retain a religious structure while rejecting some of its most intrinsic qualities.

Most significant, perhaps, is Mowrer's persistent emphasis on the importance of ethics and morality. Although psychoanalysis actually is concerned with these topics, we can agree that its concern could be more deliberate. But we must insist on preserving a clear distinction between the scientific and the ethical issues.

Despite such merits, Mowrer may be generally criticized for unfairness, exaggeration, and intolerance. He rawly restates Freud's two criteria for therapeutic success—*lieben und arbeiten* (Erikson, 1963)—as "capacity for lusty heterosexual orgasm" and "frank hostility and aggressiveness" (1960, pp. iv–v). In so doing, Mowrer has taken these terms in nothing more than their literal sense; he misses their true implication for full object love and socially oriented conduct. (*Coito ergo sum* makes an amusing play on words, but *cogito ergo sum* in its full sense is much closer to the fundamental Freudian principle.) Erikson has a much more meaningful and valid description of the implications of Freud's view of genitality in the second edition of *Childhood and Society*. He says:

> In order to be of lasting social significance, the utopia of genitality should include: 1. mutuality of orgasm; 2. with a loved partner; 3. of the other sex; 4. with whom one is able and willing to share a mutual trust; 5. and with whom one is able and willing to regulate the cycles of a. work; b. procreation; c. recreation; 6. so as to secure to the offspring, too, all the stages of a satisfactory development [Erikson, 1963, p. 266].

Mowrer repeatedly makes the point that psychoanalysis as a therapy is not successful. Since the criteria of therapeutic success are vague, this is dangerous ground on which to tread. I do not know of any truly searching studies of the effectiveness of therapy. Certainly Eysenck's (1952; 1961a,b) are not. The studies that have been done all rely on quite limited and superficial criteria which would be hardly acceptable in other fields.

In any case, the therapeutic test is far from acceptable proof of the adequacy of a theory (Munroe, 1955, p. 326 ff.). It is possible to have a theory with therapeutic *implications* which is quite sound despite its current lack of therapeutic *technique*. The therapeutic test is legitimately applied only when the argument rests on the therapeutic efficacy of the theory or the method. It is true that exaggerated claims of efficacy were early made for psychoanalysis—although not by Freud himself—and for this reason it may be fair to use the therapeutic test against psychoanalysis. Nevertheless, it is also true that in recent years such claims have decidedly diminished.

Let us now go on to the specific arguments that Mowrer raises against psychoanalysis. First, he argues strenuously against what he interprets as the emphasis of Freudian theory on biological adaptation. He does not appear to recognize that, as Rapaport (1959) indicated in "The Structure of Psychoanalytic Theory," psychoanalysis is actually stated almost entirely in behavior terms, even though original biological motivation may be postulated.

In a second point, Mowrer (1961, p. vi) hypothesizes a social basis for both the genesis and correction of psychopathology. This argument is associated with his own exclusive emphasis on the value system of the superego in relation to conflict. Neurosis is, however, much more complicated. Although some breakdowns may occur because of neglect of superego demands, they may also result from conflict due to id repression or ego weakness. As I have stated elsewhere (Shakow, 1949a), Mowrer constantly seems to be coming to the defense of the *status quo ante* superego, arguing against its being considered excessively severe, and emphasizing the needs for reliance on conscience and for assimilation of conscious values. Mowrer too strongly implies that the early-established superego is the measure of all things. However, I do not think it is doing violence to analytic theory to hold that the superego has the capacity for growth and learning.

In this connection, Kaplan points out in "Freud and Modern Philosophy" that Freud made a great contribution to the critique of conscience by recognizing its inherent destructive potentialities. Kaplan writes:

> A man may be driven by duty as much as by desire, be in bondage to his "principles" as much as to his passions. And under such compulsion he is likely to bring others to perdition and not only himself: more blood has been shed by moral zeal than in the pursuit of pleasure [Kaplan, 1957, p. 221].

Stated in the naïve dichotomous form of either "I am wrong" or "society is wrong," Mowrer's argument sounds justified. But the advancement of any society is achieved only through a proper balance between socialization and individualization (Shakow, 1949a). For psychoanalysis the initial task is the elimination of the *narrow* socialization controlling natural selfish individual tendencies. Once this is worked through, there is the possibility of achieving an optimal society, based on continued development of its individual men and stabilized through socialization.

Before specifically considering the contributions to ethics and morality of the psychoanalytic system, let me mention two common dangers in interpreting the Freudian position. The first danger, as Kaplan (1957, p. 221) so well puts it, is to mistake the amorality of objective inquiry for the immorality of tacit approval. This does not follow from a real understanding of Freud, but here, as elsewhere (Shakow & Rapaport, 1964), I take the position that Freud's theories and their implications have frequently been misunderstood.

The second danger results from the gap between psychoanalysis as developed theoretically and psychoanalysis as actually practiced. As a profession with significant social responsibility grows, certain undesirable practices frequently develop. Even some of Freud's own disciples, especially in the earlier days, practiced a "wild analysis" (Freud, 1910) that disregarded some of his most important principles. Moreover, there are still psychoanalysts who treat their patients in utter dissociation from their social and cultural environments. Although psychoanalytic training institutes have struggled with the problem of selection on both personality and intellectual grounds, they have often made errors. The self-selection of candidates, the restricted distribution of the candidates' cultural backgrounds, the less-than-satisfactory tools of selection, and the limited wisdom of the selectors, all lead to such errors. Consequently, there are psychoanalysts who practice a kind of therapy which is not oriented toward the achievement of individual integrity. And it is expressly the building of integrity that I see as a primary aim of psychoanalysis, analysis being as it is one of the most powerful weapons of psychological influence available to man.

Views on Freud's place in relation to ethics and morality have ranged from the extremes of Freud as devil to Freud as "God."

Kaufmann (1960), in his book *From Shakespeare to Existentialism*, compares Freud with Socrates and with Jesus. He points out that Freud shared with Socrates three principles: know thyself; virtue is knowledge; and the maieutic method, or the art of midwifery, which is, of course, the analytic process. Freud's aim was the achievement of true insight, which he believed called for affectively worked-through, rather than purely intellectual, knowledge about oneself. Freud pointed out in a letter to Putnam that mere intellectual knowledge was not, as Socrates and Putnam thought, enough. Freud endeavored to make what was unconscious conscious and available to reason after the unavoidably stormy period of affective living through.

Kaufmann, comparing Freud and Jesus, finds three parallels: healing through the spirit; a devotion to the outcasts of society; and the acceptance of the principle, "He that is without sin among you, let him first cast a stone."

He goes on to say that one of Freud's greatest contributions to ethics was his success in breaking down the wall between the normal and the abnormal, the respectable and the criminal, the good and the evil. Freud held that troubled persons were not possessed by the devil, but were essentially as oneself. The obvious retort is: "True, but is not Freud's contribution going in the wrong direction? Does not Freud bring the normal, the respectable and the good down to the level of the abnormal, the criminal and the evil?" This, of course, is what troubles the religiously inclined. The only answer the Freudian can make is: "Yes, I recognize your point. But is not honesty a better ground for action than illusion? If I face up to my origins honestly, there is some hope for planning my life deliberately along ethical lines; if I do not, I am likely to be buffeted about by characteristics of which I am not aware, and thus be much less likely to achieve social goals." There is much more hope for the future if outlook is based on honest inlook (Wheeler, 1921).

But Freud, particularly in his earlier days, was not much involved with the moral implications of psychoanalysis, although there were some early psychoanalysts who were—notably Putnam, Silberer, and Pfister. At that time, Freud had his eye only on the scientific aspect of psychoanalysis. He concentrated on id forces and was slow about developing an ego psychology. In the 1890's, he did formulate the foundations of an ego psychology (Freud, 1887–1902), but around 1897 he began to focus on the uncovering of the unconscious. About a quarter of a century later (Freud, 1923) he turned again to these earlier considerations, in connection with the negative therapeutic reaction. In 1926 Freud (1926 [1924]) made the crucial step toward the development of psychoanalytic ego psychology, returning to his concepts of the 1890's—a method of progress characteristic of Freud. His work contributed much to creating the atmosphere in which the ego psychologies of our day developed, but hardly at all to the *concepts* and *problems* central to present-day ego psychology. Yet it is the growth of ego psychology that has resulted in an increasing concern with problems of value, and increasing awareness within psychoanalysis itself of its implications for moral problems.

In defense of Freud's neglect, we must recognize the importance of his primary task. If he had not given detailed attention to the development of the notions of the unconscious and the id, a later ego psychology would indeed have lacked substance. We must also recognize the nature of the society in which Freud lived. His was a homogeneous culture in which social, cultural, educational, and religious support of ego and superego function was taken for granted. Freud made this point directly and indirectly on several occasions. It is his successors—Hartmann, Erikson, Kris, Loewenstein, Rapaport, *et al.*—who have been developing an ego psychology. But their work has been in keeping with Freud's belief that an ego psychology can be built only upon a consolidated knowledge of the unconscious, rather than, as in the case of some of the neo-Freudians, by essentially dispensing with the id.

Although Freud was not particularly concerned with relating his work to ethical problems, he *was* adamant about one point: that organized religion did not provide the proper foundation for ethical behavior (Herberg, 1957). It seems that he implicitly adopted two ethical imperatives for psychoanalysis: the first was not to accept the illusory; the second was that blind faith is morally wrong. As Freud stated clearly in 1932 in *New Introductory Lectures on Psychoanalysis*:

> Experience teaches us that the world is not a nursery. The ethical commands, to which religion seeks to lend its weight, *require some other foundations instead, for human society cannot do without them* [italics ours], and it is dangerous to link up obedience to them with religious belief. If one attempts to assign to religion its place in man's evolution, it seems not so much to be a lasting acquisition, as a parallel to the neurosis which the civilized individual must pass through on his way from childhood to maturity [p. 230].

If religious persons accept psychoanalysis, they do so because of the ethical aspects which are so commonly associated with religion, rather than because of the religious aspects themselves (Adler, 1919; Brophy, 1962, pp. 180–187; Erikson, 1959, pp. 64–65; Fromm, 1950, pp. 18–19; Rieff, 1959, p. xi). It is also possible that most persons still need such religious support to achieve the ethical aspects of religion.

During recent years several psychoanalytic authors have attempted to elaborate on the ethical implications of psychoanalysis. Their contributions are particularly important in the present context, but, unfortunately, we can only touch on them in bare outline.

Flugel (1955), in *Man, Morals and Society*, offers perhaps the most complete discussion of the topic of ethics and psychoanalysis in the psychoanalytic literature. He presents eight general tendencies toward moral progress which grow out of psychoanalytic principles: (1) from egocentricity to sociality; (2) from unconscious to conscious; (3) from autism to realism; (4) from moral inhibition to spontaneous "goodness"; (5) from aggression to tolerance and love; (6) from fear to security; (7) from heteronomy to autonomy; (8) from orectic or moral judgment to cognitive or psychological judgment (pp. 294–317).

Brierley, in *Trends in Psycho-Analysis*, states her set of goals for integrative development somewhat differently. They include: (1) libidinal control in relation to the development of libidinal capacity, or libidinization; (2) domestication of aggression, or its use for preventive and auxiliary purposes; (3) identification and object-love; (4) sublimation, the pilot function of ideals (Brierley, 1951, pp. 180–293).

These two sets of principles exemplify direct expansions of psychoanalytic implications in relation to morality. Somewhat less direct contributions to ethics are seen in ego-psychology, primarily in the works of Hartmann and Erikson, and in other psychoanalytic writings such as those of Frenkel-Brunswik.

Erikson, in *Childhood and Society*, presents eight phases of ego development occurring during the life cycle. With the earlier phases come: (1) basic trust as opposed to basic mistrust; (2) autonomy as opposed to shame and doubt; (3) initiative as opposed to guilt; (4) industry as opposed to inferiority. With adolescence comes: (5) identity as opposed to role confusion. With the three stages of advancing adulthood come: (6) intimacy as opposed to isolation; (7) generativity as opposed to stagnation; (8) ego integrity as opposed to despair (Erikson, 1963, pp. 247–269).

In an article in *Insight and Responsibility*, Erikson (1964, pp. 109–157) discusses the basic virtues. He parallels the eight phases of development with eight sets of virtues starting with hope in infancy, progressing through will, purpose, and competence in the school age, and going on to fidelity in adolescence, love in young adulthood, and care and wisdom in adulthood.

Else Frenkel-Brunswik also states principles of the same order. She writes:

As far as both the goals and the effective means of execution of ethics are concerned, psychoanalysis lays stress on the importance of consciousness, integration, and maturity. If we recall for a moment all that is considered an essential ingredient of maturity in psychoanalysis, such as rationality, the overcoming of aggression, the development of cooperativeness, the ability to love and to work, and the courage openly to face inside and outside threats which oppose these characteristics, we readily see that we are confronted with standards which are certainly not lower than those expounded in the traditional systems of ethics. In psychoanalysis, every neurosis is *ipso facto* considered as failure at satisfactory moral control. The traditional systems of ethics attempted to strengthen consciousness and conscience against the invasion of instincts, and that remains their important historic contribution; however, through psychoanalysis we have become aware of the fact that such strengthening can only be achieved by facing and by working through, rather than by merely condemning, the forces which threaten our conscious personal and social values. From this latter viewpoint, the mortal sin is self-deception, and lack of insight in general, rather than a lack of repression [1954, pp. 271–347].

She continues:

It is one of the greatest and least appreciated contributions of psychoanalysis to have seen that for genuinely ethical behavior not only the instincts, so far as anti-social, must be made conscious and integrated into a more encompassing system, but that the major controlling instance of the primordial id-impulses and thus the alleged major guardian of morals, the superego, also may be a source of unconscious sadistic and primitive tendencies. Thus not only the id but also the superego must in the end be subordinated to the more reasonable prescriptions of the ego [p. 335].

A number of authors from outside psychoanalysis have expressed essentially the same principles in quite other contexts. The principles are perhaps stated most clearly by G. G. Simpson, both in *The Meaning of Evolution* (Simpson, 1949) written in 1949, and in an address given to an AAAS meeting in 1959 (Simpson, 1960) on the occasion of the Darwin centenary. He wrote in the former work: "The ethical need is within and peculiar to man and its fulfillment also lies in man's nature, relative to him and to his evolution ... Man has choice and responsibility. . . ."

From Simpson's considerations come two outstanding ethical corollaries: (1) blind faith is morally wrong; (2) the maintenance of man's evolved individualization and the promotion of the integrity and dignity of the individual are morally good. Such ethics, which strongly oppose authoritarian ideologies, have wide applications for social and personal conduct. Thus, Simpson implies, socialization, a necessary human process, is ethically good when it is based on, and in turn gives, the maximum total possibility for ethically good individualization (Shakow, 1951).

In his 1959 talk, "The World into which Darwin Led Us," Simpson said:

. . . man has unique moral qualities. The evolutionary process is not moral—the word is simply irrelevant in that connection—but it has finally produced a moral animal. Conspicuous among his moral attributes is a sense of responsibility, which is probably felt in some way and to some degree by every normal human being. There has been disagreement and indeed confusion through the ages regarding to whom and for what man is responsible. The lower and the higher superstitions have produced their several answers. In the post-Darwinian world another answer seems fairly clear: man is responsible to himself and for himself. "Himself" here means the whole human species, not only the individual and certainly not just those of a certain color of hair or cast of features [1960, pp. 966–974].

Particularly relevant is his concluding thought:

A world in which man must rely on himself, in which he is not the darling of the gods but only another, albeit extraordinary, aspect of nature, is by no means congenial to the immature or the wishful thinkers. That is plainly a major reason why even now, a hundred years after *The Origin of Species*, most people have not really entered the world into which Darwin led—alas! only a minority of us. Life may conceivably be happier for some people in the older worlds of superstition . . . but adults should prefer to live in a world of reality and reason [p. 974].

In relation to individualization which is so central to Simpson's thesis, Trilling, in his *Freud and the Crisis of Our Culture* said:

I need scarcely remind you that . . . Freud is quite at one with literature. In its essence literature is concerned with the self; and the particular concern of the literature of the last two centuries has been with the self in its standing quarrel with culture . . . . This intense conviction of the existence of the self apart from culture is, as culture well knows, its noblest and most generous achievement. At the present moment it must be thought of as a liberating idea without which our developing ideal of community is bound to defeat itself. We can speak no greater praise of Freud than to say that he placed this idea at the very center of his thought [1955, pp. 58–59].

Such authors as Mowrer offer a return to the obedience of strong social norms, a return to a primitive conscience quite rigidly determined by early training. Psychoanalysis offers, in contrast, the possibility of achieving the essentials of what Thoreau fought for, what William James (1890, p. 315) some seven decades ago called the "ideal social self," what Bertrand Russell (1919) some six decades ago called "A Free Man's Worship," what Simpson (1960) has recently called "The World into which Darwin Led Us," and what I might call "The World into which Freud Leads Us." Freud's emphasis on the full use of reason, on the development of the potentialities of individual man, and on the working through of irrational origins of conduct has laid the essential foundation for a personal ethics. It remains to build upon this foundation, to develop a rational ethics, a faith suitable for scientists (Huxley, 1961, p. 7), that will enable man to enter the consciously purposive phase of evolution.

PART V

Commitment to Public Service

The following, and last, paper in this volume is of somewhat different character than those that have preceded it. Nevertheless, I believe it reflects the same spirit. The emphasis here is not on profession but rather on where one carries out one's profession. And having spent almost half a century in public institutions, it seemed reasonable to try to take stock. So when I was invited to participate in a Symposium on "Current Roles of Psychologists in Public Service" for the seventy-fifth anniversary meeting of the APA, I accepted. But the organizer of the symposium, Edwin Shneidman, and I agreed that my discussion should be focused on the *general* problems faced by professional persons working for the government. It appeared in the February, 1968, issue, of the *American Psychologist.*

27. On the Rewards (and, Alas, Frustrations) of Public Service

Over four decades—my entire professional life in fact—devoted to basic research and education in the employ of federal and state governments[1] affords some grounds for reflecting on that aspect of public service. Since inadequate information has fostered much of current, generally unfavorable, attitudes about working for the government, I believe that public professionals, especially those having favorable experiences, have a responsibility to report on these (as well as the negative ones) to their colleagues.[2]

Reprinted with permission from the *American Psychologist*, vol. 23, 1968.

[1] Twenty years at the Worcester State Hospital, eight at the Illinois Neuropsychiatric Institute of the University of Illinois, and over thirteen at the National Institute of Mental Health.

[2] In the writing of this paper I have found myself saying things which I have long thought about but which in similar vein have also been said by other persons who have written about government operations, especially about science in government. I have in mind such persons as Abelson (1966), Astin (1959), Lederberg (1967), Shannon (1967a,b). In a more general way I have found the spirit of John W. Gardner's two books (1961, 1963) inspiring and supportive, as I have Robert Livingston's annual reports as Director of Intramural Research, NIMH.

Although it is true that contributing to the public welfare is but one of the many motivations which determine a person's vocational choice, it is the one which, in the present context, I shall consider central. Such contributions need not, by any means, be made exclusively through public institutions. They may also be made by private citizens or through private organizations. The choice of where one works is, psychoanalytically speaking, in some respects "over-determined," and, non-analytically speaking, "under-determined." For this occasion, however, I shall limit myself to some of the problems involved in choosing to contribute to public service via the public sector, and share with you some experiences and observations connected with this choice.

For many of our colleagues there is something *infra dig*, or even incomprehensible, about working directly for the government. I speak from experiences in heading modest government operations and recruiting for them. I shall discuss in detail some of the actual difficulties in government service I myself have encountered. But first let me list some of the objections that I have heard commonly raised: "I want an exciting and demanding job, not a merely safe and secure one"; "Government work is bound to be mediocre work"; "Government is interested only in immediate payoffs"; "Government work is directed from above and subject to political manipulation." I am sure you can add many others. In contrast, the university setting's high standards, freedom, and opportunities are pointed to as obviously preferable. It is difficult to convince our colleagues about the stimulation that efforts to raise government operations to university levels provide. It is even more difficult for them to believe that certain parts of the government have already reached the level of some of our best universities. How can we persuade them that as citizens with special skills they have not only the opportunity, but indeed the privilege and obligation, to help raise the level of government operations as high as possible, to a level worthy of their personal identification? Is not government, after all, really a projection of ourselves? It is true that some persons do recognize these potentialities and responsibilities to some extent and are willing to accept at least a "tour of duty" with government. But, usually because of the sacrifices involved, they are not willing to make their contribution through a permanent career. Here I am concerned only with permanent, or relatively permanent, careers in government.

Of my own professional experiences let me here make a general comment and give some examples. My three work experiences have each been gratifying and exciting in both similar and different ways. They had their share of routine (how could it be otherwise?), but more important they had more than their quota of novelty. Each had its allotment of obstacles (how could we maintain our strength *without* adversity?) but, again, more important, each had more than its portion of rewards. They all happened to be in medical settings—more specifically, psychiatric settings—but this, though significant because of the range and richness of the opportunities and experiences they provided, was not their fundamental characteristic. What they had in common was that most essential quality—the compound of freedom, long-term goals, and pioneering spirit. One certainly felt that he was a participant in a group endeavor which was breaking new ground rather than in an enterprise that was directed merely at solving immediate practical problems. And as I try to analyze what were the frustrations and obstacles, but particularly why I felt so rewarded by these experiences, I come away with the feeling that each provided the same outstanding personal reward—the opportunity to contribute creatively within the limits of one's capacity to important long-range social goals. But let us get to some examples which illustrate some of these roses without neglecting some of the thorns which went with them.

At Worcester I was working in a state hospital. Anybody who knows the nature of state hospitals 30–40 years ago is acquainted with the place of the superintendent in the institution. Even in the relatively enlightened Massachusetts system the superintendent was a kind of czar who ran the institution according to his own lights. Frequently this involved more concern with the buildings or "the pigs" than with the patients. The situation at Worcester was different under William A. Bryan. The operation was patient-oriented and had a pioneering spirit which was remarkable.[3] The pioneering spirit permeated all aspects of the program, but I must not let my historical enthusiasm carry me into areas not immediately relevant. I wish particularly to select that aspect which has to do with the recognition of the proper boundaries of administrative control which I shall consider more generally later.

In order more effectively to carry out the institution's purposes, Dr. Bryan appointed a Council consisting of the Assistant Superintendent, the Clinical Director, the two Directors of Research, and the heads of the Departments of Biochemistry, Biometrics, Psychiatry, and Psychology. This was a policy-determining committee before whom all major issues of research and education for the institution came up. Frequently issues would arise with regard to both research and education which reflected a conflict between the more immediate, practical goal-seeking to which the superintendent was necessarily more sensitive, and the more remote goal-seeking of the "basic" staff. What was most remarkable about this highly "practical" administrator was his willingness to accept the majority decision and to be guided by it. In the context of what was generally prevalent in institutions of this kind, this was indeed extraordinary. It accounts perhaps for the important influence which Worcester has had in the mental health field. In such an environment one could teach both less and more advanced students and colleagues; one could carry out individual, group, and interdisciplinary research; and one could become truly and thoroughly involved with patients, so that one developed the clinical understanding which could serve as the sound foundation needed for research, teaching, and therapy.

Turning from the sublime to the "ridiculous," let me give an instance of one of the negative aspects of the Worcester situation which was a persistent torment to the professional staff. Because of the low salaries prevalent in the state system, it was especially difficult to recruit truly efficient persons at the clerical level. The hospital had an old-time telephone switchboard operator who had proved herself remarkably

[3] Cf. the first book ever written on the administrative aspects of psychiatry, Bryan's (1936) *Administrative Psychiatry*, which describes so many of the administrative innovations of the state hospital he instituted at Worcester.

able in handling telephone communications with relatives of the patients—a most important function for a hospital that was so patient-oriented. She was by far the most efficient of our telephone operators. At the same time, however, she was exceedingly insolent to staff members and their families, with resultant devastating effects on morale. Almost no day went by without her arousing the ire of one of the professionals, whether because of rudeness in relation to his professional activities or in relation to the maintenance problems of his household. In an establishment where household maintenance—home, food, laundry, and all the other extras—was part of the salary, maintenance was of almost equal importance to the professional aspect in providing that underlying peace of mind necessary for effectiveness. If you had gotten through your day without an encounter, you would come home in the evening to find your wife "in tears" because of *her* encounter. The complaints about the operator, and demands for her discharge, were constantly passed on to the Superintendent. But for years he protected her because of what he considered as her importance to the institution. She was a remarkable instance of that "insolence of office" at a low level which Graham Wallas refers to (1914, pp. 196–198) as having such devastating effects on creativity. I can vouch for at least its temporary effects on my own productivity, even in the context of the unusually favorable professional conditions.

The situation at the University of Illinois had something of the same spirit of freedom and permissiveness that I have described for Worcester. Under Francis Gerty as head of the Department of Psychiatry, the major principle was academic freedom and the liberty to carry out research as one saw fit. Dr. Gerty's policy was to recruit the most competent persons he could find to head his programs and then permit these persons complete freedom within the limits of the resources of the institution. Many were the occasions when his advice on research or teaching was sought and he would point out that the territory involved was the producer's territory and it was not for him, the manager, to say.

The situation at NIH—and now I become somewhat embarrassed at being so repetitive—also has had the same spirit of freedom and permissiveness. Under the general guidance of Dr. Shannon and Dr. Felix and the more immediate managerial supervision of Drs. Kety, Livingston, Eberhart, and Cohen (the various Directors of Research under whom I have served), there has consistently been a clear recognition of the prerogatives of the producer and the importance of long-term goals. The plaguing aspects of a large government operation I shall consider later.

So what stands out as the primary value and reward is represented by the point I have been echoing: the freedom to do one's own work as it fits into the context of the general mission of the organization with which one has associated oneself.

Let us return to our major concern. I suppose the central question to which I am addressing myself is: Does the government[4] have the obligation within its immediate

[4] In discussing "government" in this paper, I am particularly concerned with the federal government. However, the same arguments hold, if to a lesser extent, for other governmental bodies, such as state and municipal governments, and perhaps even for county governments. Actually this becomes increasingly important with the trend toward involving local governments more heavily in national programs.

domain, to support large-scale undertakings of a scientific/educational character which do not provide immediate payoffs? (Let us agree that there is little question about the desirability of government carrying out programs involving immediate and applied work.) I refer to activities that may be considered "creative"—innovative, experimental, pure, or theoretical—what in science is called "basic." Astin's definition, the "freedom to pursue a line of inquiry to the outer edge of knowledge" (1959, p. 144), is sufficiently general to suit our purposes. Although my discussion will be directed almost entirely at basic research, what I shall say applies equally to all innovative and experimental programs related to the respective missions of any of the various branches of government. I must emphasize that financial support given by the federal government to non-federal institutions or to individuals for these purposes is not what I have in mind. What I am discussing are *direct* activities carried on within the immediate structure and domain of the government.

It is evident to many of us that the government has an obligation to support a considerable share of this kind of endeavor. Many others, however, believe that it is not the business of government to "compete" in this way with either private or public educational institutions. The function of government in regard to basic studies is, they claim, merely to provide financial aid; the substantive activity itself should be carried out by the non-governmental sector. These two points of view are reflected respectively in the Long (NSF, 1955) and Wooldridge (NIH, 1965) Reports on the National Institutes of Health.

While the recent report of the Wooldridge Committee flatters the Institutes' intramural research activities, it draws a sharp distinction between what is God's and what is Caesar's—between the functions of the university and of the government. The Committee appears somewhat disconcerted that basic research can be carried out so effectively in a government operation, and they recommend not only no expansion in this direct research but even a reduction in this function, which they view as fundamentally a university responsibility.

The spirit of the Wooldridge Report is quite different from that of the Long Committee's report, which covered the same general ground ten years earlier. The members of the Long Committee saw the tremendous possibility of the intramural program of NIH "[attracting] through their facilities, conditions of employment, and freedom for individual enterprise, the most gifted medical research scientists that are available. . . .

"The federal government has," they reported, "in its ability to support individual full-time investigators at NIH, a unique opportunity to further our knowledge of disease, since very few non-governmental institutions in this country can afford to support full-time, life-long careers in research. This opportunity should be exploited to its fullest extent. There is no reason why the senior appointments at the National Institutes should not become the most sought after in the country."

My own bias, as reflected in having chosen a science career in government, is decidedly in harmony with the Long Committee's. I believe that although public service carried out in the private sector is to be highly commended, public service carried out in the public sector is worthy of at least equal, if not greater, commendation.

There are obvious reasons why the government should spend some of its resources in this way. The level of the civil service is thereby raised markedly in two respects: first, by recruiting civil servants of high quality who spend their lives dealing substantively with new and important social problems; second, through their recruitment, that considerable part of the civil service operation which has some direct or even indirect contact with them is raised. Both those colleagues who are responsible for the administrative operations and those carrying on the more routine, supportive operations and activities are thereby affected favorably. This disposition is of crucial significance because of the increasingly central role that civil servants play in our culture. (It has been estimated that at present government employs 15 per cent of the work force and that this will rise to 20 per cent "within a few short years" [Caplin, 1967]).

Also, the more responsible general citizenry can take pride in knowing that the activities of such persons are being supported by themselves as taxpayers and in this way the status of the civil servant is raised in their eyes. And, finally, the government meets an obligation to participate, even if it be on a small scale, in fostering creativity—one of society's greatest needs. It helps in this way to lay the ground for progress, a function which can be initiated only by individuals or small groups of individuals. Since government is so important in our lives, it is obligated to be among those agencies in the forefront of this effort.

I suppose I am, by this confession of faith in government, revealing that I am something of a Populist (and, some of you would add, an unsuppressible optimist). I trust, however, that you will recognize that it is not a faith in government *qua* government, but, rather, a faith in a flexible government—a government that permits competent persons full freedom to range, one that provides a *people's*, not a *patron's*, support for the creative activities of individuals.

The attitude implied in the last remark derives from a "prejudice" I have against private foundations. Experience with them as both a recipient of grants and as a member of their boards and committees has somewhat attenuated, but not entirely overcome, this prejudice. Lest I be misunderstood, I wish to emphasize that I have been highly impressed with the spirit and substance of what they do. My objection rests entirely on principle. It seems more proper for us, the people, to use our *own* money (our tax money) for the support of the common weal than to use money which has been accumulated privately. Such private funds have accrued, with fairly few exceptions, from the exploitation of *our* resources, human and material and then been returned to us for philanthropic purposes. Perhaps from these allusive statements you can sense the basis for my admittedly ambivalent prejudice.[5]

In my reference to government support of the creative activities of the individual, I see a solution, in a way, to what Freud recognized as the battle between the self and the culture (Trilling, 1955). Here is one opportunity for the culture (the government) to show that it is a community which recognizes the importance of individuality, and, at least in this area, is ready to give individuality an avenue for

[5] I feel this ambivalence even more keenly at the present moment because I am in the process of reading Wilder Penfield's (1967) biography of Alan Gregg.

expression. Unless some such view is included in our aspirations for government, it is difficult to see how government activities will avoid being doomed to mediocrity, when excellence should be its goal.

Accepting the validity of the contention that government has a responsibility to support innovative activity, how is this to be actualized? Anyone having contact with government—or for that matter with any large organization—knows that many factors are inimical to such activity. The establishment and maintenance of a creative atmosphere involves great initial travail and unceasing vigilance thereafter. It requires continuing efforts both to reduce existing negative factors and to enhance positive ones.

In considering the negative factors in government operations, what immediately comes to mind is General Stilwell's celebrated translation of his dog-Latin "personal" motto *illegitimati non carborundum* as "Don't let the bastards grind you down." Many of us in government have, on occasion, been driven to such personalizing of the workings of bureaucracy. But it would appear to be an unfair characterization of the situation and the response of the "helpless" to repeated frustration. Only in the rarest of instances are the frustrating actions the result of personal malice. Although I adopt the Stilwell term *illegitimati* in this essay for my own purposes, I emphasize that for me it merely denotes the handicaps existing in the settings and the agents but does not have the personal reference it apparently had for him. It is not improper *persons* that I am concerned with, but improper *acts*—not the *who* but the *what*.

Our behavior in any organization, aside from that portion which derives most directly from ourselves, is controlled by (1) the structure of the setting, (2) the other personnel in the operation, and (3) the attitudes we adopt. *Illegitimati* are present in each of these categories. Our problem is to eliminate, or, at least, circumvent them. Hopefully my discussion of these negative qualities will bring the problems into a remedial perspective.

Rashdall (Rashdall, Powicke & Emden, 1936, p. 3), in his notable work on medieval European universities, said: "Ideals pass into great historic forces by embodying themselves in institutions." This is indeed so and accounts for our greatest social institutions. But these institutions maintain their viability only through continuing vigilance and support. Inevitably, especially with the passage of time, there is a tendency for organizations to stray from their standards. As new people come along "who know not Moses" and do not identify with him, the spirit behind the original institutionalization gets lost. The principles are replaced by ritualistic and formal properties; the initial spirit becomes dominated by the letter.

Unfortunately no liberal supreme court is available to emphasize this fundamental spirit and to reinterpret the institutions in the light of current needs. This kind of concretization into form, itself a bastardization of the spirit, also fathers many other *illegitimati*.

Because of its size, a government necessarily has to assume some kind of structure, usually a hierarchical one. In the legitimate need for control of the myriad required personnel, the system has to depend upon certain organizational schemes, such as those embodied in a civil service system. Although these institutional arrangements have many commendable aspects which are important, for they help to run the massive operation with reasonable efficiency, they, nevertheless, remain "clerk-oriented" and handicapping to the achievement of the particular and unusual purposes we have been considering. For the kinds of persons with whom we are concerned, neither the hierarchical nor the civil service structures are satisfactory, as they may be for the overwhelming majority of government personnel. In fact, throughout my career, both in the state and federal governments, I have found myself having to battle the civil service and use all kinds of stratagems to circumvent its (inevitable?) inflexibilities. I have usually been able to win these battles, so in saying this I am revealing some kind of strength in government. But I must admit it has been at a cost in time and effort that could have been used more profitably otherwise.

A relatively recent instance of this kind is the difficulty we have had in appointing research psychologists to the proper grade level. We have been particularly interested in recruiting persons who have had *both* clinical and experimental backgrounds. But since civil service regulations essentially hold that a person with two years of experience in each of two categories gets credit not for the four years of combined experience that we consider ideal for our particular needs, but rather for only two years of either one or the other, we have been frustrated in this effort.

The hierarchical organization of government results in a degree of impersonality which leaves the "impatient" person who is trying to achieve an important goal frustrated. And creative persons are by definition impatient persons. Time is their most important commodity. The frustration comes about because so many "guards" —deputies, assistants, secretaries—are placed around the official occupants of the successively higher boxes in the organization charts. No matter how sympathetic the hierarch might be with the goals of the persons in the boxes below him, communications often do not reach him, or are, at best, much delayed in reaching him. This holds especially for written communications.

Since the kinds of persons whom we are here considering place such value on time, they tend to be as stingy about the administrator's time as they are about their own. Hence, even if they would have no difficulty about getting the ear of the administrator, especially the one whose door is "always open," they settle for getting his eye. (And government, with its preference for "memos," abets this bias for the optical.) Frequently an important communication is lost on the desk of one of the guards—buried in that vast graveyard for memos sent "upstairs." At best, it may finally return so emaciated from its long period of inanition, that even when it does come back "approved," it is no longer viable or relevant, since the original intention is no longer pertinent.

There are many other limitations, some carrying peculiarly governmental overtones, which we may mention briefly. There is the tendency of a congress (or a state legislature) to view trips to essential scientific or professional meetings—especially foreign meetings—as "junkets." Salary level offers a problem which is perennial and ubiquitous, especially at the higher levels. Other numerous privileges which universities offer are not available to government personnel: the government provides no educational allowance for children, there is much greater restriction on consultations, and there is no freedom for the private publication of books and monographs based on work even when only partly done on government time. The denial of such privileges makes the initial salary differential even more onerous for the public servant. Perhaps most difficult to bear, however, is the slowness with which clearly needed change comes about. *Patience* seems to be the primary virtue with which a government employee must be endowed, whereas *im*patience, as I have already pointed out, is one of the creative investigator's essential hallmarks.

Another difficulty in many parts of government, which is less true of universities, is the impact of the hierarchical bureaucratic structure on the importance placed upon administrative and supervisory roles. This results in insufficient attention to what should be a fundamental principle: that a person be judged by his substantive contribution, as well as, or in place of, the number of persons he supervises.

The second group of *illegitimati* are the barriers to optimal performance erected by certain personnel. Unfortunately no organization can be ideally selective about personnel. In the administrative structure there are some who provide obstacles. These persons may, like the New Hampshire men that Emerson talked about, be basically too little for the tall mountains of government. Or they may be persons who, having come into government with considerable perspective, vigor, and ideals, have gradually let themselves be worn down by the system. They become "tired radicals," preoccupied with papers rather than with human understanding. Small people in minor positions may not be responsible for decisions, but in a complex organization they can, by the support they give to the natural bureaucratic delay and indecision, contribute to what essentially becomes a negative decision. Much more serious, however, are the small men in important positions whose individual qualities do not attain the level warranted by their official status. Their value systems are rather twisted; they are the ones who "will not go beyond their father's saying."

The third group of *illegitimati* are the images or expectations we ourselves set up. A government employee not only has his direct employers, the executives over him and the Congress, he is also a public servant, so that his ultimate employer is the citizen taxpayer. The government scientist who is sensitive to the needs of the public faces a serious dilemma. Because he recognizes that the citizen (and only to a lesser extent the citizen's representative) is interested in fairly quick "results," he is tempted to be drawn away from his natural and desirable long-term view. He falls back on a more immediate and "safer" attitude, one which is much less likely to invite criticism. This can end in a kind of static, "don't rock the boat" approach to problems, rather than a forthright attack according to his knowledge and expertness, and based on his own instincts. Or, because of the conflict created between the intellectual recognition of the importance of basic research and his awareness of the multitude of afflictions from which our society suffers, the underlying guilts of most scientists (who are, of course, also citizens) are aroused because they are involving themselves with "impractical" (basic) problems. Individual scientists may then overreact and be unduly arrogant about their "purity." In the administrative sector, this sensitivity to legislative overseeing and the power of the legislature in regard to appropriations can likewise create great immobilizing caution.

Even though I had intended to be brief in the description of these *illegitimati*, I see that I have not been. Though this relatively extended listing may sound formidable, I have presented them mainly for prophylactic purposes. They are *likely* sources of difficulty, and awareness of their potential appearance may help us either to avoid them altogether or squelch them when they first raise their heads. The fact is that in good organizations they can be avoided, overcome, or at least compensated for in many ways. So let us turn to the other side of the picture—the positive, and by far the more important side.

What can we do to set up and maintain an environment of excellence comparable to the best universities? A strenuous effort toward achieving positive goals and principles is called for. Most important is the cultivation of that spirit we spoke of —the spirit of flexibility, freedom, and creativeness. Where stimulating, productive environments are found, healthy attitudes can become tradition, and spirit, not form, has the possibility of becoming established. Autonomy, support for programs and protection against interference help to develop and maintain this spirit.

One specific, underlying requirement for creating the conditions we seek is the achievement of a proper balance at the leadership level between the substantive and managerial components. Experience has convinced me that in any large-scale, knowledge-producing operation of quality there must be some division of labor between those who provide the knowledge—the producers—and those who provide the supporting structure for the development of knowledge—the managers. Although the words "producers" and "managers" have industrial connotations, they fit the needs of our present discussion admirably, so I shall employ them. I use them in their original respective senses of "begetter" and "handler." Being a good manager of such an enterprise requires profound understanding of the producers' attitudes and goals, and appreciation of the best ways of supporting them—indeed, an empathy which is a kind of creativity of its own. Managing is a full-time job in itself. I have found that those who try to combine managing with simultaneous efforts at contributing substantively, generally end up frustrated. When creative managers join together with creative producers of knowledge in setting general policy we approach the ideal situation.

While we ask the managers to understand the producers' attitudes and goals, we must also recognize that frequently administrators act in ways which work against the goals of the producers solely because of ignorance of what the producer is after. This often results from insufficient communication with the administration, either due to oversight or to reactive overemphasis by the producer on "independence." It is also important that just as he expects a sympathetic attitude from the manager, so the producer must make an effort to understand the basis for the action of the administrator before he permits himself to become frustrated.

In the end, however, the spirit of an institution derives from the *actual* persons involved in the operation. What qualities, then, should characterize the two major groups of participants—the administrators and the producers?

Eric Ashby (1964), the Master of Clare College at Cambridge, in an insightful article a few years ago stated well some of the issues with regard to university administration. He said that four qualities were essential in a good college administrator: (1) good administrators administer; (2) they refrain from making decisions which other people ought to make; (3) they conceal certain of their bright ideas; and (4) they understand and acknowledge divided loyalties. Such qualities apply equally to the government operations we are discussing.

Administrators administer. Clearly at certain times, in any large operation, the decisions come from the administrator. This is true regardless of how much common thinking through of problems has previously taken place in councils composed of senior personnel. In the end, decisions must be made by the administrator if he is to remain effective, especially decisions between different parts of the organization or those involving the organization as a whole.

Administrators refrain from making decisions which other people ought to make. Naturally, decisions like the ones just discussed are managerial territory. But decisions relating to substantive problems—such as the nature of the research, both as to subject matter and method; or the content and method of teaching—are under the producer's jurisdiction. In these areas there must be complete freedom for the producing group.

Administrators conceal their bright ideas. Good administrators are bound to have good ideas which deserve serious consideration from those who are carrying out the substantive part of the program. Because he recognizes the crucial importance of the separation of the managerial and substantive, the administrator needs to tread cautiously with what he does about such ideas. He must get them across unobtrusively, feeding them into the organization in a most tactful fashion. Sometimes he can enlist the quiet help of some of the producers to put the ideas across, either directly or in modified form. However, in the execution of his ideas it is important for him to maintain the boundaries between the managerial and the productive divisions.

Administrators acknowledge divided loyalties. Professional persons necessarily have loyalties to their professions as well as to their institutions. Ordinarily these are greater to the profession, a fact which a good institution recognizes. On occasion, especially in the context of this recognition, an institution of a pioneer nature, having its own important social goals, can build up loyalty to itself even transcending that to the producers' profession.

The good administrator recognizes that there is a natural tendency in hierarchical government operations for policy to be determined at the top and to percolate downward. He, however, does whatever he can to encourage policy to originate below at a professional level and to permit it to percolate upward. This recognition of "grass roots" opinion, as represented in assemblies of scientists, in councils, or even in the smaller group units represented, for example, by laboratories and sections, does a great deal to strengthen the morale of an institution.

We now turn to the other group in the operation—the career producer personnel. These producers should temperamentally be inner-directed, responsible "irreconcilables," restless and pioneering. More specifically, they should possess, on the one hand, the qualities that lead to high achievement, which are capacity, high aspiration levels, and high environmental expectation surrounds; and, on the other, they should also possess certain balancing superego controls, including a group superego, and two different kinds of internal superego.

Aside from the capacity, which we take for granted, two different kinds of motivating factors play a role in the goals these producers set—those coming from within and those from without. The commitments from within are closely associated with expectations from without—those set up by the environment. In regard to the former, such persons work toward aspiration levels which are in general considerably, although still realistically, above their achievement levels. They set goals and ideals which stretch them greatly, drawing them close to their capacity level. They are driven not only by intellectual demands but also by a certain kind of "guts" demand for achievement which comes from a dissatisfaction with how far their environment has been able to achieve the ultimate social goals with which they identify.

The other aspect of this motivation is the sensitivity they have to the explicit and implicit needs of the environment. One of the most striking examples of rising to almost insuperable environmental expectations—one that has for me served as *the* example of this kind of situation—is that of Cabeza de Vaca. The Indians among whom this intrepid explorer of the sixteenth century traveled, treated him as a god and expected celestial healing powers from him. And, as Terrell, one of his biographers, says, in the "most vital act of his life [he] became *Dr*. Cabeza de Vaca [1964, p. 127]." So do our producers select environments which set up extraordinary, if not such equally demanding, requirements.

But these three qualities necessary for achievement are not enough. Both the producers and the "good" environments they select afford so wide a range for individual enterprise, provide such an "abyss of freedom," that hazards are involved. To protect against these, some controls—essentially ethical ones involving the superego in some form—are needed. Such restraints come both from the person's environment and from within himself.

A major environmental control exists in the form of a group superego—the opinions and attitudes of respected colleagues working in the same institution, persons with a similar outlook who are of the same general level as oneself. Such controls are essential and are sought out by the mature person since he recognizes his own weaknesses and his need for group support.

In addition to such external control, however, one must call on internal superego controls. One form of this is the *alter ego*, which is a kind of partially externalized superego. It is constantly checking to see that we do not take ourselves too seriously, do not assume the possession of qualities beyond our capacities, qualities with which we either endow ourselves or with which the environment endows us, as in the Cabeza de Vaca example. What we are essentially dealing with here is the objectivity that comes from a good sense of humor that catches up with us every once in a while, and helps to keep us in line.

The third principle of control is another variant of the internal superego. Here I have to call, for clarification, on the Yiddish phrase: "*Es passt nit.*" A literal translation of this phrase is "It isn't appropriate" or "It isn't fitting." Although it has distinct affinity to *noblesse oblige*, for me it has both a broader and a deeper scope. It is much more democratic since it is not tied to status, either of person or class. It is impersonal, it is not demanding or peremptory, it sets up no obligations, it is not moralizing. It essentially says: "Let me call your attention to the impropriety of what you are about to do or not to do, and then *you* decide whether you still want to go ahead." It is tied up with the essence of socialization, for it implies that joining the human race automatically involved one in certain responsibilities. Sometimes "*far menshen*" (*Es passt nit far menshen*) is added to the phrase. Since "*far*" is ambiguous in Yiddish—meaning either "before" or "for"—it may also be translated: "It is inappropriate *before* people," thus carrying with it some aspect of *external* superego control—a "shame" motive. I myself favor the "for" translation "It is not the human thing to do"—thus giving it the more significant *internal* superego cast—a guilt (responsibility) motive.

Producers in whom these characteristics and these controls are coalesced are persons who can effectively carry on the type of operation we have been considering. This is especially true when they work in a group. For the kinds of functions we have been talking about, colleagues are indispensable. The functions called for are too pioneering, too demanding, and too full of frustration to be carried out alone. One needs the social support that comes from colleagues who, like oneself, are not only ready to battle the negative aspects of bureaucracy but, more important, have the same high aspirations and standards. Such persons are eternal but realistic rebels, persons who do not rebel for the sake of rebellion, but rebel in the service of the ego. Such a group only becomes complete and effective with the addition of colleagues of similar spirit who serve as managers. Then we have the makings of an "ideal" organization.

I might close with two points about the relationship between these crucial groups—the producers and the managers. First, this relationship must be founded on professional, not political, grounds—on honesty and straightforwardness with regard to scientific needs and not on the basis of presumed expediency. I believe that the producer has an obligation forthrightly to present his needs and his views as a scientist; he should deliver his punches directly and not feint. *His* decisions are not administrative decisions. He should therefore not concern himself at all with trying to outguess the various levels of administration as to their receptiveness to his requests. His responsibility is to present his *complete* and optimal program and then leave it to administrative review to determine what can or cannot be implemented. At all times, his stance is that of the *producer* of knowledge.

Second, there are always bound to be instances of disagreements between the two groups. Usually because of the nature of the division of territory, the disagreements concern issues about which the producer feels strongly but which the manager views differently. Administrative considerations are frequently present which the individual producer may not be as sensitive to as the manager, even when they are stated explicitly. Sometimes they have to remain implicit. Whatever the case, disappointment is bound to ensue. These disappointments, however, do not portend the end of the world; such occasional dark periods do pass![6] Only when these instances multiply is there basis for concern. What *is* important is that there

[6] Cf. Alan Gregg's comment about the "devouring canker, self-pitying indignation" (Penfield, 1967), and his appropriate psychosomatic quotation from Shakespeare's *Timon of Athens* (act III, sc. 5): "Ne'er prefer your injuries to your heart, lest you bring it into danger."

be complete frankness on both sides, that the producer clearly indicate his attitudes and disagreement, and that the manager be equally forthright.

I have tried in this presentation to combine the consideration of general principles and concrete illustrations. Since I have perhaps leaned more in the direction of principles, let me end up on a more concrete note. And I draw for this on my most recent experience with government, that at NIH. Despite the fact that practically all of our personnel—research personnel in our case—have had attractive offers of university positions at much higher salary and perquisite levels, relatively few have elected to leave. I have often asked myself why.

First and foremost I would put their freedom to devote themselves fully to their own research. The amount of time they wish to devote to teaching is up to them; and the administrative load, even for section chiefs, is minimal. Part of this freedom is also based on the freedom of not having periodically to send in grant proposals! Although they recognize that their salaries and perquisites are not those of the university, they also recognize that in "work assignments" they have a sabbatical perquisite which is superior to that generally available in universities. Some who have spent periods at good universities have been able to observe that the greenness of the university grass from the distance is to some extent due to the plantains it contains. Because it is so important I must, however, return to the very first point—they remain at NIH primarily because of the opportunity to devote themselves fully to their own research.

What have I essentially been saying? The many recognized defects in government can be prevented from becoming integral if constant vigilance is exercised in warding them off. We can, of course, become enchanted even with what is minimally available by comparing our situation with the opposite end of the continuum, such as the sorrowful circumstances of some Iron Curtain scientists that have recently been described. But we must not be guided by such comparisons. We can do nothing else but look in the opposite direction—set *our* aspirations for *our* government toward obtaining the utmost support for basic activities. This calls for the recruitment and support of creative producers and creative managers who, while hacking away at the underbrush of bureaucracy, are mainly occupied on the frontiers of knowledge to advance the long-term needs of the citizens.

I have been fortunate that the three government positions I have held have been in such settings. That is why I can with sincere assurance state that the ideal can be closely approximated.

Epilogue

What can I add in closing this volume in the context of today's tempestuous world —a world that has in passing disturbed the steady professional development of clinical psychology along "natural" lines while at the same time multiplying the demands for clinical psychologists to meet so widened a range of activities at all social levels. Has what I have been saying and implying about clinical psychology, about preparation for its practice, about its relationships with other professions, become largely outdated? Is it only the historical account that remains relevant? Time has indeed forcefully removed the encumbering quotes from the "perilous" of my introductory remarks.

The readers of this volume will have recognized that, at one level, this series of papers has served as a projective device. Aside from the direct personal history found in the few autobiographical bits, much of the rest has provided even more in the way of indirect hints about the personal background behind the professional opinions I have expressed. They have suggested the various positive influences that have "dogged" my career: the early involvement, the largely self-determined clinical education, the early professional functioning, the few but highly benign work environments, and the many satisfying interprofessional contacts outside the latter. But they have also hinted at negative aspects of my association with nonpsychological colleagues: the low level of response of some—whether due to ignorance or "perversity" (or both!), the regressive, defensive, "crowd" characteristics that reveal themselves even in respected associates when issues of *Fach* competition come to the fore in group assembled, and the encapsulated prejudices concerning proprietary rights in therapy or diagnosis or ethics or autonomy or administration which medical education and practice so often unfortunately encourage, at times even in highly regarded colleagues.

These negative expressions have elicited immediate challenge and disagreement from me, stated as objectively as possible. But following these rejoinders—their reasonableness often recognized and sometimes even admitted—the antagonisms have been permitted to fade into the background to take their proper place in the context of relationships so predominantly positive, exciting, and respect-inspiring. Have I been unusually fortunate in my experience? I trust not.

In any case, I can only comment on the basis of my own background. I have been consistently fortified by convictions about being a psychologist first and a clinician second, about the importance of substantial training in practice as well as in theory in optimal settings, about the necessity of a generic foundation, and about the primacy of research based on broad human field experience as the most appropriate contribution from among the several that the psychologist-clinician is prepared to make. I have, nevertheless, fought for the privilege of other clinical psychologists to make the particular contributions that their backgrounds and predilections fitted them for.

A teacher, however, always wants more than merely to express his experientially- and temperamentally-based predilections. He hopes to project his own views into his listeners, to make them over in his own image. As a pedagogic device, "Do as I do!" is obviously preferable to "Do as I say!". But there still remains a lingering doubt about its validity. What a teacher really implies by this formula is: "Observe what I do and then decide on the basis of your own background and experience what *you* should do." For aside from the differences in the complex intertwining of background and experience and temperament that lead to the formation of *Weltanschauungen*, there is always the problem of the setting in which one has to apply them. This rapidly changing world may be calling for quite different approaches and we must allow for such changes. Nevertheless, some of us believe that there *are* a few eternal verities. Among these is quality of performance.

What we need, then, is a clear strong statement from one protagonist, followed by equally clear strong statements of the differing views of his contemporaries, based, as they will be, on varying combinations of temperament, experience, and background. The conflicting positions that result must then be turned over to the current generation for their consideration and action.

Following these principles, then, I have had my say, providing in passing some suggestions as to both the explicit and implicit processes that led to the development of my views. I leave it for my contemporary oldsters to do the same for themselves. And, finally, we must leave it to the youngsters to take what they will from our respective recommendations and go on from there.

Bibliography

Abelson, P. Are the tame cats in charge? Omens of Orwell. *Saturday Review*, January 1, 1966, *49*, 100–103.

Adler, F. *An ethical philosophy of life*. New York : Appleton, 1919.

Adrian, E. D. The mental and physical origins of behavior. *International Journal of Psycho Analysis*, 1946, *27*, 1–6.

Adrian, E. D. Physiology. *Scientific American*, 1950, *183*, 71–76.

Albee, G. W. American psychology in the sixties. *American Psychologist*, 1963, *18*, 90–95.

Albee, G. W. Psychological center. In E. L. Hoch, A. O. Ross, & C. L. Winder (Eds.), *Professional preparation of clinical psychologists*. Washington : American Psychological Association, 1966. Pp. 140–142.

Allen, R. B. *Medical education and the changing order*. New York: Commonwealth Fund, 1946.

Allport, G. W. *Personality: A psychological interpretation*. New York: Holt, 1937.

Allport, G. W. The psychologist's frame of reference. *Psychological Bulletin*, 1940, *37*, 1–28.

Allport, G. W. (Ed.) Symposium: Psychoanalysis as seen by analyzed psychologists. *Journal of Abnormal and Social Psychology*, 1940, *35*, 3–55, 139–225, 305–323.

American Association for Applied Psychology, Committee on Training in Clinical (Applied) Psychology, (T. V. Moore, Chairman). Proposed program of professional training in clinical psychology. *Journal of Consulting Psychology*, 1943, *7*, 23–26.

American Psychoanalytic Association, Board on Professional Standards. Annual Report of the Committee of Training Standards in Relation to Training for Research. *Journal of the American Psychoanalytic Association*, 1957, *5*, 713.

American Psychological Association, Committee on American Board of Examiners in Professional Psychology, (C. Jacobsen, Chairman). Report. *American Psychologist*, 1946, *1*, 510–517.

American Psychological Association, Committee on Clinical Psychology (L. F. Shaffer, Chairman). Annual report, 1946. *American Psychologist*, 1946, *1*, 520–522.

American Psychological Association, Committee on Counselor Training. Recommended standards for training counseling psychologists at the doctoral level: Report of the conference on the training of counseling psychologists, Northwestern University, August 29–30, 1951. *American Psychologist*, 1952, *7*, 175–181.

American Psychological Association, Committee on the Training of Clinical Psychologists, Clinical Section, (A. W. Brown, Chairman). The definition of clinical psychology and standards of training for clinical psychologists. *Psychological Clinic*, 1935, *23*, 1–8.

American Psychological Association, Committee on Training in Clinical Psychology, (D. Shakow, Chairman). Recommended graduate training program in clinical psychology. *American Psychologist*, 1947, *2*, 539–558. (Reprinted: In V. Raimy [Ed.], *Training in clinical psychology*. New York: Prentice-Hall, 1950. Pp. 209–243.)

American Psychological Association, Committee on Training in Clinical Psychology. Clinical training facilities: 1948. *American Psychologist*, 1948, *3*, 317–318.

American Psychological Association, Committee on Training in Clinical Psychology. Doctoral training programs in clinical psychology: 1949. *American Psychologist*, 1949, *4*, 331–341.

American Psychological Association, Policy and Planning Board, (E. R. Hilgard, Chairman). Annual report, 1947. *American Psychologist*, 1947, *2*, 191–198.

American Psychological Association & American Association for Applied Psychology, Committee on Graduate and Professional Training, Subcommittee on Graduate Internship Training, (D. Shakow, Chairman). Subcommittee report on graduate internship training in psychology. *Journal of Consulting Psychology*, 1945, *9*, 243–266.

Ashby, E. A university presidency: What it takes. *Saturday Review*, November 21, 1964, *47*, 58–59, 77–78.

Astin, A. V. Basic research in government laboratories. In D. Wolfle (Ed.), *Symposium on basic research*. Washington: American Association for the Advancement of Science, 1959. Pp. 143–157.

Balint, M. On the psychoanalytic training system. *International Journal of Psycho-Analysis*, 1948, *29*, 167–173.

Balint, M. Analytic training and training analysis. *International Journal of Psycho-Analysis*, 1954, *35*, 157–162.

Barker, R. G., & Wright, H. F. Psychological ecology and the problem of psychosocial development. *Child Development*, 1949, *20*, 132–143.

Barker, R. G., & Wright, H. F. *One boy's day*. New York: Harper, 1951.

Barker, R. G., Wright, B. A., & Gonick, M. R. *Adjustment to Physical Handicap and Illness: A Survey of the Social Psychology of Physique and Disability*. Bulletin 55. New York: Social Science Research Council, 1946.

Benjamin, J. D. Methodological considerations in the validation and elaboration of psychoanalytical personality theory. *American Journal of Orthopsychiatry*, 1950, *20*, 139–156.

Bentley, A. F. The human skin: Philosophy's last line of defense. *Philosophy of Science*, 1941, *8*, 1–19.

Bergman, P. Has psychoanalysis become too complacent? Review of B. D. Lewin & H. Ross, *Psychoanalytic education in the United States*. *Contemporary Psychology*, 1961, *6*, 265–266.

Bernfeld, S. Freud's earliest theories and the school of Helmholtz. *Psychoanalytic Quarterly*, 1944, *13*, 341–362.

Binger, C. *The doctor's job*. New York: Norton, 1945.

Beverly, B. I. The effect of illness on emotional development. *Pediatrics*, 1936, *8*, 533–543.

Boring, E. G. The psychology of controversy. *Psychological Review*, 1929, *36*, 97–121.

Boring, E. G. *A history of experimental psychology.* (2nd ed.) New York: Appleton-Century-Crofts, 1950.

Born, M. Physics. *Scientific American*, 1950, *183*, 28–31.

Boston Society of Clinical Psychologists, Special Committee on the Training of Clinical Psychologists. Tentative proposals for the training of clinical psychologists. November 11, 1937. Unpublished.

Bridgman, P. W. *The logic of modern physics.* New York: Macmillan, 1928.

Brierley, M. *Trends in psychoanalysis.* London: Hogarth Press, 1951.

Broad, C. D. The "nature" of a continuant. In H. Feigl & W. Sellers, *Readings in philosophical analysis.* New York: Appleton-Century-Crofts, 1949. Pp. 472–481.

Bronowski, J. *Science and human values.* New York: Julian Messner, 1956.

Brophy, B. *Black ship to hell.* New York: Harcourt, Brace & World, 1962.

Brotemarkle, R. A. Clinical psychology, 1896–1946. *Journal of Consulting Psychology*, 1947, *11*, 1–4.

Bruner, J. S., & Krech, D. (Eds.), *Perception and personality: A symposium.* Durham, N. C.: Duke University Press, 1950.

Brunswik, E. *Systematic and representative design of psychological experiments.* Berkeley, Calif.: University of California Press, 1947.

Brunswik, E. The conceptual framework of psychology. *International Encyclopedia of Unified Sciences*, 1951, *1*, No. 10.

Bryan, W. A. *Administrative psychiatry.* New York: Norton, 1936.

Cabot, R. C. *Social work: Essays on the meeting-ground of doctor and social worker.* Boston: Houghton Mifflin, 1919.

Caplin, M. M. Personnel crisis. Letter to the editor. *The Washington Post*, August 19, 1967.

Cattell, J. McK. Retrospect: Psychology as a profession. *Journal of Consulting Psychology*, 1937, *1*, 1–3.

Commission on Graduate Medical Education. *Report.* Chicago: The Commission, 1940.

Commission on Medical Education. *Final Report.* New York: Office of the Director of the Study, 1932.

Committee on Medicine and the Changing Order. *Medicine in the changing order.* New York: Commonwealth Fund, 1947.

Conant, J. B. The role of science in our unique society. *Science*, 1948, *107*, 77–83.

Conference on an Ideal Program of Training for Psychotherapists. Gould House, Ardsley-on-Hudson, N. Y., under the sponsorship of New York University, March 21–24, 1963. New York: International Universities Press, 1969, in press.

Cook, S. W. The psychologist of the future: Scientist, professional, or both. *American Psychologist*, 1958, *13*, 635–644.

Cope, O. *Man, mind and medicine. The doctor's education.* Philadelphia: Lippincott, 1968.

Cope, O., & Zacharias, J. *Medical education reconsidered.* Philadelphia: Lippincott, 1966.

Cowles, E. The American Journal of Psychology. *American Journal of Insanity*, 1887–88, *44*, 544–546.

Cowles, E. The advancement of psychiatry in America. *American Journal of Insanity*, 1895–96, *52*, 384.

Crothers, B. (Ed.) Psychology and psychiatry in pediatrics: The problem. Report of the Subcommittee on Psychology and Psychiatry. *White House conference on child health and protection.* New York: Century, 1932.

Cutts, N. E. (Ed.) *School psychologists at mid-century.* Washington: American Psychological Association, 1955.

Darling, F. F. The ecological approach to the social sciences. *American Scientist,* 1951, *39*, 244–254.

David, H. P. Clinical psychology in other lands. In D. Brower & L. E. Abt (Eds.), *Progress in clinical psychology.* Vol. 3. New York: Grune & Stratton, 1958. Pp. 235–247.

Degan, J. W. Dimensions of functional psychoses. *Psychometric Monograph,* 1952, No. 6.

Dewey, J. *Human nature and conduct.* New York: Holt, 1922.

Dollard, J., & Miller, N. E. *Personality and psychotherapy.* New York: McGraw-Hill, 1950.

Eiseley, L. *The mind as nature.* New York: Harper & Row, 1962.

English, H. B. Fundamentals and fundamentalism in the preparation of applied psychologists. *Journal of Consulting Psychology,* 1941, *5*, 1–13.

Erikson, E. H. Growth and crises of the healthy personality. In E. H. Erikson, Identity and the life cycle. *Psychological Issues,* 1959, *1* (1, Monograph 1). Pp. 50–100.

Erikson, E. H. *Childhood and society.* (2nd ed.) New York: Norton, 1963.

Erikson, E. H. *Insight and responsibility.* New York : Norton, 1964.

Eysenck, H. J. The effects of psychotherapy: An evaluation. *Journal of Consulting Psychology,* 1952, *16*, 319–324.

Eysenck, H. J. The effects of psychotherapy. In H. J. Eysenck (Ed.), *Handbook of abnormal psychology.* New York: Basic Books, 1961. Pp. 697–725. (a)

Eysenck, H. J. (Ed.), *Handbook of abnormal psychology.* New York: Basic Books, 1961. (b)

Felix, R. H. Mental hygiene and public health. *American Journal of Orthopsychiatry,* 1948, *18*, 679–684.

Fernberger, S. W. The history of the psychological clinic. In R. A. Brotemarkle (Ed.), *Clinical psychology, studies in honor of Lightner Witmer.* Philadelphia: University of Pennsylvania Press, 1931. Pp. 10–36.

Fernberger, S. W. The American Psychological Association: A historical survey, 1892–1930. *Psychological Bulletin,* 1932, *29*, 1–89.

Finger, F. W. The certification of clinical psychologists in Virginia. *American Psychologist,* 1946, *1*, 395–398.

Fisher, R. A. *The design of experiments.* (2nd ed.) Edinburgh: Oliver & Boyd, 1937.

Flexner, A. *Medical education in the United States and Canada.* Bulletin No. 4. New York: Carnegie Foundation for the Advancement of Teaching, 1910.

Flexner, A. *Medical education.* New York: Macmillan, 1925.

Flugel, J. C. *A hundred years of psychology.* London: Duckworth, 1951.

Flugel, J. C. *Man, morals and society.* London: Penguin, 1955.

Frankfurter, F. *Felix Frankfurter reminisces.* (Recorded in talks with H. B. Phillips) Garden City, N. Y.: Doubleday, 1962.

French, L. M. *Psychiatric social work.* New York: Commonwealth Fund, 1940.

Frenkel-Brunswik, E. Contributions to the analysis and synthesis of knowledge. *Proceedings of the American Academy of Arts and Sciences,* 1954, *80*, 271–347.

Freud, S. (1887–1902) *The origins of psychoanalysis: Letters to Wilhelm Fliess, drafts and notes: 1887–1902.* London: Imago, 1954.

Freud, S. (1910) "Wild" psychoanalysis. *Standard edition.* Vol. 11. London: Hogarth Press, 1957. Pp. 219–227.

Freud, S. (1923) The ego and the id. *Standard edition.* Vol. 19. London: Hogarth Press, 1961. Pp. 1–66.

Freud, S. (1926 [1924]) Inhibitions, symptoms and anxiety. *Standard edition.* Vol. 20. London: Hogarth Press, 1959. Pp. 75–175.

Freud, S. (1926) The question of lay analysis. *Standard edition.* Vol. 20. London: Hogarth Press, 1959. Pp. 177–258.

Freud, S. (1932) *New introductory lectures on psychoanalysis.* New York: Norton, 1933.

Freud, S. (1938) Splitting of the ego in the defensive process. *Collected papers.* Vol. 5 London: Hogarth Press, 1950. Pp. 372–375.

Freud, S. (1940 [1938]) *An outline of psychoanalysis.* New York: Norton, 1949.

Fromm, E. *Psychoanalysis and religion.* New Haven: Yale University Press, 1950.

Gardner, J. W. *Excellence: Can we be equal and excellent too?* New York: Harper & Row, 1961.

Gardner, J. W. *Self-renewal: The individual and the innovative society.* New York: Harper & Row, 1963.

Ginsburg, E. L. The training and function of a psychiatric social worker in a clinical setting. In M. R. Harrower (Ed.), *Training in clinical psychology.* New York: Josiah Macy, Jr., Foundation, 1947. Pp. 31–40.

Glover, E. Medical psychology or academic (normal) psychology: A problem in orientation. *British Journal of Medical Psychology,* 1934, *14,* 31–49.

Goddard, H. H. In the beginning. *Training School Bulletin,* 1943, *40,* 154–161.

Gregg, A. *The furtherance of medical research.* New Haven: Yale University Press, 1941.

Gregg, A. (Chairman) *The place of psychology in an ideal university.* The report of the University Commission to advise on the future of psychology at Harvard. Cambridge: Harvard University Press, 1947.

Gregg, A. The limitations of psychiatry. *American Journal of Psychiatry,* 1948, *104,* 513–522.

Gregg, A. The place of psychoanalysis in medicine. In F. Alexander & H. Ross (Eds.), *Twenty years of psychoanalysis.* New York: Norton, 1953. Pp. 28–49.

Group for the Advancement of Psychiatry. *Report of the committee on psychiatric social work* (Report No. 2), 1948. (a)

Group for the Advancement of Psychiatry. *Report on medical education* (Report No. 3), March, 1948. (b)

Hall, G. S. Laboratory of the McLean Hospital, Somerville, Mass. *American Journal of Insanity,* 1894–95, *51,* 358–364.

Hanfmann, E., & Kasanin, J. Conceptual thinking in schizophrenia. *Nervous and Mental Disease Monographs,* 1942, No. 67.

Harlow, H. F. The formation of learning sets. *Psychological Review,* 1949, *56,* 51–65.

Harrower, M. R. (Ed.), *Training in clinical psychology: Minutes of the first conference.* New York: Josiah Macy, Jr., Foundation, 1947.

Hartmann, H. Psychoanalysis and moral values. New York: International Universities Press, 1960.

Hartwell, S. W. *Fifty-five "bad" boys.* New York: Knopf, 1931.

Healy, W. *The individual delinquent.* Boston: Little, Brown, 1915.

Healy, W. Twenty-five years of child guidance. In *Studies from the Institute for Juvenile Research*, Series C, No. 256. Chicago: Illinois Department of Public Welfare, 1934. Pp. 1–2.

Hebb, D. O. *The organization of behavior*. New York: Wiley, 1949.

Heiser, K. F. Certification of psychologists in Connecticut. *Psychological Bulletin*, 1945, *42*, 624–630.

Hendrick, I. Primary facilities in psychoanalytic psychiatry. In M. R. Harrower (Ed.), *Training in clinical psychology*. New York: Josiah Macy, Jr., Foundation, 1947. Pp. 74–79.

Herberg, W. Freud, the revisionists, and social reality. In B. Nelson (Ed.), *Freud and the 20th century*. New York: Meridian, 1957. Pp. 143–163.

Hilgard, E. R. *Theories of learning*. New York: Appleton-Century-Crofts, 1948.

Hoch, A. Kraepelin on psychological experimentation in psychiatry. *American Journal of Insanity*, 1895–96, *52*, 387–396.

Hoch, E. L., & Darley, J. G. A case at law. *American Psychologist*, 1962, *17*, 623–654.

Hoch, E. L., Ross, A. O., & Winder, C. L. (Eds.) *Professional preparation of clinical psychologists*. (Proceedings of the Conference on the Professional Preparation of Clinical Psychologists meeting at the Center for Continuing Education, Chicago, Ill., Aug. 27–Sept. 1, 1965.) Washington: American Psychological Association, 1966.

Holmes, A. *The conservation of the child*. Philadelphia: Lippincott, 1912.

Hoskins, R. G. *The biology of schizophrenia*. New York: Norton, 1946.

Hull, C. L. *Principles of behavior*. New York: Appleton-Century, 1943.

Hunter, W. S. On the professional training of psychologists. *Psychological Review*, 1941, *48*, 498–523.

Hurd, H. M. The new McLean Hospital. *American Journal of Insanity*, 1895–96, *52*, 502.

Hurd, H. M. *The institutional care of the insane in the United States and Canada*. Baltimore: Johns Hopkins Press, 1916.

Huston, P. E. The reflex time of the patellar tendon reflex in normal and schizophrenic subjects. *Journal of General Psychology*, 1935, *13*, 3–41.

Huston, P. E. An orientation for clinical psychology. *Journal of Consulting Psychology*, 1948, *12*, 221–227.

Huston, P. E., & Shakow, D. Learning capacity in schizophrenia. *American Journal of Psychiatry*, 1949, *105*, 881–888.

Huston, P. E., Shakow, D., & Erickson, M. H. A study of hypnotically induced complexes by means of the Luria technique. *Journal of General Psychology*, 1934, *11*, 65–97.

Huston, P. E., Shakow, D., & Riggs, L. A. Studies of motor function in schizophrenia. II. Reaction time. *Journal of General Psychology*, 1937, *16*, 39–82.

Huxley, J. Preface. In J. Huxley (Ed.), *The humanist frame*. New York: Harper, 1961. Pp. 5–7.

International Psycho-analytical Association. (Various authors.) Discussion of lay analysis. *International Journal of Psycho-Analysis*, 1927, *8*, 174–283, 392–401.

Israel, H. E., & Goldstein, B. Operationism in psychology. *Psychological Review*, 1944, *51*, 177–188.

Jacobsen, C. F., Wolfe, J. B., & Jackson, T. A. An experimental analysis of the functions of the frontal association areas in primates. *Journal of Nervous and Mental Disease*, 1935, *82*, 1–14.

James, H. (Ed.) *Letters of William James.* Vol. 2. Boston: Atlantic Monthly Press, 1920.

James, W. *The principles of psychology.* Vol. 1. New York: Holt, 1890.

Joint Commission on Mental Illness and Health. *Action for mental health.* New York: Basic Books, 1961.

Jones, E. *Sigmund Freud: Life and work.* Vol. 3. *The last phase, 1919–1939.* London: Hogarth Press, 1957.

Jones, H. E. *Development in adolescence.* New York: Appleton-Century, 1943.

Kaplan, A. Freud and modern philosophy. In B. Nelson (Ed.), *Freud and the 20th century.* New York: Meridian, 1957. Pp. 209–229.

Kaufmann, W. *From Shakespeare to existentialism.* New York: Doubleday (Anchor), 1960.

Kelly, E. L. Research on the selection of clinical psychologists. *Journal of Clinical Psychology,* 1947, *3,* 39–42.

Kelly, E. L. Clinical psychology—1960: Report of survey findings. *American Psychological Association Division of Clinical Psychology Newsletter,* 1961, *14* (1), 1–11.

Klopfer, B., & Kelley, D. M. *The Rorschach technique.* Yonkers-on-Hudson, N. Y.: World Book, 1942.

Kluckhohn, C., & Murray, H. A. (Eds.), *Personality in nature, society and culture.* New York: Knopf, 1948.

Koch, S. Epilogue. In S. Koch (Ed.), *Psychology: A study of a science.* Vol. 5. New York: McGraw-Hill, 1959. Pp. 729–788.

Köhler, W. The obsessions of normal people. Paper presented at the inauguration of the Graduate School of Arts and Sciences, Brandeis University, Waltham, Mass., 1958.

Krech, D. Notes toward a psychological theory. *Journal of Personality,* 1949, *18,* 66–87.

Krech, D. Dynamic systems as open neurological systems. *Psychological Review,* 1950, *57,* 345–361. (a)

Krech, D. Dynamic systems, psychological fields, and hypothetical constructs. *Psychological Review,* 1950, *57,* 283–290. (b)

Kris, E. The significance of Freud's earliest studies. *International Journal of Psychoanalysis,* 1950, *31,* 1–9.

Kubie, L. S. Elements in the medical curriculum which are essential in the training for psychotherapy. In M. R. Harrower (Ed.), *Training in clinical psychology.* New York: Josiah Macy, Jr., Foundation, 1947. Pp. 46–51.

Kubie, L. S. The pros and cons of a new profession: A doctorate in medical psychology. *Texas Reports on Biology and Medicine,* 1954, *12,* 692–737.

LaPiere, R. *The Freudian ethic.* London: Allen & Unwin, 1960.

Laski, H. *The American democracy.* New York: Viking Press, 1948.

Lederberg, J. Some problems of instant medicine. *Saturday Review,* May 6, 1967, *50,* 66–70.

Levy, D. Experiments on the sucking reflex and social behavior of dogs. *American Journal of Orthopsychiatry,* 1934, *4,* 203–224.

Lewin, B. D., & Ross, H. *Psychoanalytic education in the United States.* New York: Norton, 1960.

Lewin, K. Vorsatz, Wille und Bedürfnis. *Psychologische Forschung,* 1926, *7,* 294–385. (Reprinted: Will and needs. In W. D. Ellis, *A source book of Gestalt psychology.* New York: Humanities Press, 1950.)

Lewin, K. *A dynamic theory of personality.* New York: McGraw-Hill, 1935. (a)

Lewin, K. The research center for group dynamics at the Massachusetts Institute of Technology. *Sociometry*, 1935, *8*, 126–136. (b)

Lewin, K. *Principles of topological psychology*. New York: McGraw-Hill, 1936.

Liddell, H. S. Conditioned reflex method and experimental neurosis. In J. McV. Hunt, *Personality and the behavior disorders*. Vol. 1. New York: Ronald Press, 1944. Pp. 389–412.

Lippitt, R. An experimental study of the effect of democratic and authoritarian group atmospheres. *University of Iowa Studies in Child Welfare*, 1940, *16*, (3), 43–198.

Louttit, C. M. The nature of clinical psychology. *Psychological Bulletin*, 1939, *36*, 361–389.

Lowrey, L. G. Orthopsychiatric treatment. In L. G. Lowrey & V. Sloane (Eds.), *Orthopsychiatry, 1923–1948: Retrospect and prospect*. New York: American Orthopsychiatric Association, 1948. Pp. 524–549.

MacCorquodale, K., & Meehl, P. E. On a distinction between hypothetical constructs and intervening variables. *Psychological Review*, 1948, *55*, 95–107.

MacFarlane, J. W. Studies in child guidance: I. Methodology of data collection and organization. *Monographs of the Society for Research in Child Development*, 1938, *3*, No. 6.

MacFarlane, J. W. Looking ahead in orthopsychiatric research. *American Journal of Orthopsychiatry*, 1950, *20*, 85–91.

Maier, N. R. F. & Klee, J. B. Studies of abnormal behavior in the rat. *Journal of Psychology*, 1945, *19*, 133–163.

McGinnies, E. Psychology in Japan: 1960. *American Psychologist*, 1960, *15*, 556–562.

Meehl, P. E. The cognitive activity of the clinician. *American Psychologist*, 1960, *15*, 19–27. (Reprinted: In J. R. Braun [Ed.], *Clinical psychology in transition*. Cleveland, Ohio: Howard Allen, 1961. Pp. 35–43.)

Menninger, W. *Psychiatry in a troubled world*. New York: Macmillan, 1948. (a)

Menninger, W. *Psychiatry: Its evolution and present status*. Ithaca, N. Y.: Cornell University Press, 1948. (b)

Merlan, P. Brentano and Freud. *Journal of the History of Ideas*, 1945, *6*, 375–377.

Merlan, P. Brentano and Freud—A sequel. *Journal of the History of Ideas*, 1949, *10*, 451.

Mettler, F. A. (Ed.), *Selective partial ablation of the frontal cortex*. New York: Hoeber, 1949.

Meyer, A. In memoriam, G. Stanley Hall. *American Journal of Psychiatry*, 1924–25, *4*, 151–153.

Meyer, A. The organization of community facilities for prevention, care and treatment of nervous and mental diseases. In *Proceedings of the first international congress on mental hygiene*. New York: International Congress for Mental Hygiene, 1932. Pp. 237–257.

Miles, W. R. Age and human ability. *Psychological Review*, 1933, *40*, 99–123.

Miles, W. R. Psychological aspects of aging. In E. V. Cowdry (Ed.), *Problems of aging*. Baltimore: Williams & Wilkins, 1939. Pp. 535–571.

Miles, W. R. A year of state certification of psychologists. *American Psychologist*, 1946, *1*, 393–394.

Miller, G. A., & Frick, F. C. Statistical behavioristics and sequences of responses. *Psychological Review*, 1949, *56*, 311–324.

Miller, J. G. Clinical psychology in the Veterans Administration. *American Psychologist*, 1946, *1*, 181–189.

Miller, J. G. Elements in the medical curriculum which should be incorporated in the training of the clinical psychologist. In M. R. Harrower (Ed.), *Training in clinical psychology*. New York: Josiah Macy, Jr., Foundation, 1947. Pp. 41–46.

Moore, T. V. The essential psychoses and their fundamental syndromes. *Studies in Psychiatry and Psychology from the Catholic University of America*, 1933, *3*, No. 3.

Morrow, W. R. The development of psychological internship training. *Journal of Consulting Psychology*, 1946, *10*, 165–183.

Mowrer, O. H. *Learning theory and personality dynamics*. New York: Ronald Press, 1950.

Mowrer, O. H. *Learning theory and the symbolic processes*. New York: Wiley, 1960.

Mowrer, O. H. *The crisis in psychiatry and religion*. Princeton, N. J.: Van Nostrand (Insight Books), 1961.

Munroe, R. L. *Schools of psychoanalytic thought*. New York: Dryden, 1955.

Murchison, C. (Ed.) *History of psychology in autobiography*. Vol. 3. Worcester, Mass.: Clark University Press, 1936.

Murray, H. A. *Explorations in personality: A clinical and experimental study of fifty men of college age*. New York: Oxford University Press, 1938.

Murray, H. A. *Thematic apperception test*. Cambridge, Mass.: Harvard University Press, 1943.

National Institutes of Health Study Committee (D. E. Wooldridge, Chairman). *Biomedical science and its administration*. Report to the President. Washington: United States Government Printing Office, 1965.

National Research Council, Division of Medical Sciences and Division of Anthropology and Psychology, (C. Wissler, Chairman). Conference on relations of psychiatry to psychology, Washington, D. C., April 30, 1921.

National Science Foundation, Special Committee on Medical Research, (C. N. H. Long, Chairman). Medical research activities of the Department of Health, Education and Welfare. December, 1955. Unpublished.

New York City Committee on Mental Hygiene. *Standards of training of professional personnel in psychiatric clinics*. New York, 1935 (second printing, 1938).

New York State Association for Applied Psychology, Special Committee on School Psychologists. Report on the functions, training, and employment opportunities of school psychologists. *Journal of Consulting Psychology*, 1943, *7*, 230–243.

Parloff, M. B., Goldstein, N., & Iflund, B. Communication of values and therapeutic change. *A.M.A. Archives of General Psychiatry*, 1960, *2*, 300–304.

Parsons, T., & Shils, E. A. *Toward a general theory of action*. Cambridge, Mass.: Harvard University Press, 1951.

Penfield, W. *The difficult art of giving: The epic of Alan Gregg*. Boston: Little, Brown, 1967.

Perry, R. B. *The thought and character of William James*. Vol. 2. Boston: Little, Brown, 1935.

Perry, R. B. *In the spirit of William James*. New Haven: Yale University Press, 1938.

Poffenberger, A. T. The training of the clinical psychologist. *Journal of Consulting Psychology*, 1938, *2*, 1–6.

Pratt, C. C. *The logic of modern psychology*. New York: Macmillan, 1939.

Pressey, S. L. On the committee vs. the scientific approach to problems of professional training. *American Psychologist*, 1948, *3*, 176–177.

Proceedings of the 55th annual business meeting of the American Psychological Association, Detroit, Michigan. *American Psychologist*, 1947, *2*, 468–510.

Raimy, V. C. (Ed.) *Training in clinical psychology*. (Conference on graduate education in clinical psychology, Boulder, Colo.) New York: Prentice-Hall, 1950.

Rapaport, D. The conceptual model of psychoanalysis. *Journal of Personality*, 1951, *20*, 56–81.

Rapaport, D. The structure of psychoanalytic theory: A systematizing attempt. In S. Koch (Ed.), *Psychology: A study of a science*. Vol. 3. New York: McGraw-Hill, 1959. Pp. 55–183. (Reprinted: In *Psychological Issues*, 1960, *2* (2, Monograph 6).)

Rashdall, H., Powicke, F. M., & Emden, A. B. (Eds.), *The universities of Europe in the Middle Ages*. Vol. 3. Oxford: Clarendon Press, 1936.

Reid, J. R. The problem of values in psychoanalysis. *American Journal of Psychoanalysis*, 1955, *15*, 115–122.

Rennie, T. A. C., & Woodward, L. E. *Mental health in modern society*. New York: Commonwealth Fund, 1948.

Report of Committee on Training Standards to the Board on Professional Standards. *Journal of the American Psychoanalytic Association*, 1957, *5*, 713.

Report of Conference on an ideal training program for psychotherapy. *American Psychologist*, 1963, *18*, 677–679.

Rickers-Ovsiankina, M. Studies on the personality structure of schizophrenic individuals. I. The accessibility of schizophrenics to environmental influences. *Journal of General Psychology*, 1937, *16*, 153–178.

Rieff, P. *Freud: The mind of the moralist*. New York: Viking Press, 1959.

Riessman, F., & National Institute of Labor Education. New approaches to mental health treatment for labor and low income groups. Report No. 2, 1964, National Institute of Labor Education, Mental Health Program, New York. Unpublished.

Rioch, M., Elkes, C., Flint, A., Sweet, B., Newman, R., & Silber, E. National Institute of Mental Health pilot project in training mental health counselors. (USPHS Publ. No. 1254) Washington: United States Government Printing Office, 1965.

Rioch, M. J., Elkes, C., Flint, A. A., Usdansky, B. S., Newman, R. G., & Silber, E. National Institute of Mental Health pilot study in training mental health counselors. *American Journal of Orthopsychiatry*, 1963, *33*, 678–689.

Roe, A. Analysis of Group Rorschachs of psychologists and anthropologists and a comparison with biological and physical scientists. *Psychological Monographs*, 1953, *67*, No. 2.

Roe, A. (Ed.) *Graduate education in psychology*. (Report of the Conference on Graduate Education in Psychology, sponsored by the Education and Training Board of the APA, held at Miami Beach, Fla., Nov. 29–Dec. 7, 1958.) Washington: American Psychological Association, 1959.

Roe, A., & Shakow, D. Intelligence in mental disorder. *Annals of the New York Academy of Science*, 1942, *42*, 361–490.

Rogers, C. R., Raskin, N. J., Seeman, J., Sheerer, E. T., Stock, D., Haigh, G., Hoffman, A. E., & Carr, A. C. A coordinated research in psychotherapy. *Journal of Consulting Psychology*, 1949, *13*, 149–220.

Rosenthal, D. Changes in some moral values following psychotherapy. *Journal of Consulting Psychology*, 1955, *19*, 431–436.

Rosenzweig, S. *Psychodiagnosis*. New York: Grune & Stratton, 1949.

Rosenzweig, S. Topograph bolder: The three-and-six plan for the training of clinical psychologists. *American Psychologist*, 1967, *22*, 801–802.

Ross, S. APA-approved doctoral programs in clinical and in counseling psychology: 1963. *American Psychologist*, 1963, *18*, 309–310.

Russell, B. A free man's worship. In B. Russell, *Mysticism and logic*. London: Longmans Green, 1919. Pp. 46–57.

Russell, B. *A history of western philosophy*. New York: Simon & Schuster, 1945.

Sanborn, F. B. (Ed.) *Familiar letters of Henry David Thoreau*. Boston: Houghton Mifflin, 1894.

Schutz, W. C. Theory and methodology of content analysis. Unpublished doctoral dissertation, University of California at Los Angeles, 1951.

Sears, R. R. Clinical training facilities: 1947. A report from the Committee on Graduate and Professional Training. *American Psychologist*, 1947, *2*, 199–205.

Seashore, C. E. *Pioneering in psychology*. Iowa City: University of Iowa Press, 1942.

Shakow, D. An internship year for psychologists (with special reference to psychiatric hospitals). *Journal of Consulting Psychology*, 1938, *2*, 73–76.

Shakow, D. The functions of the psychologist in the state hospital. *Journal of Consulting Psychology*, 1939, *3*, 20–23.

Shakow, D. One psychologist as analysand. *Journal of Abnormal and Social Psychology*, 1940, *35*, 198–211.

Shakow, D. The training of the clinical psychologist. *Journal of Consulting Psychology*, 1942, *6*, 277–288.

Shakow, D. One hundred years of American psychiatry—A special review. *Psychological Bulletin*, 1945, *42*, 423–432. (a)

Shakow, D. Training in clinical psychology—A note on trends. *Journal of Consulting Psychology*, 1945, *9*, 240–242. (b)

Shakow, D. The Worcester internship program. *Journal of Consulting Psychology*, 1946, *10*, 191–200.

Shakow, D. Training for the clinical application of test techniques. In M. R. Harrower (Ed.), *Training in clinical psychology*. New York: Josiah Macy, Jr., Foundation, 1947. Pp. 21–27.

Shakow, D. Clinical psychology: An evaluation. In L. G. Lowrey & V. Sloane (Eds.), *Orthopsychiatry, 1923–1948: Retrospect and prospect*. New York: American Orthopsychiatric Association, 1948. Pp. 231–247. (a)

Shakow, D. The psychologist in the clinic setting. Round table, 1947, *American Journal of Orthopsychiatry*, 1948, *18*, 514–517. (b)

Shakow, D. Discussion of O. H. Mowrer: Some hypotheses concerning psychology and learning. Paper presented at Midwestern Psychological Association, Chicago, April 29, 1949. (a)

Shakow, D. The objective evaluation of psychotherapy. The evaluation of the procedure. *American Journal of Orthopsychiatry*, 1949, *19*, 471–481. (b)

Shakow, D. Psychology and psychiatry: A dialogue. Part I & Part II. *American Journal of Orthopsychiatry*, 1949, *19*, 191–208, 381–396. (c)

Shakow, D. Review of G. G. Simpson, *The meaning of evolution*. *Journal of Abnormal and Social Psychology*, 1951, *46*, 271–273.

Shakow, D. Discussion. In F. Alexander & H. Ross (Eds.), *Twenty years of psychoanalysis*. New York: Norton, 1953. Pp. 216–226. (a)

Shakow, D. Some aspects of mid-century psychiatry: Experimental psychology. In

R. R. Grinker (Ed.), *Mid-century psychiatry*. Springfield, Ill.: Charles C. Thomas, 1953. Pp. 76–103. (b)

Shakow, D. The improvement of practicum training and facilities. In C. Strother (Ed.), *Psychology and mental health*. Washington: American Psychological Association, 1957. Pp. 53–75.

Shakow, D. The recorded psychoanalytic interview as an objective approach to research in psychoanalysis. *Psychoanalytic Quarterly*, 1960, *29*, 82–97.

Shakow, D. Seventeen years later: Clinical psychology in the light of the 1947 committee on training in clinical psychology report. *American Psychologist*, 1965, *20*, 353–362.

Shakow, D. Schools of Psychology: Psychoanalysis. In D. Krantz (Ed.), *Systems of Psychology: A Symposium in the History of Psychology*. New York: Appleton-Century-Crofts, 1969.

Shakow, D., Dolkart, M. B., & Goldman, R. The memory function in psychoses of the aged. *Diseases of the Nervous System*, 1941, *2*, 43–48.

Shakow, D. & Rapaport, D. The influence of Freud on American psychology. *Psychological Issues*, 1964, *4*, (1, Monograph 13). (also Cleveland: World Publishing Co., 1968.)

Shakow, D., Rodnick, E. H., & Lebeaux, T. A psychological study of a schizophrenic: Exemplification of a method. *Journal of Abnormal and Social Psychology*, 1945, *40*, 154–174.

Shannon, J. A. The advancement of medical research: A twenty-year view of the role of the National Institutes of Health. *Journal of Medical Education*, 1967, *42*, 97–108. (a)

Shannon, J. A. Some further thoughts on the relationships between science and federal programs. Paper presented at the meeting of the Federation of American Societies for Experimental Biology, Chicago, April 1967. Unpublished. (b)

Sigerist, H. E. *The great doctors*. New York: Norton, 1939.

Simpson, G. G. *The meaning of evolution*. New Haven: Yale University Press, 1949.

Simpson, G. G. The world into which Darwin led us. *Science*, 1960, *131*, 966–974.

Skinner, B. F. *The behavior of organisms*. New York: Appleton-Century-Crofts, 1938.

Stein, M. I. *Volunteers for peace; the first group of Peace Corps volunteers in a rural community development program in Colombia, South America*. New York: Wiley, 1966.

Stephenson, W. The significance of Q technique for the study of personality. In M. L. Reymert (Ed.), *Feelings and emotions*. The Mooseheart Symposium. New York: McGraw-Hill, 1950. Pp. 552–570.

Stevens, S. S. Psychology and the science of science. *Psychological Bulletin*, 1939, *36*, 221–263.

Stevens, S. S. (Ed.), *Handbook of experimental psychology*. New York: Wiley, 1951.

Stevenson, G. S. & Smith, G. *Child guidance clinics: A quarter century of development*. New York: Commonwealth Fund, 1934.

Strother, C. R. (Ed.) *Psychology and mental health*. (A report of the Institute on Education and Training for Psychological Contributions to Mental Health, held at Stanford University in Aug., 1955.) Washington: American Psychological Association, 1956.

Summerfield, A. Clinical psychology in Britain. *American Psychologist*, 1958, *13*, 171–176.

Symonds, J. P. Ten years of journalism in psychology, 1937–1946. *Journal of Consulting Psychology*, 1946, *10*, 335–374.

Symposium on certification and licensing. *Journal of Consulting Psychology*, 1941, *5*, 49–79.

Szasz, T. Psychoanalytic training. *International Journal of Psycho-Analysis*, 1958, *39*, 598–613.

Terman, L. M. *The measurement of intelligence*. Boston: Houghton Mifflin, 1916.

Terman, L. M. & Merrill, M. A. *Measuring intelligence*. Boston: Houghton Mifflin, 1937.

Terrell, J. U. *Journey into darkness*. London: Jarrolds, 1964.

Thurstone, C. C. *Multiple factor analysis*. Chicago: University of Chicago Press, 1947.

Tolman, E. C. *Purposive behavior in animals and men*. New York: Century, 1932.

Tolman, E. C. The determiners of behavior at a choice point. *Psychological Review*, 1938, *45*, 1–41.

Tolman, E. C. Discussion. *Journal of Personality*, 1949, *18*, 48–50.

Trilling, L. *Freud and the crisis of our culture*. Boston: Beacon Press, 1955.

Tryon, R. C. Psychology in flux: The academic-professional bipolarity. *American Psychologist*, 1963, *18*, 134–143.

Wallas, G. *The great society: A psychological analysis*. London: Macmillan, 1914.

Wallin, J. E. W. *The mental health of the school child*. New Haven: Yale University Press, 1914.

Watson, R. I. *Readings in the clinical method in psychology*. New York: Harper & Bros., 1949.

Weaver, W. Science and complexity. *American Scientist*, 1948, *36*, 536–544.

Wechsler, D. *The measurement of adult intelligence*. (3rd. ed.) Baltimore: Williams & Wilkins, 1944.

Weiss, P. A. *Principles of development*. New York: Holt, 1939.

Wells, F. L. Psychology in medical education. *Archives of Neurology and Psychiatry*, 1936, *35*, 631–638.

Wheeler, W. M. On instincts. *Journal of Abnormal Psychology*, 1921, *15*, 295–318.

White, W. A. *Forty years of psychiatry*. New York: Nervous and Mental Diseases Publishing Co., 1933.

Whitehead, A. N. *The aims of education and other essays*. New York: Mentor Books, 1949. (Intro. by Felix Frankfurter.)

Whitehorn, J. C. The meaning of medical education in our society. *American Journal of Psychiatry*, 1952, *109*, 81–88.

Witmer, H. L. *Psychiatric clinics for children*. New York: Commonwealth Fund, 1940.

Witmer, H. L. (Ed.), *Teaching psychotherapeutic medicine*. New York: Commonwealth Fund, 1947.

Wright, E. The influence of frustration upon the social relations of young children. *Character and Personality*, 1942, *12*, 111–122.

Yerkes, R. M. Psychology and defense. *Proceedings of the American Philosophical Society*, 1941, *84*, 1–16.

Zimet, C. N. Conference on the professional preparation of clinical psychologists: A progress report. *American Psychologist*, 1965, *20*, 232–233.

Name Index

Subject Index

For Product Safety Concerns and Information please contact our EU
representative GPSR@taylorandfrancis.com
Taylor & Francis Verlag GmbH, Kaufingerstraße 24, 80331 München, Germany

www.ingramcontent.com/pod-product-compliance
Ingram Content Group UK Ltd.
Pitfield, Milton Keynes, MK11 3LW, UK
UKHW040107200926
475702UK00011B/1280

* 9 7 8 0 2 0 2 3 0 8 9 0 6 *